WRITING, ART, COLORS, DESIGN & LETTERS BY

KENNY KEIL

EDITED BY

AMANDA MEADOWS

WRITING, ART, COLORS, LETTERS, AND DESIGN BY KENNY KEIL
EDITED BY AMANDA MEADOWS

PUBLISHED BY ONI-LION FORGE PUBLISHING GROUP, LLC

JAMES LUCAS JONES
president & publisher
SARAH GAYDOS
editor in chief
CHARLIE CHU
e.v.p. of creative &
business development
BRAD ROOKS
director of operations
AMBER O'NEILL
special projects manager
HARRIS FISH
events manager
MARGOT WOOD
director of marketing & sales
DEVIN FUNCHES
sales & marketing manager
KATIE SAINZ
marketing manager

TARA LEHMANN
publicist
TROY LOOK
director of design & production
KATE Z. STONE
senior graphic designer
SONJA SYNAK
graphic designer
HILARY THOMPSON
graphic designer
SARAH ROCKWELL
junior graphic designer
ANGIE KNOWLES
digital prepress lead
VINCENT KUKUA
digital prepress technician
JASMINE AMIRI
senior editor

SHAWNA GORE
senior editor
AMANDA MEADOWS
senior editor
ROBERT MEYERS
senior editor, licensing
GRACE BORNHOFT
editor
ZACK SOTO
editor
CHRIS CERASI
editorial coordinator
STEVE ELLIS
vice president of games
BEN EISNER
game developer
MICHELLE NGUYEN
executive assistant
JUNG LEE
logistics coordinator

JOE NOZEMACK
publisher emeritus

1319 SE Martin Luther King, Jr. Blvd.
Suite 240
Portland, OR 97214

First Edition: September 2020
ISBN 978-1-62010-781-2
eISBN 978-1-62010-802-4

Library of Congress Control Number: 2020934174

Printed in South Korea through
Four Colour Print Group, Louisville, KY.

ONIPRESS.COM
FACEBOOK.COM/ONIPRESS
TWITTER.COM/ONIPRESS
ONIPRESS.TUMBLR.COM
INSTAGRAM.COM/ONIPRESS

KENNYKEIL.COM
TWITTER.COM/KENNYKEIL
INSTAGRAM.COM/KENNYKEIL

1 2 3 4 5 6 7 8 9 10

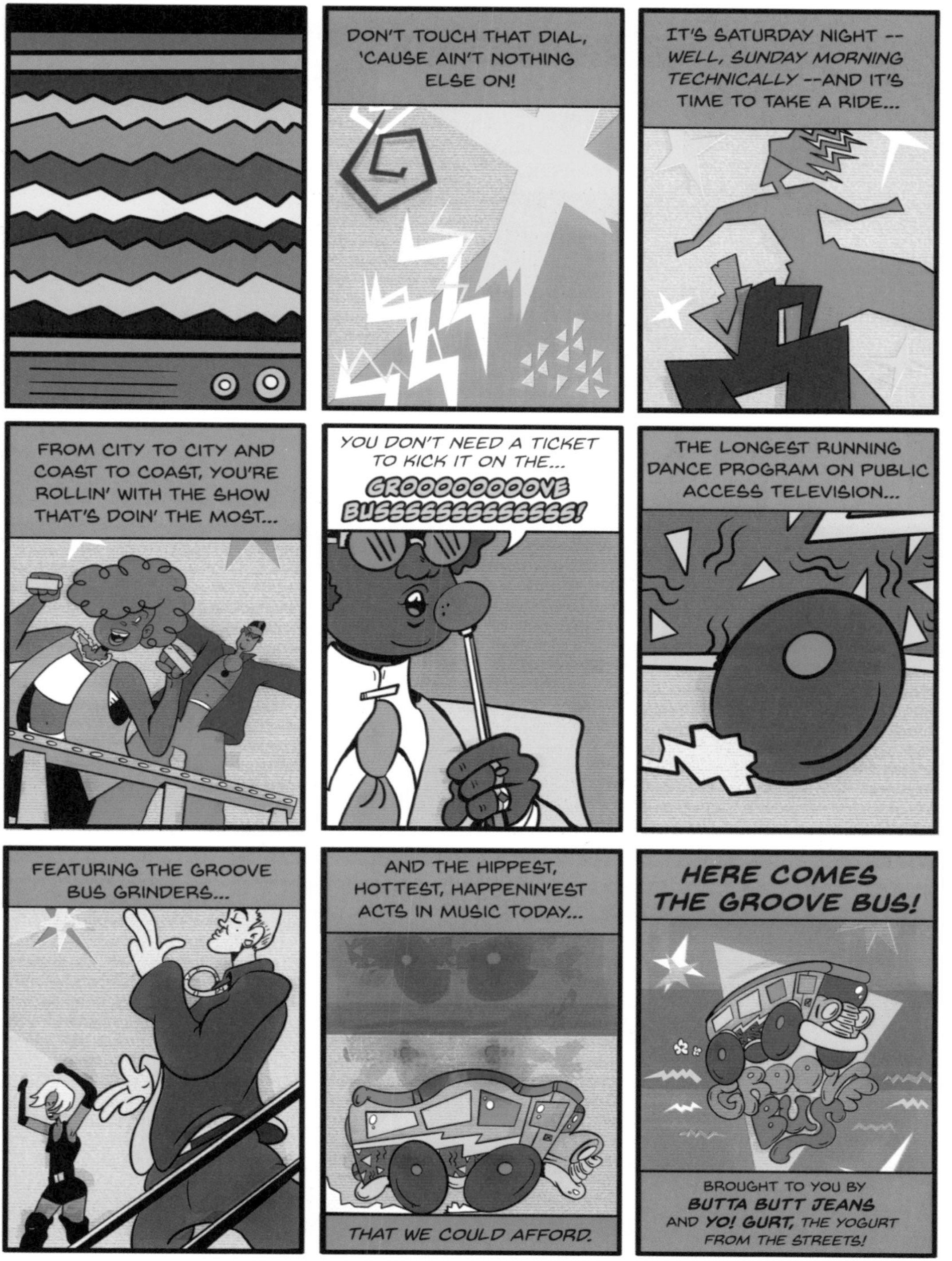
DON'T TOUCH THAT DIAL, 'CAUSE AIN'T NOTHING ELSE ON!
IT'S SATURDAY NIGHT -- WELL, SUNDAY MORNING TECHNICALLY --AND IT'S TIME TO TAKE A RIDE...
FROM CITY TO CITY AND COAST TO COAST, YOU'RE ROLLIN' WITH THE SHOW THAT'S DOIN' THE MOST...
YOU DON'T NEED A TICKET TO KICK IT ON THE...
GROOOOOOOOOVE BUSSSSSSSSSSSSSS!
THE LONGEST RUNNING DANCE PROGRAM ON PUBLIC ACCESS TELEVISION...
FEATURING THE GROOVE BUS GRINDERS...
AND THE HIPPEST, HOTTEST, HAPPENIN'EST ACTS IN MUSIC TODAY...
THAT WE COULD AFFORD.
HERE COMES THE GROOVE BUS!
GROOVE BUS
BROUGHT TO YOU BY BUTTA BUTT JEANS AND YO! GURT, THE YOGURT FROM THE STREETS!

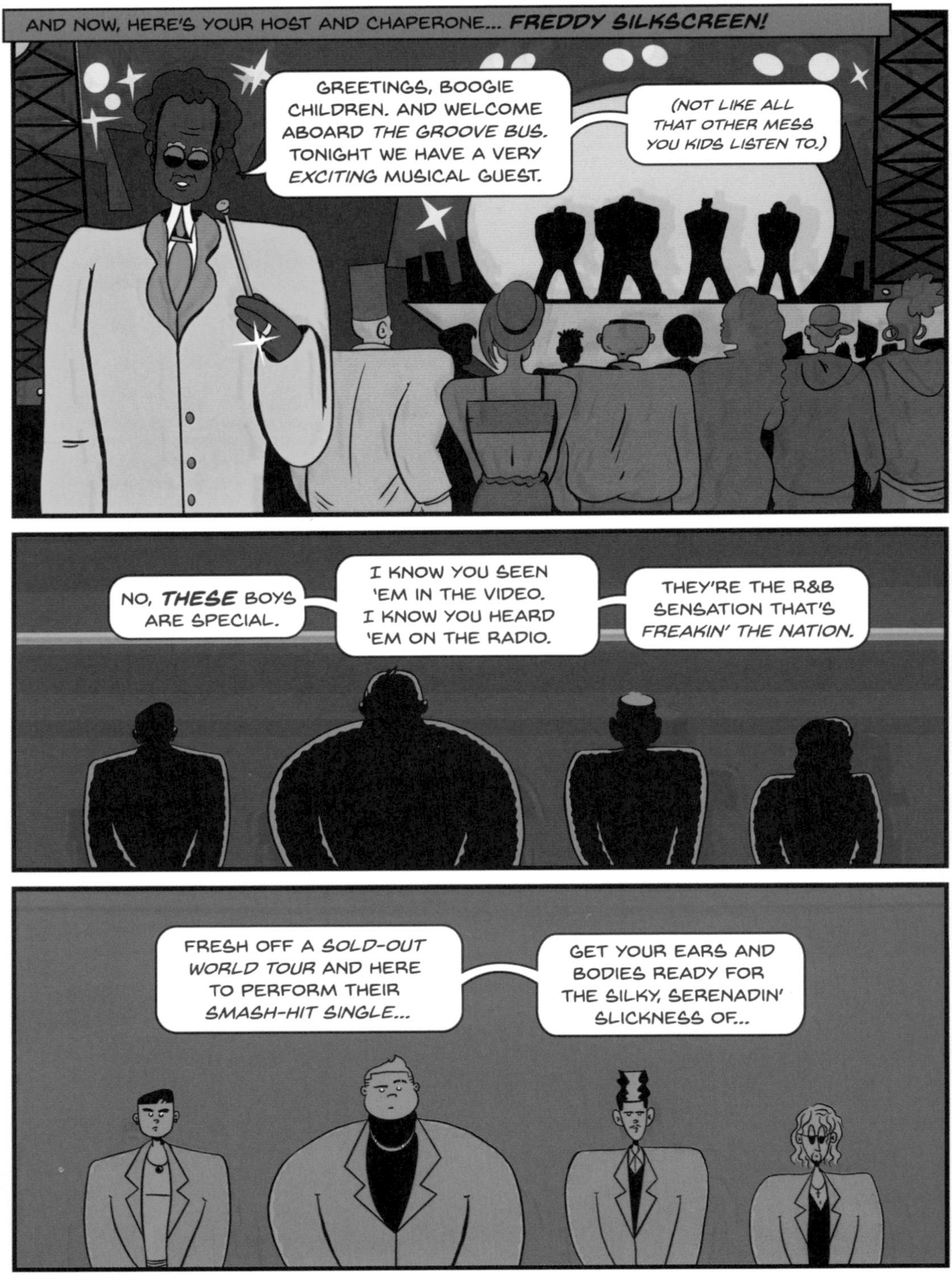
AND NOW, HERE'S YOUR HOST AND CHAPERONE... FREDDY SILKSCREEN!
GREETINGS, BOOGIE CHILDREN. AND WELCOME ABOARD THE GROOVE BUS. TONIGHT WE HAVE A VERY EXCITING MUSICAL GUEST.
(NOT LIKE ALL THAT OTHER MESS YOU KIDS LISTEN TO.)
NO, THESE BOYS ARE SPECIAL.
I KNOW YOU SEEN 'EM IN THE VIDEO. I KNOW YOU HEARD 'EM ON THE RADIO.
THEY'RE THE R&B SENSATION THAT'S FREAKIN' THE NATION.
FRESH OFF A SOLD-OUT WORLD TOUR AND HERE TO PERFORM THEIR SMASH-HIT SINGLE...
GET YOUR EARS AND BODIES READY FOR THE SILKY, SERENADIN' SLICKNESS OF...

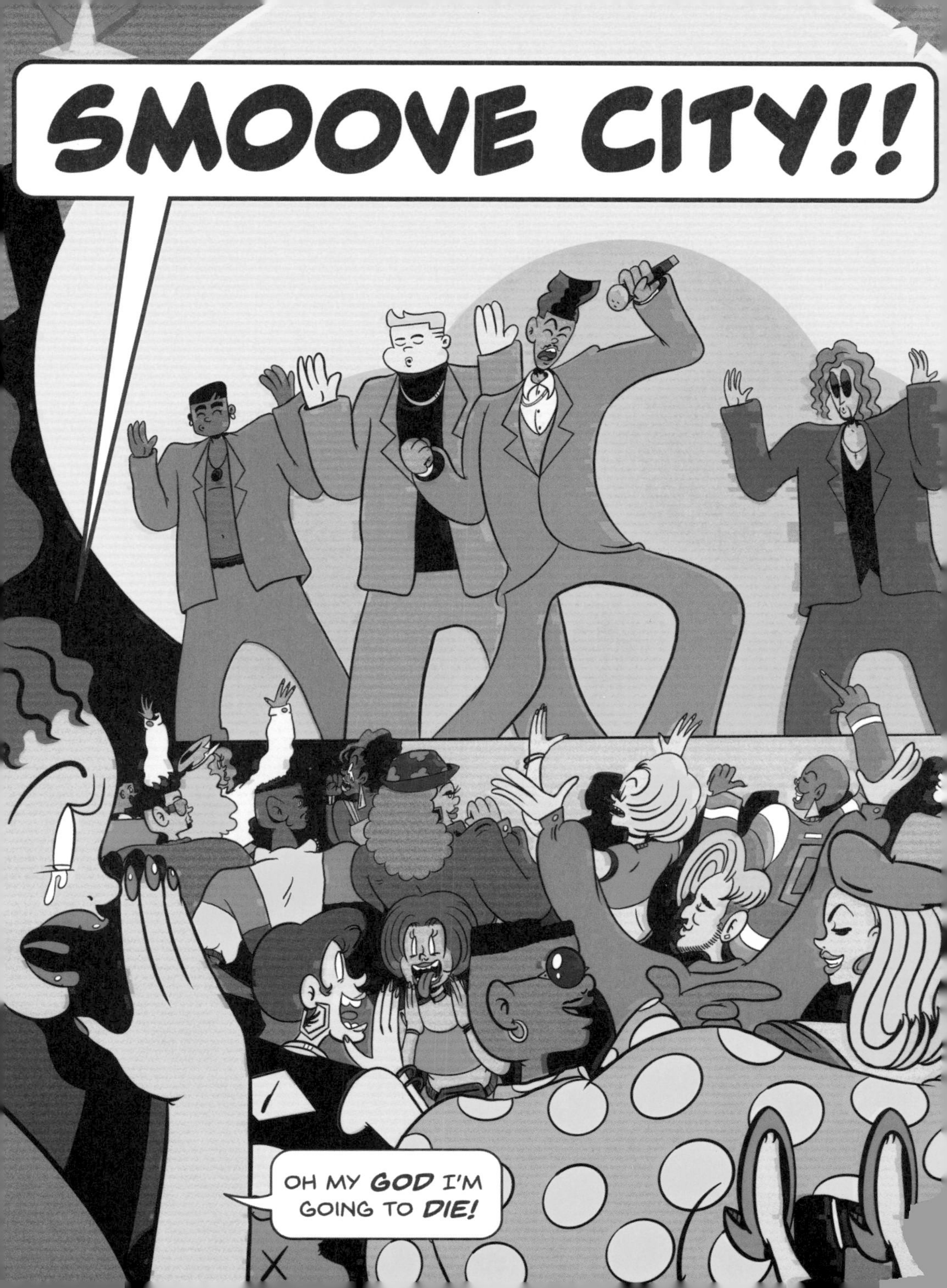
SMOOVE CITY!!
OH MY GOD I'M GOING TO DIE!

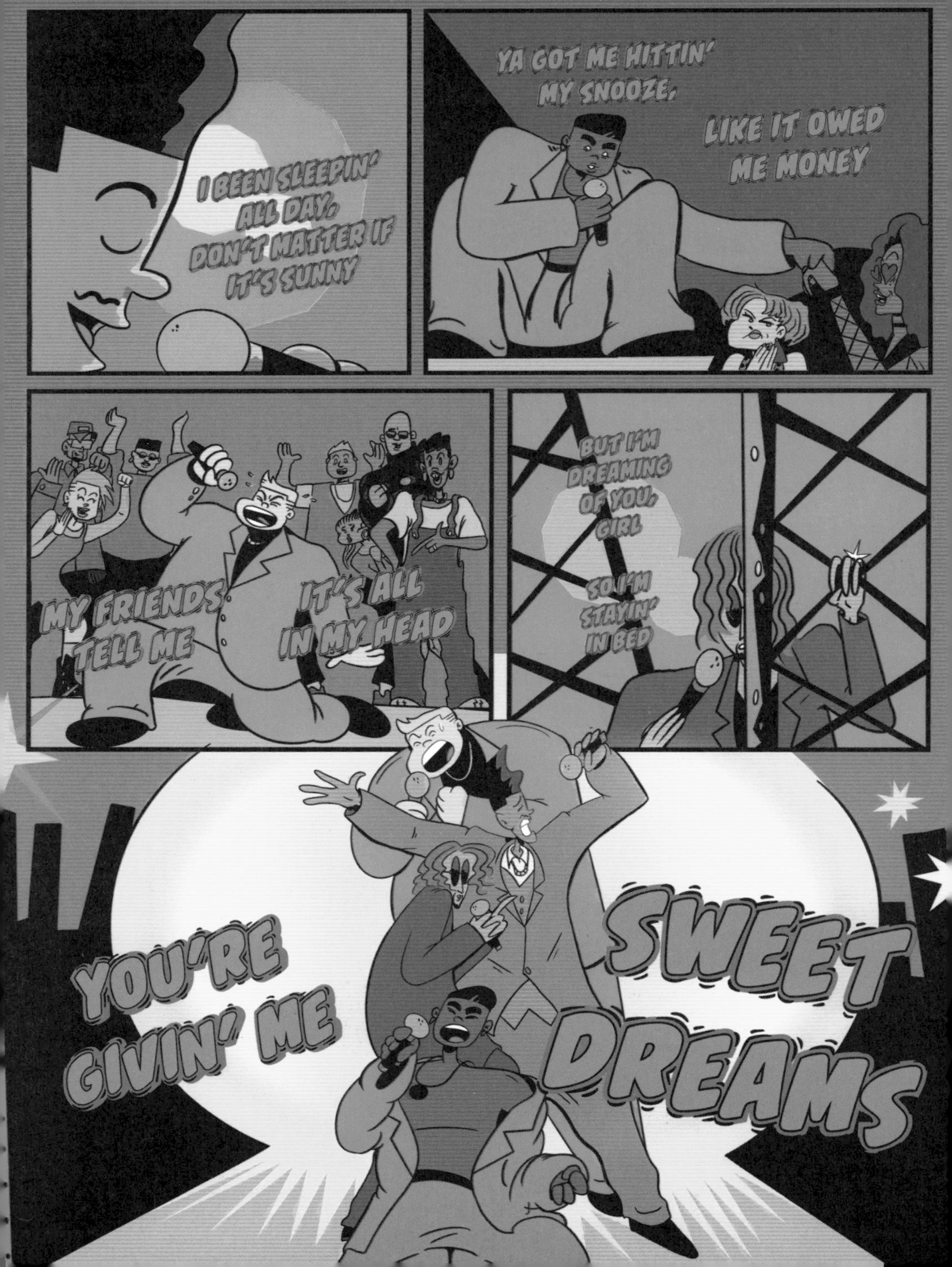
I BEEN SLEEPIN' ALL DAY, DON'T MATTER IF IT'S SUNNY
YA GOT ME HITTIN' MY SNOOZE,
LIKE IT OWED ME MONEY
MY FRIENDS TELL ME
IT'S ALL IN MY HEAD
BUT I'M DREAMING OF YOU, GIRL
SO I'M STAYIN' IN BED
YOU'RE GIVIN' ME
SWEET DREAMS

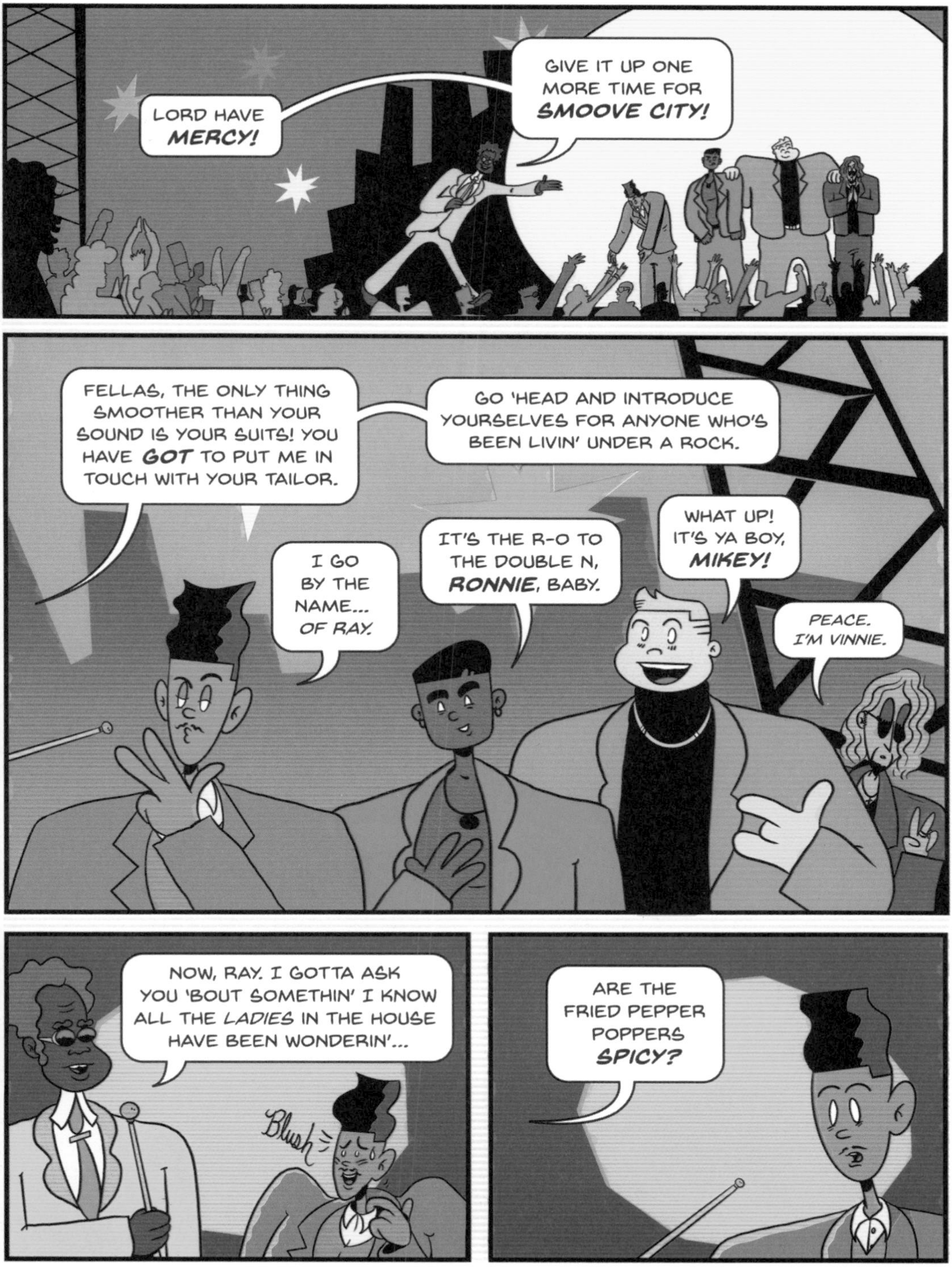
LORD HAVE MERCY!
GIVE IT UP ONE MORE TIME FOR SMOOVE CITY!
FELLAS, THE ONLY THING SMOOTHER THAN YOUR SOUND IS YOUR SUITS! YOU HAVE GOT TO PUT ME IN TOUCH WITH YOUR TAILOR.
GO 'HEAD AND INTRODUCE YOURSELVES FOR ANYONE WHO'S BEEN LIVIN' UNDER A ROCK.
I GO BY THE NAME... OF RAY.
IT'S THE R-O TO THE DOUBLE N, RONNIE, BABY.
WHAT UP! IT'S YA BOY, MIKEY!
PEACE. I'M VINNIE.
NOW, RAY. I GOTTA ASK YOU 'BOUT SOMETHIN' I KNOW ALL THE LADIES IN THE HOUSE HAVE BEEN WONDERIN'...
Blush
ARE THE FRIED PEPPER POPPERS SPICY?

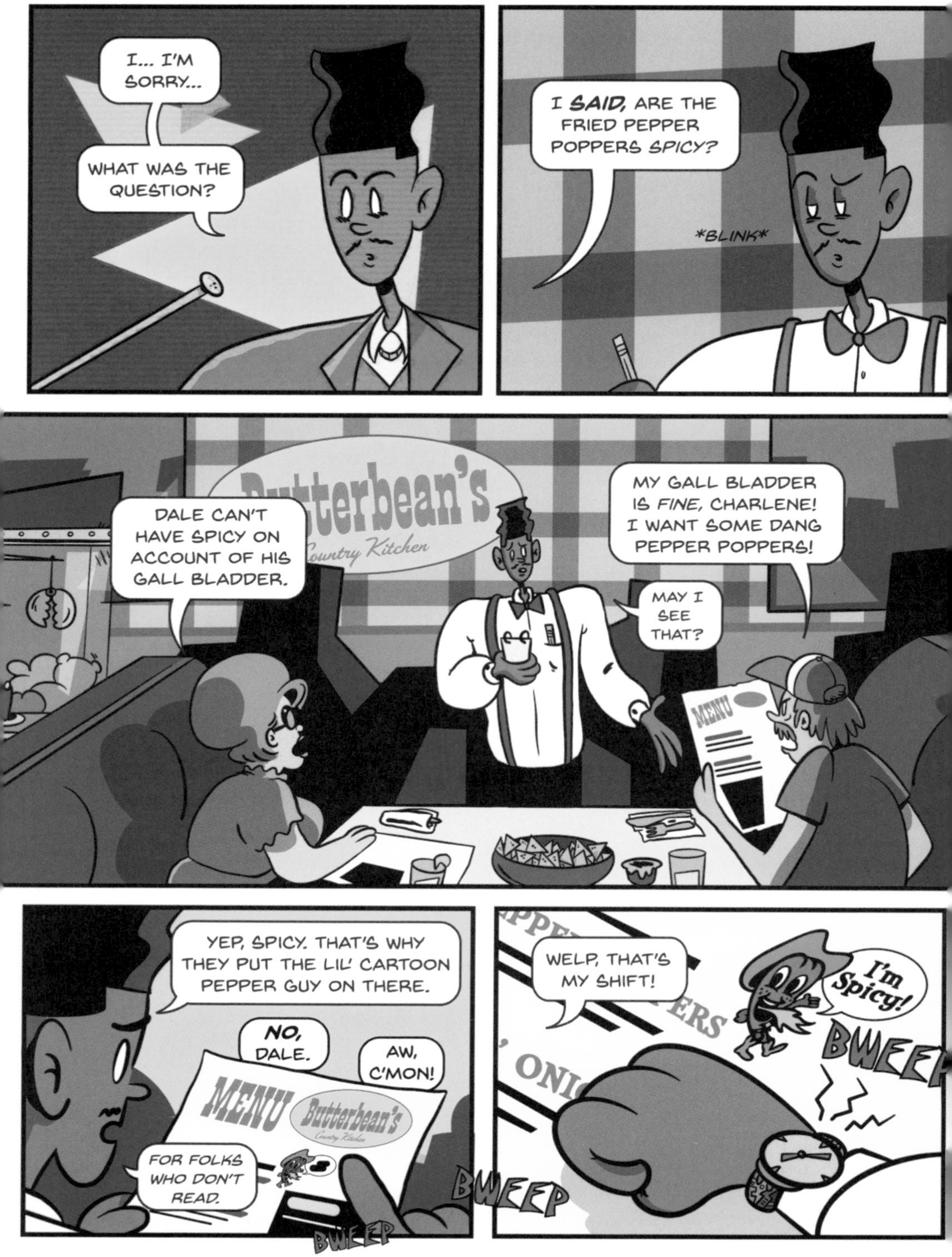
I... I'M SORRY...
WHAT WAS THE QUESTION?
I SAID, ARE THE FRIED PEPPER POPPERS SPICY?
BLINK
Butterbean's Country Kitchen
DALE CAN'T HAVE SPICY ON ACCOUNT OF HIS GALL BLADDER.
MY GALL BLADDER IS FINE, CHARLENE! I WANT SOME DANG PEPPER POPPERS!
MAY I SEE THAT?
MENU
YEP, SPICY. THAT'S WHY THEY PUT THE LIL' CARTOON PEPPER GUY ON THERE.
NO, DALE.
AW, C'MON!
MENU Butterbean's Country Kitchen
FOR FOLKS WHO DON'T READ.
BWEEP
BWEEP
WELP, THAT'S MY SHIFT!
I'm Spicy!
BWEEP

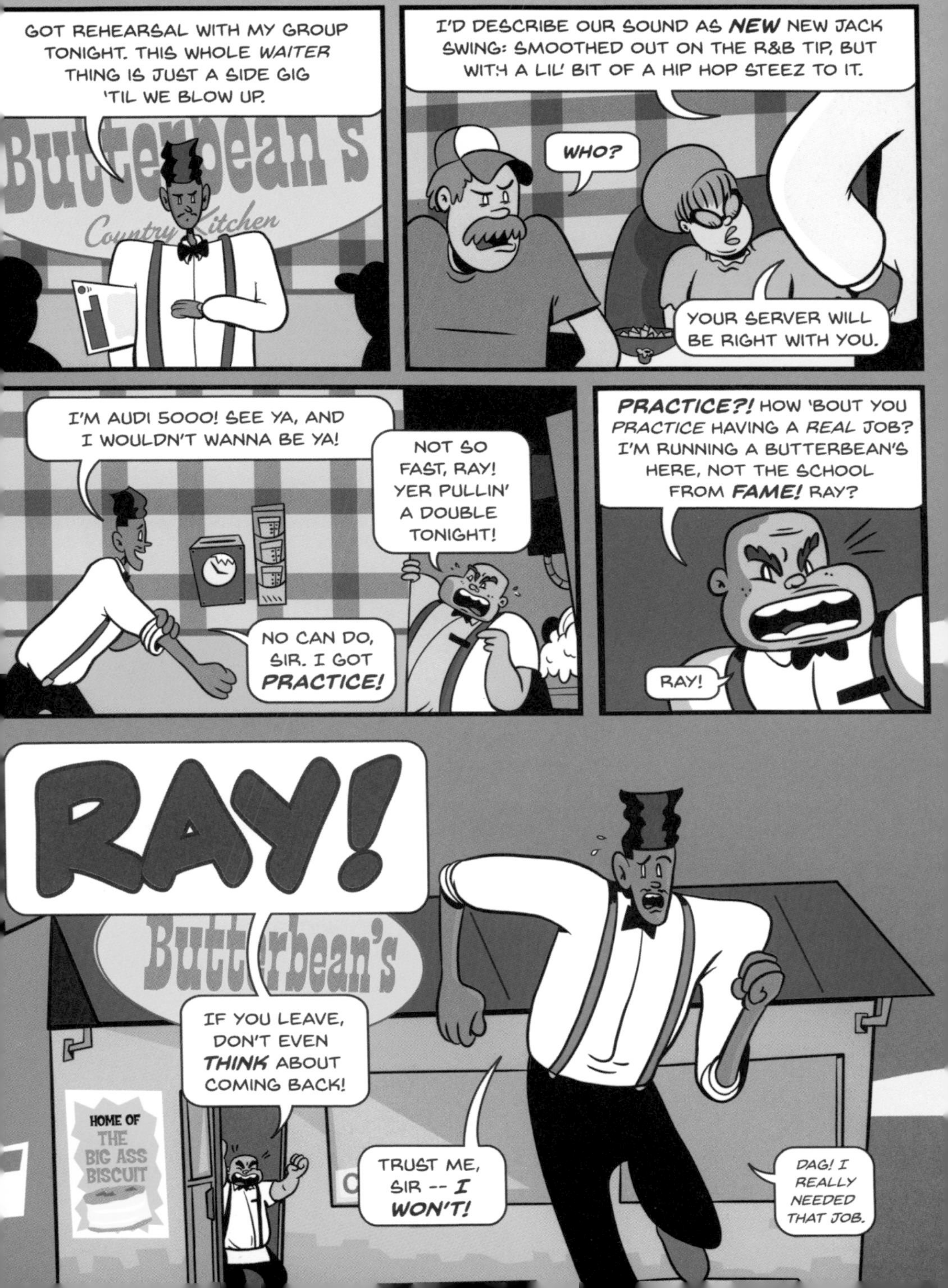
GOT REHEARSAL WITH MY GROUP TONIGHT. THIS WHOLE WAITER THING IS JUST A SIDE GIG 'TIL WE BLOW UP.
Butterbean's Country Kitchen
I'D DESCRIBE OUR SOUND AS NEW NEW JACK SWING: SMOOTHED OUT ON THE R&B TIP, BUT WITH A LIL' BIT OF A HIP HOP STEEZ TO IT.
WHO?
YOUR SERVER WILL BE RIGHT WITH YOU.
I'M AUDI 5000! SEE YA, AND I WOULDN'T WANNA BE YA!
NOT SO FAST, RAY! YER PULLIN' A DOUBLE TONIGHT!
NO CAN DO, SIR. I GOT PRACTICE!
PRACTICE?! HOW 'BOUT YOU PRACTICE HAVING A REAL JOB? I'M RUNNING A BUTTERBEAN'S HERE, NOT THE SCHOOL FROM FAME! RAY?
RAY!
RAY!
Butterbean's
IF YOU LEAVE, DON'T EVEN THINK ABOUT COMING BACK!
HOME OF THE BIG ASS BISCUIT
TRUST ME, SIR -- I WON'T!
DAG! I REALLY NEEDED THAT JOB.

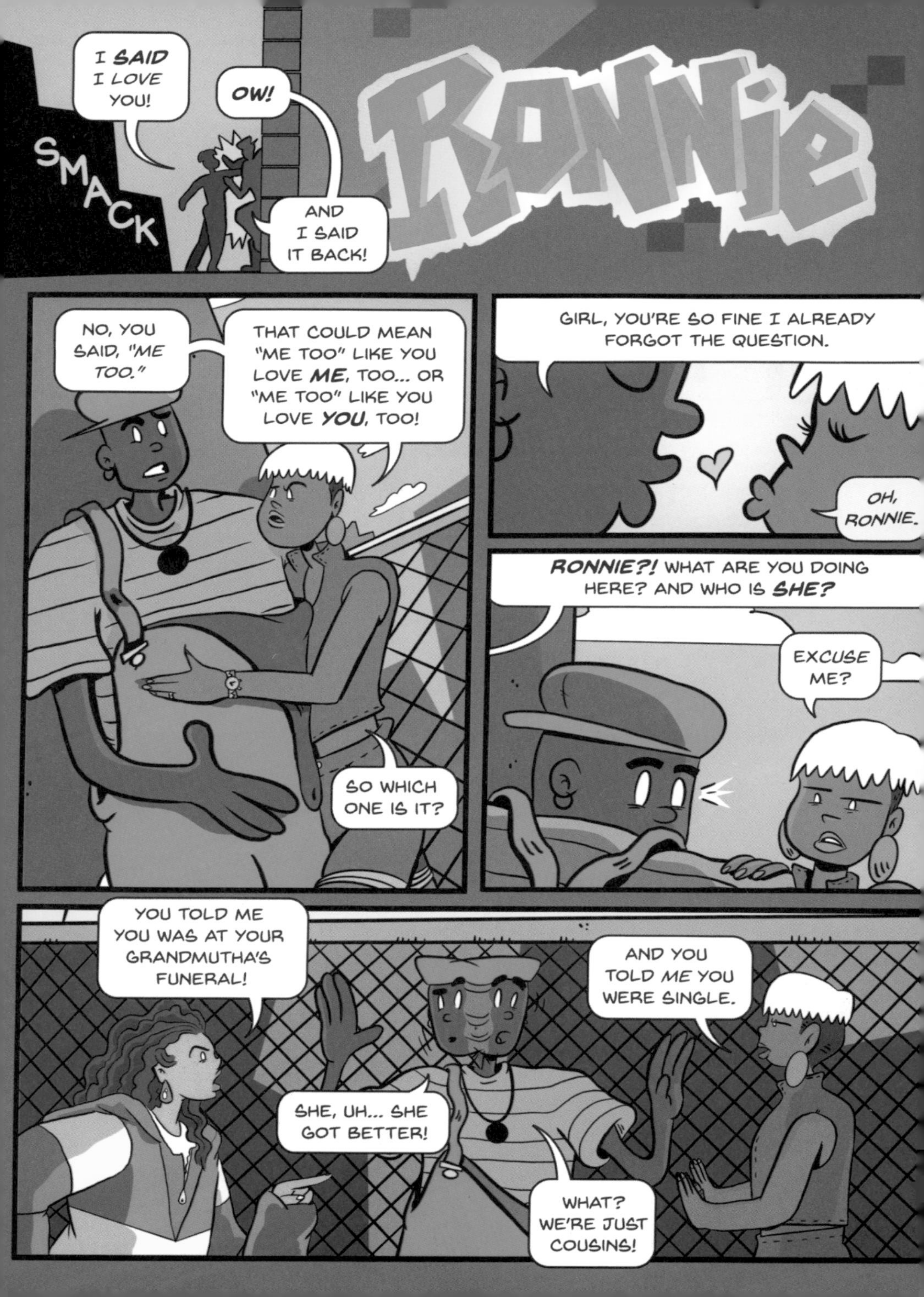
I SAID I LOVE YOU!
SMACK
OW!
AND I SAID IT BACK!
RONNIE
NO, YOU SAID, "ME TOO."
THAT COULD MEAN "ME TOO" LIKE YOU LOVE ME, TOO... OR "ME TOO" LIKE YOU LOVE YOU, TOO!
SO WHICH ONE IS IT?
GIRL, YOU'RE SO FINE I ALREADY FORGOT THE QUESTION.
OH, RONNIE.
RONNIE?! WHAT ARE YOU DOING HERE? AND WHO IS SHE?
EXCUSE ME?
YOU TOLD ME YOU WAS AT YOUR GRANDMUTHA'S FUNERAL!
AND YOU TOLD ME YOU WERE SINGLE.
SHE, UH... SHE GOT BETTER!
WHAT? WE'RE JUST COUSINS!

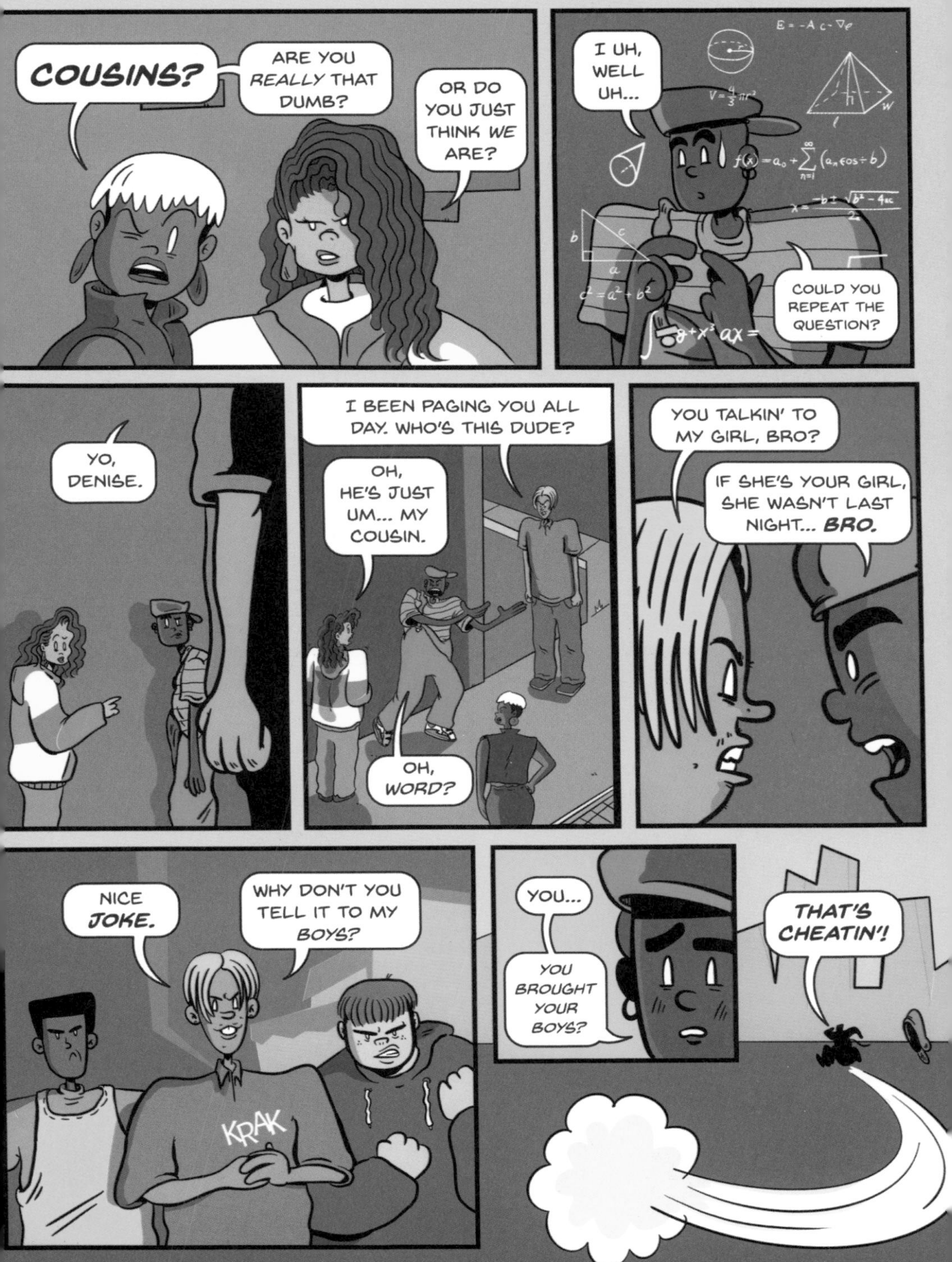
COUSINS?
ARE YOU REALLY THAT DUMB?
OR DO YOU JUST THINK WE ARE?
I UH, WELL UH...
COULD YOU REPEAT THE QUESTION?
YO, DENISE.
I BEEN PAGING YOU ALL DAY. WHO'S THIS DUDE?
OH, HE'S JUST UM... MY COUSIN.
OH, WORD?
YOU TALKIN' TO MY GIRL, BRO?
IF SHE'S YOUR GIRL, SHE WASN'T LAST NIGHT... BRO.
NICE JOKE.
WHY DON'T YOU TELL IT TO MY BOYS?
KRAK
YOU...
YOU BROUGHT YOUR BOYS?
THAT'S CHEATIN'!

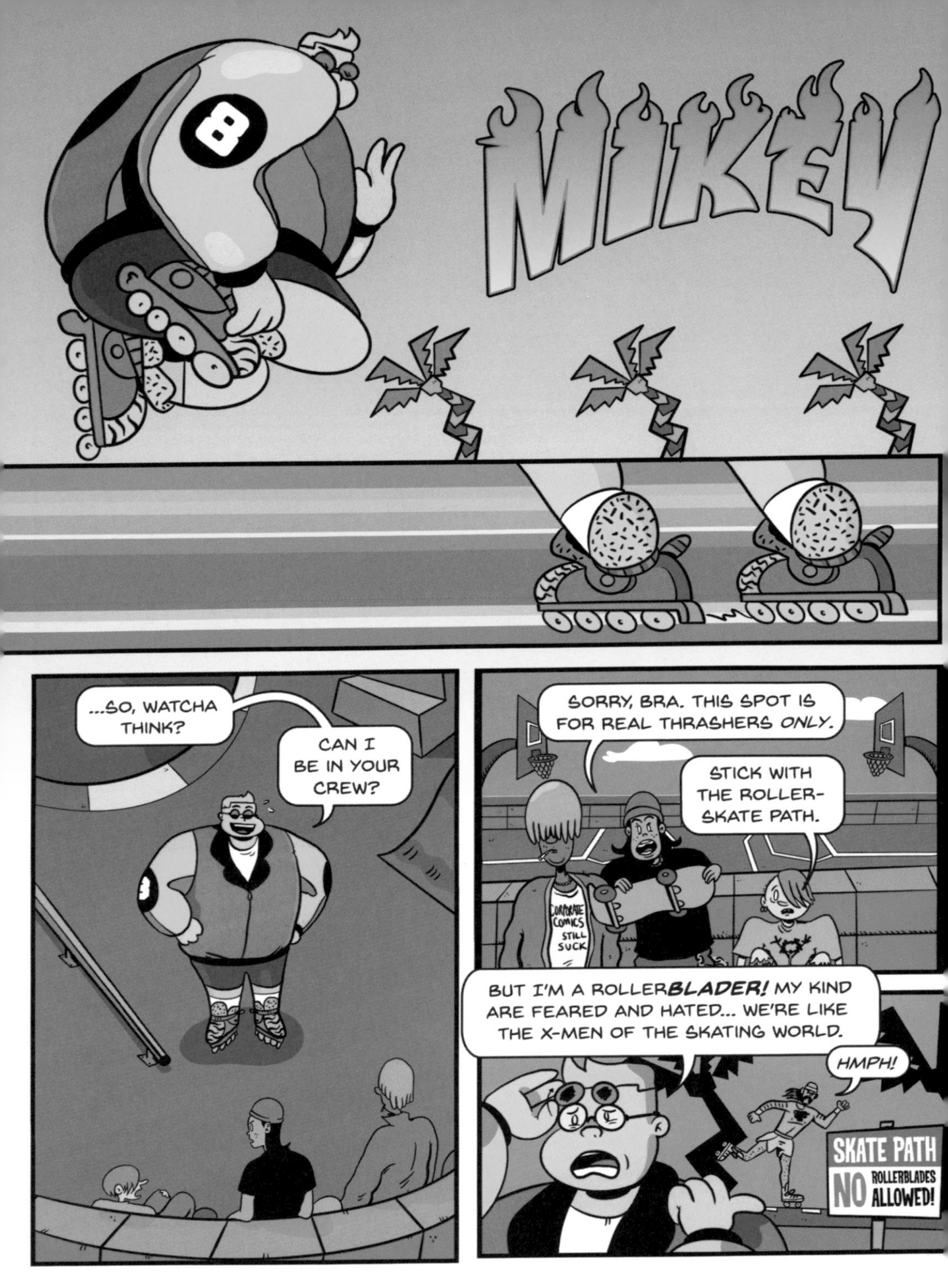
MIKEY
...SO, WATCHA THINK?
CAN I BE IN YOUR CREW?
SORRY, BRA. THIS SPOT IS FOR REAL THRASHERS *ONLY*.
STICK WITH THE ROLLER-SKATE PATH.
CORPORATE COMICS STILL SUCK
BUT I'M A ROLLER**BLADER!** MY KIND ARE FEARED AND HATED... WE'RE LIKE THE X-MEN OF THE SKATING WORLD.
HMPH!
SKATE PATH NO ROLLERBLADES ALLOWED!

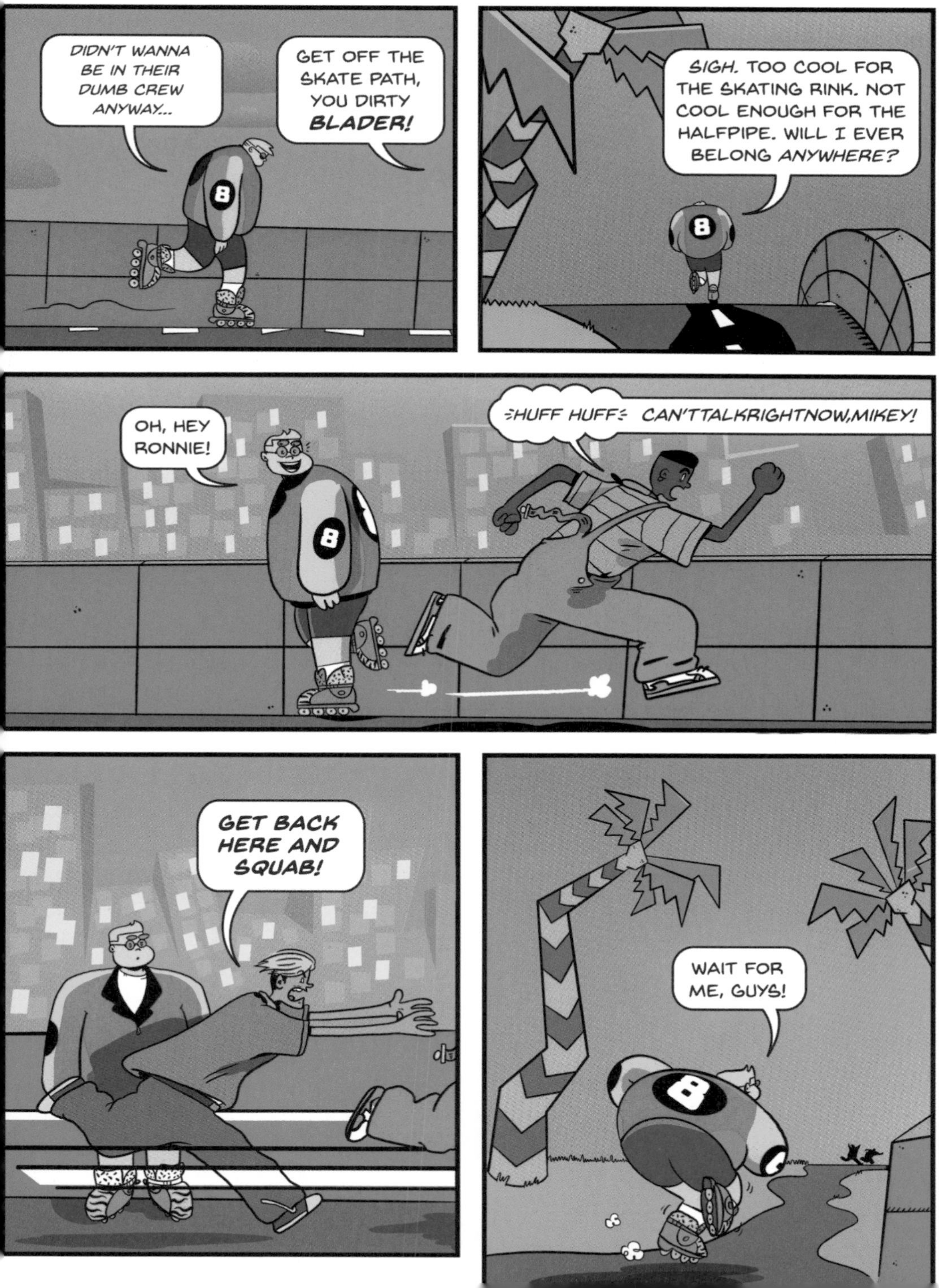
DIDN'T WANNA BE IN THEIR DUMB CREW ANYWAY...
GET OFF THE SKATE PATH, YOU DIRTY BLADER!
SIGH. TOO COOL FOR THE SKATING RINK. NOT COOL ENOUGH FOR THE HALFPIPE. WILL I EVER BELONG ANYWHERE?
OH, HEY RONNIE!
HUFF HUFF CAN'TTALKRIGHTNOW,MIKEY!
GET BACK HERE AND SQUAB!
WAIT FOR ME, GUYS!

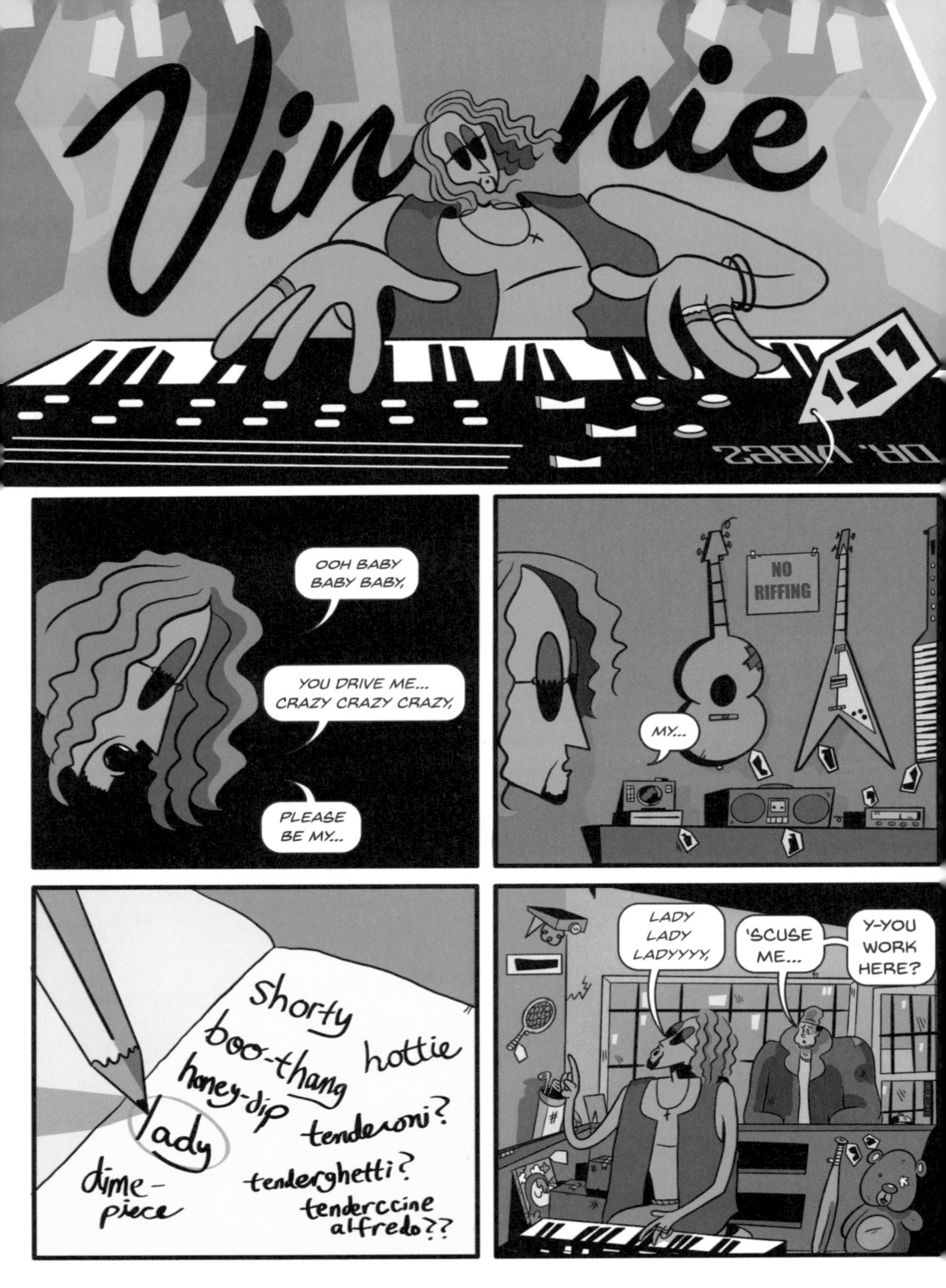
Vinnie
OOH BABY BABY BABY,
YOU DRIVE ME... CRAZY CRAZY CRAZY,
PLEASE BE MY...
NO RIFFING
MY...
shorty
boo-thang
hottie
honey-dip
lady
tenderoni?
dime-piece
tenderghetti?
tenderccine alfredo??
LADY LADY LADYYYY,
'SCUSE ME...
Y-YOU WORK HERE?

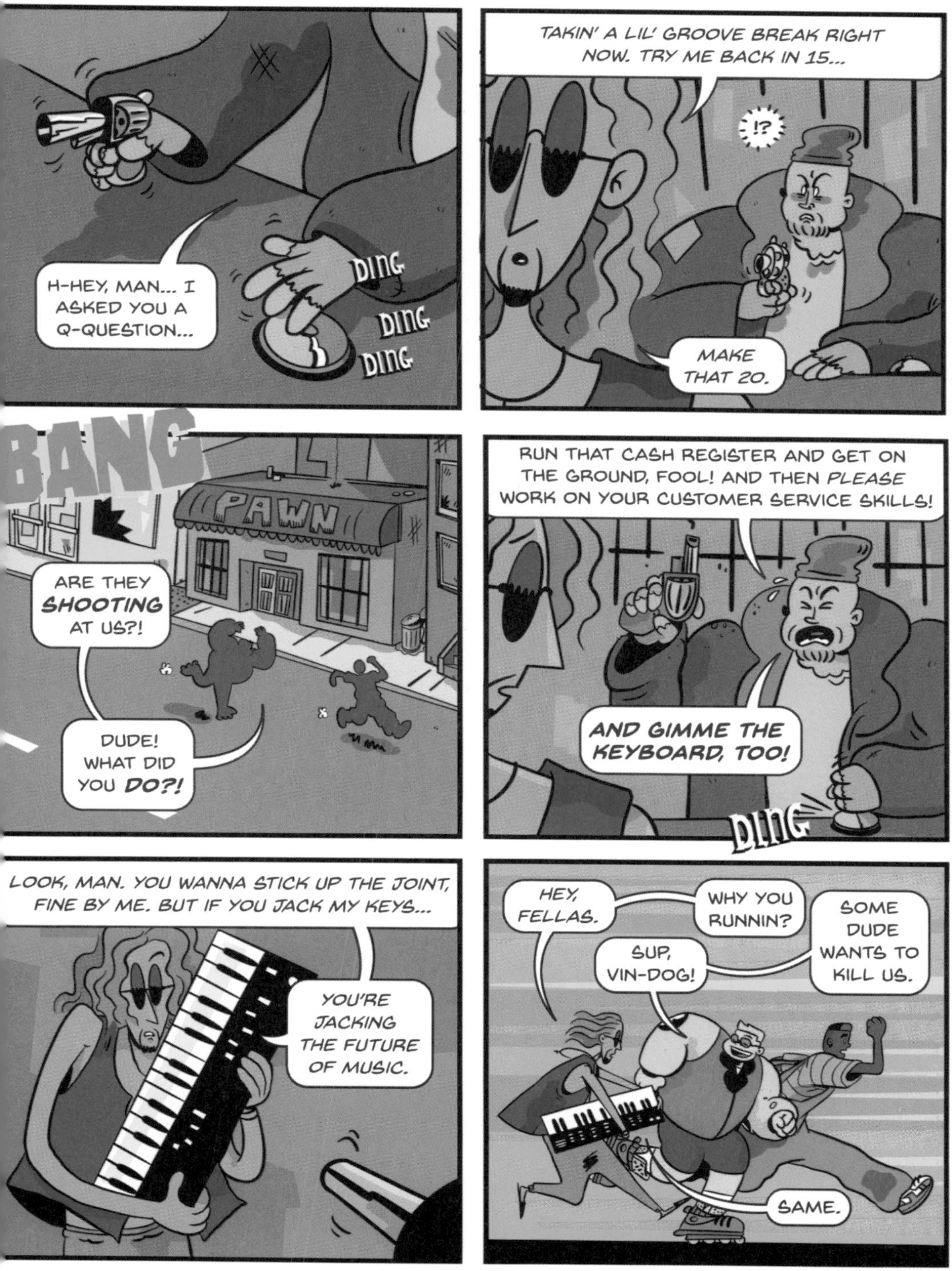

H-HEY, MAN... I ASKED YOU A Q-QUESTION...
DING
DING
DING
TAKIN' A LIL' GROOVE BREAK RIGHT NOW. TRY ME BACK IN 15...
!?
MAKE THAT 20.
BANG
PAWN
ARE THEY *SHOOTING* AT US?!
DUDE! WHAT DID YOU *DO?!*
RUN THAT CASH REGISTER AND GET ON THE GROUND, FOOL! AND THEN *PLEASE* WORK ON YOUR CUSTOMER SERVICE SKILLS!
AND GIMME THE KEYBOARD, TOO!
DING
LOOK, MAN. YOU WANNA STICK UP THE JOINT, FINE BY ME. BUT IF YOU JACK MY KEYS...
YOU'RE JACKING THE FUTURE OF MUSIC.
HEY, FELLAS.
WHY YOU RUNNIN?
SUP, VIN-DOG!
SOME DUDE WANTS TO KILL US.
SAME.

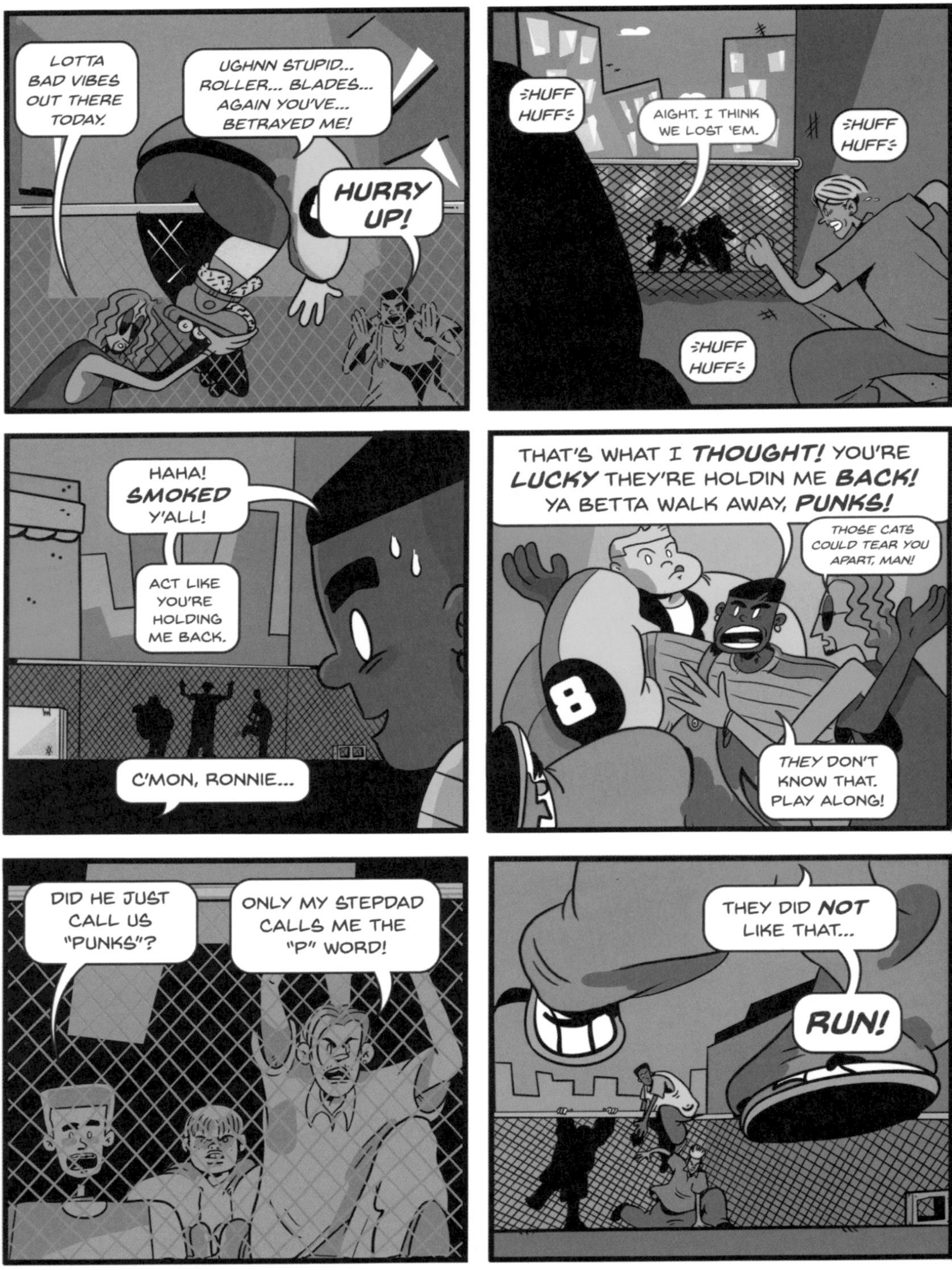
LOTTA BAD VIBES OUT THERE TODAY.
UGHNN STUPID... ROLLER... BLADES... AGAIN YOU'VE... BETRAYED ME!
HURRY UP!
HUFF HUFF
AIGHT. I THINK WE LOST 'EM.
HUFF HUFF
HUFF HUFF
HAHA! SMOKED Y'ALL!
ACT LIKE YOU'RE HOLDING ME BACK.
C'MON, RONNIE...
THAT'S WHAT I THOUGHT! YOU'RE LUCKY THEY'RE HOLDIN ME BACK! YA BETTA WALK AWAY, PUNKS!
THOSE CATS COULD TEAR YOU APART, MAN!
THEY DON'T KNOW THAT. PLAY ALONG!
DID HE JUST CALL US "PUNKS"?
ONLY MY STEPDAD CALLS ME THE "P" WORD!
THEY DID NOT LIKE THAT...
RUN!

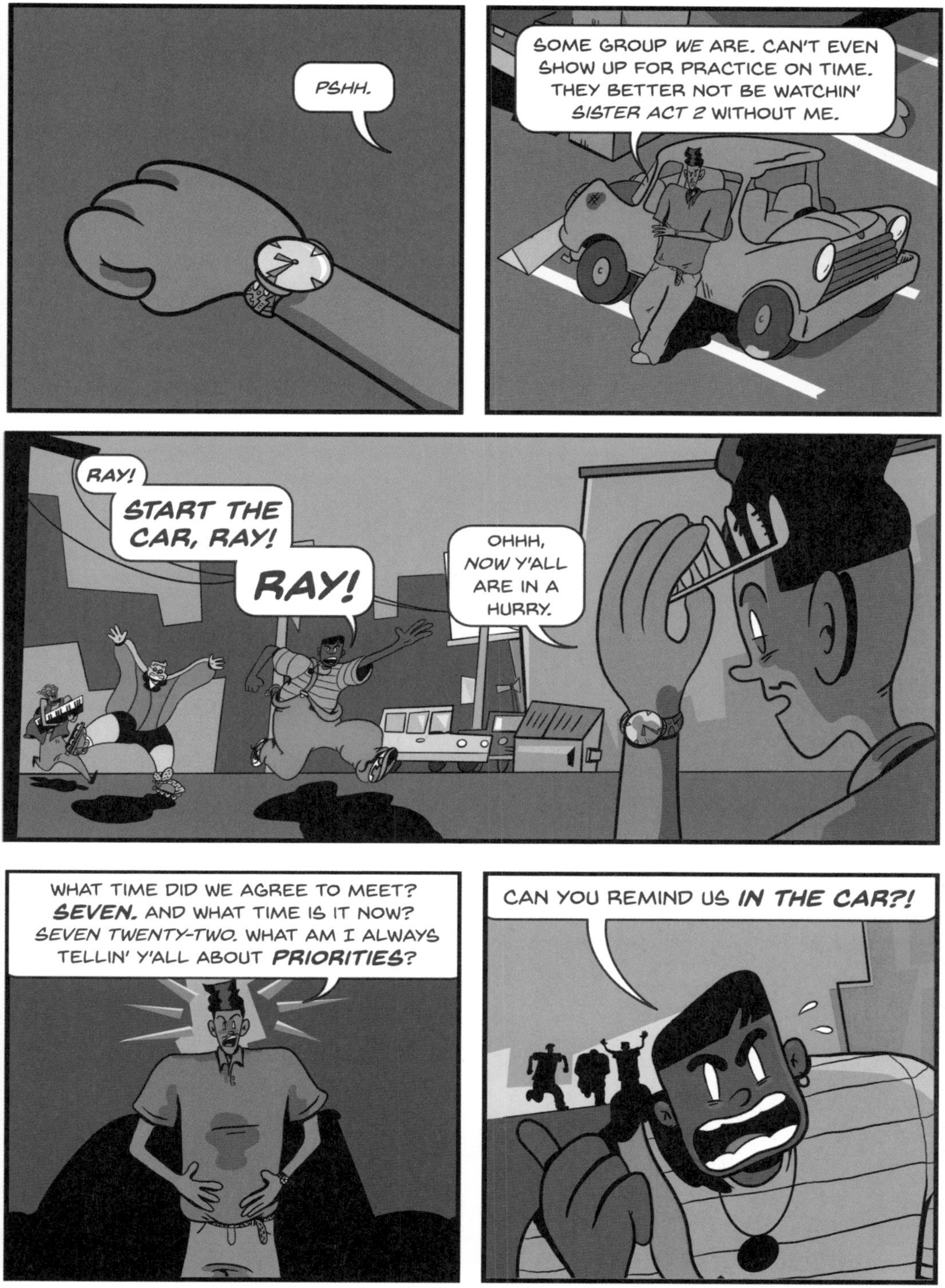
PSHH.
SOME GROUP WE ARE. CAN'T EVEN SHOW UP FOR PRACTICE ON TIME. THEY BETTER NOT BE WATCHIN' SISTER ACT 2 WITHOUT ME.
RAY!
START THE CAR, RAY!
RAY!
OHHH, NOW Y'ALL ARE IN A HURRY.
WHAT TIME DID WE AGREE TO MEET? SEVEN. AND WHAT TIME IS IT NOW? SEVEN TWENTY-TWO. WHAT AM I ALWAYS TELLIN' Y'ALL ABOUT PRIORITIES?
CAN YOU REMIND US IN THE CAR?!

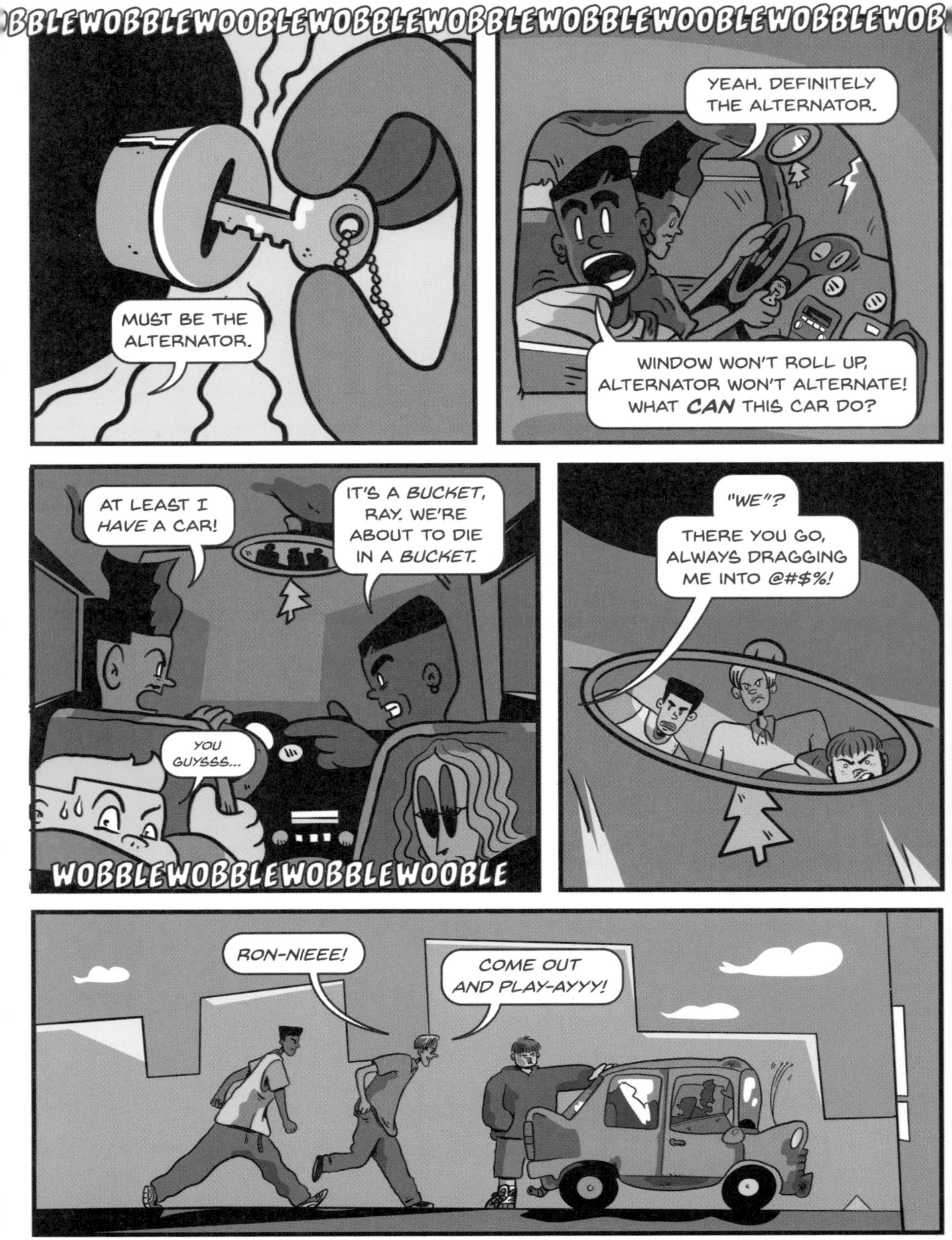
BBLEWOBBLEWOOBLEWOBBLEWOBBLEWOBBLEWOOBLEWOBBLEWOB
MUST BE THE ALTERNATOR.
YEAH. DEFINITELY THE ALTERNATOR.
WINDOW WON'T ROLL UP, ALTERNATOR WON'T ALTERNATE! WHAT CAN THIS CAR DO?
AT LEAST I HAVE A CAR!
IT'S A BUCKET, RAY. WE'RE ABOUT TO DIE IN A BUCKET.
YOU GUYSSS...
WOBBLEWOBBLEWOBBLEWOOBLE
"WE"?
THERE YOU GO, ALWAYS DRAGGING ME INTO @#$%!
RON-NIEEE!
COME OUT AND PLAY-AYYY!

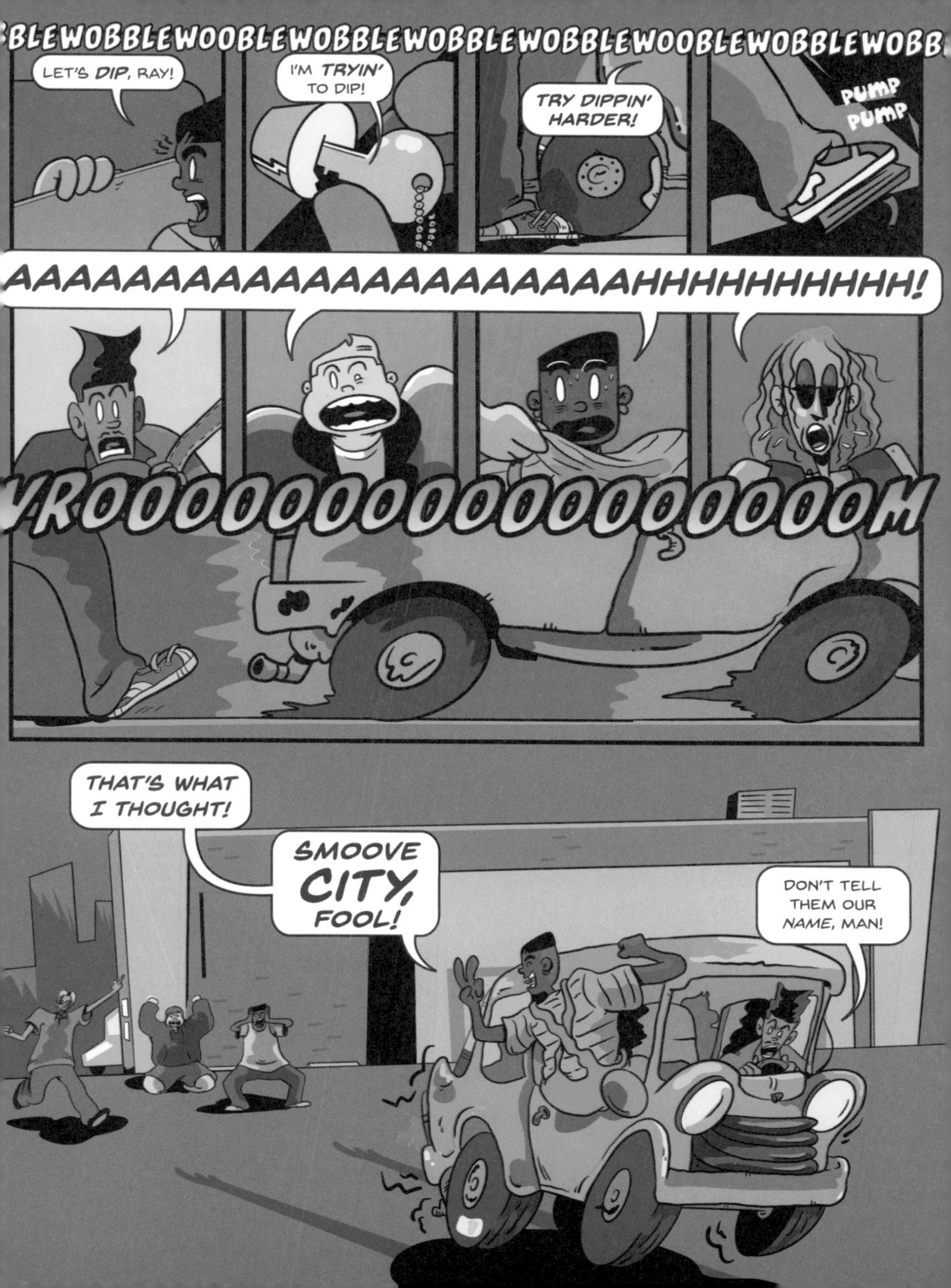
BLEWOBBLEWOOBLEWOBBLEWOBBLEWOBBLEWOOBLEWOBBLEWOBB
LET'S DIP, RAY!
I'M TRYIN' TO DIP!
TRY DIPPIN' HARDER!
PUMP PUMP
AAAAAAAAAAAAAAAAAAAAAAAHHHHHHHHHH!
VROOOOOOOOOOOOOOOOOOM
THAT'S WHAT I THOUGHT!
SMOOVE CITY, FOOL!
DON'T TELL THEM OUR NAME, MAN!

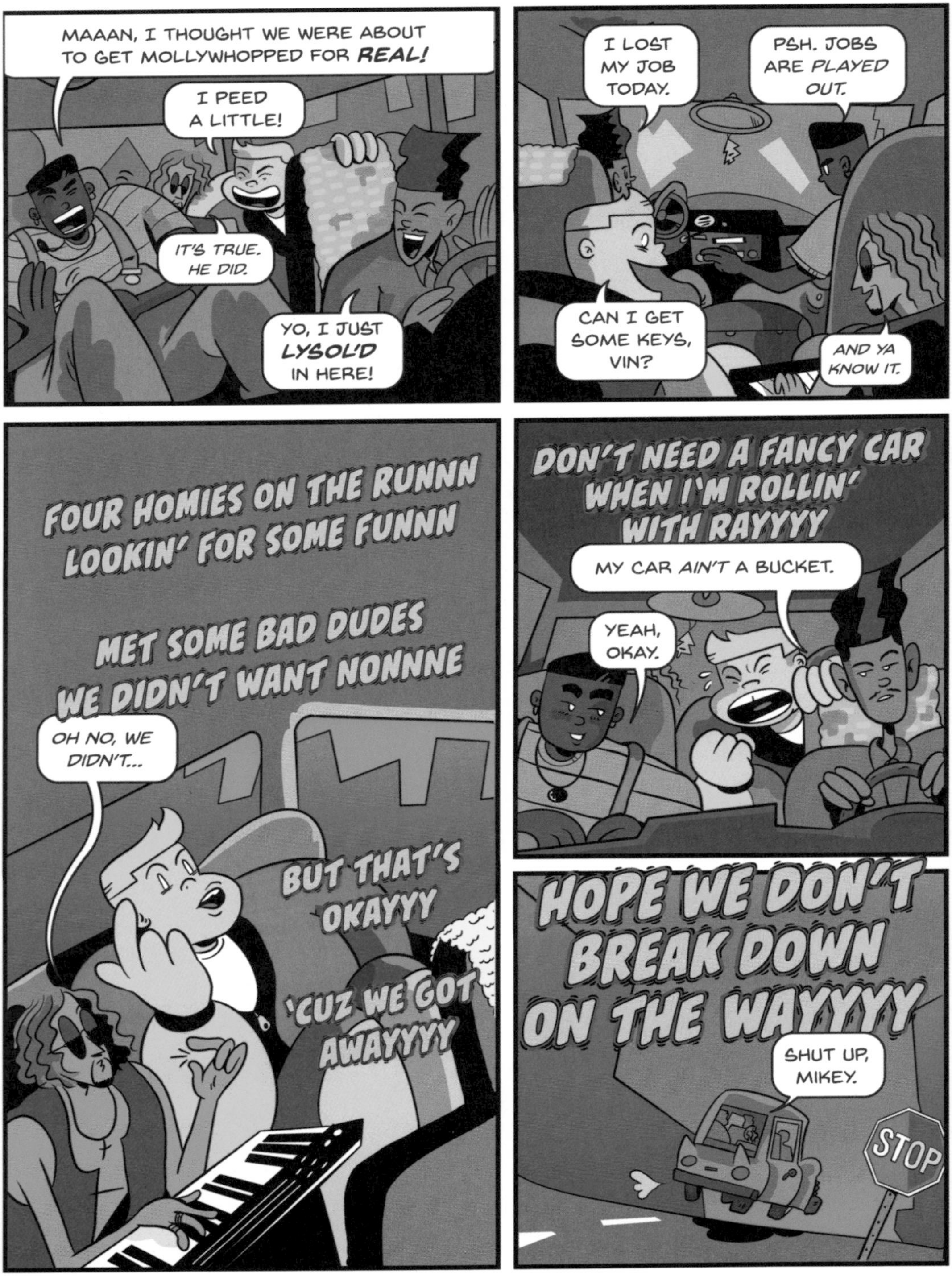
MAAAN, I THOUGHT WE WERE ABOUT TO GET MOLLYWHOPPED FOR REAL!
I PEED A LITTLE!
IT'S TRUE. HE DID.
YO, I JUST LYSOL'D IN HERE!
I LOST MY JOB TODAY.
PSH. JOBS ARE PLAYED OUT.
CAN I GET SOME KEYS, VIN?
AND YA KNOW IT.
FOUR HOMIES ON THE RUNNN LOOKIN' FOR SOME FUNNN
MET SOME BAD DUDES WE DIDN'T WANT NONNNE
OH NO, WE DIDN'T...
BUT THAT'S OKAYYY
'CUZ WE GOT AWAYYYY
DON'T NEED A FANCY CAR WHEN I'M ROLLIN' WITH RAYYYY
MY CAR AIN'T A BUCKET.
YEAH, OKAY.
HOPE WE DON'T BREAK DOWN ON THE WAYYYY
SHUT UP, MIKEY.
STOP

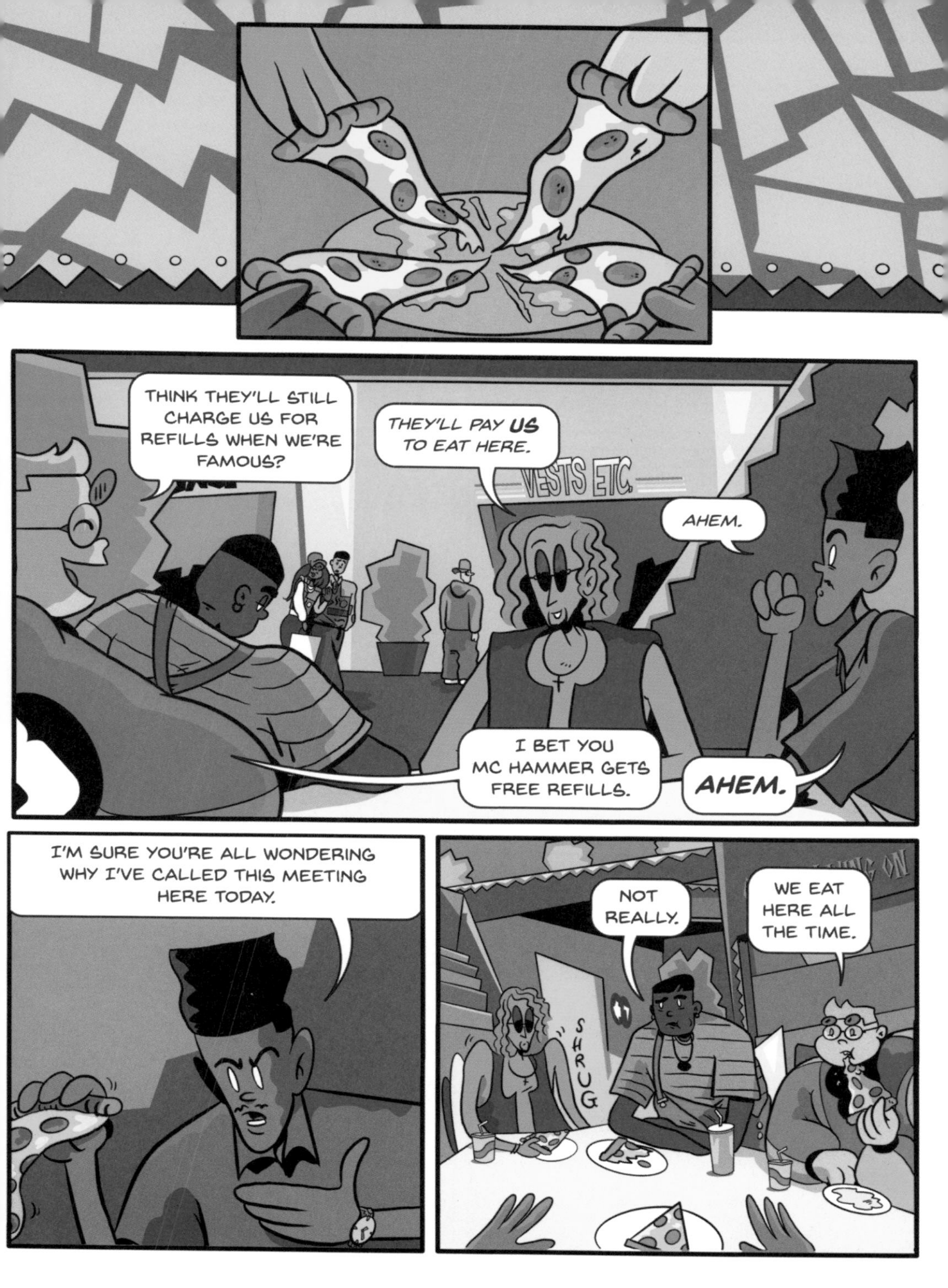
THINK THEY'LL STILL CHARGE US FOR REFILLS WHEN WE'RE FAMOUS?
THEY'LL PAY **US** TO EAT HERE.
VESTS ETC.
AHEM.
I BET YOU MC HAMMER GETS FREE REFILLS.
AHEM.
I'M SURE YOU'RE ALL WONDERING WHY I'VE CALLED THIS MEETING HERE TODAY.
NOT REALLY.
WE EAT HERE ALL THE TIME.
SHRUG

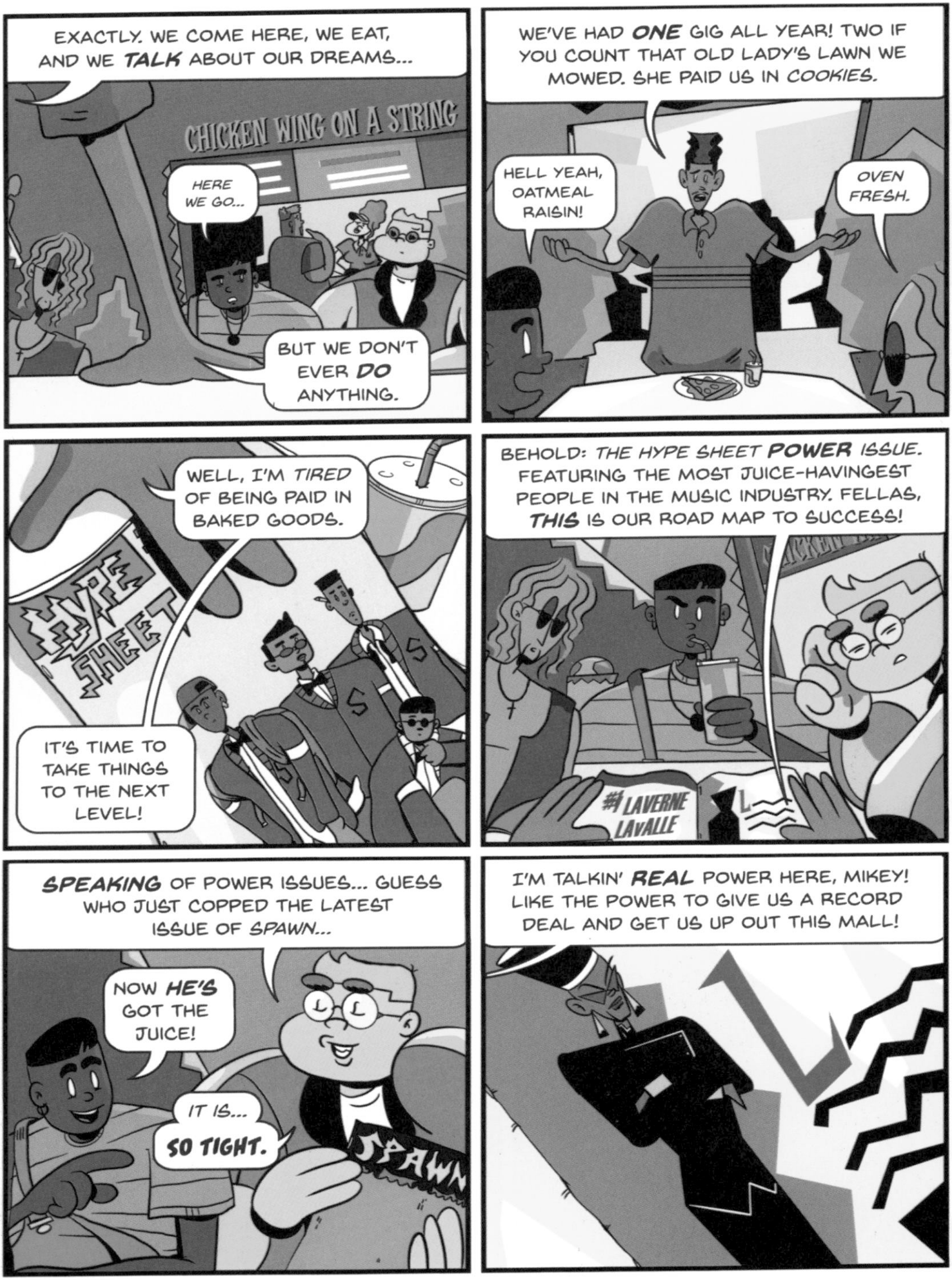
EXACTLY. WE COME HERE, WE EAT, AND WE TALK ABOUT OUR DREAMS...
CHICKEN WING ON A STRING
HERE WE GO...
BUT WE DON'T EVER DO ANYTHING.
WE'VE HAD ONE GIG ALL YEAR! TWO IF YOU COUNT THAT OLD LADY'S LAWN WE MOWED. SHE PAID US IN COOKIES.
HELL YEAH, OATMEAL RAISIN!
OVEN FRESH.
WELL, I'M TIRED OF BEING PAID IN BAKED GOODS.
HYPE SHEET
IT'S TIME TO TAKE THINGS TO THE NEXT LEVEL!
BEHOLD: THE HYPE SHEET POWER ISSUE. FEATURING THE MOST JUICE-HAVINGEST PEOPLE IN THE MUSIC INDUSTRY. FELLAS, THIS IS OUR ROAD MAP TO SUCCESS!
#1 LAVERNE LAVALLE
SPEAKING OF POWER ISSUES... GUESS WHO JUST COPPED THE LATEST ISSUE OF SPAWN...
NOW HE'S GOT THE JUICE!
IT IS...
SO TIGHT.
SPAWN
I'M TALKIN' REAL POWER HERE, MIKEY! LIKE THE POWER TO GIVE US A RECORD DEAL AND GET US UP OUT THIS MALL!

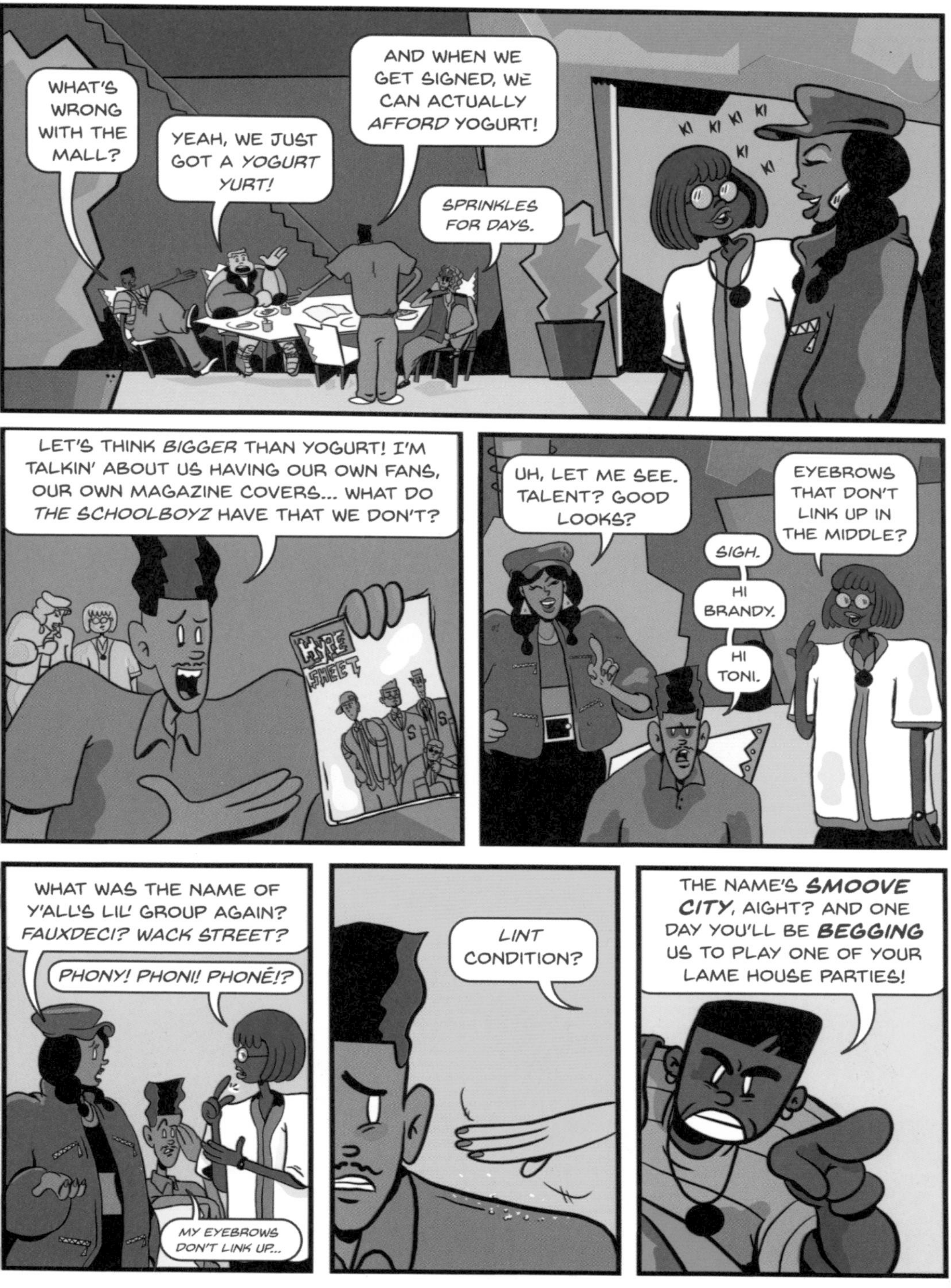
WHAT'S WRONG WITH THE MALL?
YEAH, WE JUST GOT A *YOGURT* YURT!
AND WHEN WE GET SIGNED, WE CAN ACTUALLY *AFFORD* YOGURT!
SPRINKLES FOR DAYS.
KI KI KI KI KI KI
LET'S THINK *BIGGER* THAN YOGURT! I'M TALKIN' ABOUT US HAVING OUR OWN FANS, OUR OWN MAGAZINE COVERS... WHAT DO *THE SCHOOLBOYZ* HAVE THAT WE DON'T?
HYPE SHEET
UH, LET ME SEE. TALENT? GOOD LOOKS?
EYEBROWS THAT DON'T LINK UP IN THE MIDDLE?
SIGH.
HI BRANDY.
HI TONI.
WHAT WAS THE NAME OF Y'ALL'S LIL' GROUP AGAIN? *FAUXDECI? WACK STREET?*
PHONY! PHONI! PHONÉ!?
MY EYEBROWS DON'T LINK UP...
LINT CONDITION?
THE NAME'S ***SMOOVE CITY***, AIGHT? AND ONE DAY YOU'LL BE ***BEGGING*** US TO PLAY ONE OF YOUR LAME HOUSE PARTIES!

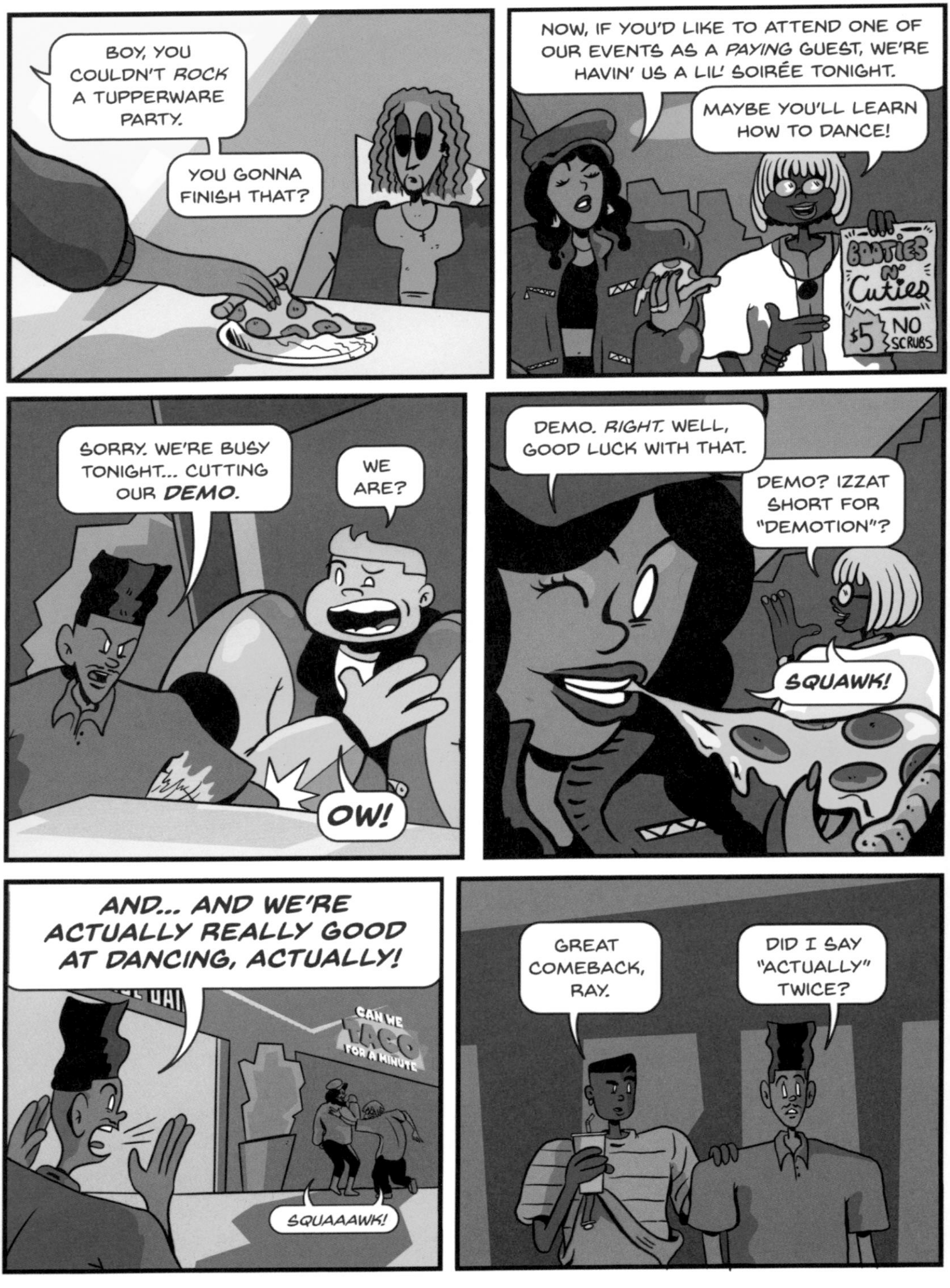
BOY, YOU COULDN'T *ROCK* A TUPPERWARE PARTY.
YOU GONNA FINISH THAT?
NOW, IF YOU'D LIKE TO ATTEND ONE OF OUR EVENTS AS A *PAYING* GUEST, WE'RE HAVIN' US A LIL' SOIRÉE TONIGHT.
MAYBE YOU'LL LEARN HOW TO DANCE!
BOOTIES N' Cuties
$5 NO SCRUBS
SORRY. WE'RE BUSY TONIGHT... CUTTING OUR ***DEMO.***
WE ARE?
OW!
DEMO. *RIGHT.* WELL, GOOD LUCK WITH THAT.
DEMO? IZZAT SHORT FOR "DEMOTION"?
SQUAWK!
AND... AND WE'RE ACTUALLY REALLY GOOD AT DANCING, ACTUALLY!
CAN WE TACO FOR A MINUTE
SQUAAAWK!
GREAT COMEBACK, RAY.
DID I SAY "ACTUALLY" TWICE?

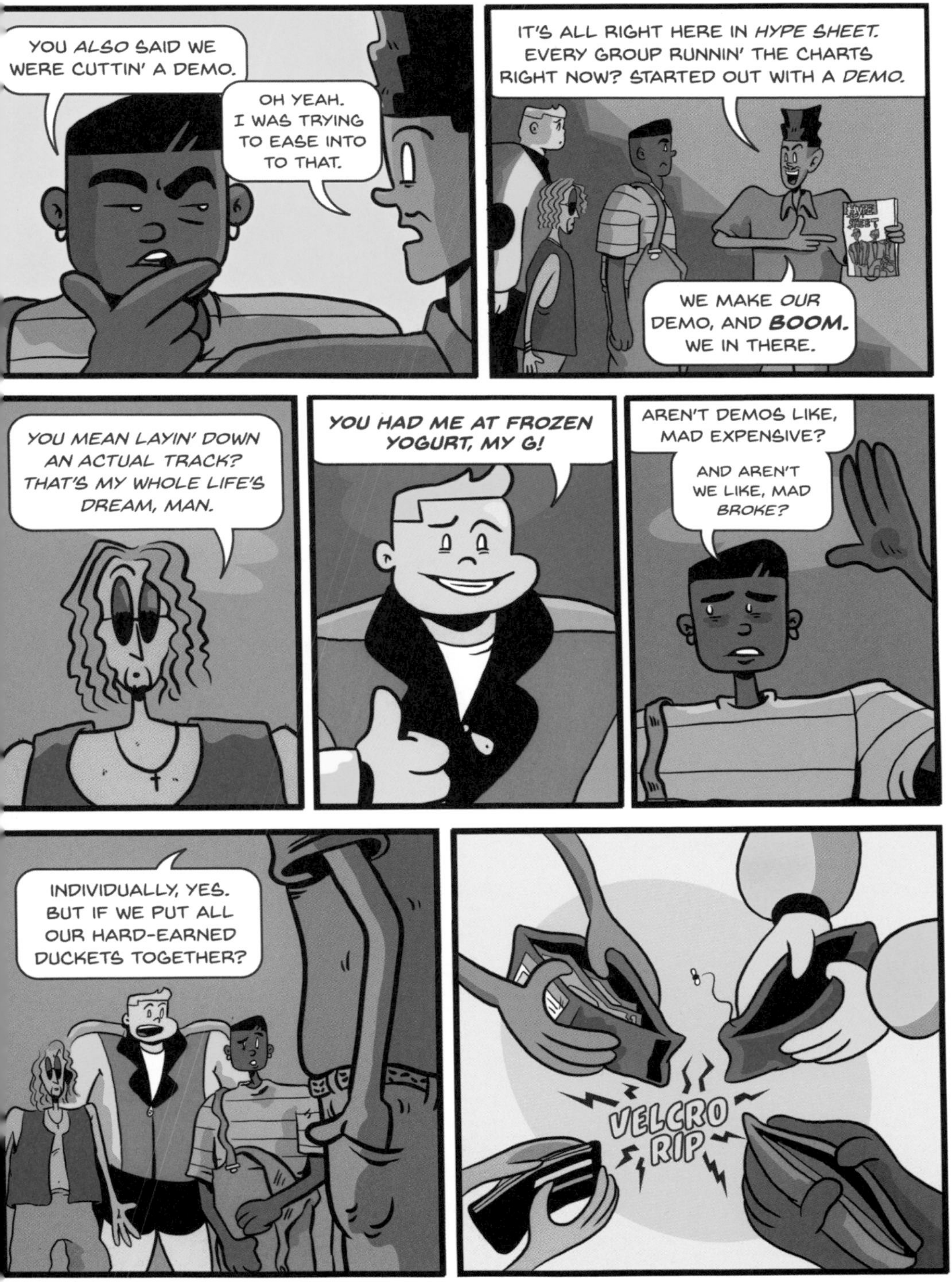
YOU *ALSO* SAID WE WERE CUTTIN' A DEMO.
OH YEAH. I WAS TRYING TO EASE INTO TO THAT.
IT'S ALL RIGHT HERE IN *HYPE SHEET.* EVERY GROUP RUNNIN' THE CHARTS RIGHT NOW? STARTED OUT WITH A *DEMO.*
HYPE SHEET
WE MAKE *OUR* DEMO, AND ***BOOM.*** WE IN THERE.
YOU MEAN LAYIN' DOWN AN ACTUAL TRACK? THAT'S MY WHOLE LIFE'S DREAM, MAN.
YOU HAD ME AT FROZEN YOGURT, MY G!
AREN'T DEMOS LIKE, MAD EXPENSIVE?
AND AREN'T WE LIKE, MAD *BROKE?*
INDIVIDUALLY, YES. BUT IF WE PUT ALL OUR HARD-EARNED DUCKETS TOGETHER?
VELCRO RIP

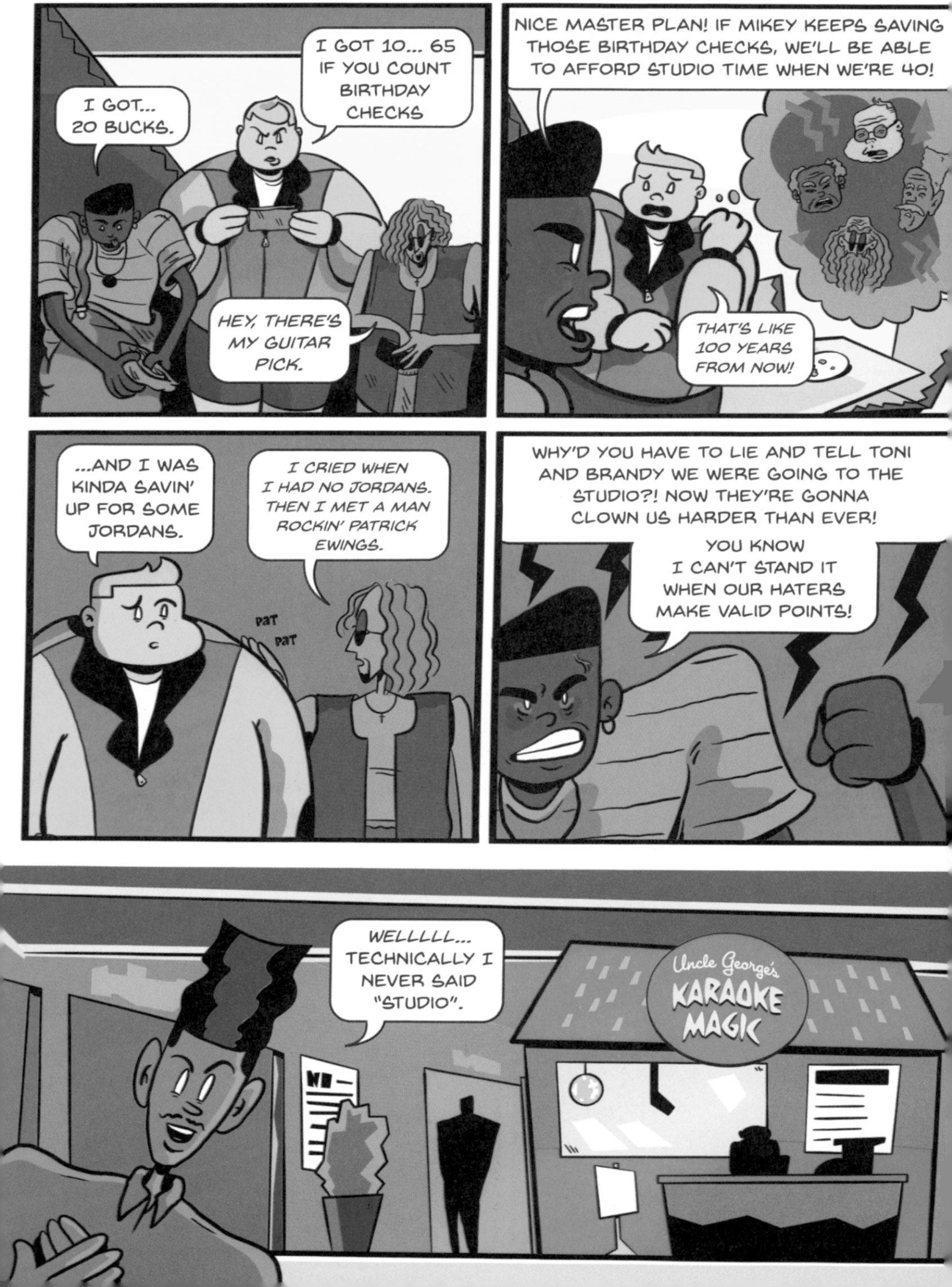
I GOT... 20 BUCKS.
I GOT 10... 65 IF YOU COUNT BIRTHDAY CHECKS
HEY, THERE'S MY GUITAR PICK.
NICE MASTER PLAN! IF MIKEY KEEPS SAVING THOSE BIRTHDAY CHECKS, WE'LL BE ABLE TO AFFORD STUDIO TIME WHEN WE'RE 40!
THAT'S LIKE 100 YEARS FROM NOW!
...AND I WAS KINDA SAVIN' UP FOR SOME JORDANS.
I CRIED WHEN I HAD NO JORDANS. THEN I MET A MAN ROCKIN' PATRICK EWINGS.
PAT
PAT
WHY'D YOU HAVE TO LIE AND TELL TONI AND BRANDY WE WERE GOING TO THE STUDIO?! NOW THEY'RE GONNA CLOWN US HARDER THAN EVER!
YOU KNOW I CAN'T STAND IT WHEN OUR HATERS MAKE VALID POINTS!
WELLLLL... TECHNICALLY I NEVER SAID "STUDIO".
Uncle George's
KARAOKE MAGIC

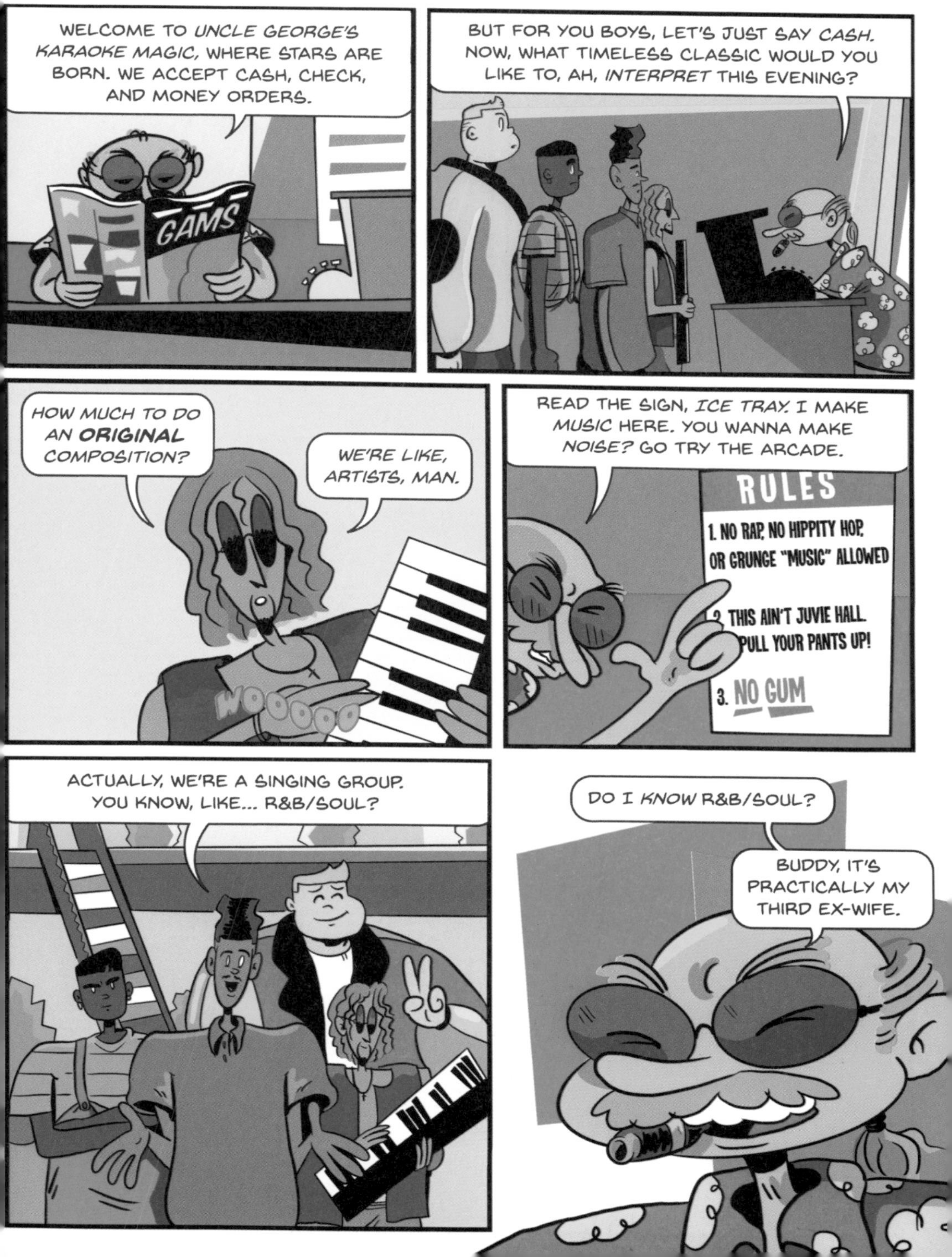
WELCOME TO *UNCLE GEORGE'S KARAOKE MAGIC*, WHERE STARS ARE BORN. WE ACCEPT CASH, CHECK, AND MONEY ORDERS.
GAMS
BUT FOR YOU BOYS, LET'S JUST SAY *CASH*. NOW, WHAT TIMELESS CLASSIC WOULD YOU LIKE TO, AH, *INTERPRET* THIS EVENING?
HOW MUCH TO DO AN **ORIGINAL** COMPOSITION?
WE'RE LIKE, ARTISTS, MAN.
WOOOOOO
READ THE SIGN, *ICE TRAY*. I MAKE *MUSIC* HERE. YOU WANNA MAKE *NOISE?* GO TRY THE ARCADE.
RULES
1. NO RAP, NO HIPPITY HOP, OR GRUNGE "MUSIC" ALLOWED
2. THIS AIN'T JUVIE HALL. PULL YOUR PANTS UP!
3. NO GUM
ACTUALLY, WE'RE A SINGING GROUP. YOU KNOW, LIKE... R&B/SOUL?
DO I *KNOW* R&B/SOUL?
BUDDY, IT'S PRACTICALLY MY THIRD EX-WIFE.

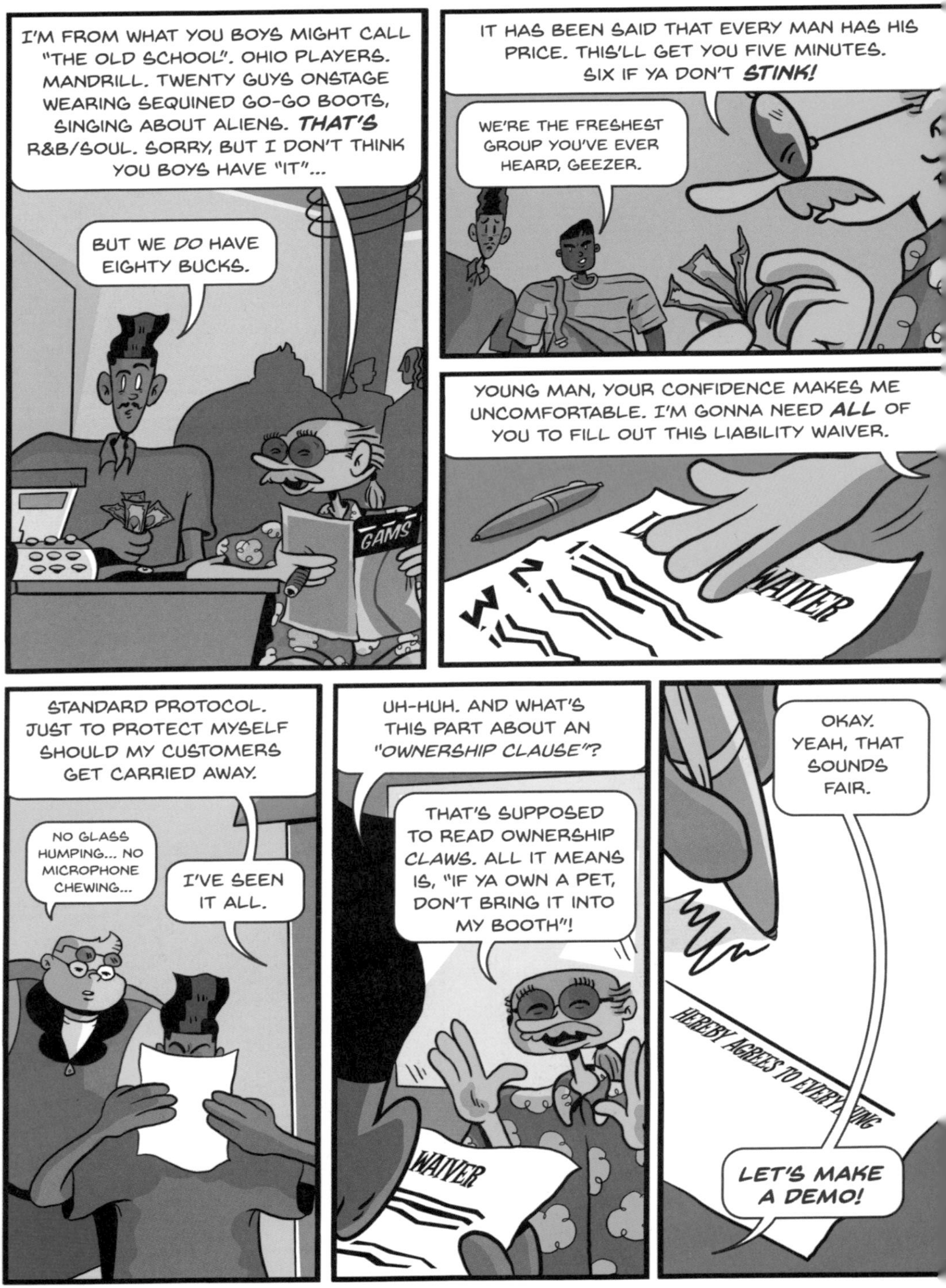
I'M FROM WHAT YOU BOYS MIGHT CALL "THE OLD SCHOOL". OHIO PLAYERS. MANDRILL. TWENTY GUYS ONSTAGE WEARING SEQUINED GO-GO BOOTS, SINGING ABOUT ALIENS. THAT'S R&B/SOUL. SORRY, BUT I DON'T THINK YOU BOYS HAVE "IT"...
BUT WE DO HAVE EIGHTY BUCKS.
GAMS
IT HAS BEEN SAID THAT EVERY MAN HAS HIS PRICE. THIS'LL GET YOU FIVE MINUTES. SIX IF YA DON'T STINK!
WE'RE THE FRESHEST GROUP YOU'VE EVER HEARD, GEEZER.
YOUNG MAN, YOUR CONFIDENCE MAKES ME UNCOMFORTABLE. I'M GONNA NEED ALL OF YOU TO FILL OUT THIS LIABILITY WAIVER.
WAIVER
STANDARD PROTOCOL. JUST TO PROTECT MYSELF SHOULD MY CUSTOMERS GET CARRIED AWAY.
NO GLASS HUMPING... NO MICROPHONE CHEWING...
I'VE SEEN IT ALL.
UH-HUH. AND WHAT'S THIS PART ABOUT AN "OWNERSHIP CLAUSE"?
THAT'S SUPPOSED TO READ OWNERSHIP CLAWS. ALL IT MEANS IS, "IF YA OWN A PET, DON'T BRING IT INTO MY BOOTH"!
WAIVER
OKAY. YEAH, THAT SOUNDS FAIR.
HEREBY AGREES TO EVERY
LET'S MAKE A DEMO!

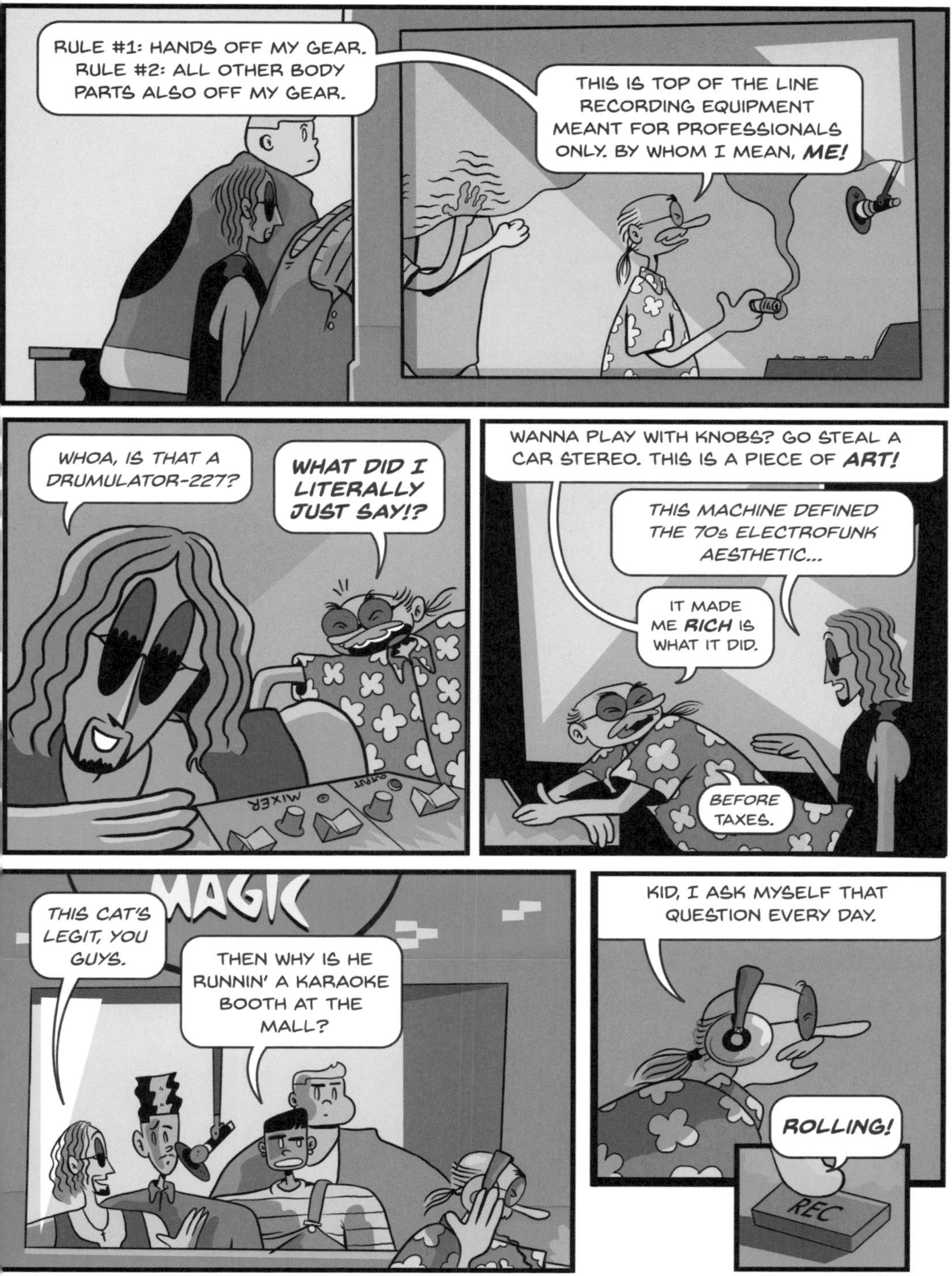
RULE #1: HANDS OFF MY GEAR. RULE #2: ALL OTHER BODY PARTS ALSO OFF MY GEAR.
THIS IS TOP OF THE LINE RECORDING EQUIPMENT MEANT FOR PROFESSIONALS ONLY. BY WHOM I MEAN, ME!
WHOA, IS THAT A DRUMULATOR-227?
WHAT DID I LITERALLY JUST SAY!?
MIXER
WANNA PLAY WITH KNOBS? GO STEAL A CAR STEREO. THIS IS A PIECE OF ART!
THIS MACHINE DEFINED THE 70s ELECTROFUNK AESTHETIC...
IT MADE ME RICH IS WHAT IT DID.
BEFORE TAXES.
MAGIC
THIS CAT'S LEGIT, YOU GUYS.
THEN WHY IS HE RUNNIN' A KARAOKE BOOTH AT THE MALL?
KID, I ASK MYSELF THAT QUESTION EVERY DAY.
ROLLING!
REC

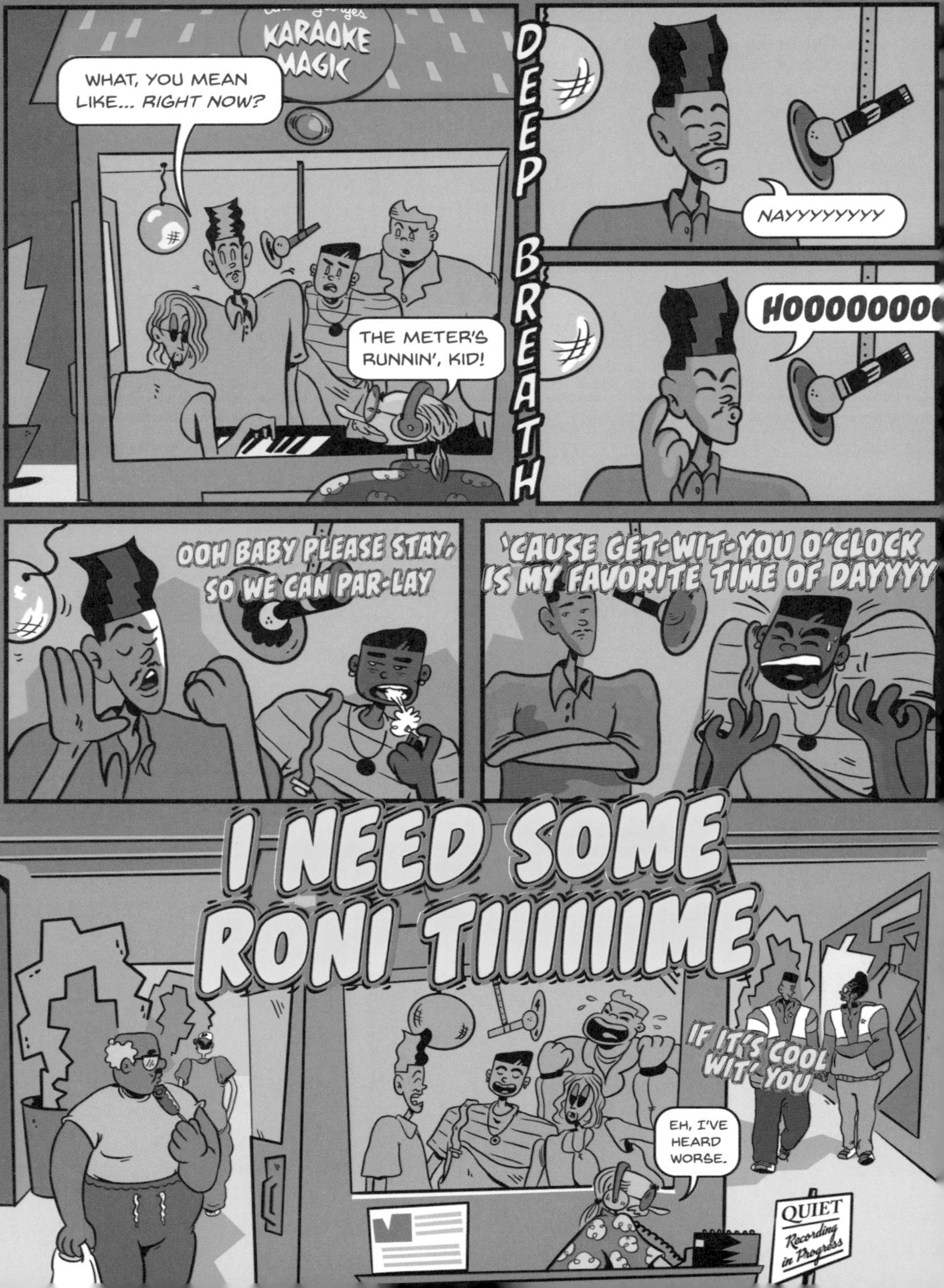
KARAOKE MAGIC
WHAT, YOU MEAN LIKE... RIGHT NOW?
THE METER'S RUNNIN', KID!
DEEP BREATH
NAYYYYYYYY
HOOOOOOOO
OOH BABY PLEASE STAY, SO WE CAN PAR-LAY
'CAUSE GET-WIT-YOU O'CLOCK IS MY FAVORITE TIME OF DAYYYY
I NEED SOME RONI TIIIIIIME
IF IT'S COOL WIT' YOU
EH, I'VE HEARD WORSE.
QUIET Recording in Progress

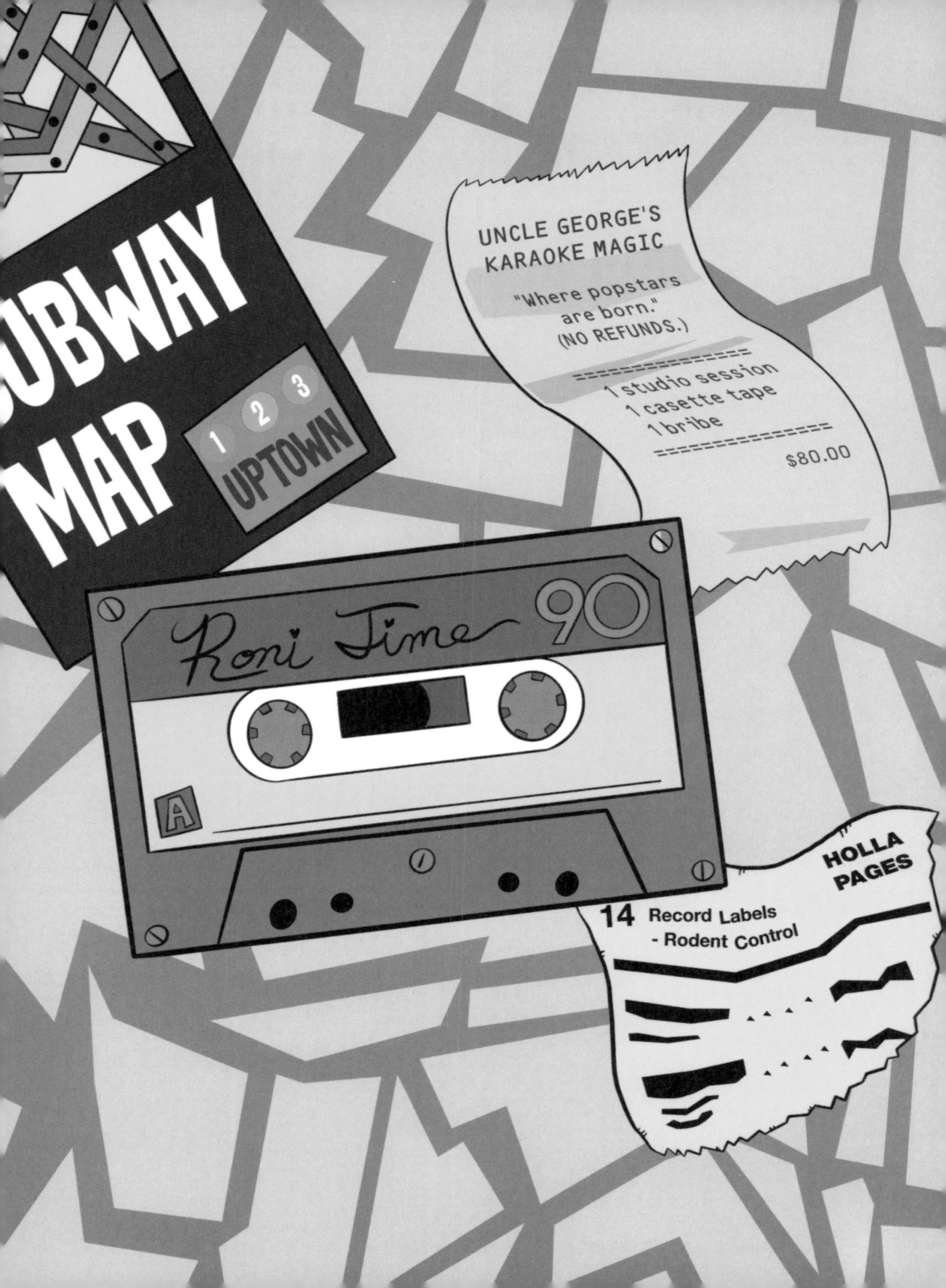
SUBWAY
MAP
1 2 3
UPTOWN
UNCLE GEORGE'S
KARAOKE MAGIC
"Where popstars
are born."
(NO REFUNDS.)
1 studio session
1 casette tape
1 bribe
$80.00
Roni Time
90
A
HOLLA
PAGES
14 Record Labels
- Rodent Control

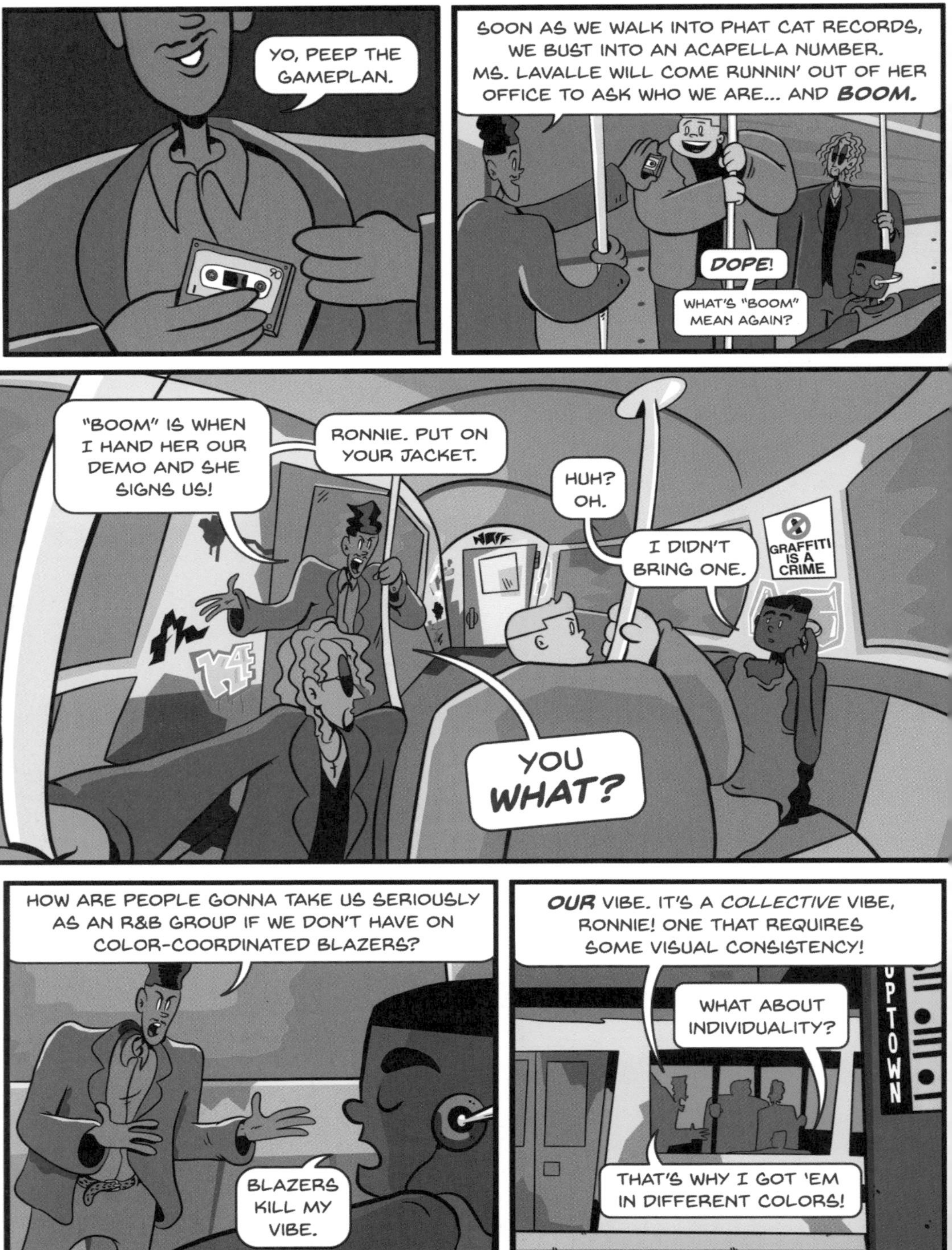
YO, PEEP THE GAMEPLAN.
SOON AS WE WALK INTO PHAT CAT RECORDS, WE BUST INTO AN ACAPELLA NUMBER. MS. LAVALLE WILL COME RUNNIN' OUT OF HER OFFICE TO ASK WHO WE ARE... AND *BOOM.*
DOPE!
WHAT'S "BOOM" MEAN AGAIN?
"BOOM" IS WHEN I HAND HER OUR DEMO AND SHE SIGNS US!
RONNIE. PUT ON YOUR JACKET.
HUH? OH.
I DIDN'T BRING ONE.
GRAFFITI IS A CRIME
YOU *WHAT?*
HOW ARE PEOPLE GONNA TAKE US SERIOUSLY AS AN R&B GROUP IF WE DON'T HAVE ON COLOR-COORDINATED BLAZERS?
BLAZERS KILL MY VIBE.
OUR VIBE. IT'S A *COLLECTIVE* VIBE, RONNIE! ONE THAT REQUIRES SOME VISUAL CONSISTENCY!
UPTOWN
WHAT ABOUT INDIVIDUALITY?
THAT'S WHY I GOT 'EM IN DIFFERENT COLORS!

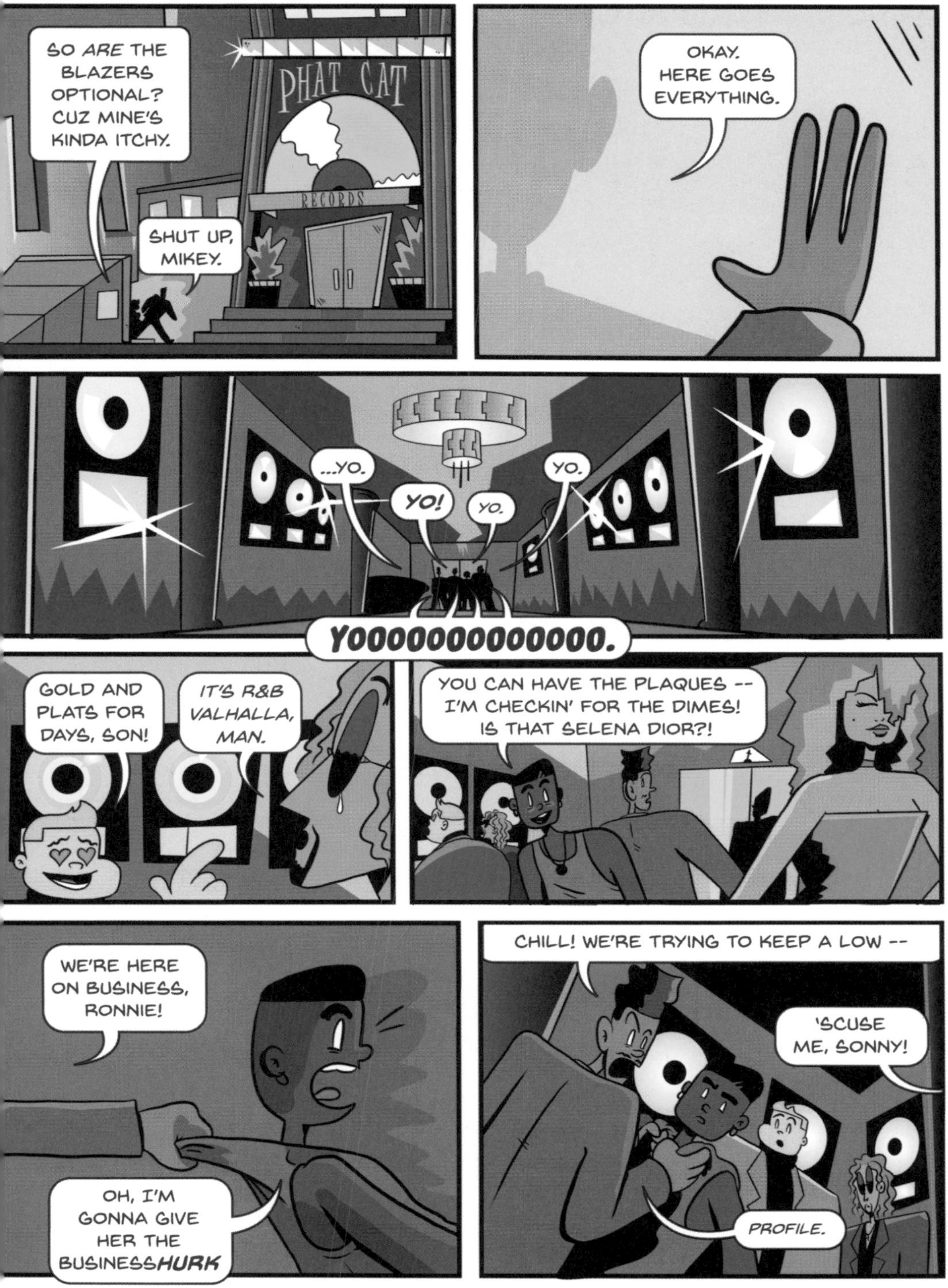
SO ARE THE BLAZERS OPTIONAL? CUZ MINE'S KINDA ITCHY.
PHAT CAT
RECORDS
SHUT UP, MIKEY.
OKAY. HERE GOES EVERYTHING.
...YO.
YO!
YO.
YO.
YOOOOOOOOOOOOO.
GOLD AND PLATS FOR DAYS, SON!
IT'S R&B VALHALLA, MAN.
YOU CAN HAVE THE PLAQUES -- I'M CHECKIN' FOR THE DIMES! IS THAT SELENA DIOR?!
WE'RE HERE ON BUSINESS, RONNIE!
OH, I'M GONNA GIVE HER THE BUSINESSHURK
CHILL! WE'RE TRYING TO KEEP A LOW --
'SCUSE ME, SONNY!
PROFILE.

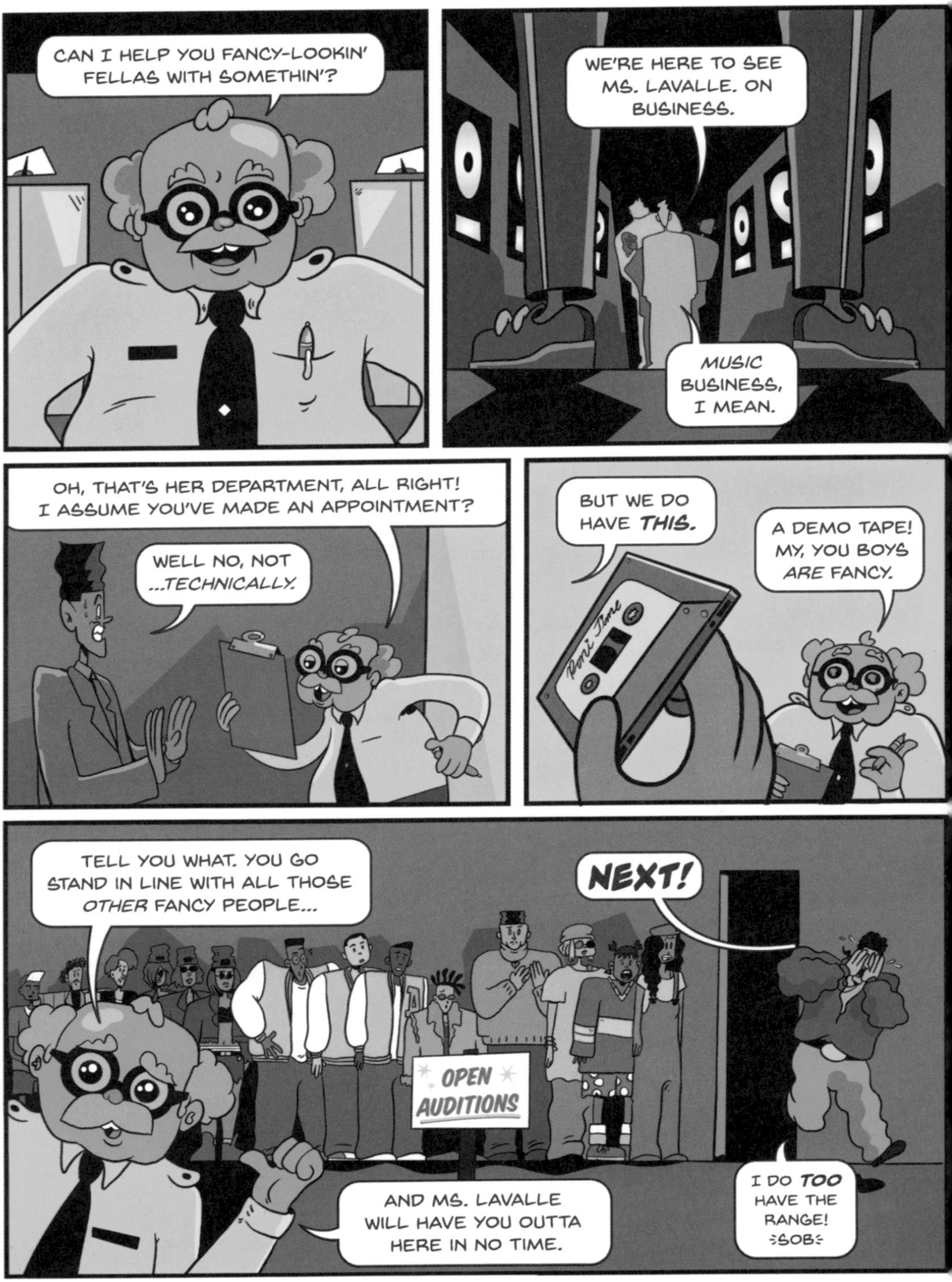
CAN I HELP YOU FANCY-LOOKIN' FELLAS WITH SOMETHIN'?
WE'RE HERE TO SEE MS. LAVALLE. ON BUSINESS.
MUSIC BUSINESS, I MEAN.
OH, THAT'S HER DEPARTMENT, ALL RIGHT! I ASSUME YOU'VE MADE AN APPOINTMENT?
WELL NO, NOT ...TECHNICALLY.
BUT WE DO HAVE THIS.
Roni Time
A DEMO TAPE! MY, YOU BOYS ARE FANCY.
TELL YOU WHAT. YOU GO STAND IN LINE WITH ALL THOSE OTHER FANCY PEOPLE...
NEXT!
OPEN AUDITIONS
AND MS. LAVALLE WILL HAVE YOU OUTTA HERE IN NO TIME.
I DO TOO HAVE THE RANGE! SOB

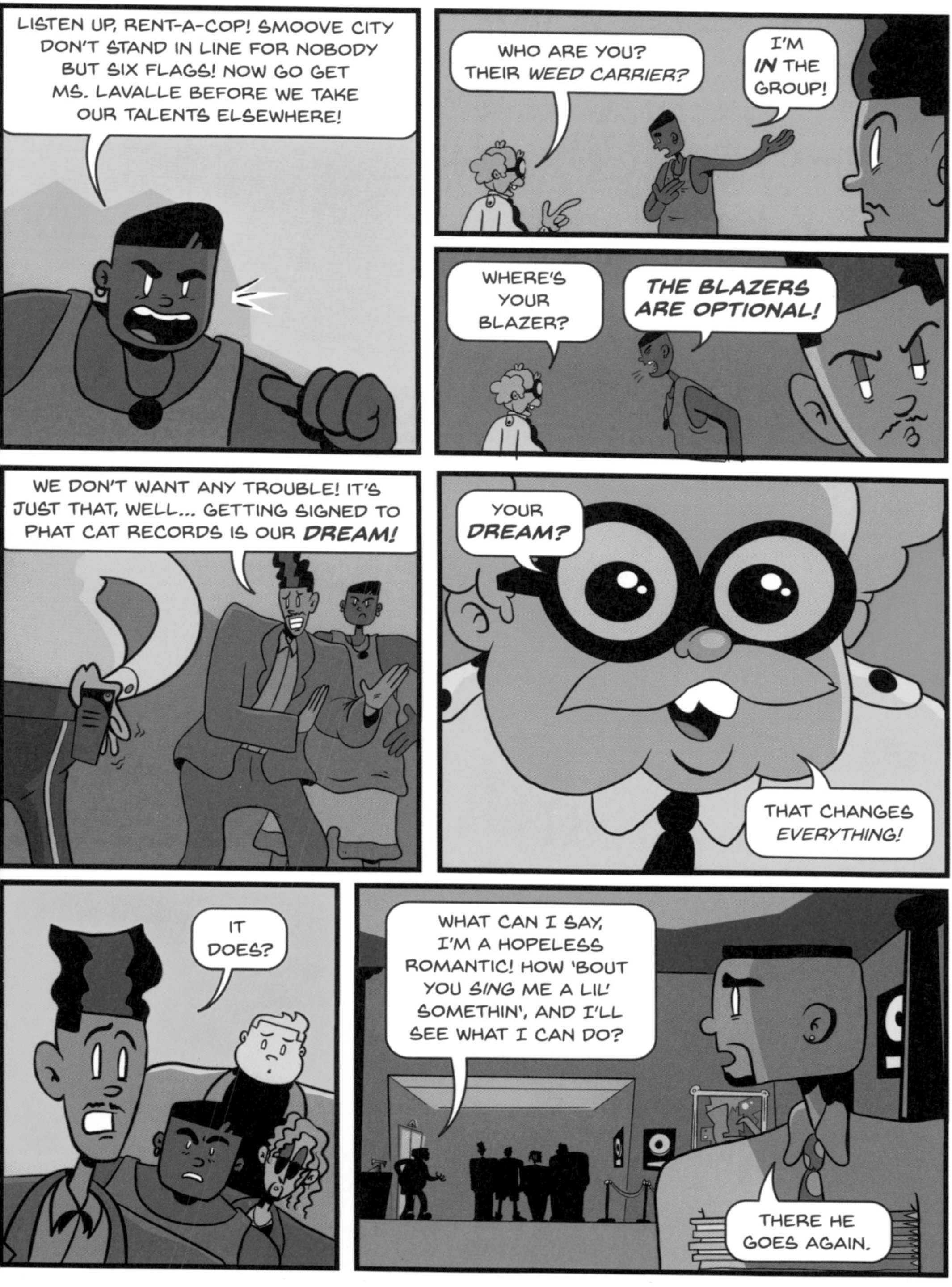

LISTEN UP, RENT-A-COP! SMOOVE CITY DON'T STAND IN LINE FOR NOBODY BUT SIX FLAGS! NOW GO GET MS. LAVALLE BEFORE WE TAKE OUR TALENTS ELSEWHERE!
WHO ARE YOU? THEIR *WEED CARRIER?*
I'M ***IN*** THE GROUP!
WHERE'S YOUR BLAZER?
THE BLAZERS ARE OPTIONAL!
WE DON'T WANT ANY TROUBLE! IT'S JUST THAT, WELL... GETTING SIGNED TO PHAT CAT RECORDS IS OUR ***DREAM!***
YOUR ***DREAM?***
THAT CHANGES *EVERYTHING!*
IT DOES?
WHAT CAN I SAY, I'M A HOPELESS ROMANTIC! HOW 'BOUT YOU *SING* ME A LIL' SOMETHIN', AND I'LL SEE WHAT I CAN DO?
THERE HE GOES AGAIN.

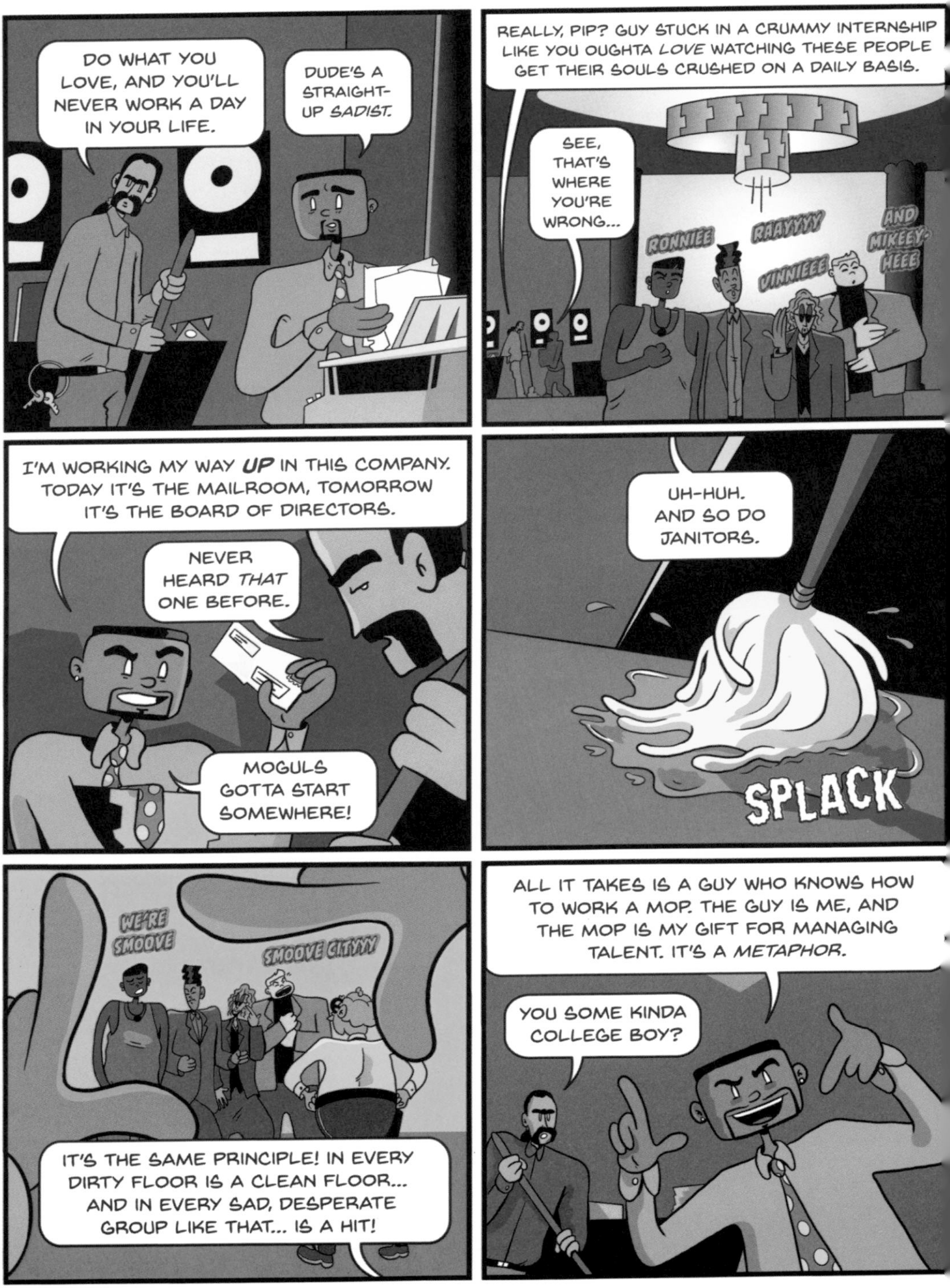
DO WHAT YOU LOVE, AND YOU'LL NEVER WORK A DAY IN YOUR LIFE.
DUDE'S A STRAIGHT-UP *SADIST.*
REALLY, PIP? GUY STUCK IN A CRUMMY INTERNSHIP LIKE YOU OUGHTA *LOVE* WATCHING THESE PEOPLE GET THEIR SOULS CRUSHED ON A DAILY BASIS.
SEE, THAT'S WHERE YOU'RE WRONG...
RONNIEE
RAAYYYY
VINNIEEE
AND MIKEEY-HEEE
I'M WORKING MY WAY **UP** IN THIS COMPANY. TODAY IT'S THE MAILROOM, TOMORROW IT'S THE BOARD OF DIRECTORS.
NEVER HEARD *THAT* ONE BEFORE.
MOGULS GOTTA START SOMEWHERE!
UH-HUH. AND SO DO JANITORS.
SPLACK
WE'RE SMOOVE
SMOOVE CITYYY
IT'S THE SAME PRINCIPLE! IN EVERY DIRTY FLOOR IS A CLEAN FLOOR... AND IN EVERY SAD, DESPERATE GROUP LIKE THAT... IS A HIT!
ALL IT TAKES IS A GUY WHO KNOWS HOW TO WORK A MOP. THE GUY IS ME, AND THE MOP IS MY GIFT FOR MANAGING TALENT. IT'S A *METAPHOR.*
YOU SOME KINDA COLLEGE BOY?

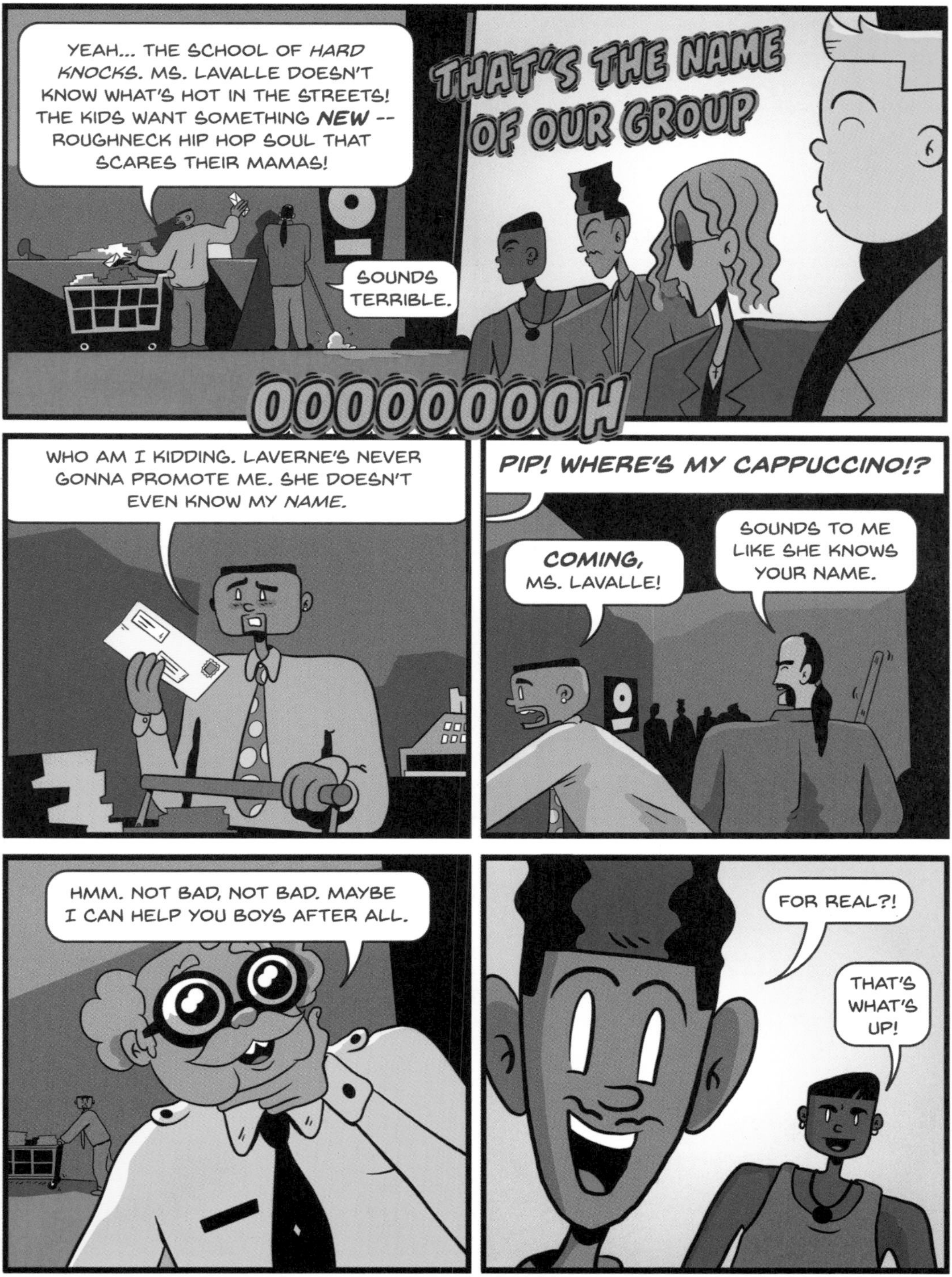
YEAH... THE SCHOOL OF HARD KNOCKS. MS. LAVALLE DOESN'T KNOW WHAT'S HOT IN THE STREETS! THE KIDS WANT SOMETHING NEW -- ROUGHNECK HIP HOP SOUL THAT SCARES THEIR MAMAS!
SOUNDS TERRIBLE.
THAT'S THE NAME OF OUR GROUP
OOOOOOOOH
WHO AM I KIDDING. LAVERNE'S NEVER GONNA PROMOTE ME. SHE DOESN'T EVEN KNOW MY NAME.
PIP! WHERE'S MY CAPPUCCINO!?
COMING, MS. LAVALLE!
SOUNDS TO ME LIKE SHE KNOWS YOUR NAME.
HMM. NOT BAD, NOT BAD. MAYBE I CAN HELP YOU BOYS AFTER ALL.
FOR REAL?!
THAT'S WHAT'S UP!

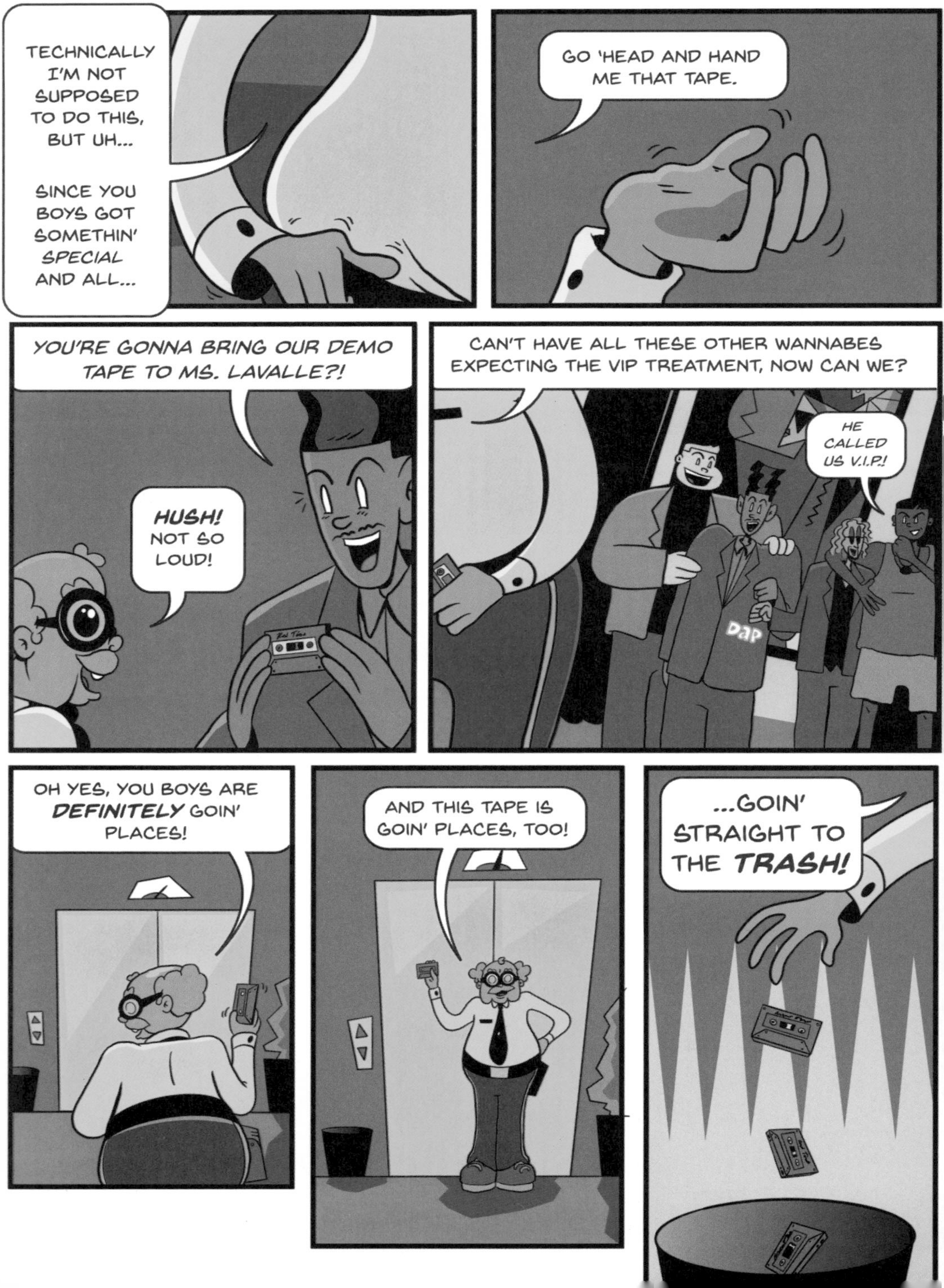
TECHNICALLY I'M NOT SUPPOSED TO DO THIS, BUT UH...
SINCE YOU BOYS GOT SOMETHIN' SPECIAL AND ALL...
GO 'HEAD AND HAND ME THAT TAPE.
YOU'RE GONNA BRING OUR DEMO TAPE TO MS. LAVALLE?!
HUSH! NOT SO LOUD!
CAN'T HAVE ALL THESE OTHER WANNABES EXPECTING THE VIP TREATMENT, NOW CAN WE?
HE CALLED US V.I.P.!
DAP
OH YES, YOU BOYS ARE DEFINITELY GOIN' PLACES!
AND THIS TAPE IS GOIN' PLACES, TOO!
...GOIN' STRAIGHT TO THE TRASH!

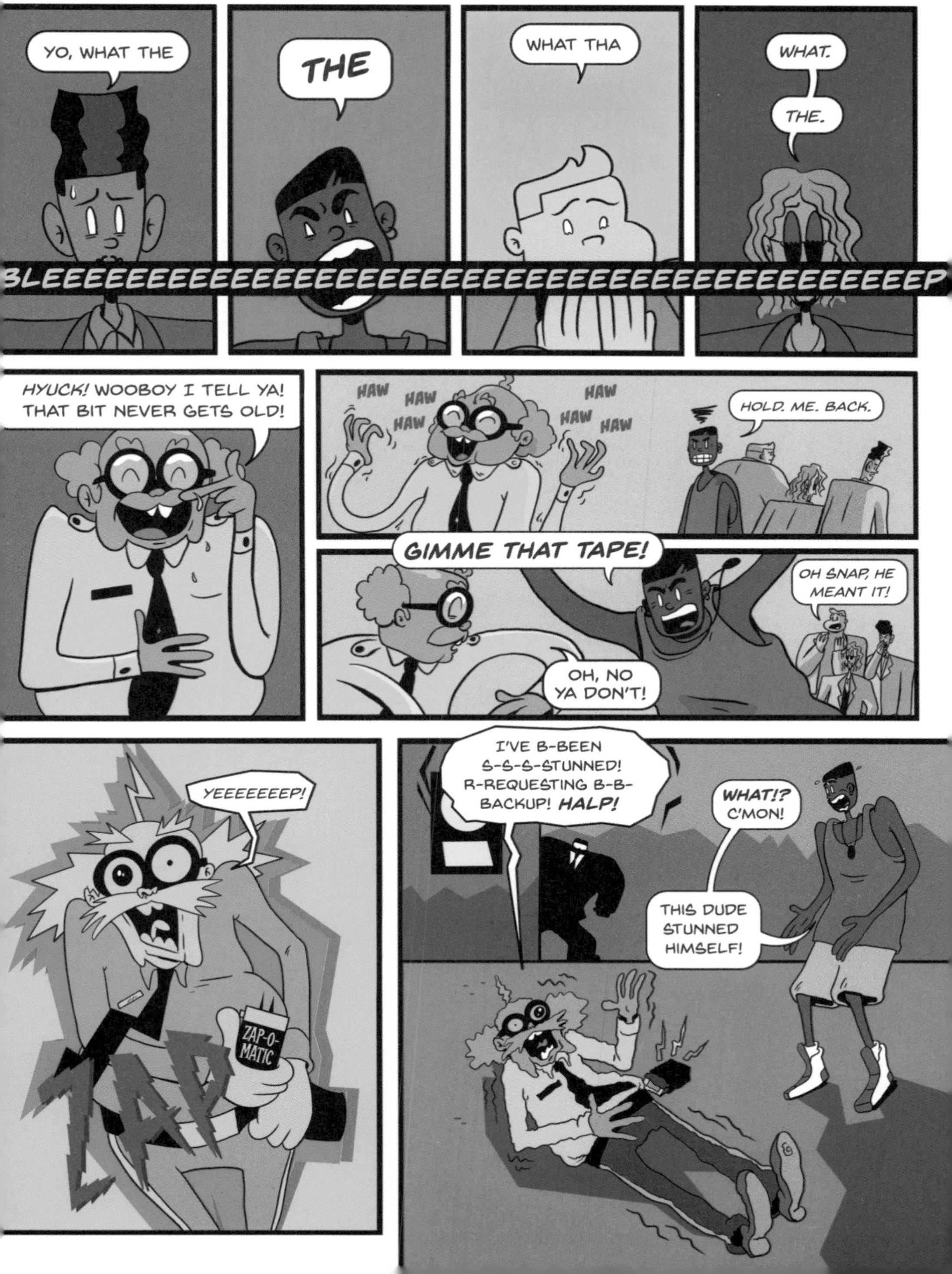
YO, WHAT THE
THE
WHAT THA
WHAT.
THE.
BLEEEEEEEEEEEEEEEEEEEEEEEEEEEEEEEEEEEEEEEEEEEEEEP
HYUCK! WOOBOY I TELL YA! THAT BIT NEVER GETS OLD!
HAW HAW HAW HAW HAW HAW
HOLD. ME. BACK.
GIMME THAT TAPE!
OH SNAP, HE MEANT IT!
OH, NO YA DON'T!
YEEEEEEEP!
ZAP-O-MATIC
ZAP
I'VE B-BEEN S-S-S-STUNNED! R-REQUESTING B-B-BACKUP! HALP!
WHAT!? C'MON!
THIS DUDE STUNNED HIMSELF!

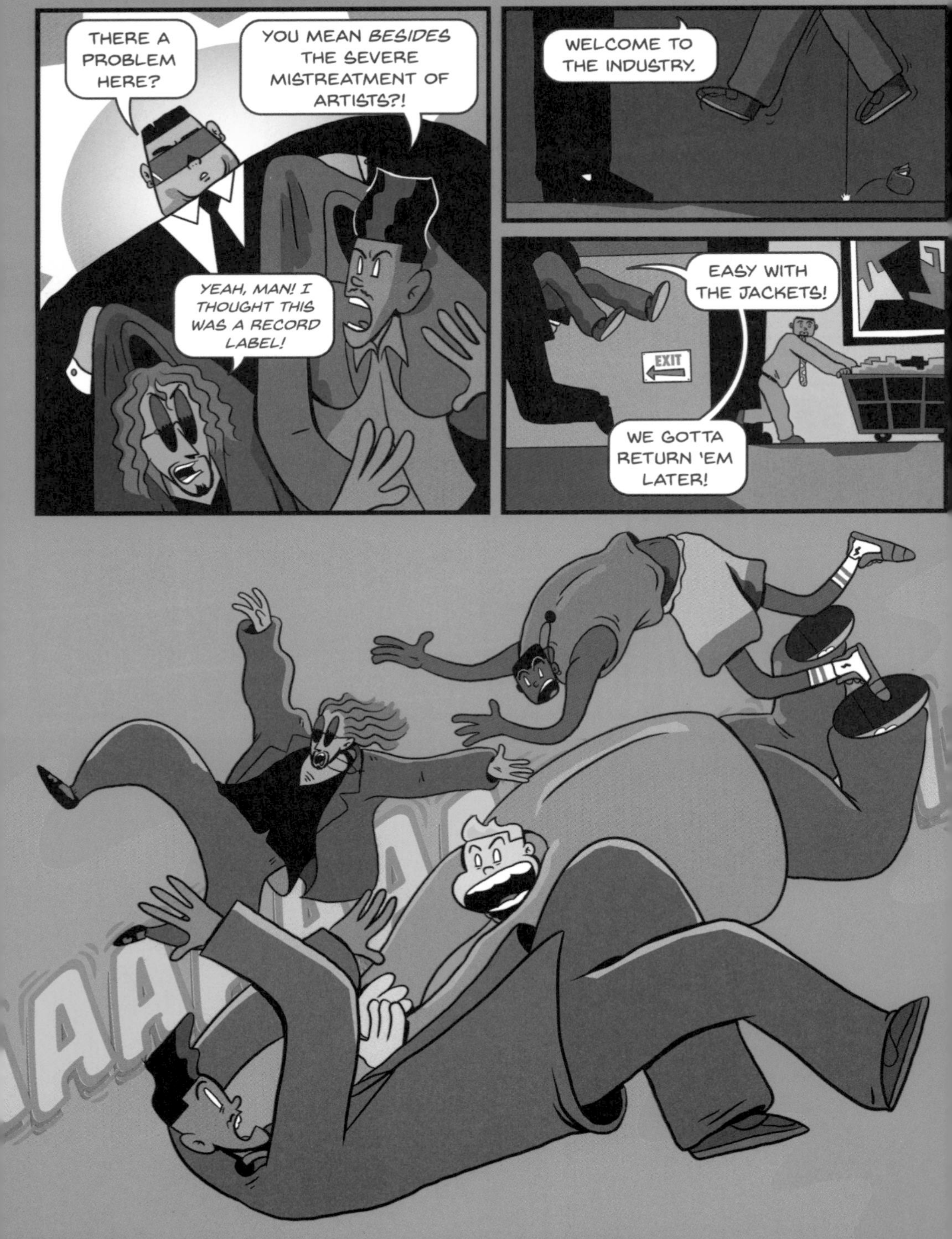
THERE A PROBLEM HERE?
YOU MEAN *BESIDES* THE SEVERE MISTREATMENT OF ARTISTS?!
YEAH, MAN! I THOUGHT THIS WAS A RECORD LABEL!
WELCOME TO THE INDUSTRY.
EASY WITH THE JACKETS!
EXIT
WE GOTTA RETURN 'EM LATER!

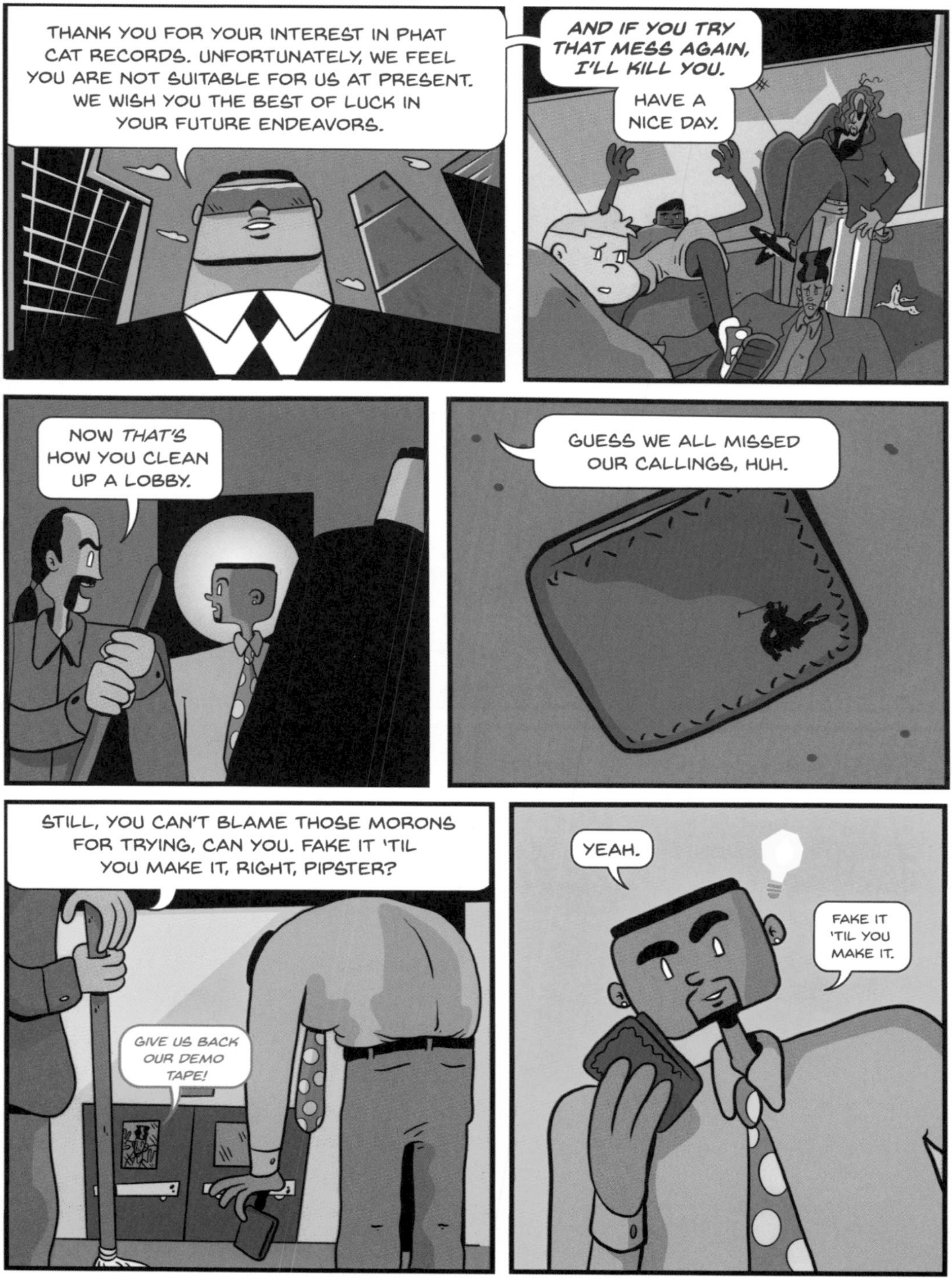
THANK YOU FOR YOUR INTEREST IN PHAT CAT RECORDS. UNFORTUNATELY, WE FEEL YOU ARE NOT SUITABLE FOR US AT PRESENT. WE WISH YOU THE BEST OF LUCK IN YOUR FUTURE ENDEAVORS.
AND IF YOU TRY THAT MESS AGAIN, I'LL KILL YOU.
HAVE A NICE DAY.
NOW *THAT'S* HOW YOU CLEAN UP A LOBBY.
GUESS WE ALL MISSED OUR CALLINGS, HUH.
STILL, YOU CAN'T BLAME THOSE MORONS FOR TRYING, CAN YOU. FAKE IT 'TIL YOU MAKE IT, RIGHT, PIPSTER?
GIVE US BACK OUR DEMO TAPE!
YEAH.
FAKE IT 'TIL YOU MAKE IT.

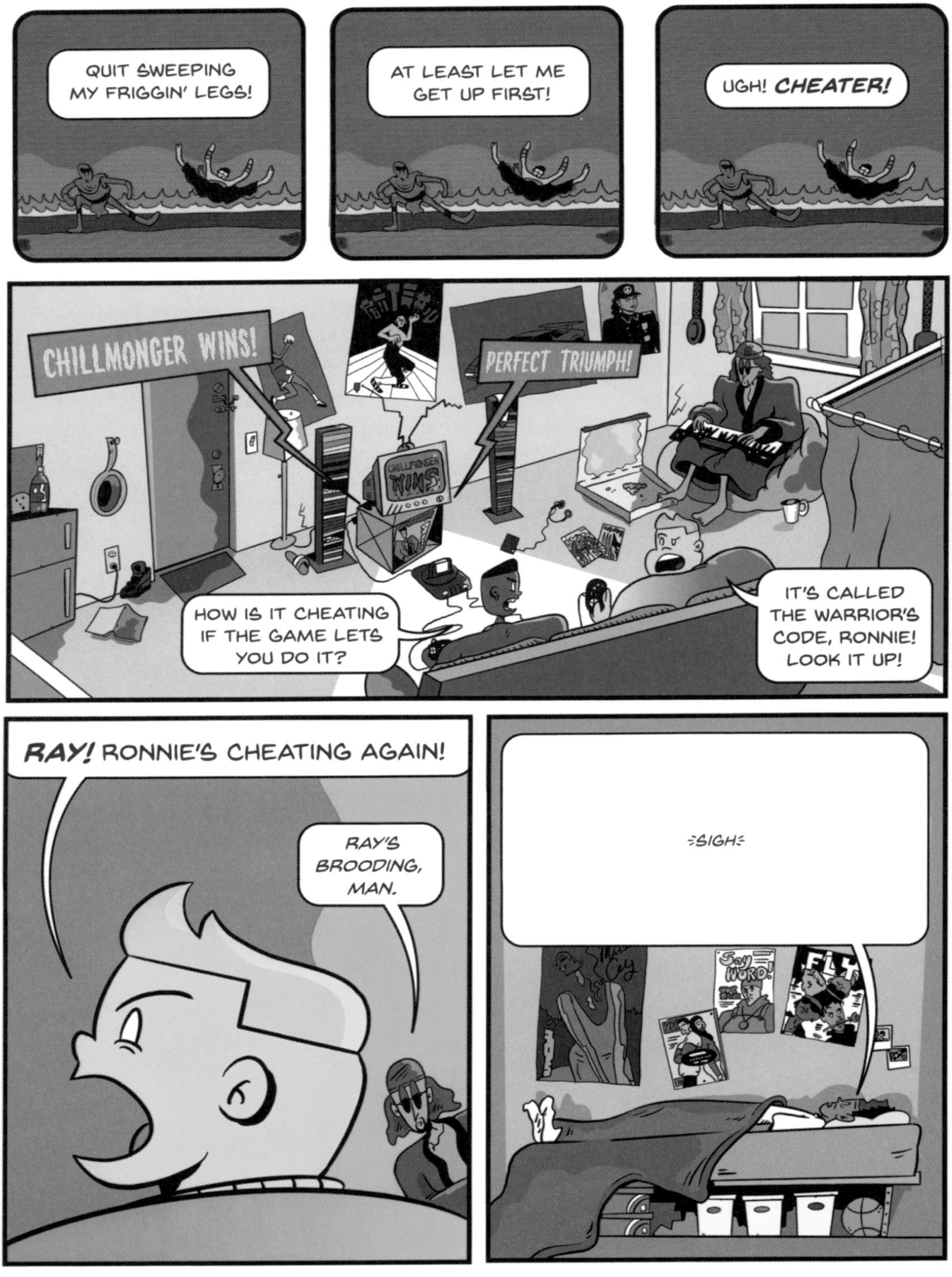
QUIT SWEEPING MY FRIGGIN' LEGS!
AT LEAST LET ME GET UP FIRST!
UGH! ***CHEATER!***
CHILLMONGER WINS!
PERFECT TRIUMPH!
HOW IS IT CHEATING IF THE GAME LETS YOU DO IT?
IT'S CALLED THE WARRIOR'S CODE, RONNIE! LOOK IT UP!
RAY! RONNIE'S CHEATING AGAIN!
RAY'S BROODING, MAN.
SIGH

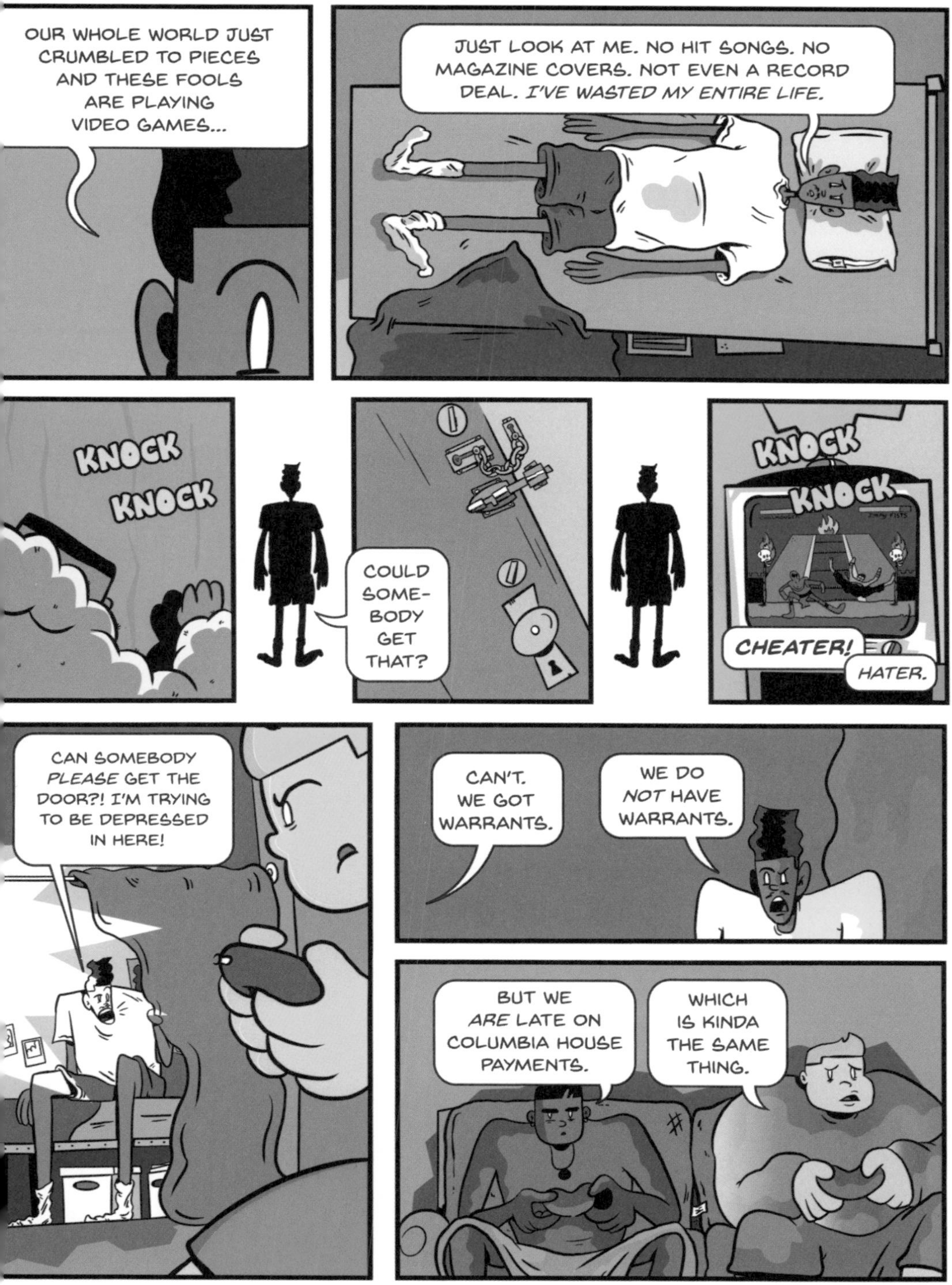
OUR WHOLE WORLD JUST CRUMBLED TO PIECES AND THESE FOOLS ARE PLAYING VIDEO GAMES...
JUST LOOK AT ME. NO HIT SONGS. NO MAGAZINE COVERS. NOT EVEN A RECORD DEAL. *I'VE WASTED MY ENTIRE LIFE.*
KNOCK
KNOCK
COULD SOME-BODY GET THAT?
KNOCK
KNOCK
CHEATER!
HATER.
CAN SOMEBODY *PLEASE* GET THE DOOR?! I'M TRYING TO BE DEPRESSED IN HERE!
CAN'T. WE GOT WARRANTS.
WE DO *NOT* HAVE WARRANTS.
BUT WE *ARE* LATE ON COLUMBIA HOUSE PAYMENTS.
WHICH IS KINDA THE SAME THING.

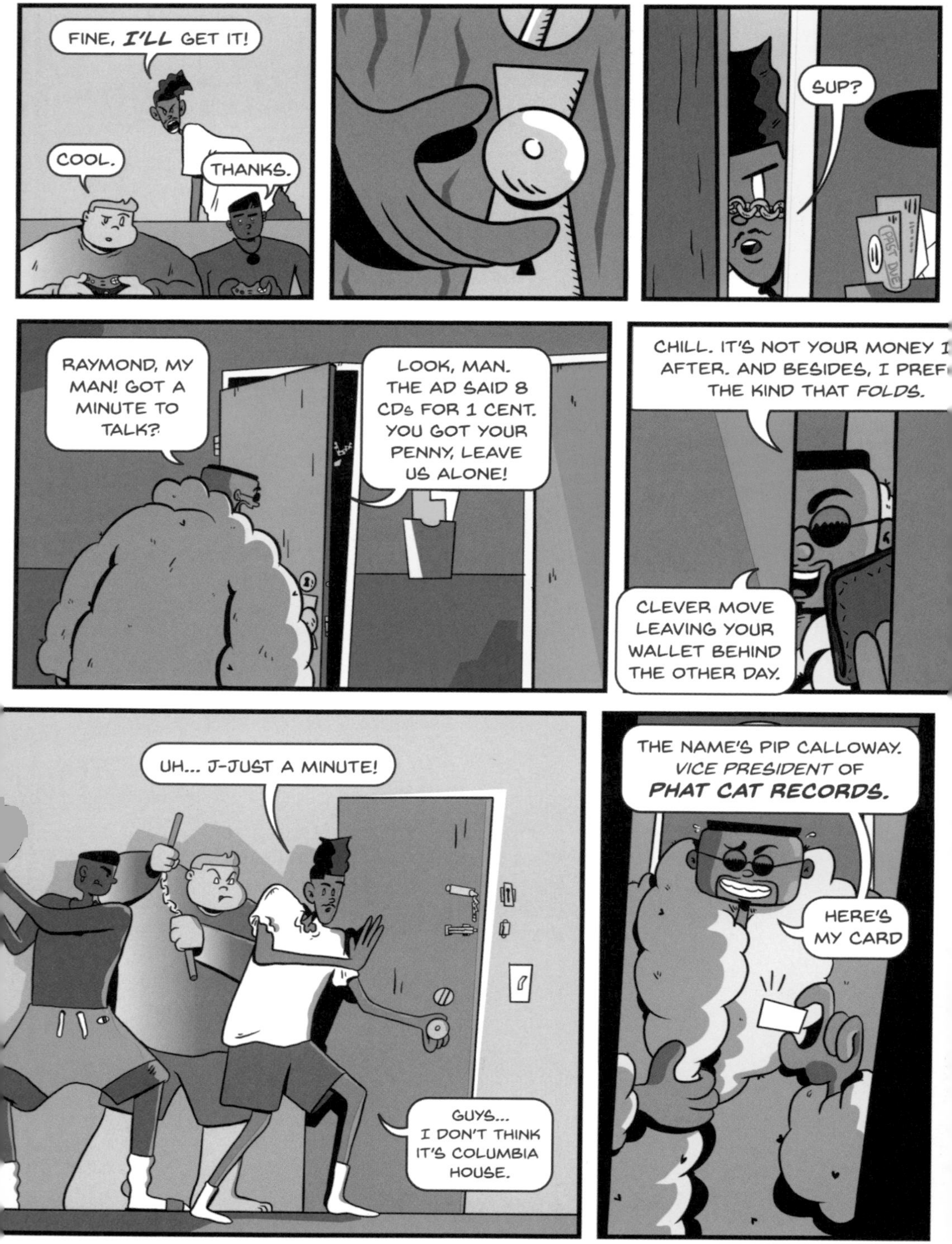

FINE, *I'LL* GET IT!
COOL.
THANKS.
PAST DUE
SUP?
RAYMOND, MY MAN! GOT A MINUTE TO TALK?
LOOK, MAN. THE AD SAID 8 CDs FOR 1 CENT. YOU GOT YOUR PENNY, LEAVE US ALONE!
CHILL. IT'S NOT YOUR MONEY I AFTER. AND BESIDES, I PREF THE KIND THAT *FOLDS*.
CLEVER MOVE LEAVING YOUR WALLET BEHIND THE OTHER DAY.
UH... J-JUST A MINUTE!
GUYS... I DON'T THINK IT'S COLUMBIA HOUSE.
THE NAME'S PIP CALLOWAY. *VICE PRESIDENT* OF **PHAT CAT RECORDS.**
HERE'S MY CARD

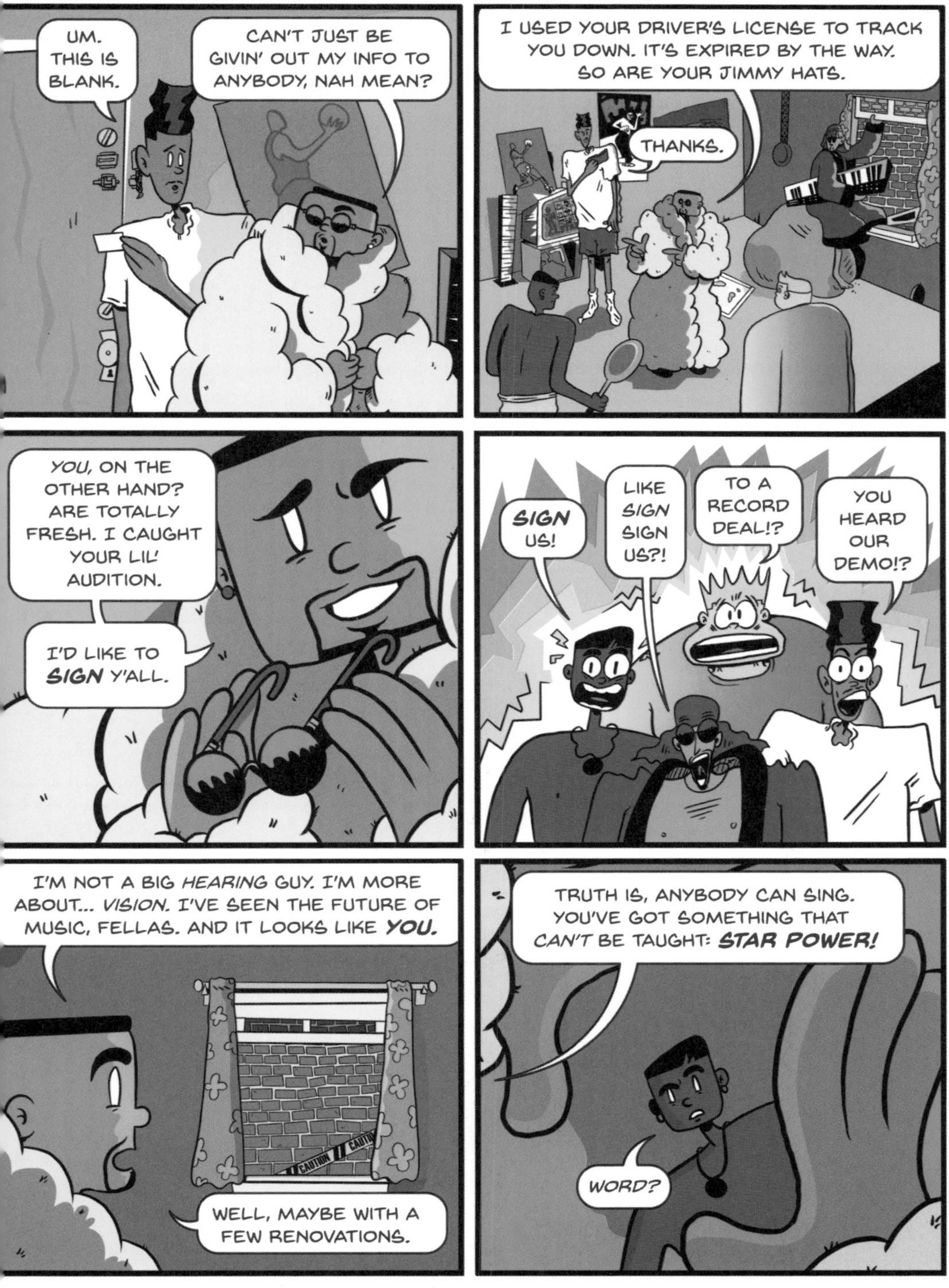
UM. THIS IS BLANK.
CAN'T JUST BE GIVIN' OUT MY INFO TO ANYBODY, NAH MEAN?
I USED YOUR DRIVER'S LICENSE TO TRACK YOU DOWN. IT'S EXPIRED BY THE WAY. SO ARE YOUR JIMMY HATS.
THANKS.
YOU, ON THE OTHER HAND? ARE TOTALLY FRESH. I CAUGHT YOUR LIL' AUDITION.
I'D LIKE TO SIGN Y'ALL.
SIGN US!
LIKE SIGN SIGN US?!
TO A RECORD DEAL!?
YOU HEARD OUR DEMO!?
I'M NOT A BIG HEARING GUY. I'M MORE ABOUT... VISION. I'VE SEEN THE FUTURE OF MUSIC, FELLAS. AND IT LOOKS LIKE YOU.
CAUTION CAUTION
WELL, MAYBE WITH A FEW RENOVATIONS.
TRUTH IS, ANYBODY CAN SING. YOU'VE GOT SOMETHING THAT CAN'T BE TAUGHT: STAR POWER!
WORD?

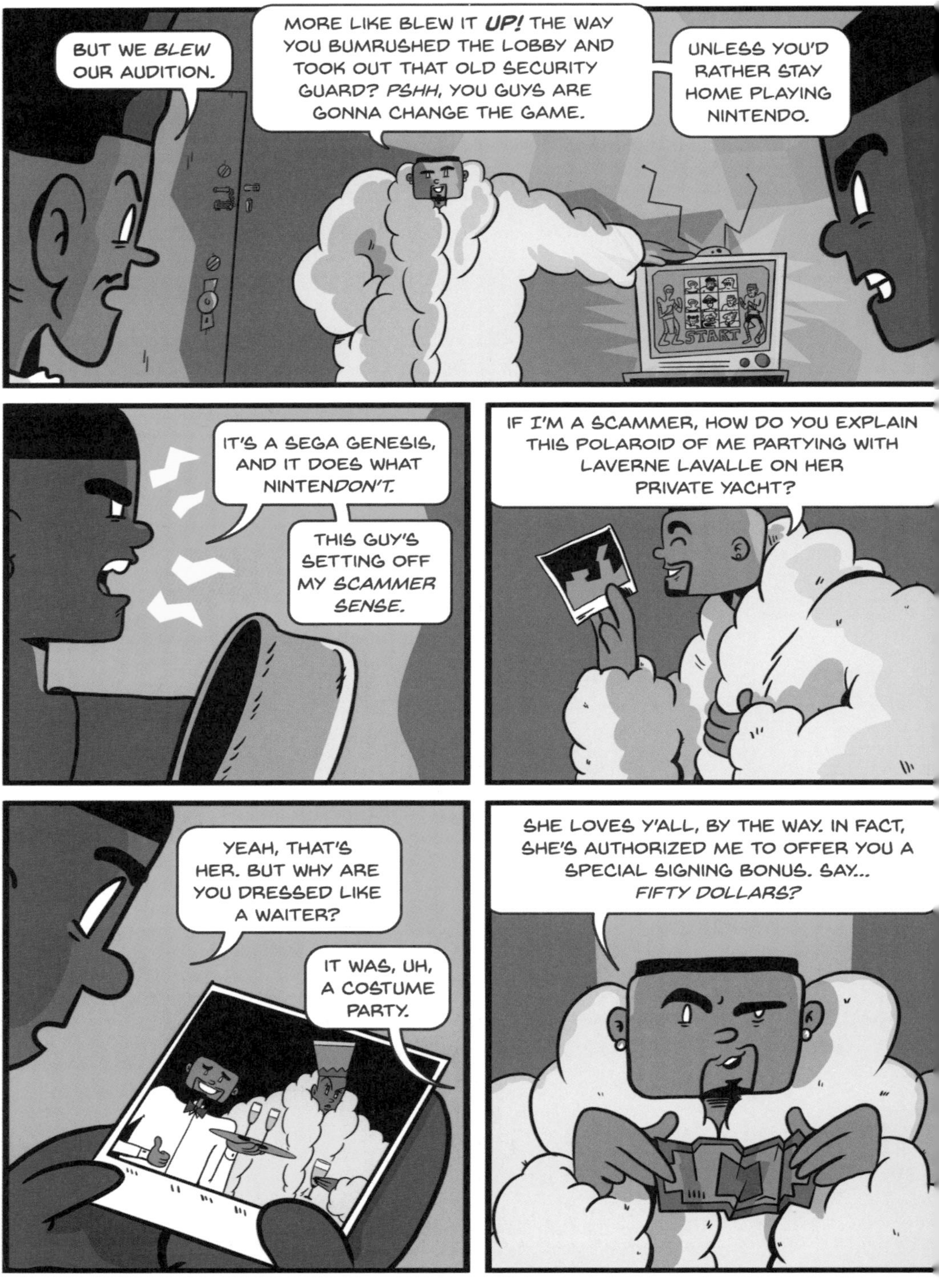
BUT WE *BLEW* OUR AUDITION.
MORE LIKE BLEW IT ***UP!*** THE WAY YOU BUMRUSHED THE LOBBY AND TOOK OUT THAT OLD SECURITY GUARD? *PSHH*, YOU GUYS ARE GONNA CHANGE THE GAME.
UNLESS YOU'D RATHER STAY HOME PLAYING NINTENDO.
START
IT'S A SEGA GENESIS, AND IT DOES WHAT NINTEN*DON'T*.
THIS GUY'S SETTING OFF MY *SCAMMER SENSE*.
IF I'M A SCAMMER, HOW DO YOU EXPLAIN THIS POLAROID OF ME PARTYING WITH LAVERNE LAVALLE ON HER PRIVATE YACHT?
YEAH, THAT'S HER. BUT WHY ARE YOU DRESSED LIKE A WAITER?
IT WAS, UH, A COSTUME PARTY.
SHE LOVES Y'ALL, BY THE WAY. IN FACT, SHE'S AUTHORIZED ME TO OFFER YOU A SPECIAL SIGNING BONUS. SAY... *FIFTY DOLLARS?*

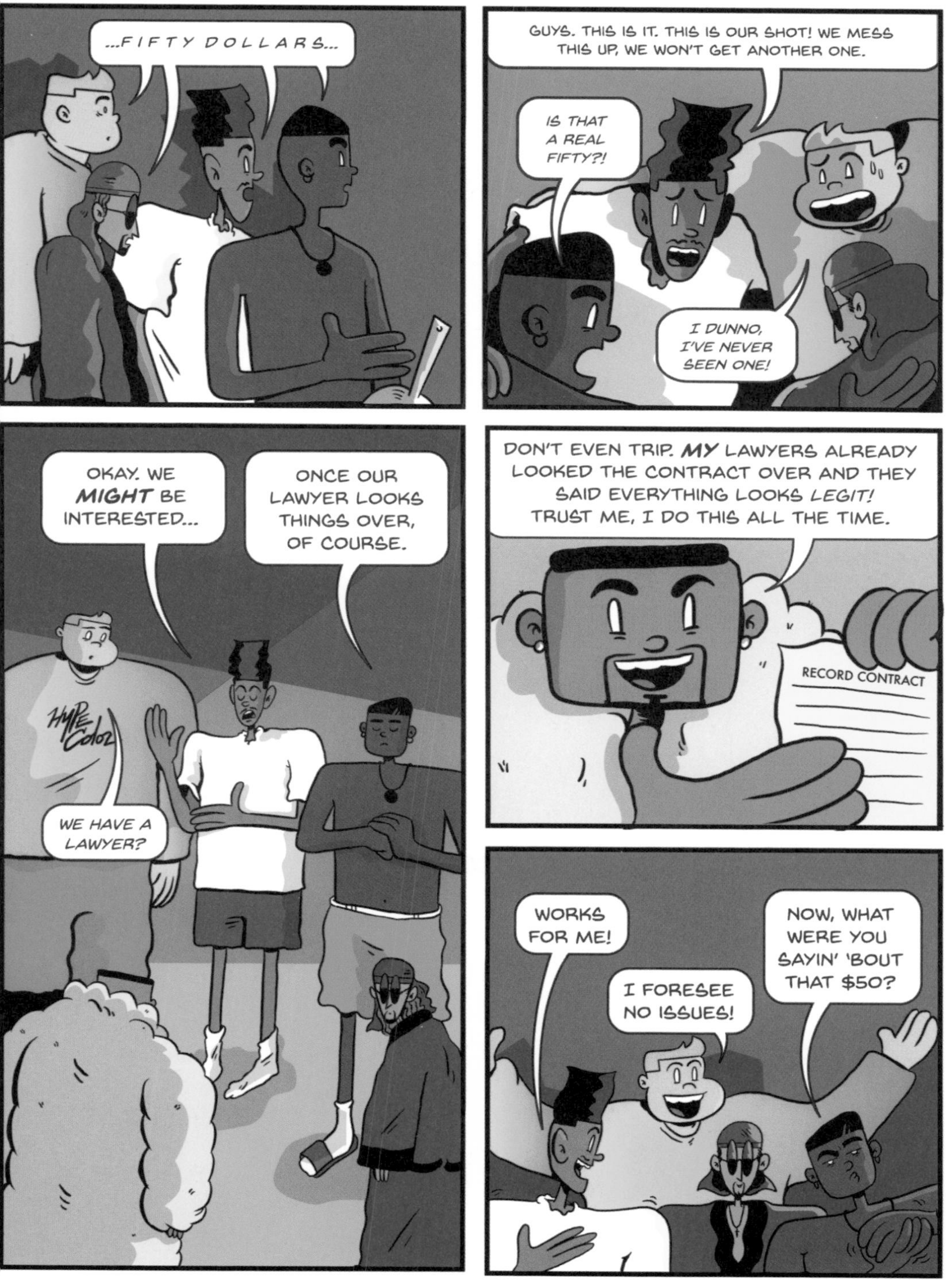
...FIFTY DOLLARS...
GUYS. THIS IS IT. THIS IS OUR SHOT! WE MESS THIS UP, WE WON'T GET ANOTHER ONE.
IS THAT A REAL FIFTY?!
I DUNNO, I'VE NEVER SEEN ONE!
OKAY. WE MIGHT BE INTERESTED...
ONCE OUR LAWYER LOOKS THINGS OVER, OF COURSE.
WE HAVE A LAWYER?
HYPE COLOR
DON'T EVEN TRIP. MY LAWYERS ALREADY LOOKED THE CONTRACT OVER AND THEY SAID EVERYTHING LOOKS LEGIT! TRUST ME, I DO THIS ALL THE TIME.
RECORD CONTRACT
WORKS FOR ME!
I FORESEE NO ISSUES!
NOW, WHAT WERE YOU SAYIN' 'BOUT THAT $50?

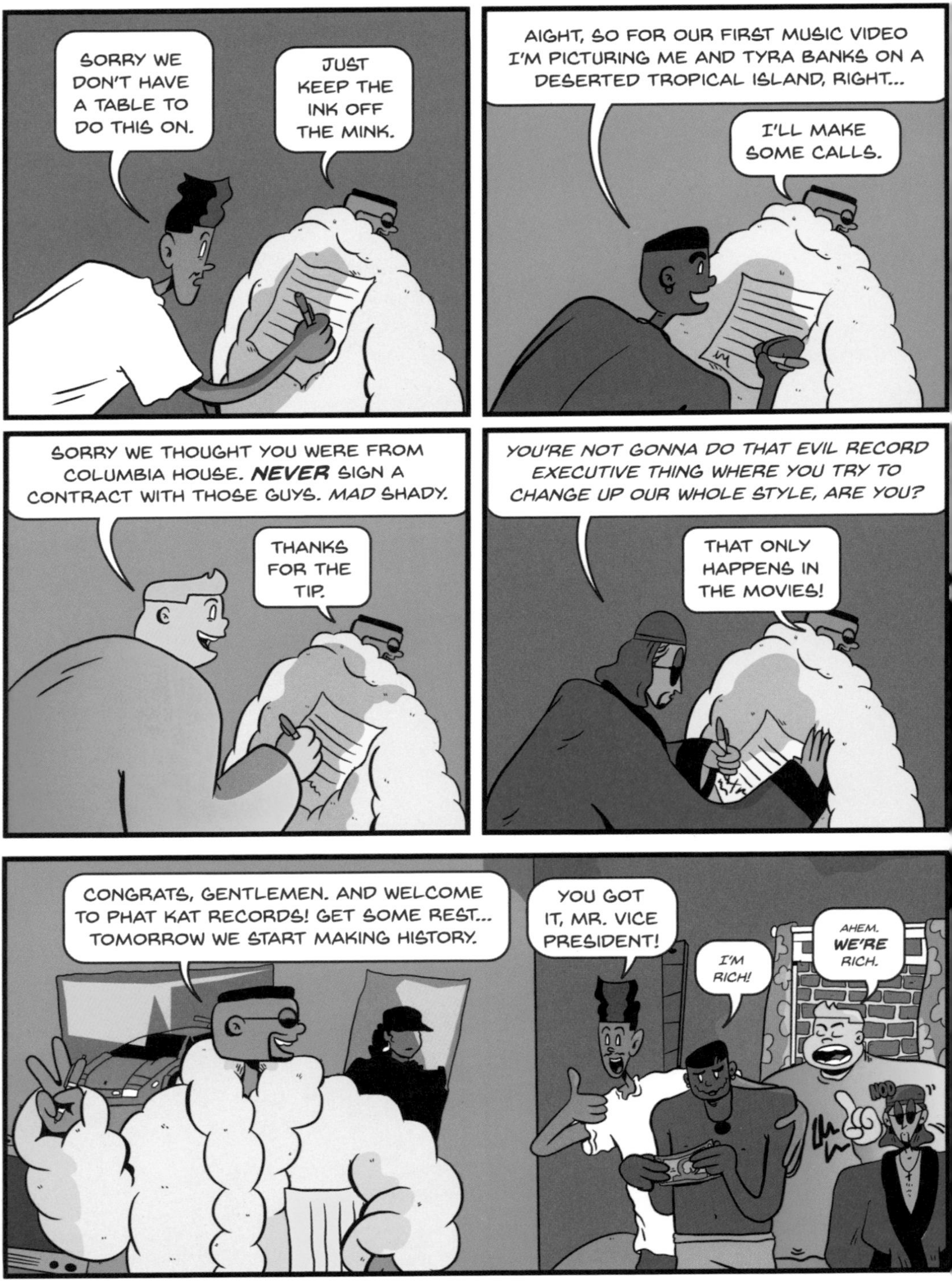
SORRY WE DON'T HAVE A TABLE TO DO THIS ON.
JUST KEEP THE INK OFF THE MINK.
AIGHT, SO FOR OUR FIRST MUSIC VIDEO I'M PICTURING ME AND TYRA BANKS ON A DESERTED TROPICAL ISLAND, RIGHT...
I'LL MAKE SOME CALLS.
SORRY WE THOUGHT YOU WERE FROM COLUMBIA HOUSE. **NEVER** SIGN A CONTRACT WITH THOSE GUYS. *MAD SHADY.*
THANKS FOR THE TIP.
YOU'RE NOT GONNA DO THAT EVIL RECORD EXECUTIVE THING WHERE YOU TRY TO CHANGE UP OUR WHOLE STYLE, ARE YOU?
THAT ONLY HAPPENS IN THE MOVIES!
CONGRATS, GENTLEMEN. AND WELCOME TO PHAT KAT RECORDS! GET SOME REST... TOMORROW WE START MAKING HISTORY.
YOU GOT IT, MR. VICE PRESIDENT!
I'M RICH!
AHEM. **WE'RE** RICH.

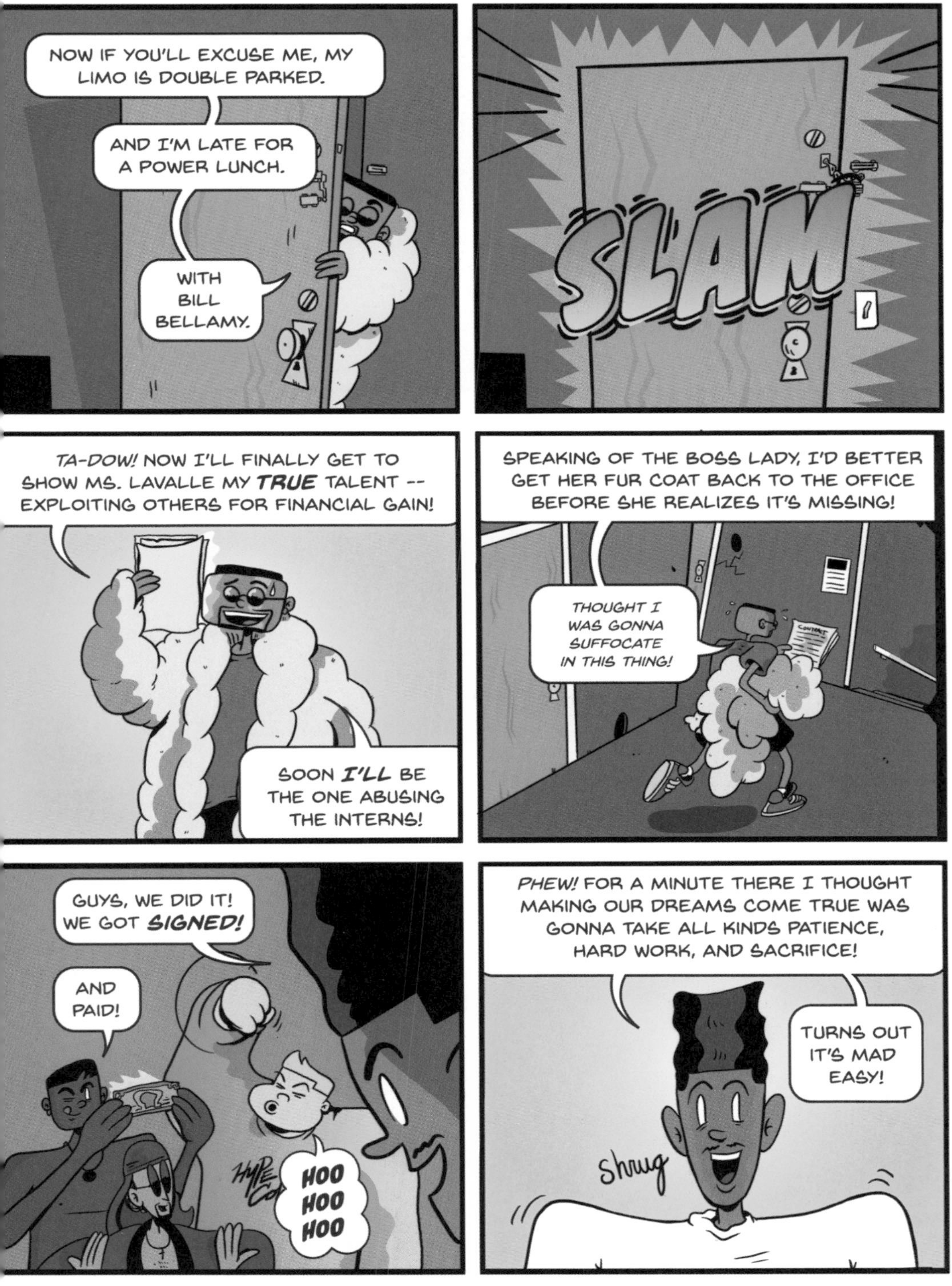
NOW IF YOU'LL EXCUSE ME, MY LIMO IS DOUBLE PARKED.
AND I'M LATE FOR A POWER LUNCH.
WITH BILL BELLAMY.
SLAM
TA-DOW! NOW I'LL FINALLY GET TO SHOW MS. LAVALLE MY ***TRUE*** TALENT -- EXPLOITING OTHERS FOR FINANCIAL GAIN!
SOON ***I'LL*** BE THE ONE ABUSING THE INTERNS!
SPEAKING OF THE BOSS LADY, I'D BETTER GET HER FUR COAT BACK TO THE OFFICE BEFORE SHE REALIZES IT'S MISSING!
THOUGHT I WAS GONNA SUFFOCATE IN THIS THING!
GUYS, WE DID IT! WE GOT ***SIGNED!***
AND PAID!
HOO HOO HOO
PHEW! FOR A MINUTE THERE I THOUGHT MAKING OUR DREAMS COME TRUE WAS GONNA TAKE ALL KINDS PATIENCE, HARD WORK, AND SACRIFICE!
TURNS OUT IT'S MAD EASY!
Shrug

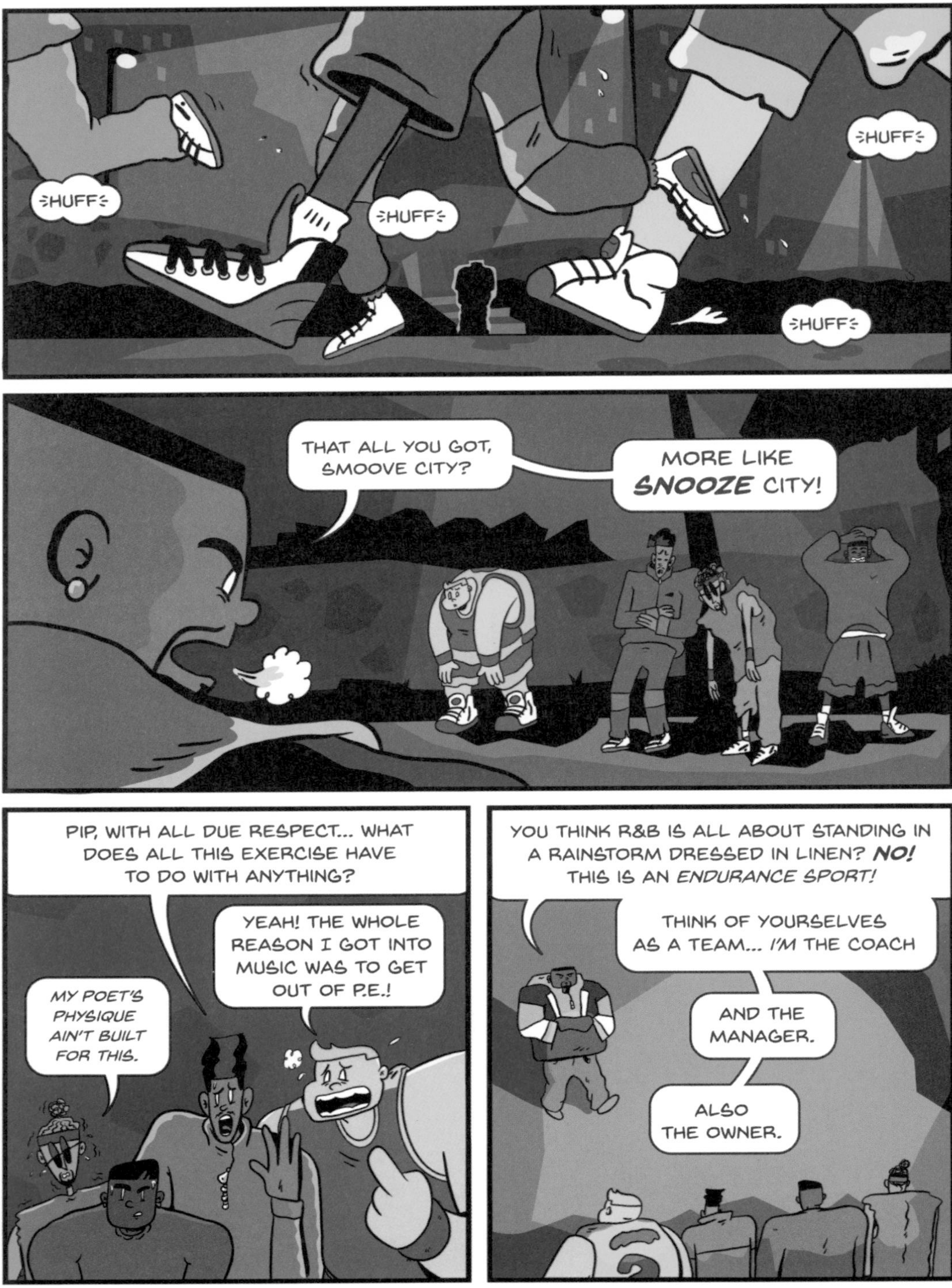
HUFF
HUFF
HUFF
HUFF
THAT ALL YOU GOT, SMOOVE CITY?
MORE LIKE SNOOZE CITY!
PIP, WITH ALL DUE RESPECT... WHAT DOES ALL THIS EXERCISE HAVE TO DO WITH ANYTHING?
YEAH! THE WHOLE REASON I GOT INTO MUSIC WAS TO GET OUT OF P.E.!
MY POET'S PHYSIQUE AIN'T BUILT FOR THIS.
YOU THINK R&B IS ALL ABOUT STANDING IN A RAINSTORM DRESSED IN LINEN? NO! THIS IS AN ENDURANCE SPORT!
THINK OF YOURSELVES AS A TEAM... I'M THE COACH
AND THE MANAGER.
ALSO THE OWNER.

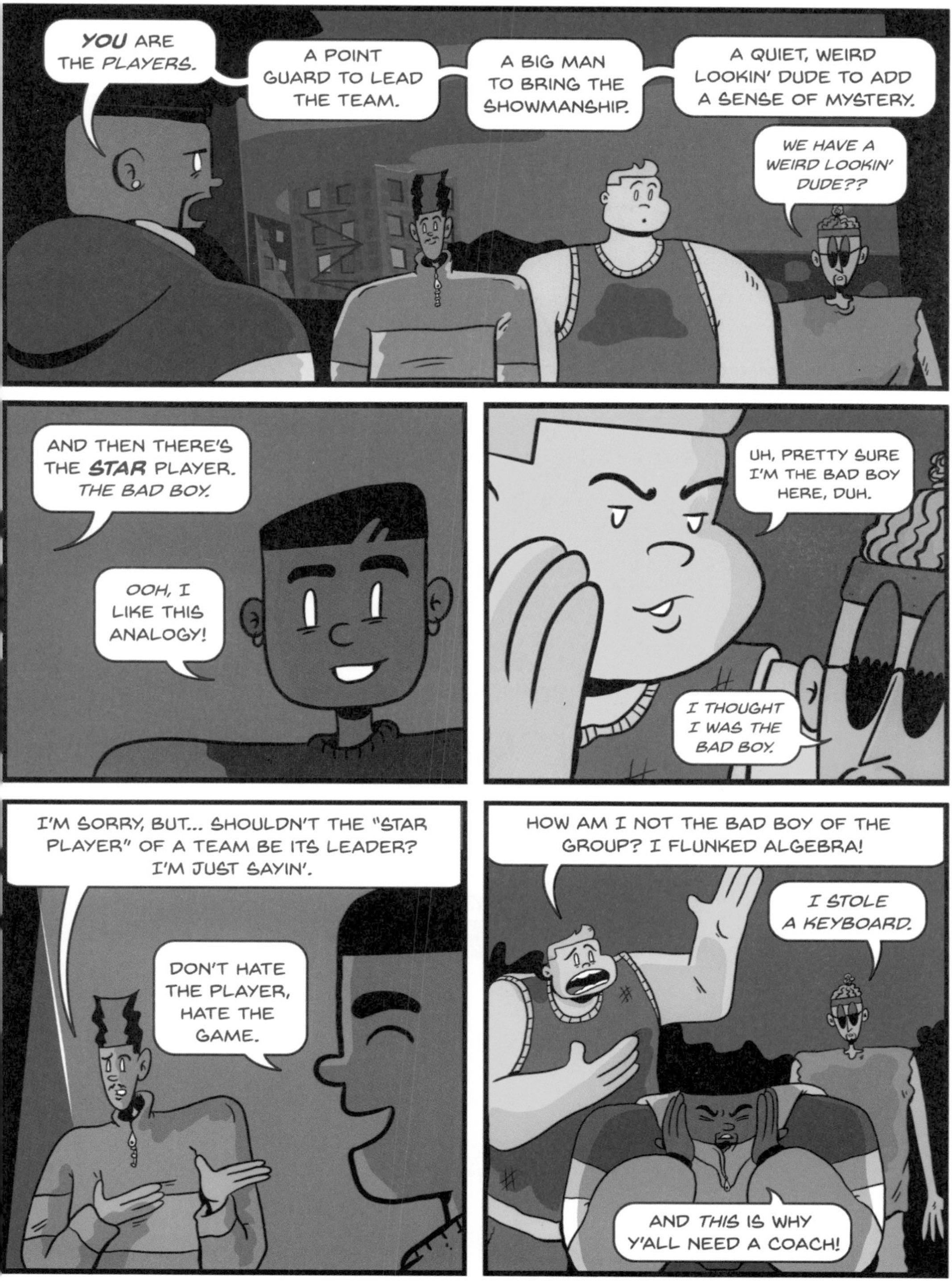
YOU ARE THE PLAYERS.
A POINT GUARD TO LEAD THE TEAM.
A BIG MAN TO BRING THE SHOWMANSHIP.
A QUIET, WEIRD LOOKIN' DUDE TO ADD A SENSE OF MYSTERY.
WE HAVE A WEIRD LOOKIN' DUDE??
AND THEN THERE'S THE STAR PLAYER. THE BAD BOY.
OOH, I LIKE THIS ANALOGY!
UH, PRETTY SURE I'M THE BAD BOY HERE, DUH.
I THOUGHT I WAS THE BAD BOY.
I'M SORRY, BUT... SHOULDN'T THE "STAR PLAYER" OF A TEAM BE ITS LEADER? I'M JUST SAYIN'.
DON'T HATE THE PLAYER, HATE THE GAME.
HOW AM I NOT THE BAD BOY OF THE GROUP? I FLUNKED ALGEBRA!
I STOLE A KEYBOARD.
AND THIS IS WHY Y'ALL NEED A COACH!

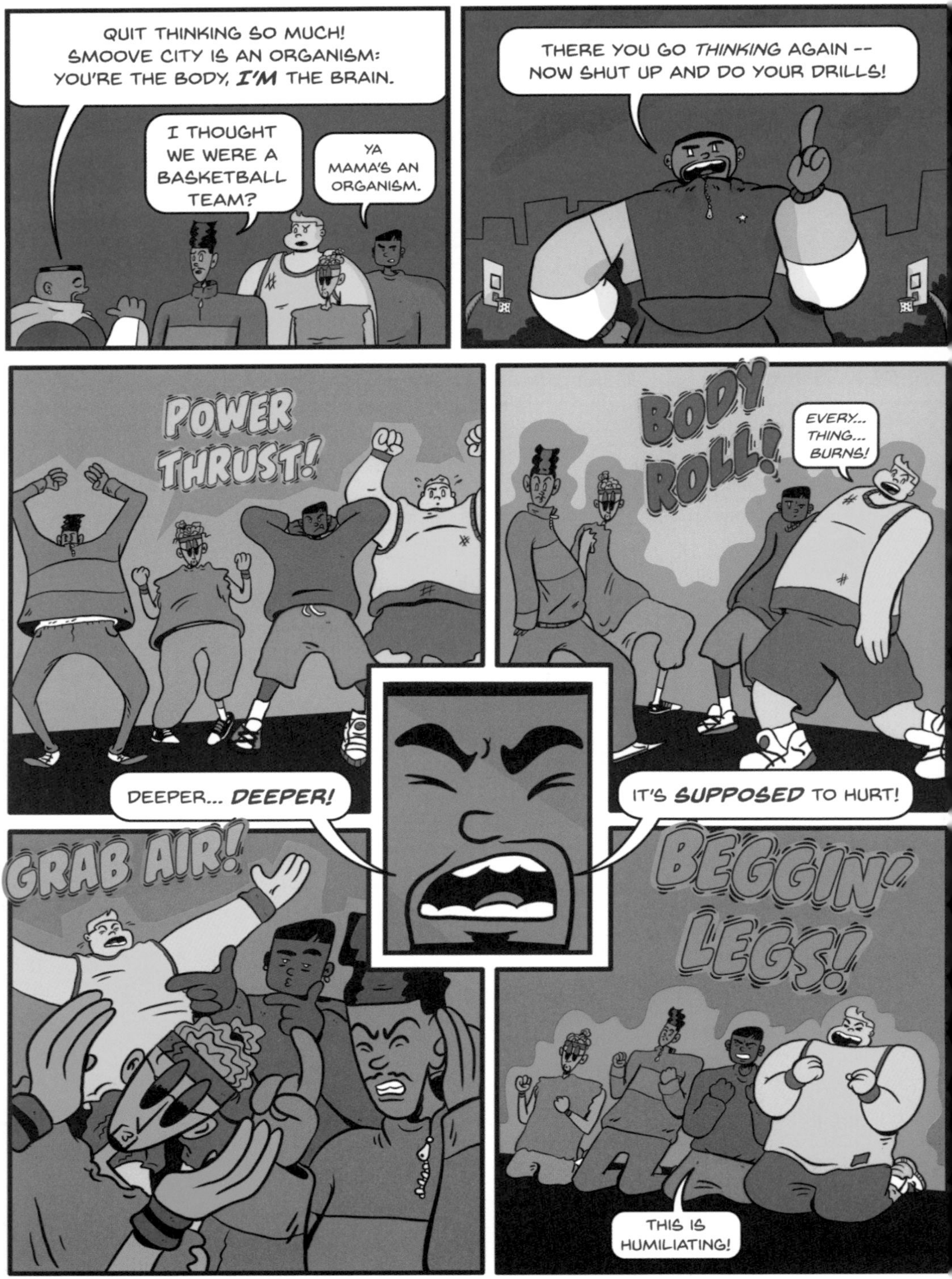
QUIT THINKING SO MUCH! SMOOVE CITY IS AN ORGANISM: YOU'RE THE BODY, *I'M* THE BRAIN.
I THOUGHT WE WERE A BASKETBALL TEAM?
YA MAMA'S AN ORGANISM.
THERE YOU GO *THINKING* AGAIN -- NOW SHUT UP AND DO YOUR DRILLS!
POWER THRUST!
BODY ROLL!
EVERY... THING... BURNS!
DEEPER... *DEEPER!*
IT'S *SUPPOSED* TO HURT!
GRAB AIR!
BEGGIN' LEGS!
THIS IS HUMILIATING!

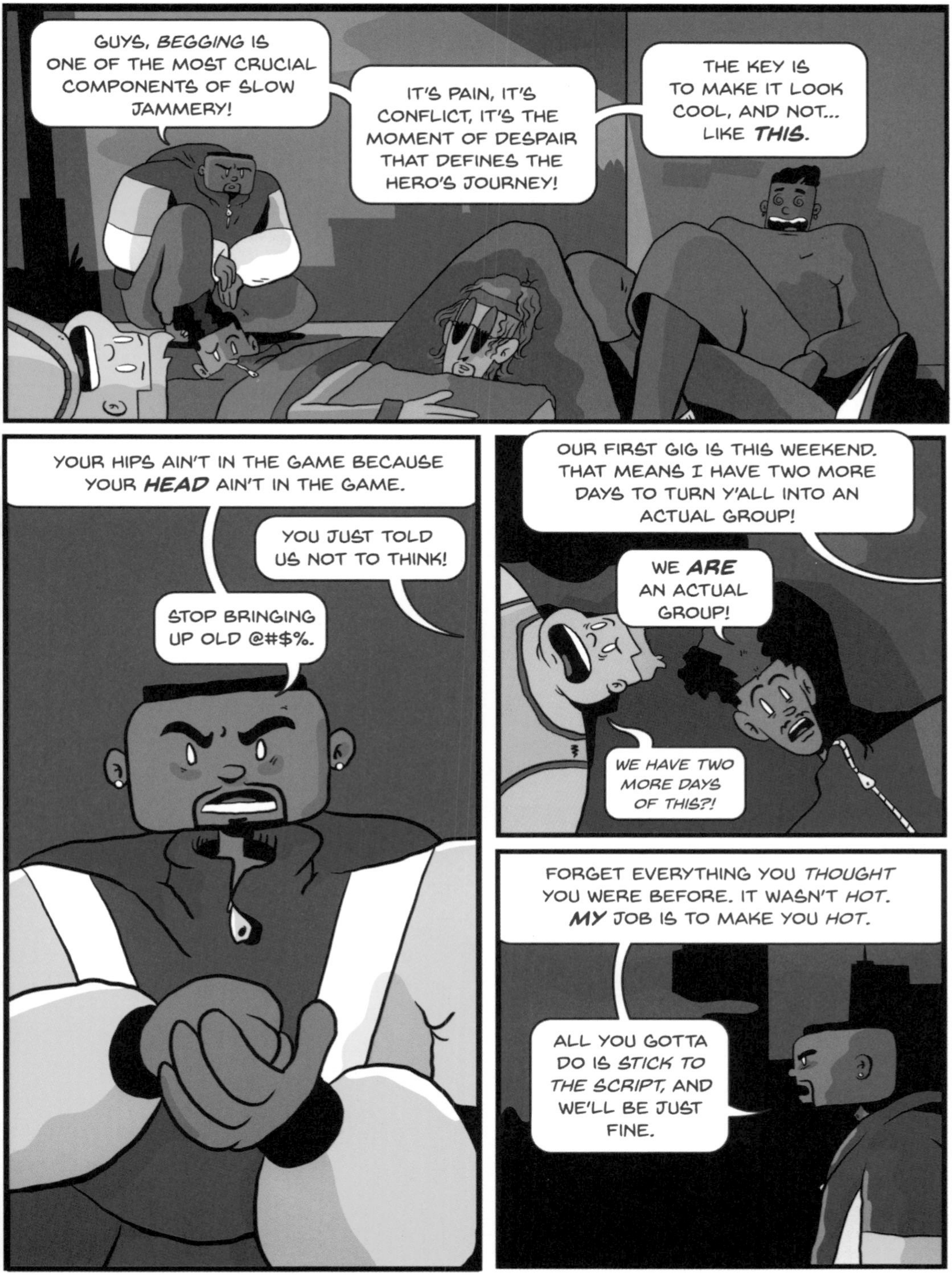
GUYS, *BEGGING* IS ONE OF THE MOST CRUCIAL COMPONENTS OF SLOW JAMMERY!
IT'S PAIN, IT'S CONFLICT, IT'S THE MOMENT OF DESPAIR THAT DEFINES THE HERO'S JOURNEY!
THE KEY IS TO MAKE IT LOOK COOL, AND NOT... LIKE ***THIS***.
YOUR HIPS AIN'T IN THE GAME BECAUSE YOUR ***HEAD*** AIN'T IN THE GAME.
YOU JUST TOLD US NOT TO THINK!
STOP BRINGING UP OLD @#$%.
OUR FIRST GIG IS THIS WEEKEND. THAT MEANS I HAVE TWO MORE DAYS TO TURN Y'ALL INTO AN ACTUAL GROUP!
WE ***ARE*** AN ACTUAL GROUP!
WE HAVE TWO MORE DAYS OF THIS?!
FORGET EVERYTHING YOU *THOUGHT* YOU WERE BEFORE. IT WASN'T *HOT*. ***MY*** JOB IS TO MAKE YOU *HOT*.
ALL YOU GOTTA DO IS *STICK TO THE SCRIPT*, AND WE'LL BE JUST FINE.

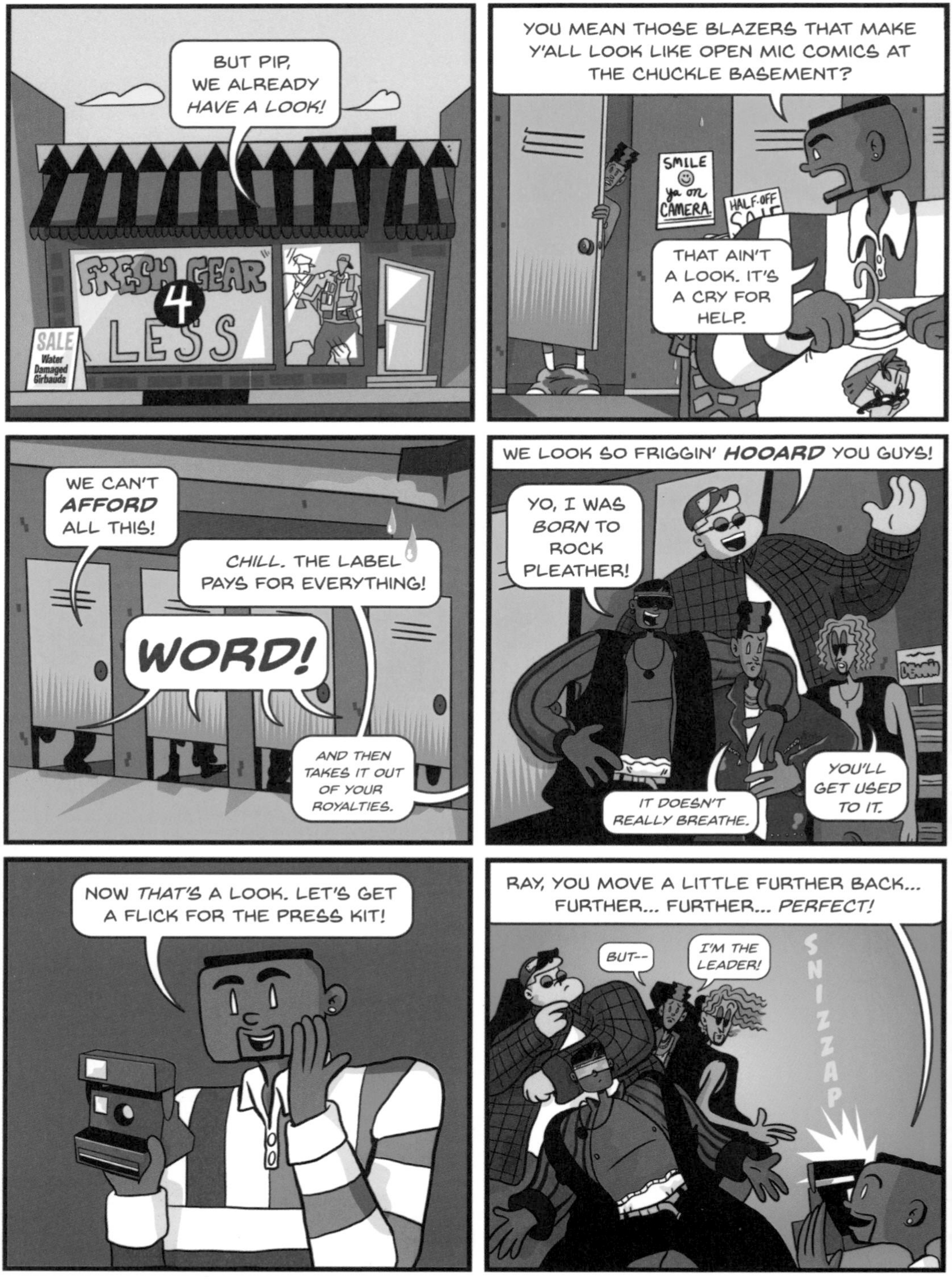
BUT PIP, WE ALREADY HAVE A LOOK!
FRESH GEAR 4 LESS
SALE Water Damaged Girbauds
YOU MEAN THOSE BLAZERS THAT MAKE Y'ALL LOOK LIKE OPEN MIC COMICS AT THE CHUCKLE BASEMENT?
SMILE ya on CAMERA.
HALF-OFF SALE
THAT AIN'T A LOOK. IT'S A CRY FOR HELP.
WE CAN'T AFFORD ALL THIS!
CHILL. THE LABEL PAYS FOR EVERYTHING!
WORD!
AND THEN TAKES IT OUT OF YOUR ROYALTIES.
WE LOOK SO FRIGGIN' HOOARD YOU GUYS!
YO, I WAS BORN TO ROCK PLEATHER!
IT DOESN'T REALLY BREATHE.
YOU'LL GET USED TO IT.
NOW THAT'S A LOOK. LET'S GET A FLICK FOR THE PRESS KIT!
RAY, YOU MOVE A LITTLE FURTHER BACK... FURTHER... FURTHER... PERFECT!
BUT--
I'M THE LEADER!
SNIZZAP

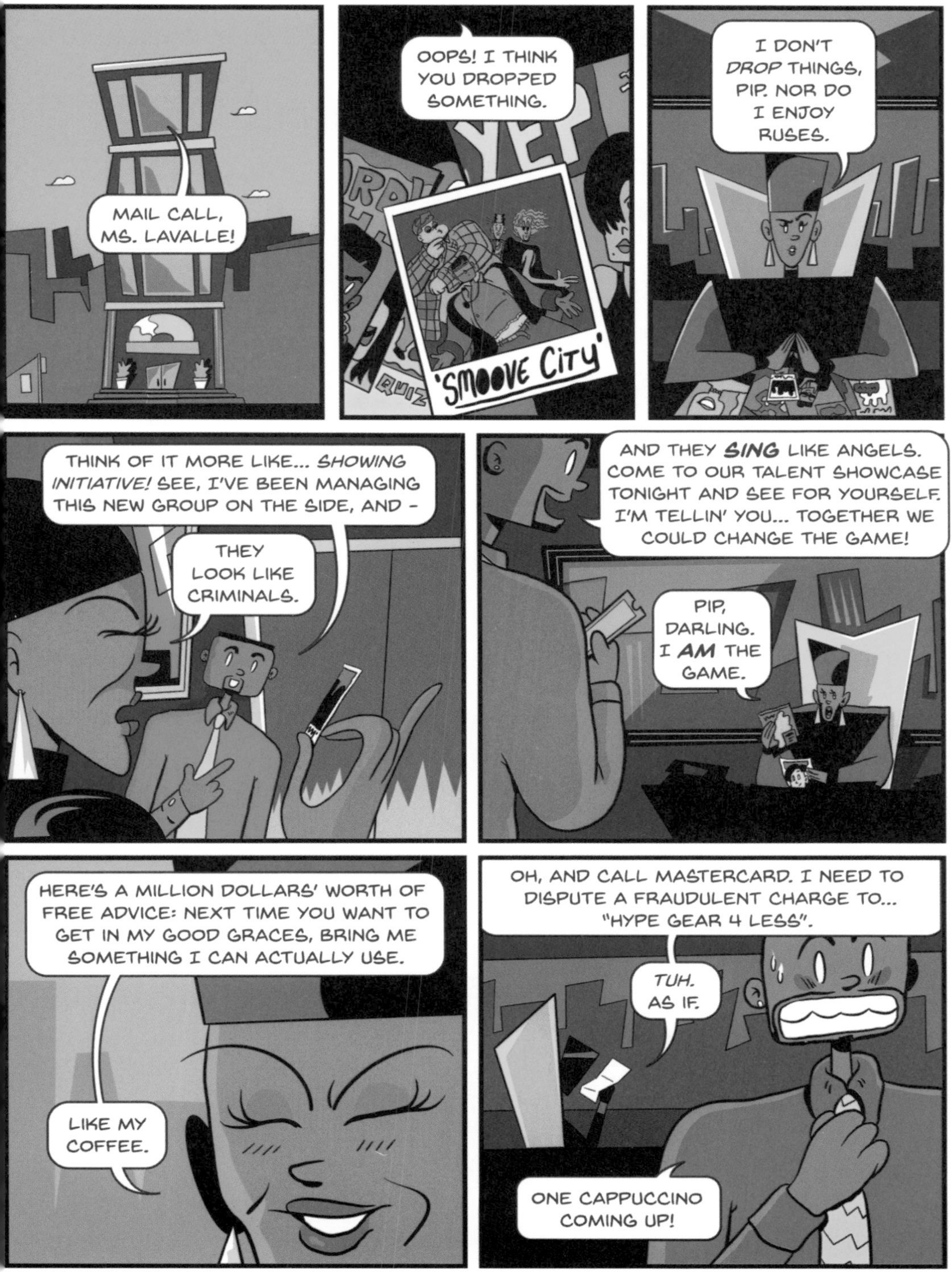
MAIL CALL, MS. LAVALLE!
OOPS! I THINK YOU DROPPED SOMETHING.
'SMOOVE CITY'
I DON'T *DROP* THINGS, PIP. NOR DO I ENJOY RUSES.
THINK OF IT MORE LIKE... *SHOWING INITIATIVE!* SEE, I'VE BEEN MANAGING THIS NEW GROUP ON THE SIDE, AND -
THEY LOOK LIKE CRIMINALS.
AND THEY ***SING*** LIKE ANGELS. COME TO OUR TALENT SHOWCASE TONIGHT AND SEE FOR YOURSELF. I'M TELLIN' YOU... TOGETHER WE COULD CHANGE THE GAME!
PIP, DARLING. I **AM** THE GAME.
HERE'S A MILLION DOLLARS' WORTH OF FREE ADVICE: NEXT TIME YOU WANT TO GET IN MY GOOD GRACES, BRING ME SOMETHING I CAN ACTUALLY USE.
LIKE MY COFFEE.
OH, AND CALL MASTERCARD. I NEED TO DISPUTE A FRAUDULENT CHARGE TO... "HYPE GEAR 4 LESS".
TUH. AS IF.
ONE CAPPUCCINO COMING UP!

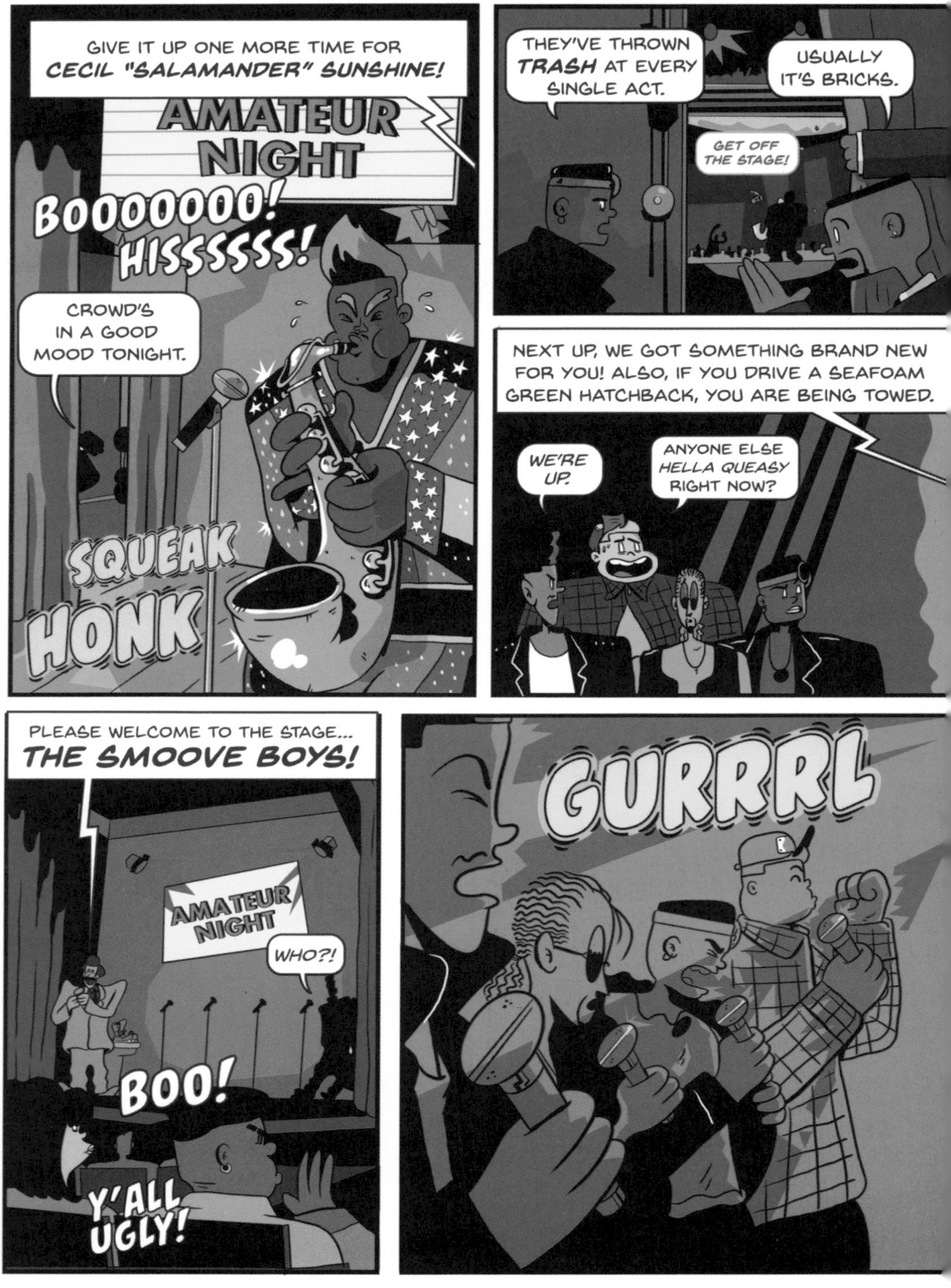

GIVE IT UP ONE MORE TIME FOR CECIL "SALAMANDER" SUNSHINE!
AMATEUR NIGHT
BOOOOOOO! HISSSSS!
CROWD'S IN A GOOD MOOD TONIGHT.
SQUEAK
HONK
THEY'VE THROWN TRASH AT EVERY SINGLE ACT.
USUALLY IT'S BRICKS.
GET OFF THE STAGE!
NEXT UP, WE GOT SOMETHING BRAND NEW FOR YOU! ALSO, IF YOU DRIVE A SEAFOAM GREEN HATCHBACK, YOU ARE BEING TOWED.
WE'RE UP.
ANYONE ELSE HELLA QUEASY RIGHT NOW?
PLEASE WELCOME TO THE STAGE... THE SMOOVE BOYS!
AMATEUR NIGHT
WHO?!
BOO!
Y'ALL UGLY!
GURRRL

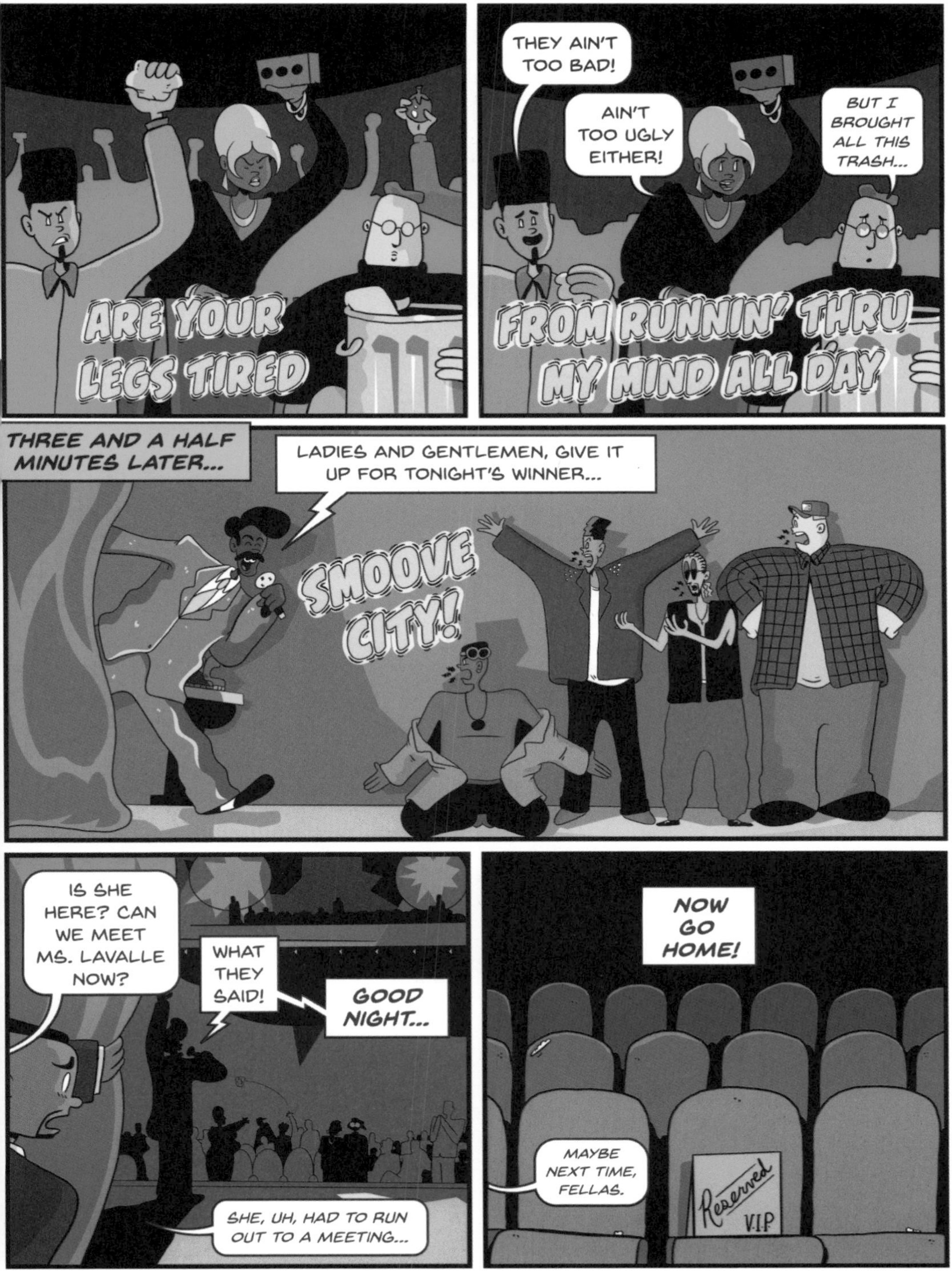
ARE YOUR LEGS TIRED
THEY AIN'T TOO BAD!
AIN'T TOO UGLY EITHER!
BUT I BROUGHT ALL THIS TRASH...
FROM RUNNIN' THRU MY MIND ALL DAY
THREE AND A HALF MINUTES LATER...
LADIES AND GENTLEMEN, GIVE IT UP FOR TONIGHT'S WINNER...
SMOOVE CITY!
IS SHE HERE? CAN WE MEET MS. LAVALLE NOW?
WHAT THEY SAID!
GOOD NIGHT...
SHE, UH, HAD TO RUN OUT TO A MEETING...
NOW GO HOME!
MAYBE NEXT TIME, FELLAS.
Reserved
V.I.P.

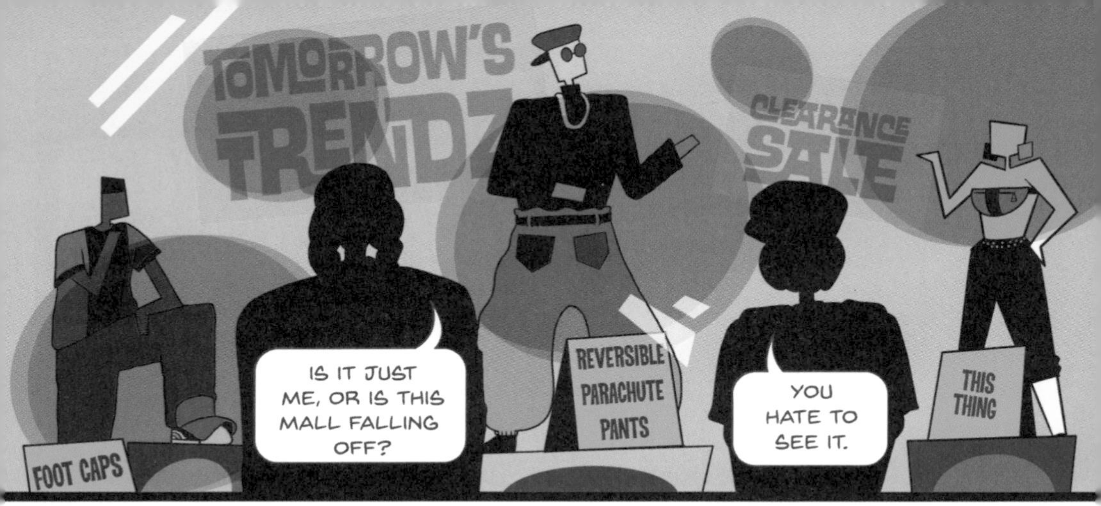
TOMORROW'S TRENDZ
CLEARANCE SALE
FOOT CAPS
IS IT JUST ME, OR IS THIS MALL FALLING OFF?
REVERSIBLE PARACHUTE PANTS
YOU HATE TO SEE IT.
THIS THING

TONI+BRANDY

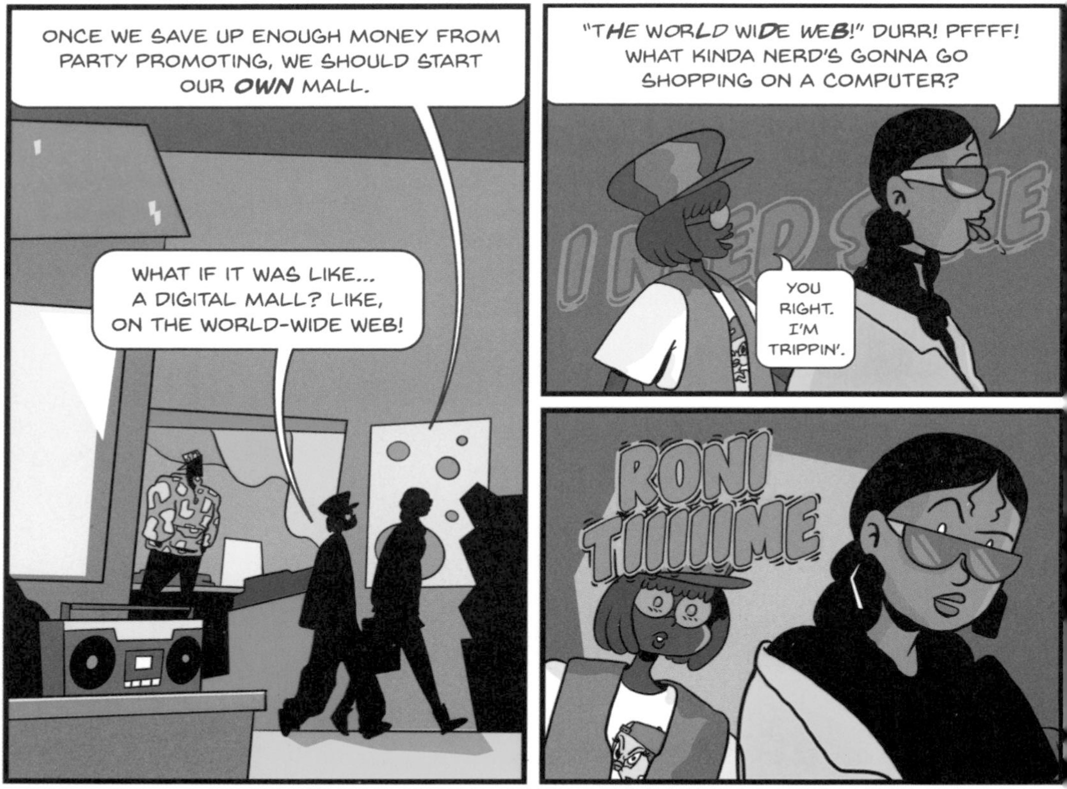
ONCE WE SAVE UP ENOUGH MONEY FROM PARTY PROMOTING, WE SHOULD START OUR ***OWN*** MALL.
WHAT IF IT WAS LIKE... A DIGITAL MALL? LIKE, ON THE WORLD-WIDE WEB!
"THE WORLD WIDE WEB!" DURR! PFFFF! WHAT KINDA NERD'S GONNA GO SHOPPING ON A COMPUTER?
YOU RIGHT. I'M TRIPPIN'.
RONI TIIIIIME

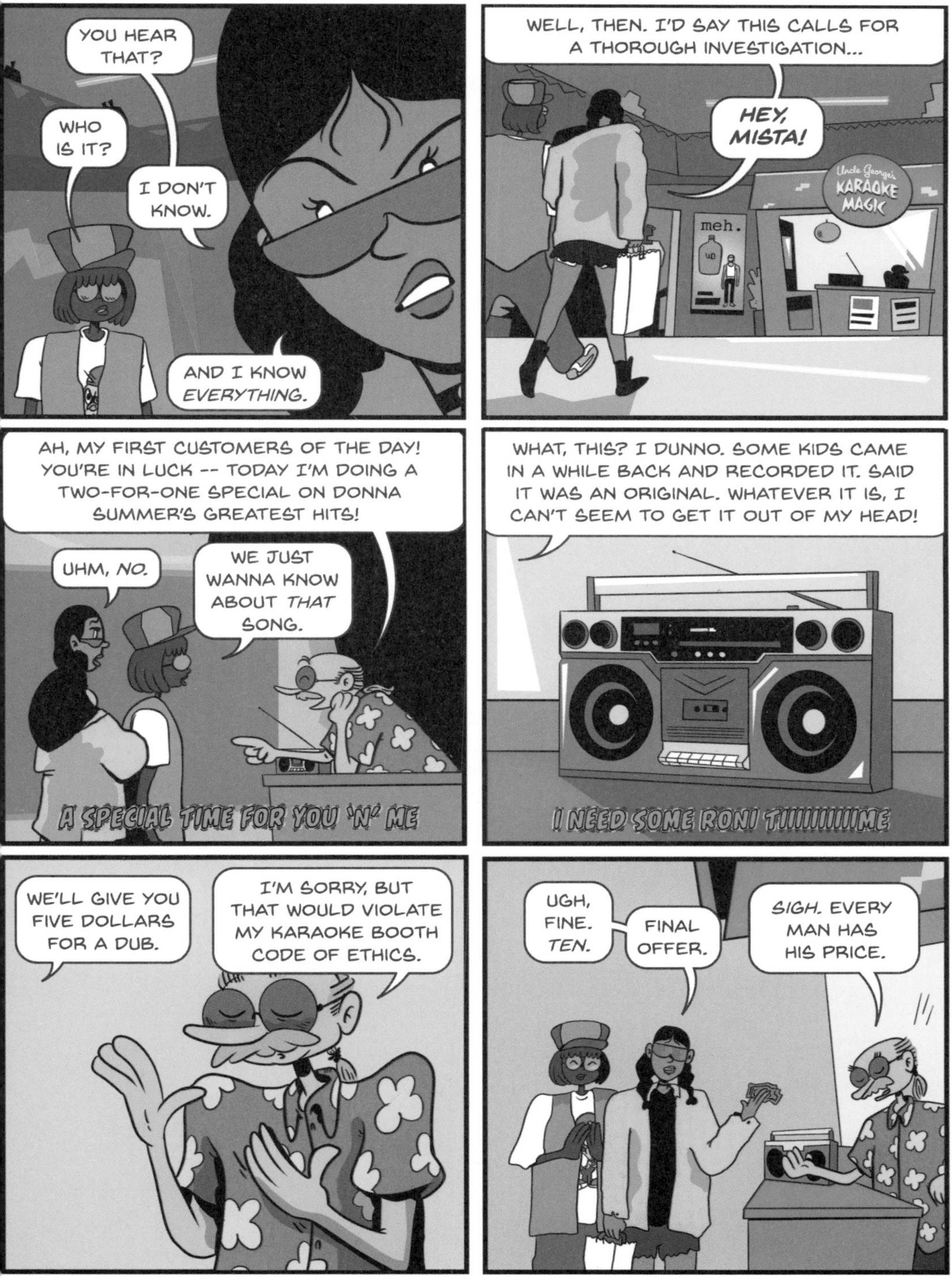
YOU HEAR THAT?
WHO IS IT?
I DON'T KNOW.
AND I KNOW *EVERYTHING.*
WELL, THEN. I'D SAY THIS CALLS FOR A THOROUGH INVESTIGATION...
HEY, MISTA!
meh.
Uncle George's KARAOKE MAGIC
AH, MY FIRST CUSTOMERS OF THE DAY! YOU'RE IN LUCK -- TODAY I'M DOING A TWO-FOR-ONE SPECIAL ON DONNA SUMMER'S GREATEST HITS!
UHM, *NO.*
WE JUST WANNA KNOW ABOUT *THAT* SONG.
A SPECIAL TIME FOR YOU 'N' ME
WHAT, THIS? I DUNNO. SOME KIDS CAME IN A WHILE BACK AND RECORDED IT. SAID IT WAS AN ORIGINAL. WHATEVER IT IS, I CAN'T SEEM TO GET IT OUT OF MY HEAD!
I NEED SOME RONI TIIIIIIIIIME
WE'LL GIVE YOU FIVE DOLLARS FOR A DUB.
I'M SORRY, BUT THAT WOULD VIOLATE MY KARAOKE BOOTH CODE OF ETHICS.
UGH, FINE. *TEN.*
FINAL OFFER.
SIGH. EVERY MAN HAS HIS PRICE.

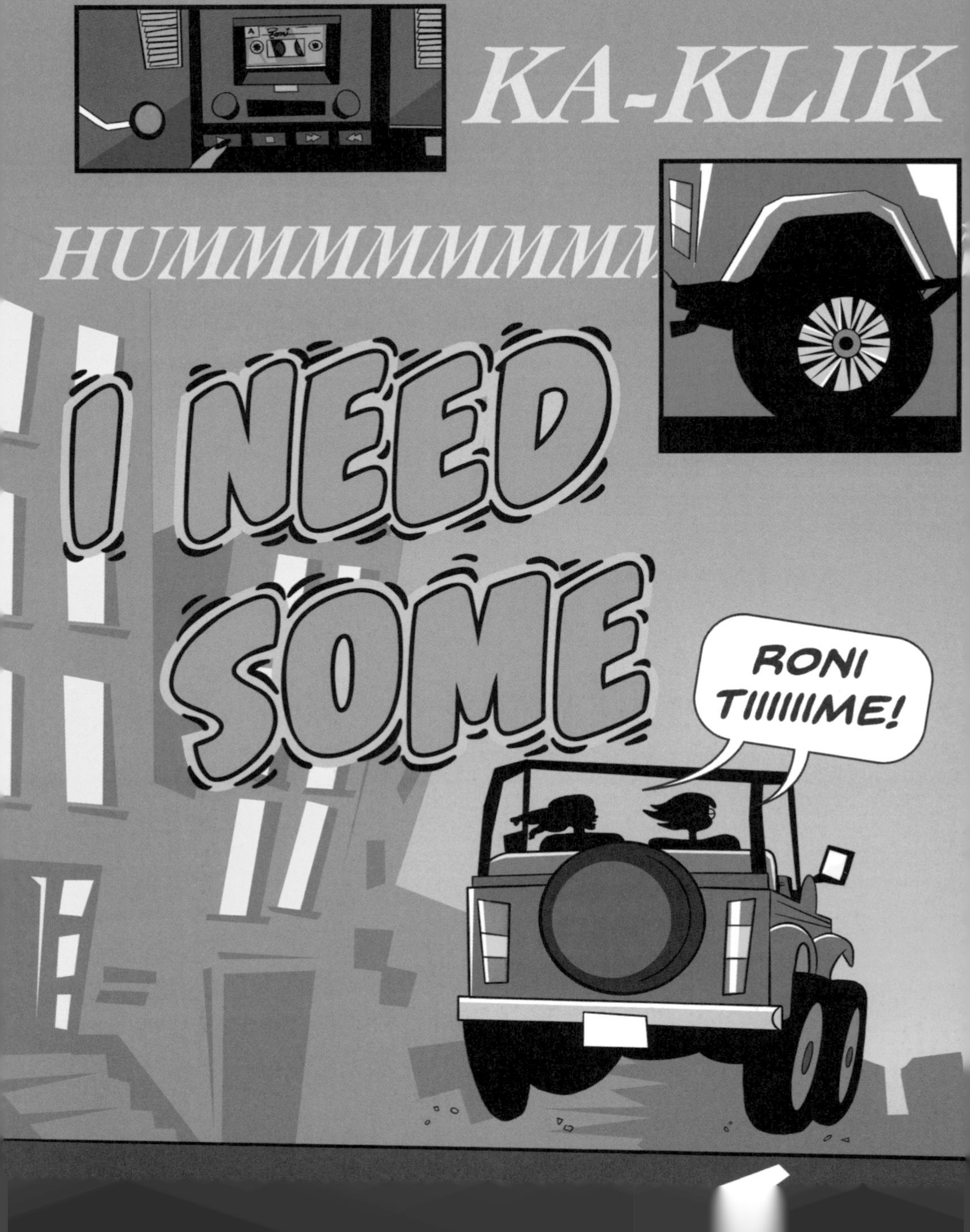
KA-KLIK
HUMMMMMMMMM
I NEED SOME
RONI TIIIIIME!

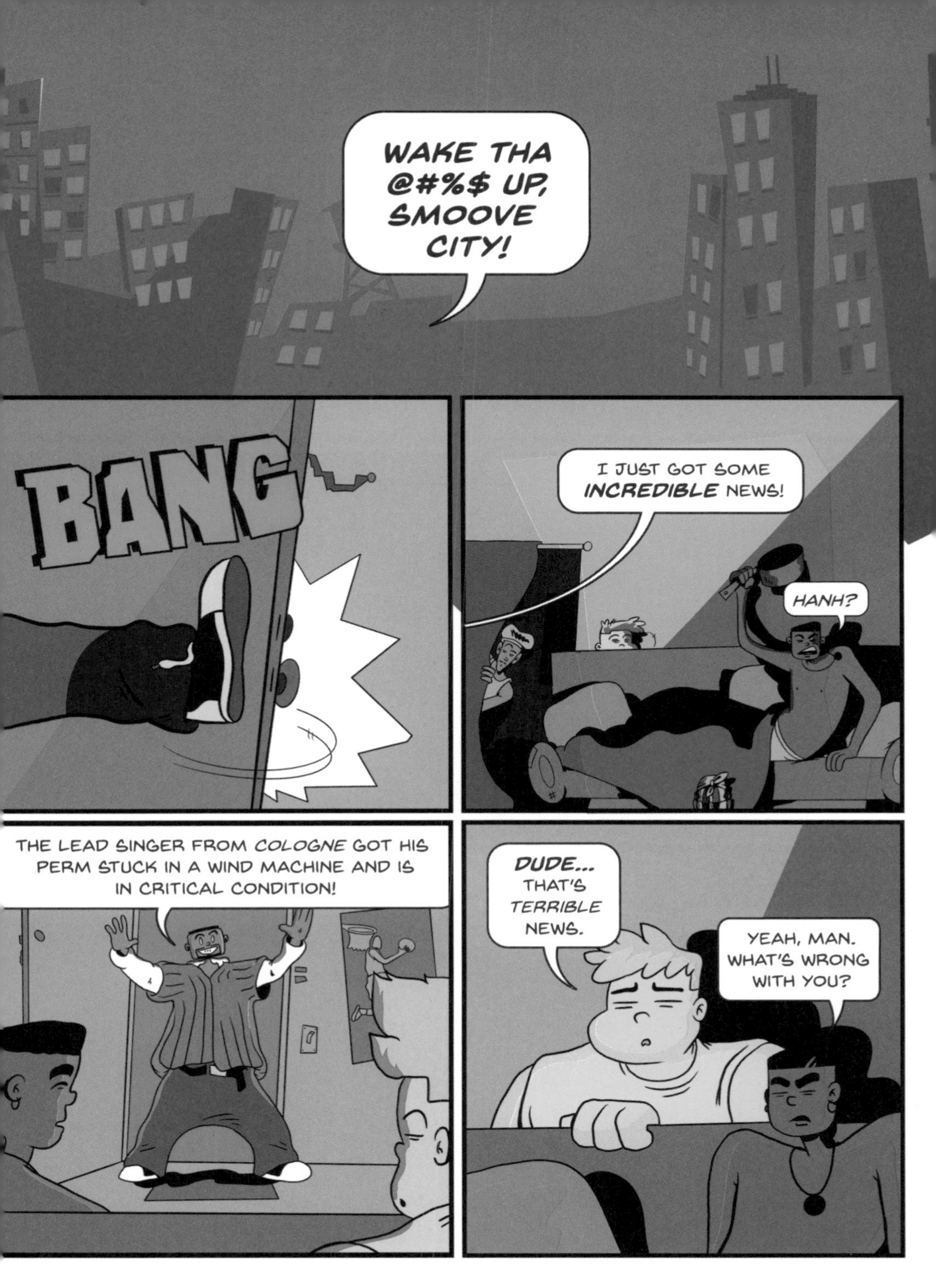
WAKE THA @#%$ UP, SMOOVE CITY!
BANG
I JUST GOT SOME INCREDIBLE NEWS!
HANH?
THE LEAD SINGER FROM COLOGNE GOT HIS PERM STUCK IN A WIND MACHINE AND IS IN CRITICAL CONDITION!
DUDE... THAT'S TERRIBLE NEWS.
YEAH, MAN. WHAT'S WRONG WITH YOU?

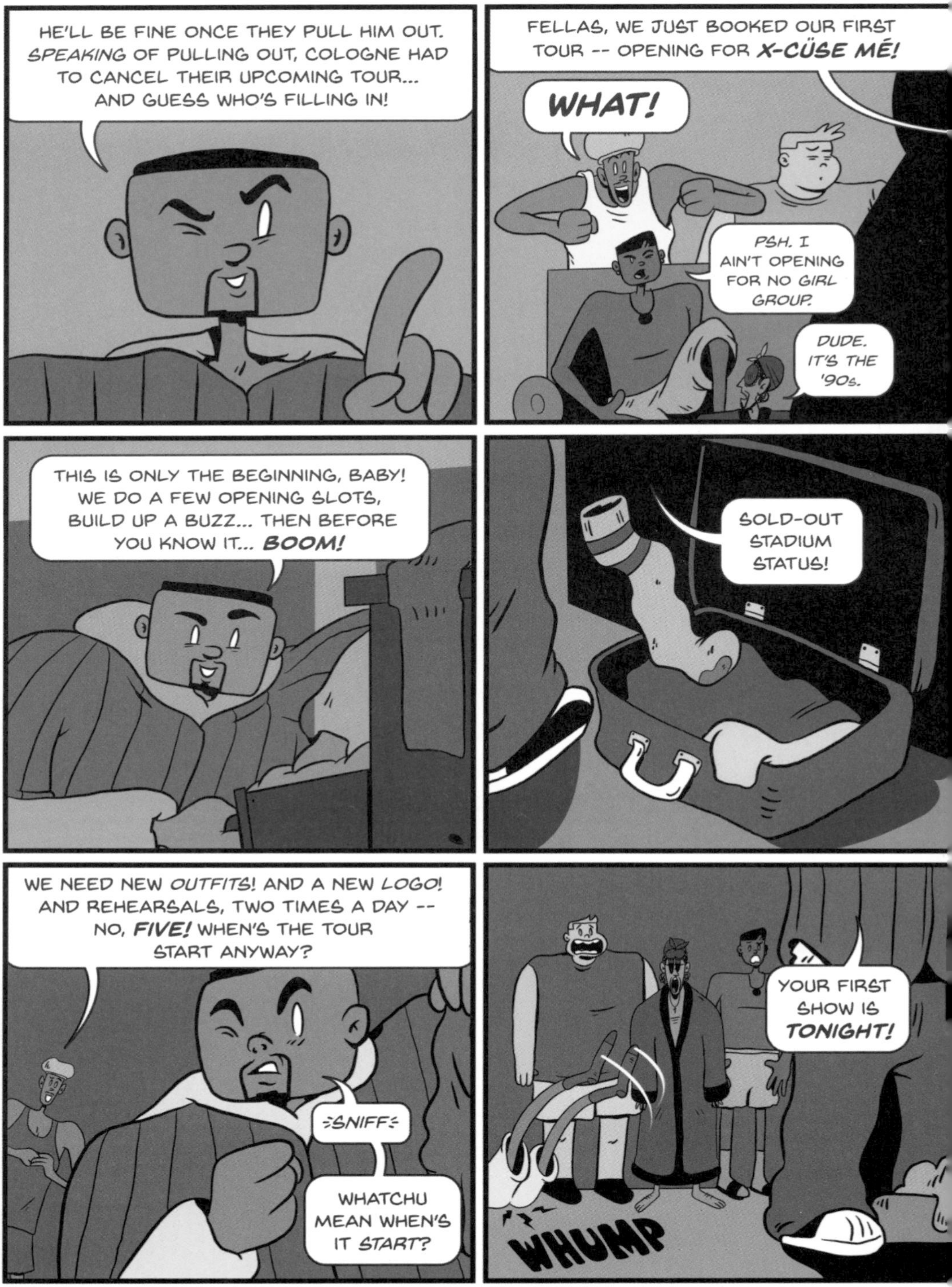
HE'LL BE FINE ONCE THEY PULL HIM OUT. SPEAKING OF PULLING OUT, COLOGNE HAD TO CANCEL THEIR UPCOMING TOUR... AND GUESS WHO'S FILLING IN!
FELLAS, WE JUST BOOKED OUR FIRST TOUR -- OPENING FOR X-CÜSE MÉ!
WHAT!
PSH. I AIN'T OPENING FOR NO GIRL GROUP.
DUDE. IT'S THE '90s.
THIS IS ONLY THE BEGINNING, BABY! WE DO A FEW OPENING SLOTS, BUILD UP A BUZZ... THEN BEFORE YOU KNOW IT... BOOM!
SOLD-OUT STADIUM STATUS!
WE NEED NEW OUTFITS! AND A NEW LOGO! AND REHEARSALS, TWO TIMES A DAY -- NO, FIVE! WHEN'S THE TOUR START ANYWAY?
SNIFF
WHATCHU MEAN WHEN'S IT START?
YOUR FIRST SHOW IS TONIGHT!
WHUMP

SO, ARE WE FLYIN' FIRST CLASS OR PRIVATE?

OOH! CAN WE GET A HELICOPTER?

DICEY CAB "Roll At Your Own Risk"

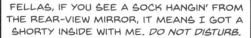

UH, THIS ONE'S MORE OF A *GROUND* TOUR. I WANNA GIVE Y'ALL A LITTLE TASTE OF THAT ROCKSTAR ROAD LIFE.

YOU GOT US A TOUR BUS?!

TIGHT.

FELLAS, IF YOU SEE A SOCK HANGIN' FROM THE REAR-VIEW MIRROR, IT MEANS I GOT A SHORTY INSIDE WITH ME. *DO NOT DISTURB.*

DID WE PACK SOCKS?

THIS IS ABOUT TO BE THE *GREATEST SUMMER* OF OUR *ENTIRE LIVES!*

BUS STATION

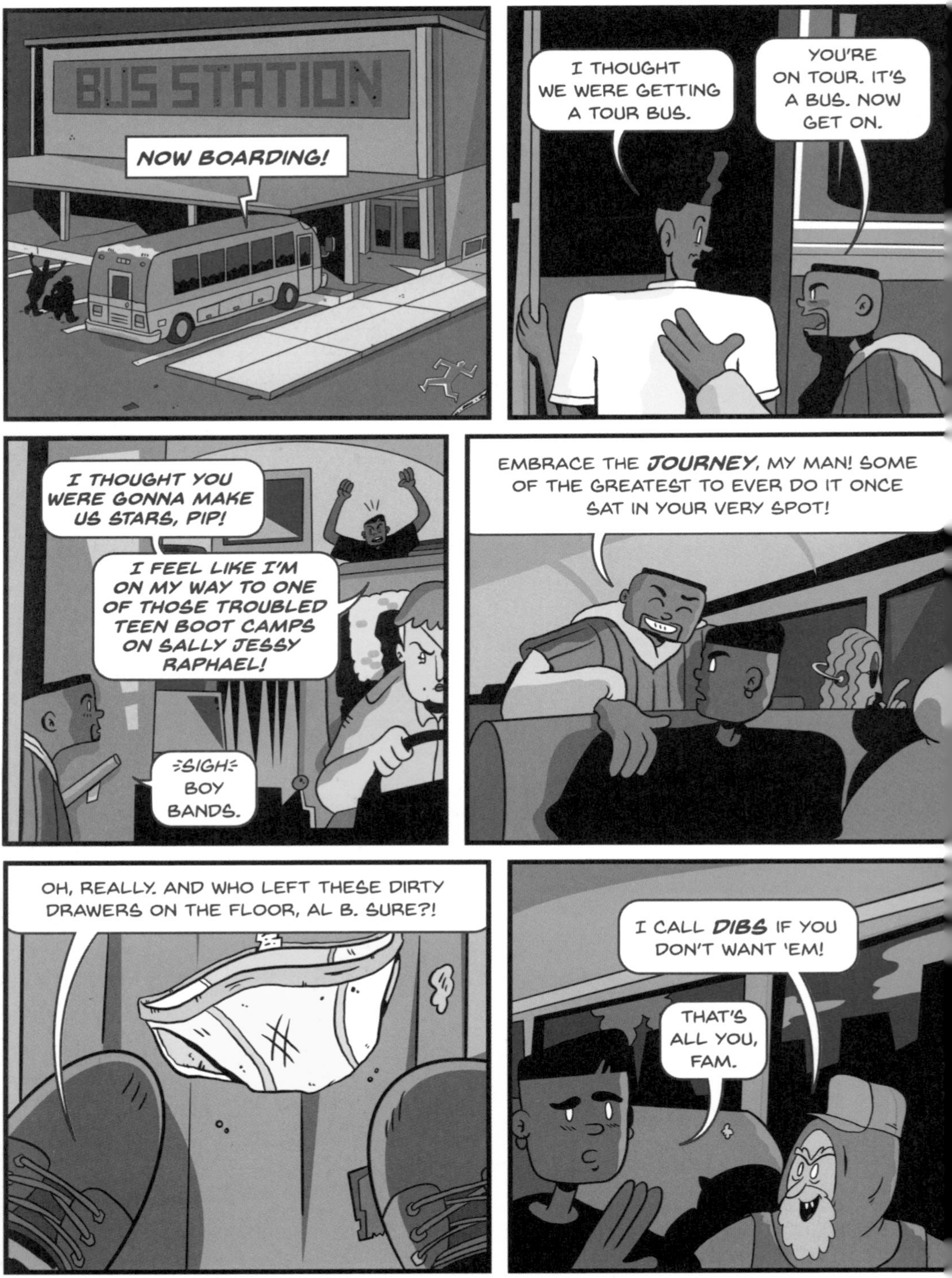
BUS STATION
NOW BOARDING!
I THOUGHT WE WERE GETTING A TOUR BUS.
YOU'RE ON TOUR. IT'S A BUS. NOW GET ON.
I THOUGHT YOU WERE GONNA MAKE US STARS, PIP!
I FEEL LIKE I'M ON MY WAY TO ONE OF THOSE TROUBLED TEEN BOOT CAMPS ON SALLY JESSY RAPHAEL!
SIGH BOY BANDS.
EMBRACE THE JOURNEY, MY MAN! SOME OF THE GREATEST TO EVER DO IT ONCE SAT IN YOUR VERY SPOT!
OH, REALLY. AND WHO LEFT THESE DIRTY DRAWERS ON THE FLOOR, AL B. SURE?!
I CALL DIBS IF YOU DON'T WANT 'EM!
THAT'S ALL YOU, FAM.

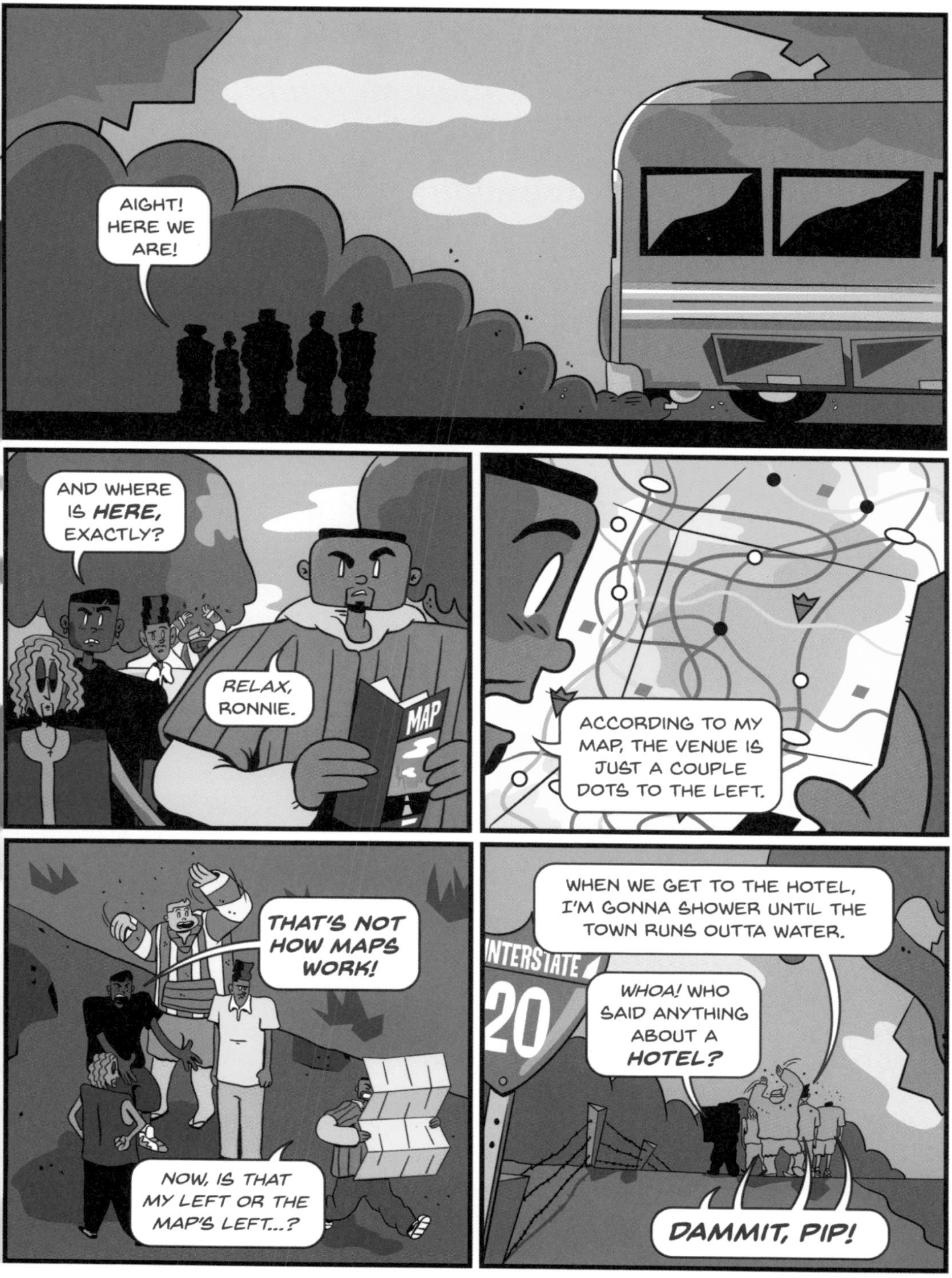
AIGHT! HERE WE ARE!
AND WHERE IS *HERE,* EXACTLY?
RELAX, RONNIE.
MAP
ACCORDING TO MY MAP, THE VENUE IS JUST A COUPLE DOTS TO THE LEFT.
THAT'S NOT HOW MAPS WORK!
NOW, IS THAT MY LEFT OR THE MAP'S LEFT...?
WHEN WE GET TO THE HOTEL, I'M GONNA SHOWER UNTIL THE TOWN RUNS OUTTA WATER.
INTERSTATE
20
WHOA! WHO SAID ANYTHING ABOUT A *HOTEL?*
DAMMIT, PIP!

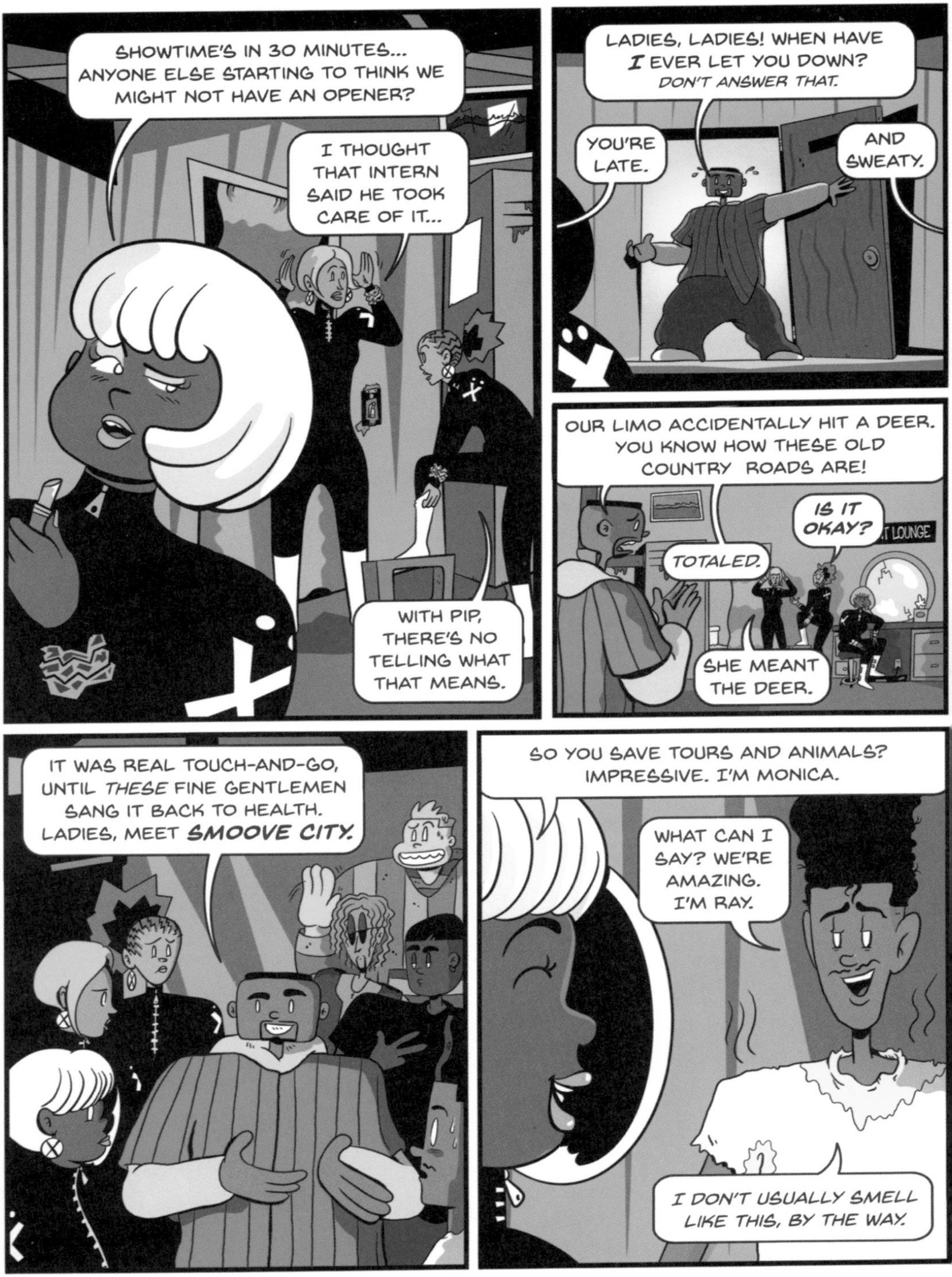

SHOWTIME'S IN 30 MINUTES... ANYONE ELSE STARTING TO THINK WE MIGHT NOT HAVE AN OPENER?
I THOUGHT THAT INTERN SAID HE TOOK CARE OF IT...
WITH PIP, THERE'S NO TELLING WHAT THAT MEANS.
LADIES, LADIES! WHEN HAVE *I* EVER LET YOU DOWN? *DON'T ANSWER THAT.*
YOU'RE LATE.
AND SWEATY.
OUR LIMO ACCIDENTALLY HIT A DEER. YOU KNOW HOW THESE OLD COUNTRY ROADS ARE!
IS IT OKAY?
TOTALED.
SHE MEANT THE DEER.
IT WAS REAL TOUCH-AND-GO, UNTIL *THESE* FINE GENTLEMEN SANG IT BACK TO HEALTH. LADIES, MEET ***SMOOVE CITY.***
SO YOU SAVE TOURS AND ANIMALS? IMPRESSIVE. I'M MONICA.
WHAT CAN I SAY? WE'RE AMAZING. I'M RAY.
I DON'T USUALLY SMELL LIKE THIS, BY THE WAY.

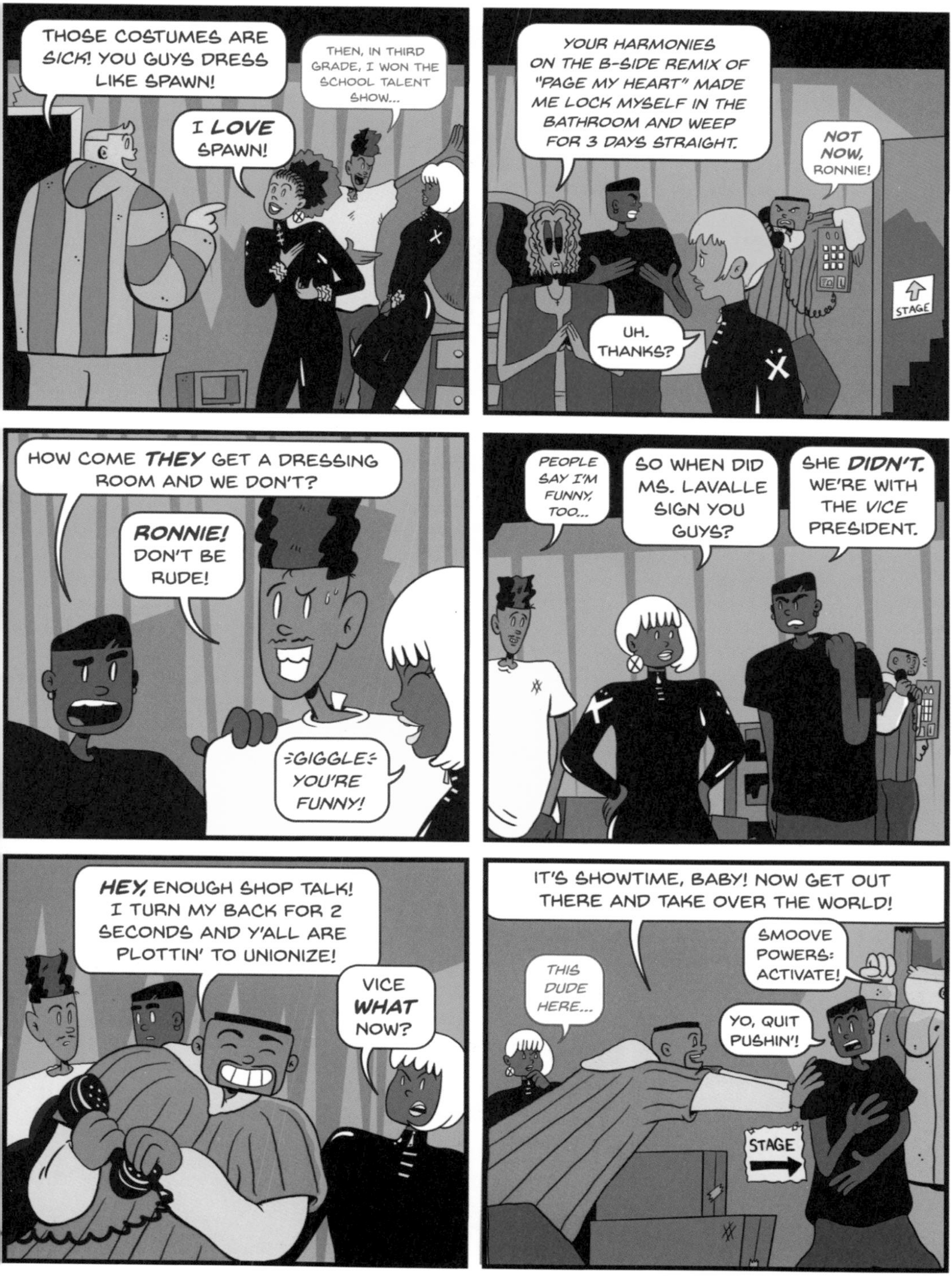
THOSE COSTUMES ARE SICK! YOU GUYS DRESS LIKE SPAWN!
THEN, IN THIRD GRADE, I WON THE SCHOOL TALENT SHOW...
I LOVE SPAWN!
YOUR HARMONIES ON THE B-SIDE REMIX OF "PAGE MY HEART" MADE ME LOCK MYSELF IN THE BATHROOM AND WEEP FOR 3 DAYS STRAIGHT.
NOT NOW, RONNIE!
UH. THANKS?
STAGE
HOW COME THEY GET A DRESSING ROOM AND WE DON'T?
RONNIE! DON'T BE RUDE!
GIGGLE YOU'RE FUNNY!
PEOPLE SAY I'M FUNNY, TOO...
SO WHEN DID MS. LAVALLE SIGN YOU GUYS?
SHE DIDN'T. WE'RE WITH THE VICE PRESIDENT.
HEY, ENOUGH SHOP TALK! I TURN MY BACK FOR 2 SECONDS AND Y'ALL ARE PLOTTIN' TO UNIONIZE!
VICE WHAT NOW?
IT'S SHOWTIME, BABY! NOW GET OUT THERE AND TAKE OVER THE WORLD!
SMOOVE POWERS: ACTIVATE!
THIS DUDE HERE...
YO, QUIT PUSHIN'!
STAGE

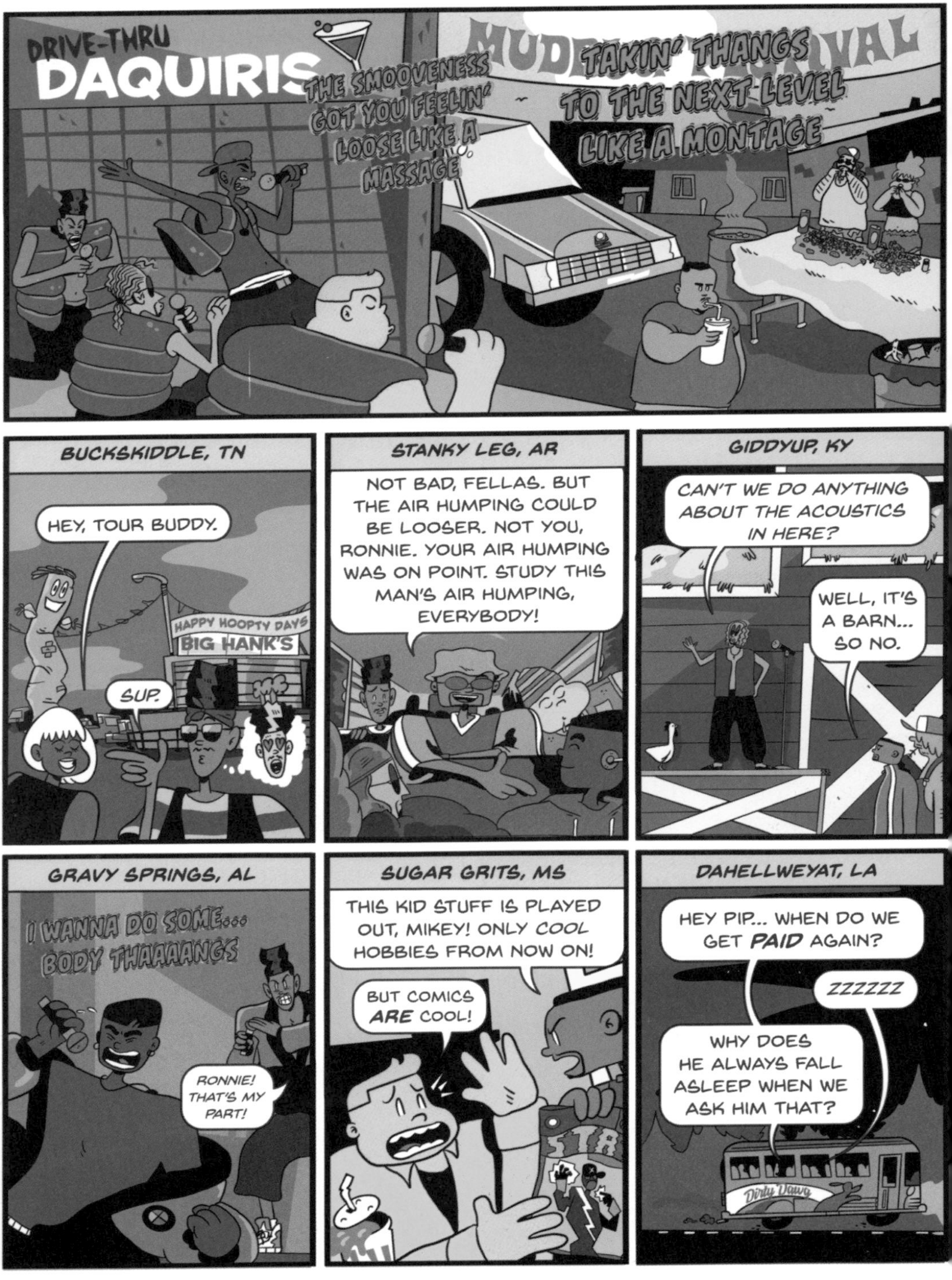
DRIVE-THRU
DAQUIRIS
THE SMOOVENESS GOT YOU FEELIN' LOOSE LIKE A MASSAGE
TAKIN' THANGS TO THE NEXT LEVEL LIKE A MONTAGE
BUCKSKIDDLE, TN
HEY, TOUR BUDDY.
HAPPY HOOPTY DAYS
BIG HANK'S
SUP.
STANKY LEG, AR
NOT BAD, FELLAS. BUT THE AIR HUMPING COULD BE LOOSER. NOT YOU, RONNIE. YOUR AIR HUMPING WAS ON POINT. STUDY THIS MAN'S AIR HUMPING, EVERYBODY!
GIDDYUP, KY
CAN'T WE DO ANYTHING ABOUT THE ACOUSTICS IN HERE?
WELL, IT'S A BARN... SO NO.
GRAVY SPRINGS, AL
I WANNA DO SOME... BODY THAAAANGS
RONNIE! THAT'S MY PART!
SUGAR GRITS, MS
THIS KID STUFF IS PLAYED OUT, MIKEY! ONLY COOL HOBBIES FROM NOW ON!
BUT COMICS ARE COOL!
DAHELLWEYAT, LA
HEY PIP... WHEN DO WE GET PAID AGAIN?
ZZZZZZ
WHY DOES HE ALWAYS FALL ASLEEP WHEN WE ASK HIM THAT?
Dirty Dawg

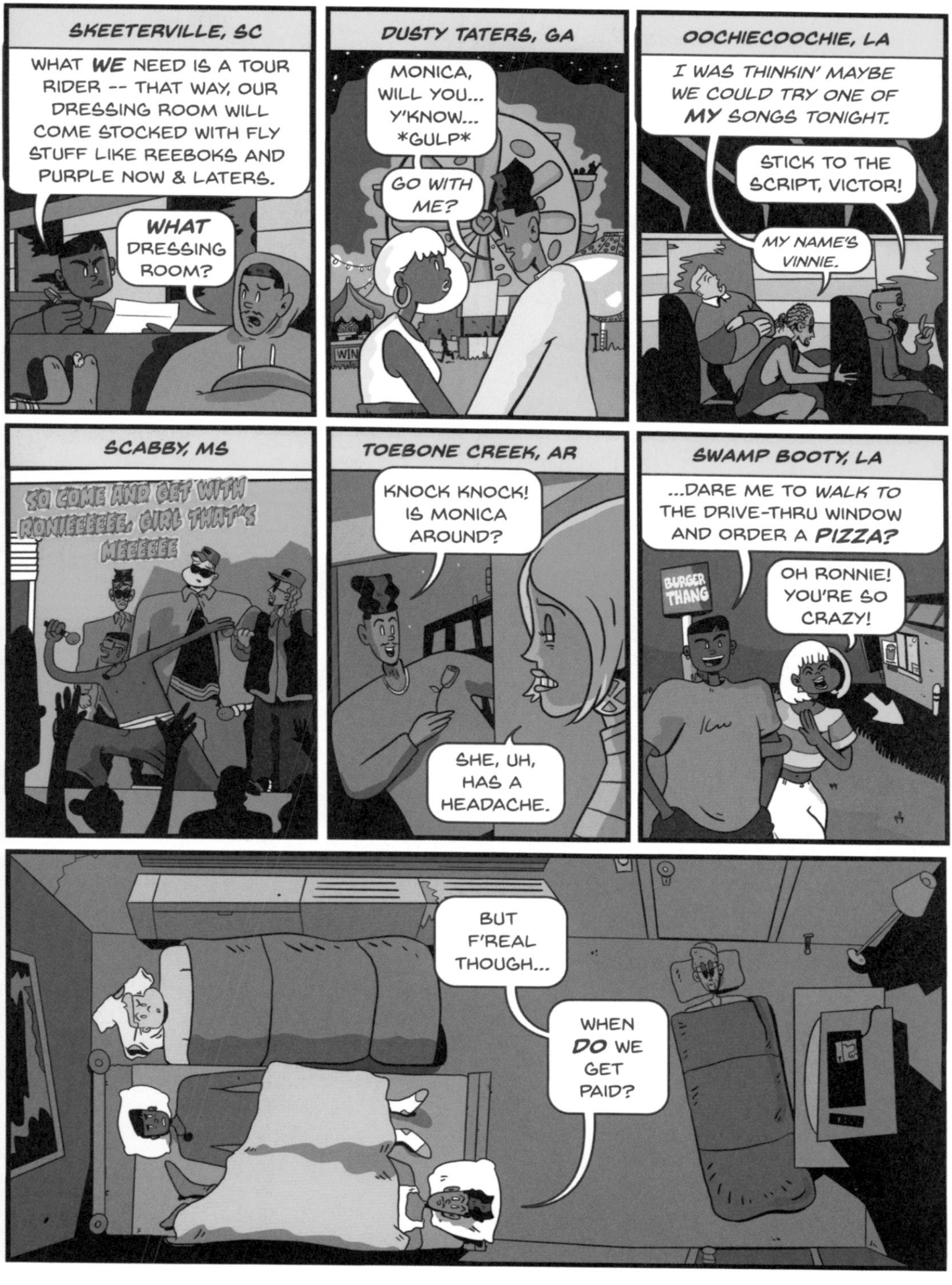
SKEETERVILLE, SC
WHAT WE NEED IS A TOUR RIDER -- THAT WAY, OUR DRESSING ROOM WILL COME STOCKED WITH FLY STUFF LIKE REEBOKS AND PURPLE NOW & LATERS.
WHAT DRESSING ROOM?
DUSTY TATERS, GA
MONICA, WILL YOU... Y'KNOW... *GULP*
GO WITH ME?
OOCHIECOOCHIE, LA
I WAS THINKIN' MAYBE WE COULD TRY ONE OF MY SONGS TONIGHT.
STICK TO THE SCRIPT, VICTOR!
MY NAME'S VINNIE.
SCABBY, MS
SO COME AND GET WITH RONIEEEEEE, GIRL THAT'S MEEEEEE
TOEBONE CREEK, AR
KNOCK KNOCK! IS MONICA AROUND?
SHE, UH, HAS A HEADACHE.
SWAMP BOOTY, LA
...DARE ME TO WALK TO THE DRIVE-THRU WINDOW AND ORDER A PIZZA?
BURGER THANG
OH RONNIE! YOU'RE SO CRAZY!
BUT F'REAL THOUGH...
WHEN DO WE GET PAID?

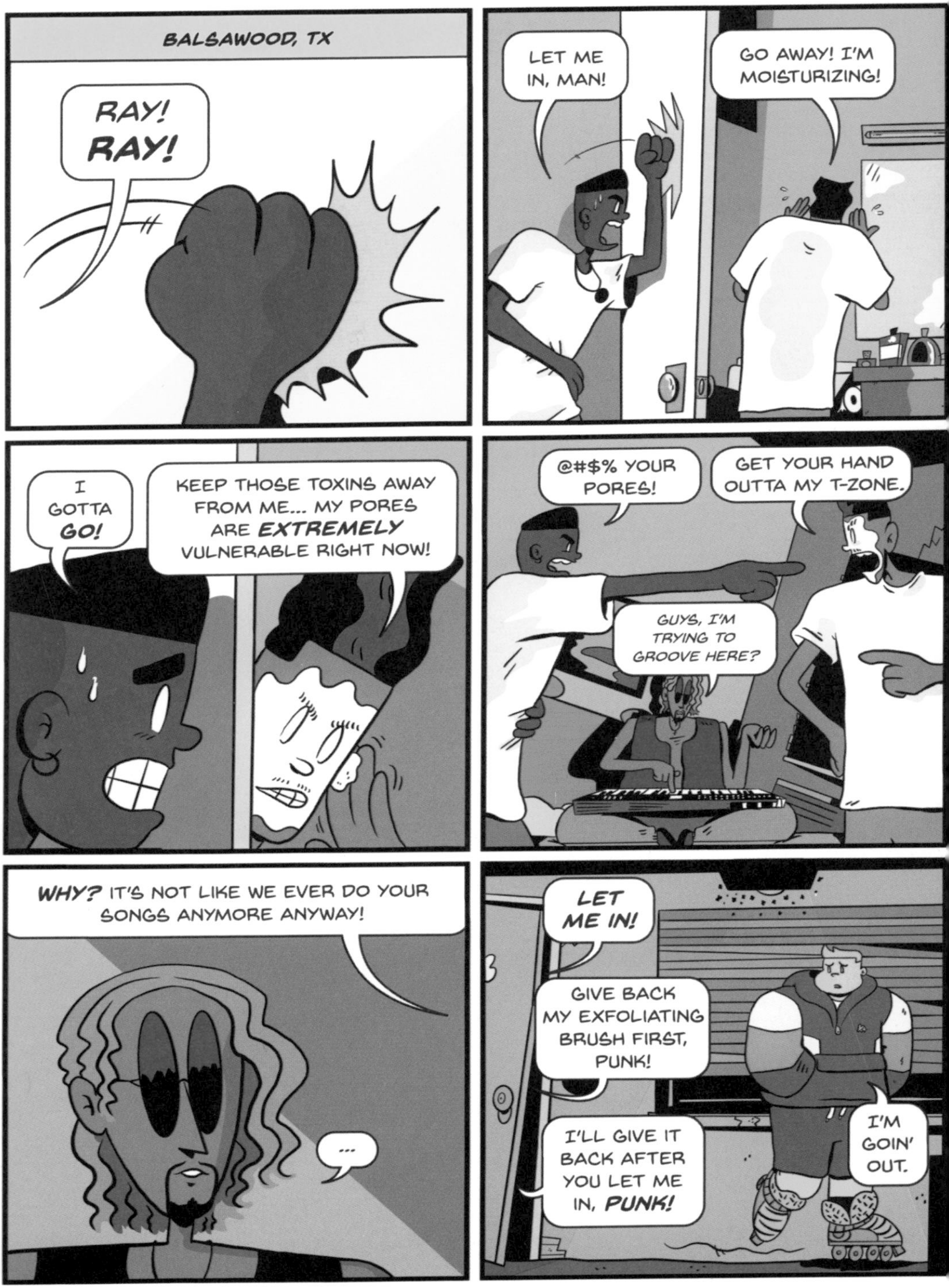
BALSAWOOD, TX
RAY! RAY!
LET ME IN, MAN!
GO AWAY! I'M MOISTURIZING!
I GOTTA GO!
KEEP THOSE TOXINS AWAY FROM ME... MY PORES ARE EXTREMELY VULNERABLE RIGHT NOW!
@#$% YOUR PORES!
GET YOUR HAND OUTTA MY T-ZONE.
GUYS, I'M TRYING TO GROOVE HERE?
WHY? IT'S NOT LIKE WE EVER DO YOUR SONGS ANYMORE ANYWAY!
...
LET ME IN!
GIVE BACK MY EXFOLIATING BRUSH FIRST, PUNK!
I'LL GIVE IT BACK AFTER YOU LET ME IN, PUNK!
I'M GOIN' OUT.

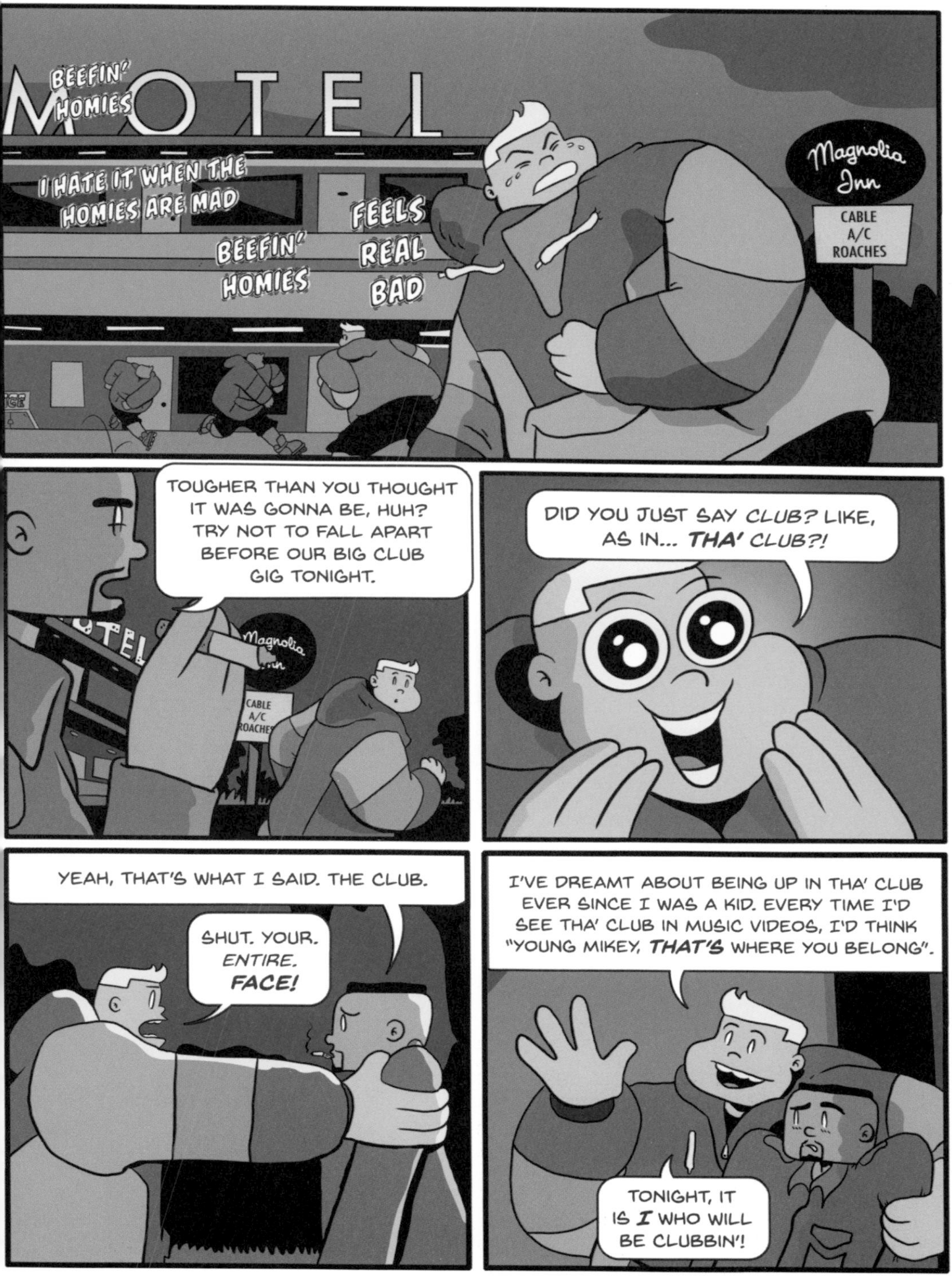
MOTEL
BEEFIN' HOMIES
I HATE IT WHEN THE HOMIES ARE MAD
BEEFIN' HOMIES
FEELS REAL BAD
Magnolia Inn
CABLE
A/C
ROACHES
TOUGHER THAN YOU THOUGHT IT WAS GONNA BE, HUH? TRY NOT TO FALL APART BEFORE OUR BIG CLUB GIG TONIGHT.
DID YOU JUST SAY CLUB? LIKE, AS IN... THA' CLUB?!
YEAH, THAT'S WHAT I SAID. THE CLUB.
SHUT. YOUR. ENTIRE. FACE!
I'VE DREAMT ABOUT BEING UP IN THA' CLUB EVER SINCE I WAS A KID. EVERY TIME I'D SEE THA' CLUB IN MUSIC VIDEOS, I'D THINK "YOUNG MIKEY, THAT'S WHERE YOU BELONG".
TONIGHT, IT IS I WHO WILL BE CLUBBIN'!

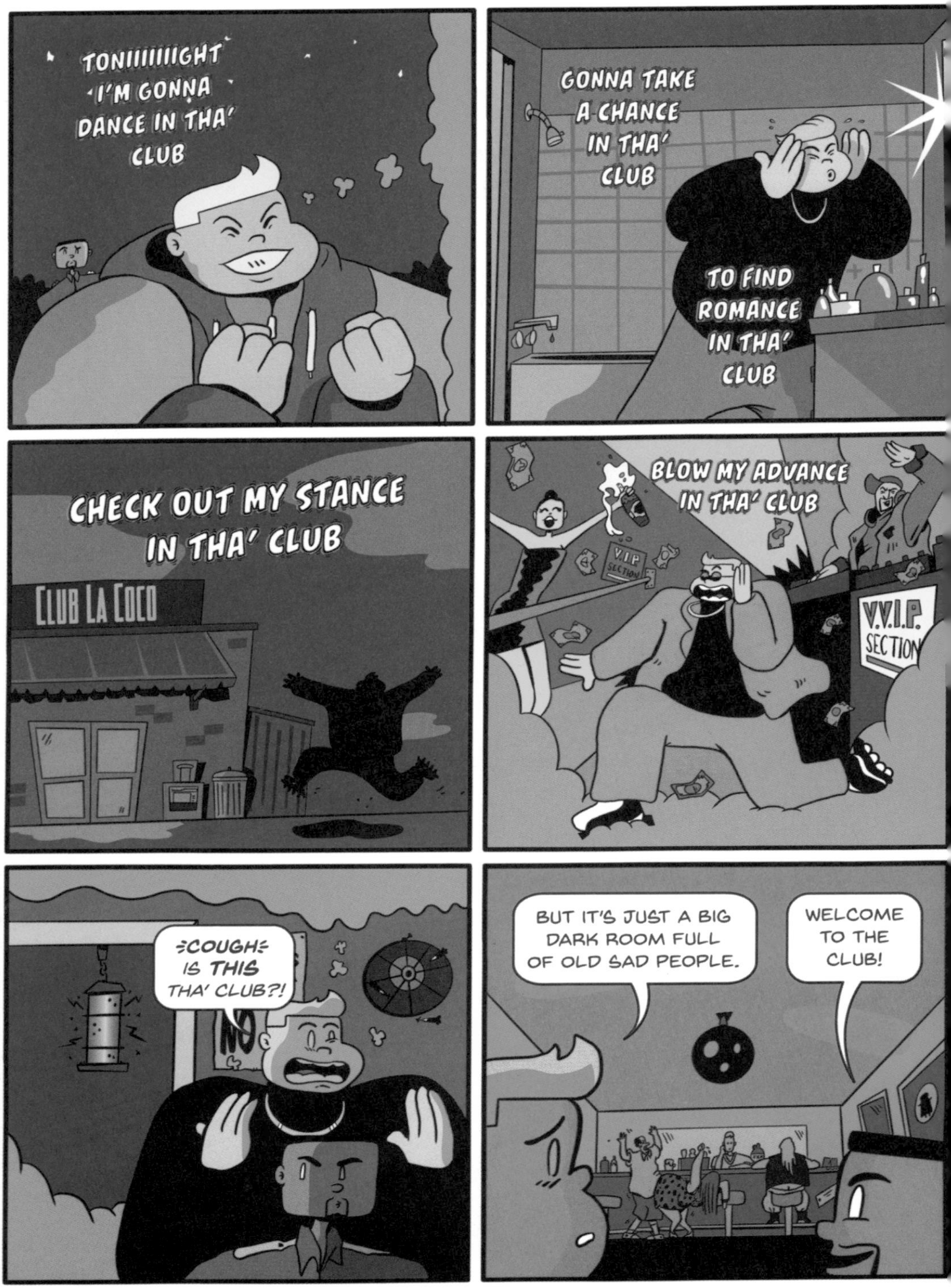
TONIIIIIIIGHT I'M GONNA DANCE IN THA' CLUB
GONNA TAKE A CHANCE IN THA' CLUB
TO FIND ROMANCE IN THA' CLUB
CHECK OUT MY STANCE IN THA' CLUB
CLUB LA COCO
BLOW MY ADVANCE IN THA' CLUB
VIP SECTION
V.V.I.P. SECTION
COUGH IS THIS THA' CLUB?!
NO
BUT IT'S JUST A BIG DARK ROOM FULL OF OLD SAD PEOPLE.
WELCOME TO THE CLUB!

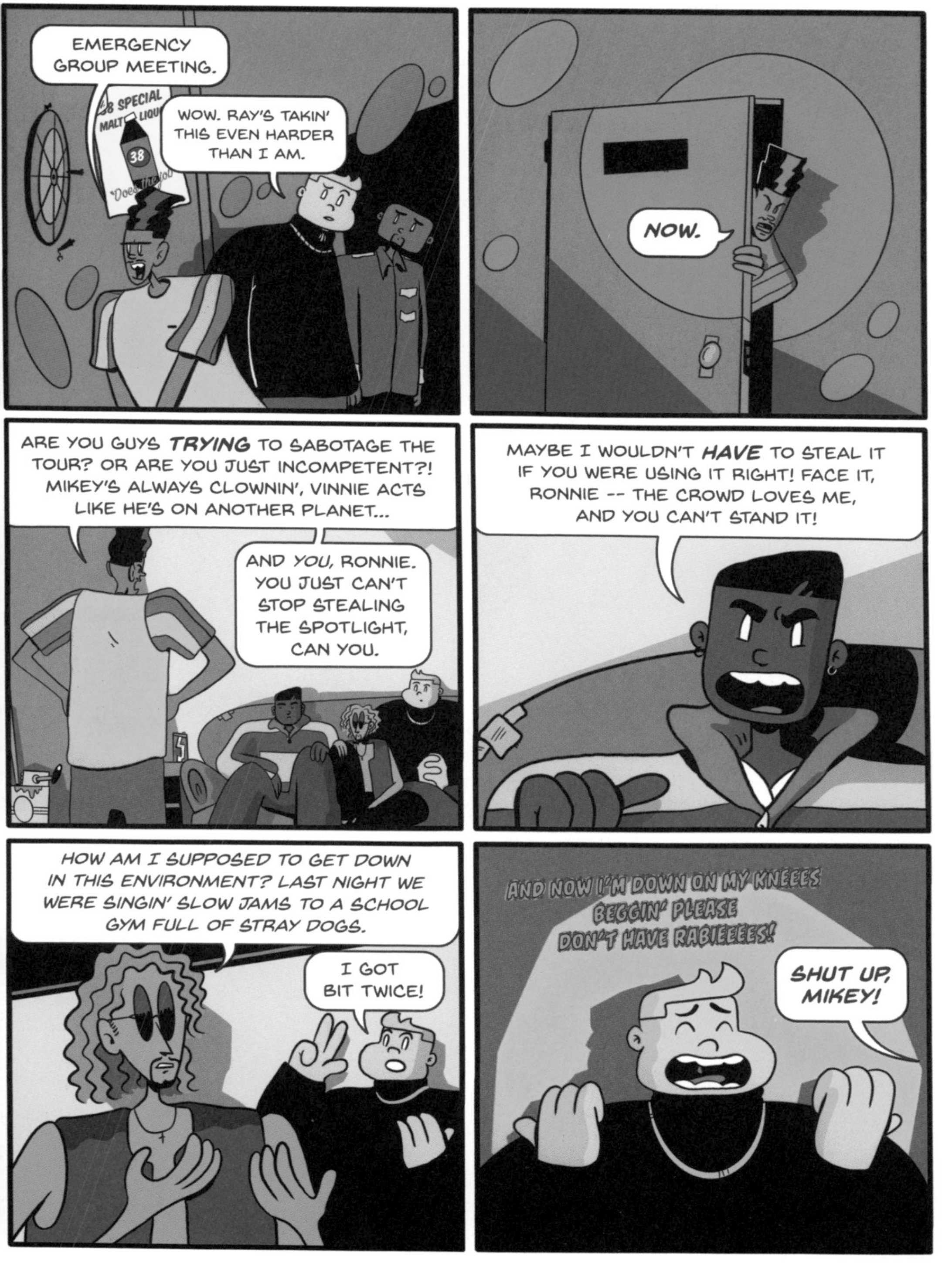
EMERGENCY GROUP MEETING.
38 SPECIAL MALT LIQU
38
WOW. RAY'S TAKIN' THIS EVEN HARDER THAN I AM.
NOW.
ARE YOU GUYS TRYING TO SABOTAGE THE TOUR? OR ARE YOU JUST INCOMPETENT?! MIKEY'S ALWAYS CLOWNIN', VINNIE ACTS LIKE HE'S ON ANOTHER PLANET...
AND YOU, RONNIE. YOU JUST CAN'T STOP STEALING THE SPOTLIGHT, CAN YOU.
MAYBE I WOULDN'T HAVE TO STEAL IT IF YOU WERE USING IT RIGHT! FACE IT, RONNIE -- THE CROWD LOVES ME, AND YOU CAN'T STAND IT!
HOW AM I SUPPOSED TO GET DOWN IN THIS ENVIRONMENT? LAST NIGHT WE WERE SINGIN' SLOW JAMS TO A SCHOOL GYM FULL OF STRAY DOGS.
I GOT BIT TWICE!
AND NOW I'M DOWN ON MY KNEEES BEGGIN' PLEASE DON'T HAVE RABIEEEES!
SHUT UP, MIKEY!

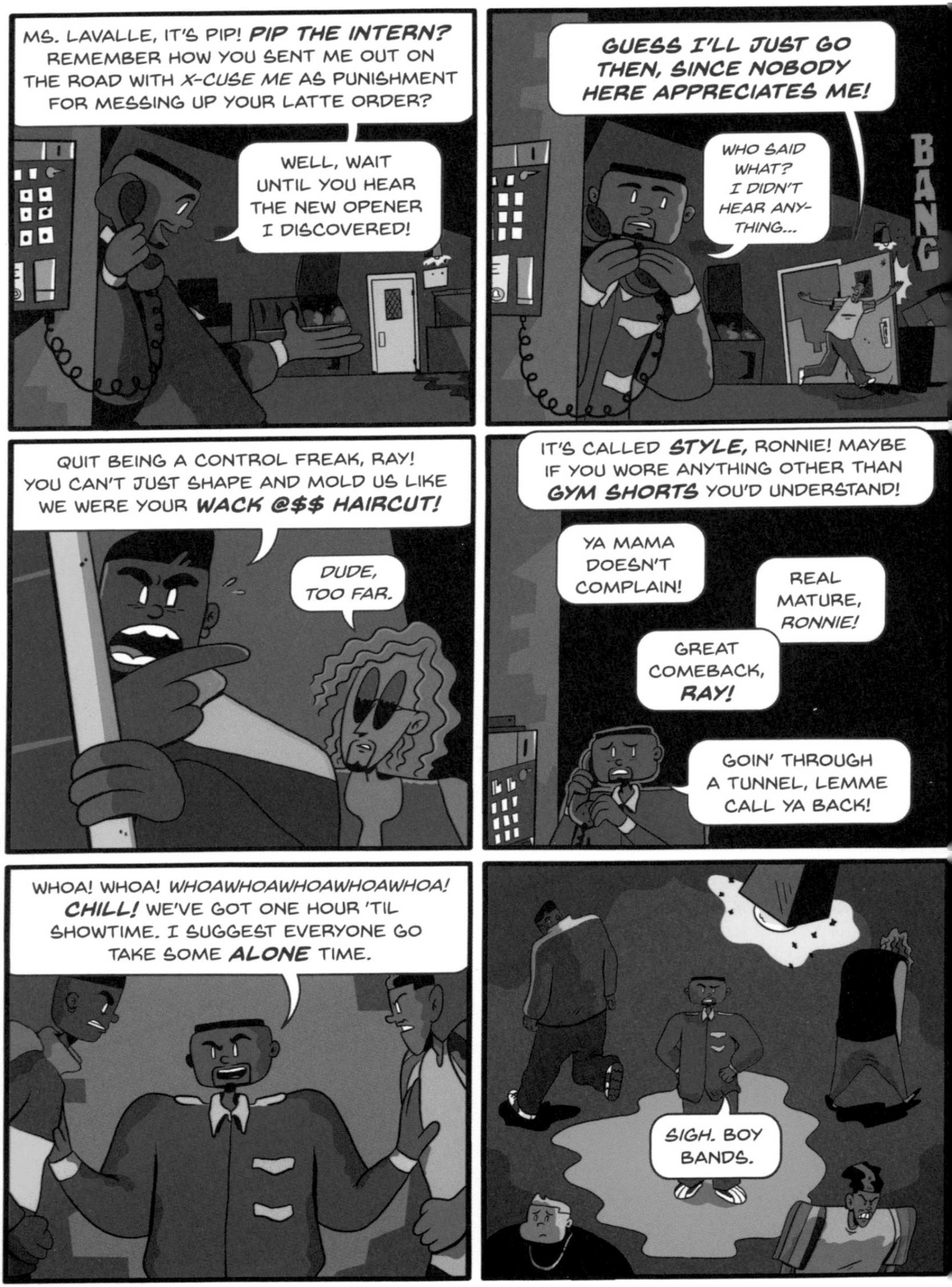
MS. LAVALLE, IT'S PIP! PIP THE INTERN? REMEMBER HOW YOU SENT ME OUT ON THE ROAD WITH X-CUSE ME AS PUNISHMENT FOR MESSING UP YOUR LATTE ORDER?
WELL, WAIT UNTIL YOU HEAR THE NEW OPENER I DISCOVERED!
GUESS I'LL JUST GO THEN, SINCE NOBODY HERE APPRECIATES ME!
WHO SAID WHAT? I DIDN'T HEAR ANY-THING...
BANG
QUIT BEING A CONTROL FREAK, RAY! YOU CAN'T JUST SHAPE AND MOLD US LIKE WE WERE YOUR WACK @$$ HAIRCUT!
DUDE, TOO FAR.
IT'S CALLED STYLE, RONNIE! MAYBE IF YOU WORE ANYTHING OTHER THAN GYM SHORTS YOU'D UNDERSTAND!
YA MAMA DOESN'T COMPLAIN!
REAL MATURE, RONNIE!
GREAT COMEBACK, RAY!
GOIN' THROUGH A TUNNEL, LEMME CALL YA BACK!
WHOA! WHOA! WHOAWHOAWHOAWHOAWHOA! CHILL! WE'VE GOT ONE HOUR 'TIL SHOWTIME. I SUGGEST EVERYONE GO TAKE SOME ALONE TIME.
SIGH. BOY BANDS.

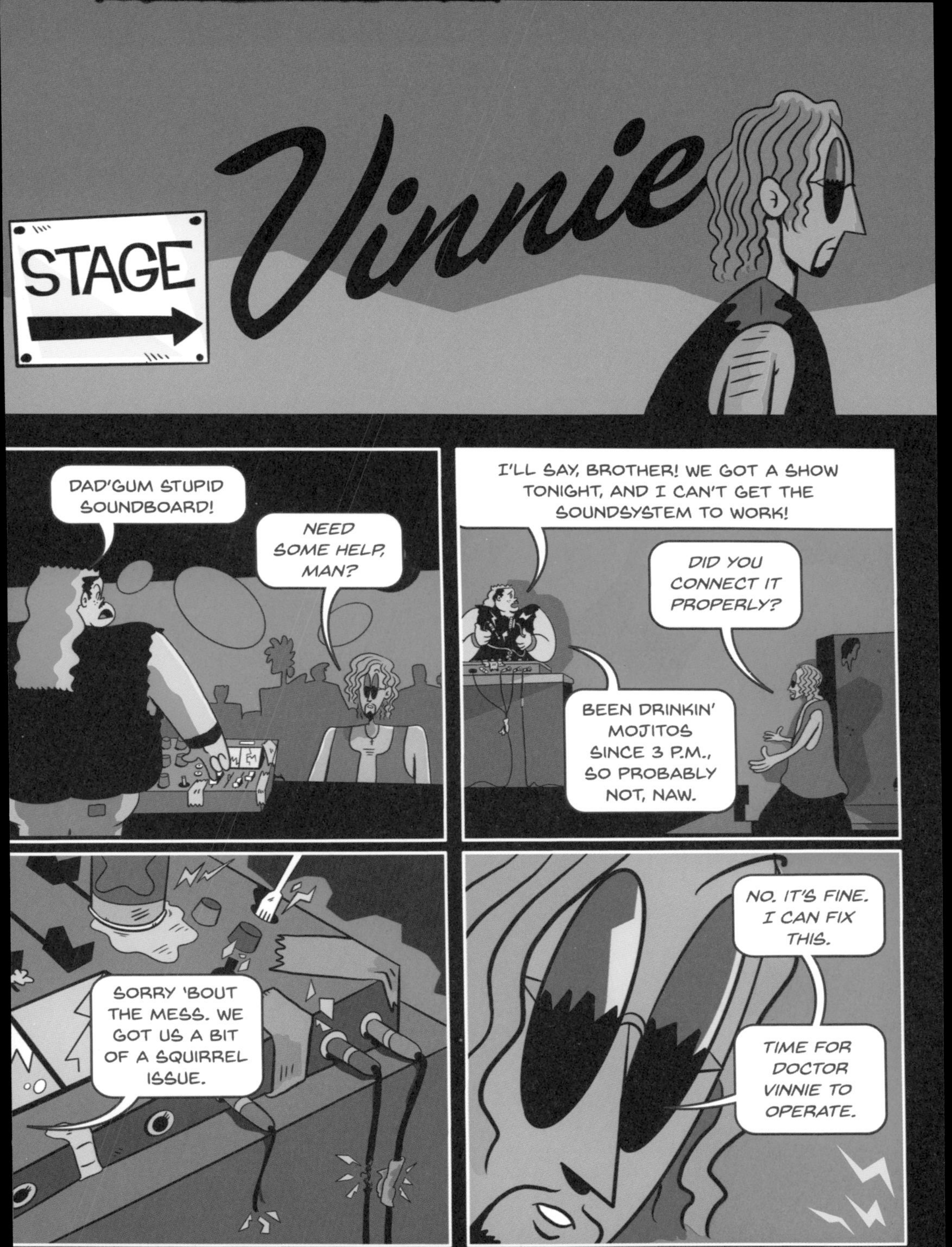

STAGE
Vinnie
DAD'GUM STUPID SOUNDBOARD!
NEED SOME HELP, MAN?
I'LL SAY, BROTHER! WE GOT A SHOW TONIGHT, AND I CAN'T GET THE SOUNDSYSTEM TO WORK!
DID YOU CONNECT IT PROPERLY?
BEEN DRINKIN' MOJITOS SINCE 3 P.M., SO PROBABLY NOT, NAW.
SORRY 'BOUT THE MESS. WE GOT US A BIT OF A SQUIRREL ISSUE.
NO. IT'S FINE. I CAN FIX THIS.
TIME FOR DOCTOR VINNIE TO OPERATE.

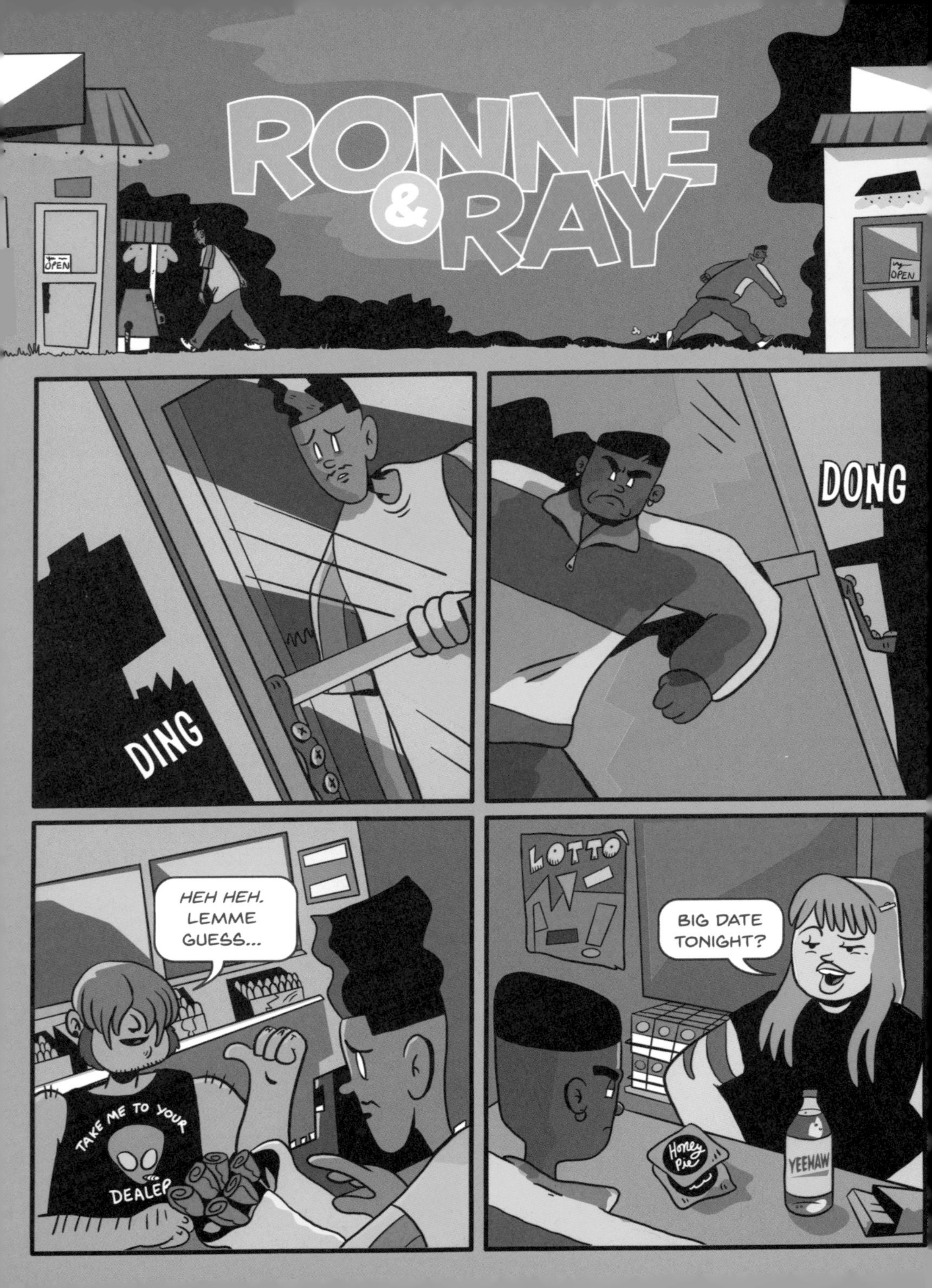
RONNIE & RAY
OPEN
OPEN
DING
DONG
HEH HEH. LEMME GUESS...
TAKE ME TO YOUR DEALER
LOTTO
BIG DATE TONIGHT?
Honey Pie
YEEHAW

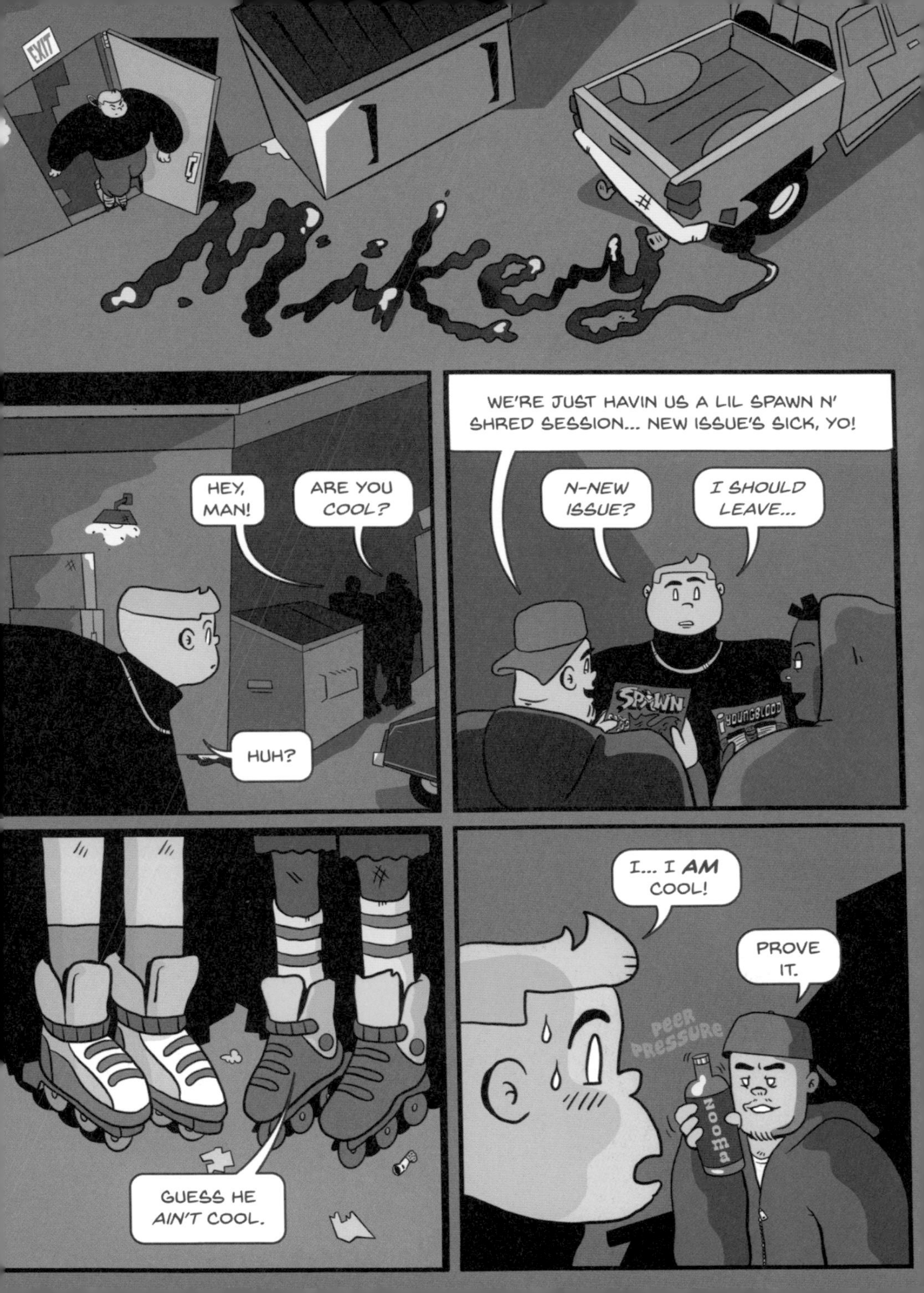
EXIT
MIKEY
HEY, MAN!
ARE YOU COOL?
HUH?
WE'RE JUST HAVIN US A LIL SPAWN N' SHRED SESSION... NEW ISSUE'S SICK, YO!
N-NEW ISSUE?
I SHOULD LEAVE...
SPAWN
YOUNGBLOOD
GUESS HE AIN'T COOL.
I... I **AM** COOL!
PROVE IT.
PEER PRESSURE
HOOCH

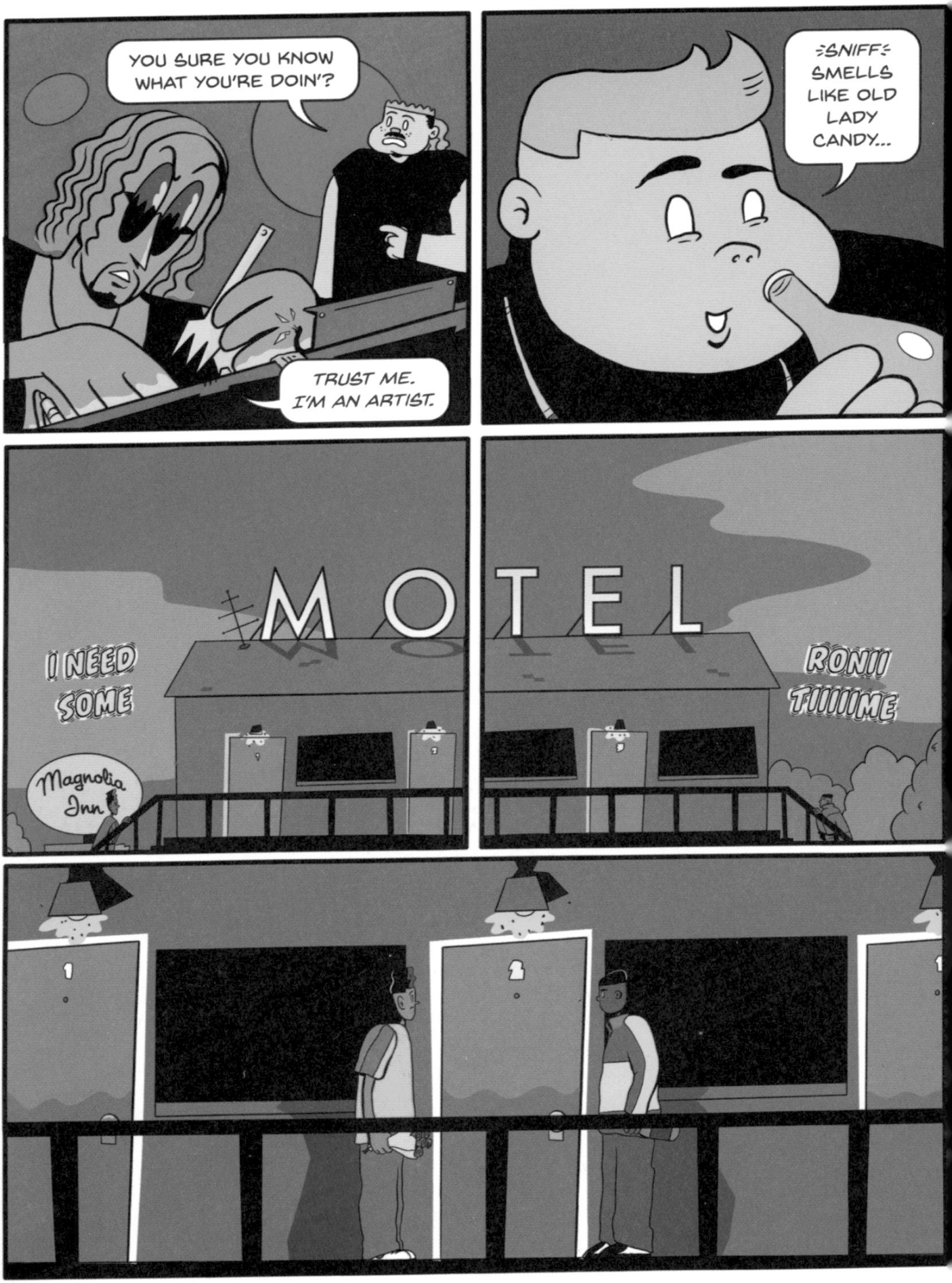
YOU SURE YOU KNOW WHAT YOU'RE DOIN'?
TRUST ME. I'M AN ARTIST.
=SNIFF= SMELLS LIKE OLD LADY CANDY...
MOTEL
I NEED SOME
RONII TIIIIIME
Magnolia Inn
1
2
1

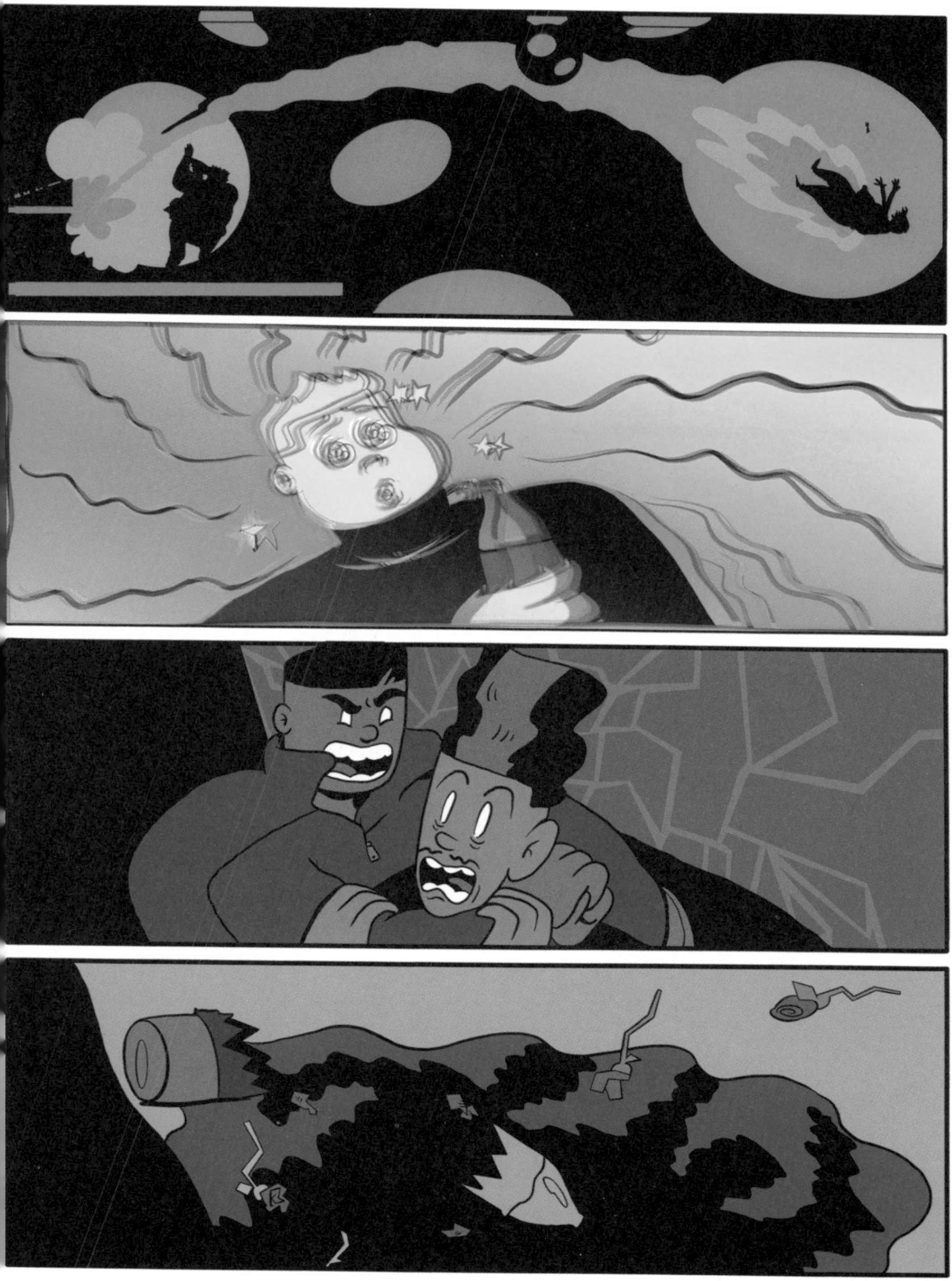

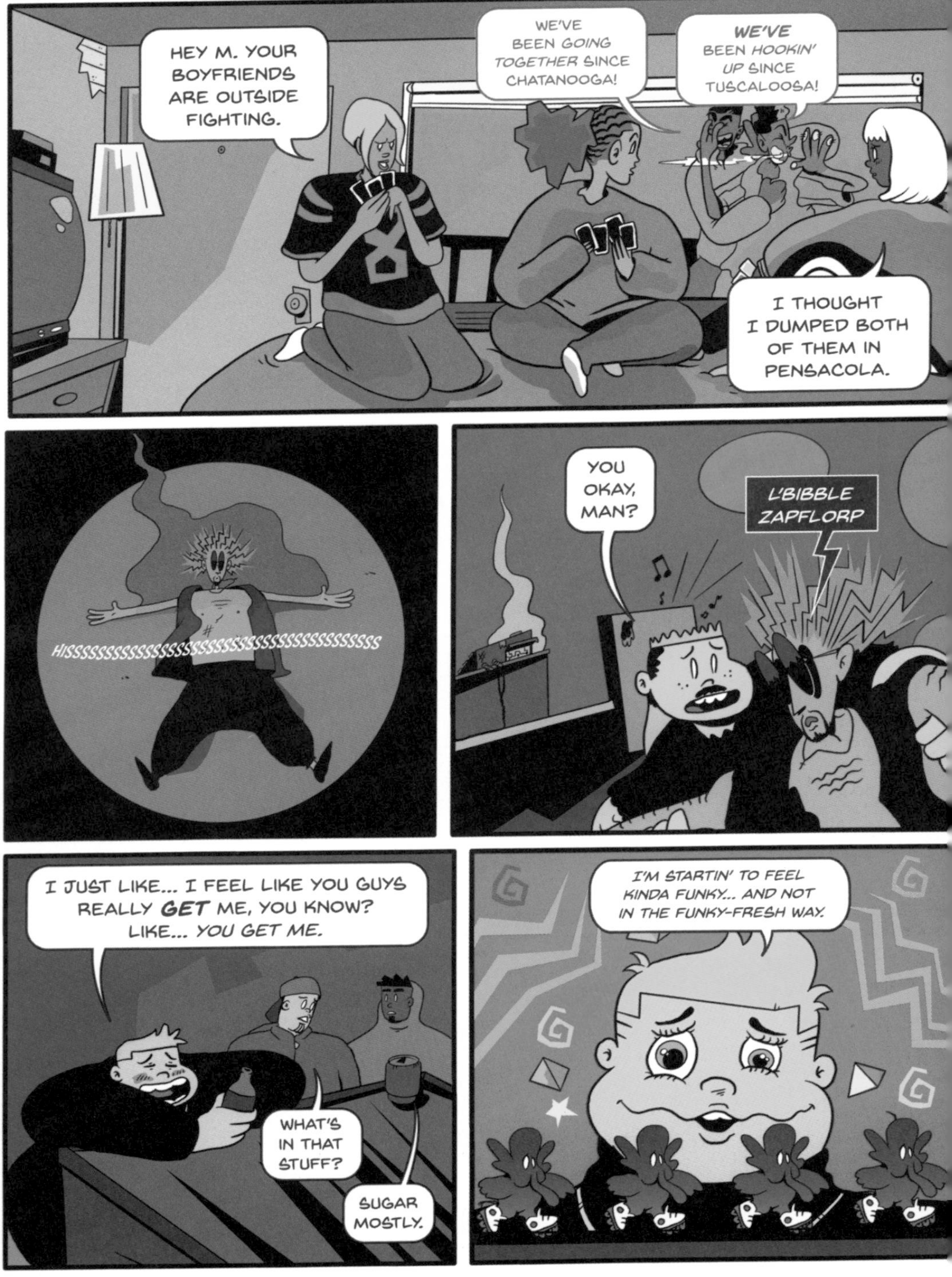
HEY M. YOUR BOYFRIENDS ARE OUTSIDE FIGHTING.
WE'VE BEEN GOING TOGETHER SINCE CHATANOOGA!
WE'VE BEEN HOOKIN' UP SINCE TUSCALOOSA!
I THOUGHT I DUMPED BOTH OF THEM IN PENSACOLA.
HISSSSSSSSSSSSSSSSSSSSSSSSSSSSSSSSSSSSSSSSS
YOU OKAY, MAN?
L'BIBBLE ZAPFLORP
I JUST LIKE... I FEEL LIKE YOU GUYS REALLY GET ME, YOU KNOW? LIKE... YOU GET ME.
WHAT'S IN THAT STUFF?
SUGAR MOSTLY.
I'M STARTIN' TO FEEL KINDA FUNKY... AND NOT IN THE FUNKY-FRESH WAY.

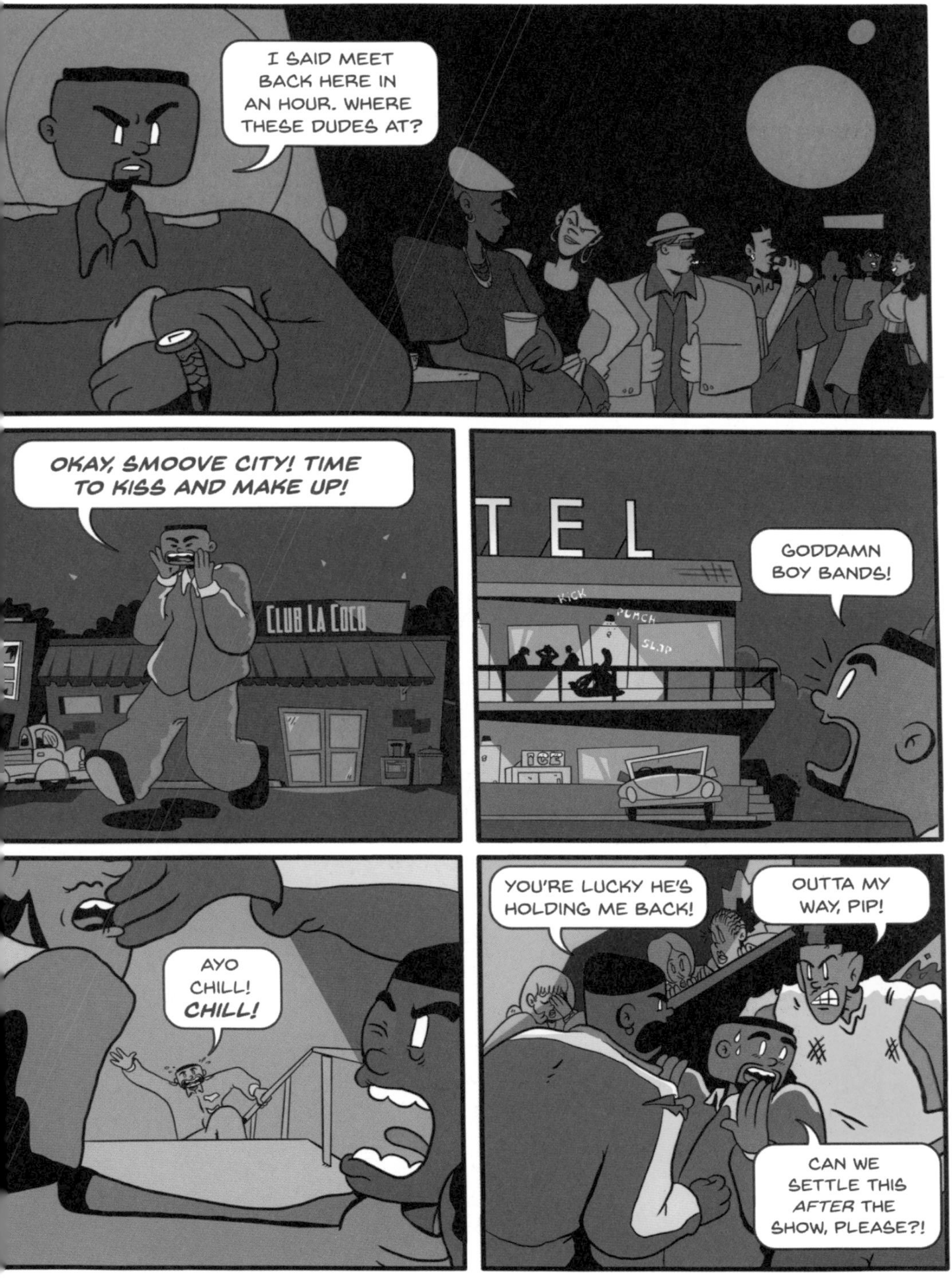

I SAID MEET BACK HERE IN AN HOUR. WHERE THESE DUDES AT?
OKAY, SMOOVE CITY! TIME TO KISS AND MAKE UP!
CLUB LA COCO
TEL
KICK
PUNCH
SLAP
ICE
GODDAMN BOY BANDS!
AYO CHILL! CHILL!
YOU'RE LUCKY HE'S HOLDING ME BACK!
OUTTA MY WAY, PIP!
CAN WE SETTLE THIS AFTER THE SHOW, PLEASE?!

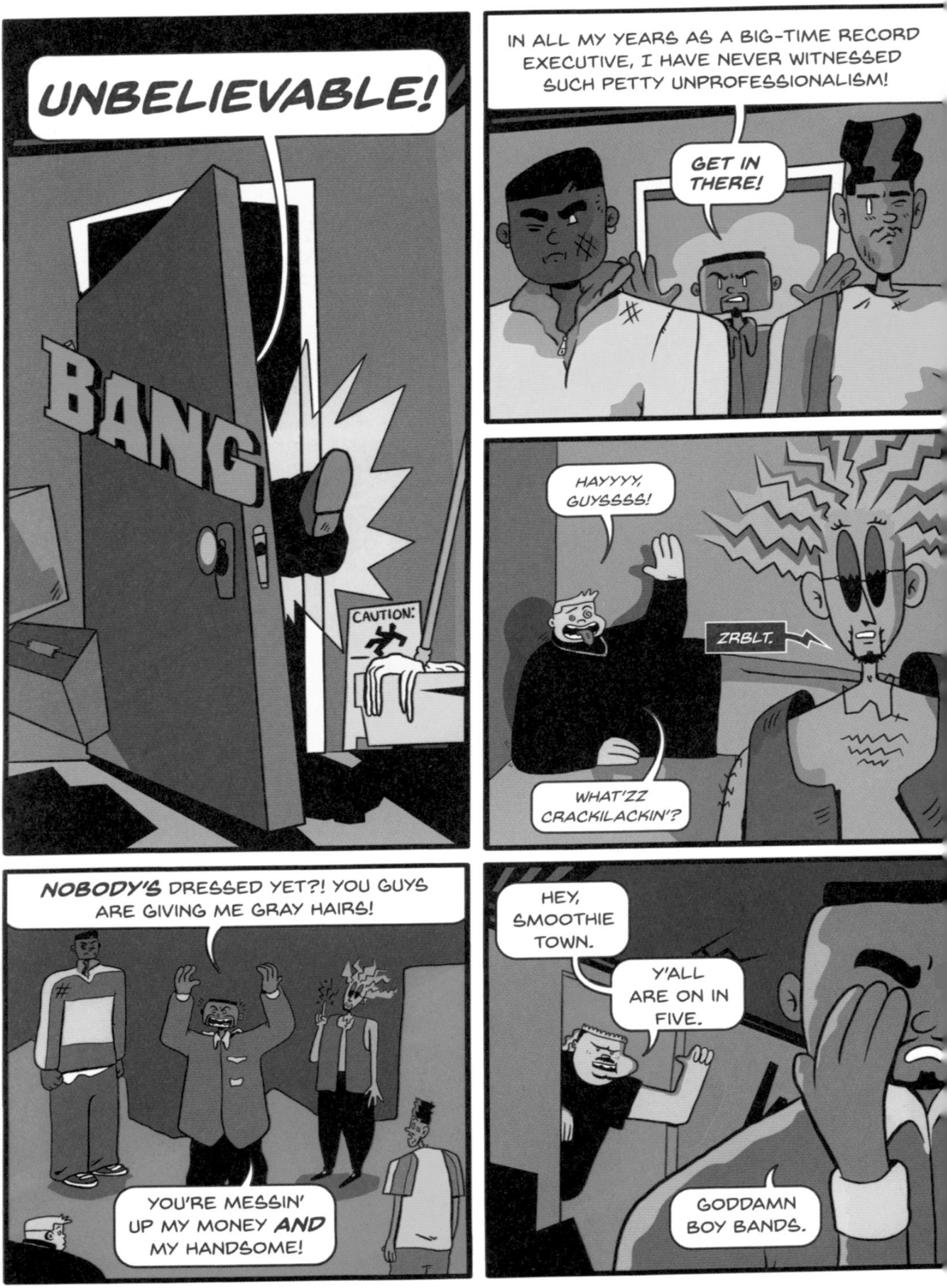
UNBELIEVABLE!
BANG
CAUTION:
IN ALL MY YEARS AS A BIG-TIME RECORD EXECUTIVE, I HAVE NEVER WITNESSED SUCH PETTY UNPROFESSIONALISM!
GET IN THERE!
HAYYYY, GUYSSSS!
ZRBLT.
WHAT'ZZ CRACKILACKIN'?
NOBODY'S DRESSED YET?! YOU GUYS ARE GIVING ME GRAY HAIRS!
YOU'RE MESSIN' UP MY MONEY AND MY HANDSOME!
HEY, SMOOTHIE TOWN.
Y'ALL ARE ON IN FIVE.
GODDAMN BOY BANDS.

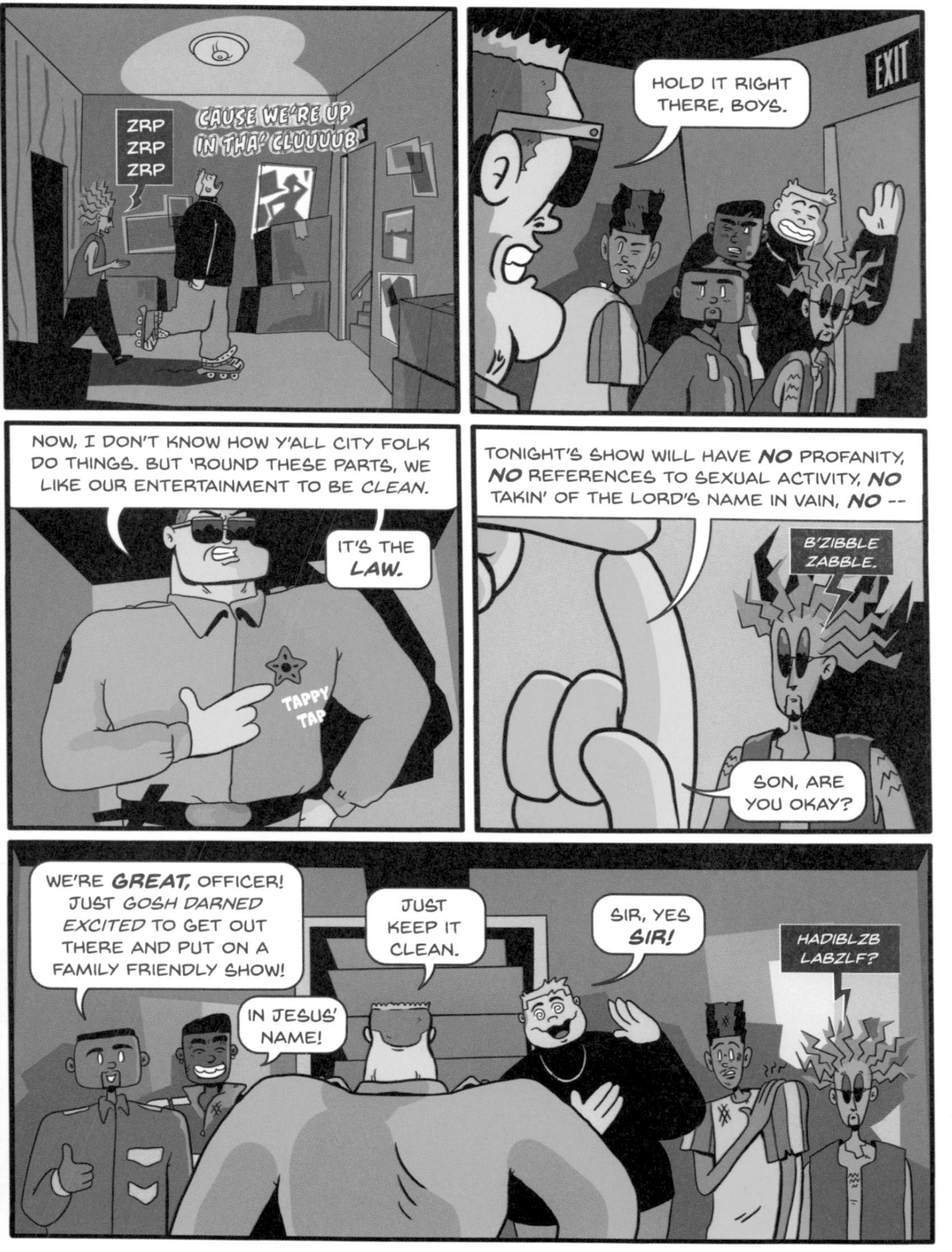
ZRP
ZRP
ZRP
CAUSE WE'RE UP IN THA' CLUUUUB
HOLD IT RIGHT THERE, BOYS.
EXIT
NOW, I DON'T KNOW HOW Y'ALL CITY FOLK DO THINGS. BUT 'ROUND THESE PARTS, WE LIKE OUR ENTERTAINMENT TO BE CLEAN.
IT'S THE LAW.
TAPPY TAP
TONIGHT'S SHOW WILL HAVE NO PROFANITY, NO REFERENCES TO SEXUAL ACTIVITY, NO TAKIN' OF THE LORD'S NAME IN VAIN, NO --
B'ZIBBLE ZABBLE.
SON, ARE YOU OKAY?
WE'RE GREAT, OFFICER! JUST GOSH DARNED EXCITED TO GET OUT THERE AND PUT ON A FAMILY FRIENDLY SHOW!
JUST KEEP IT CLEAN.
IN JESUS' NAME!
SIR, YES SIR!
HADIBLZB LABZLF?

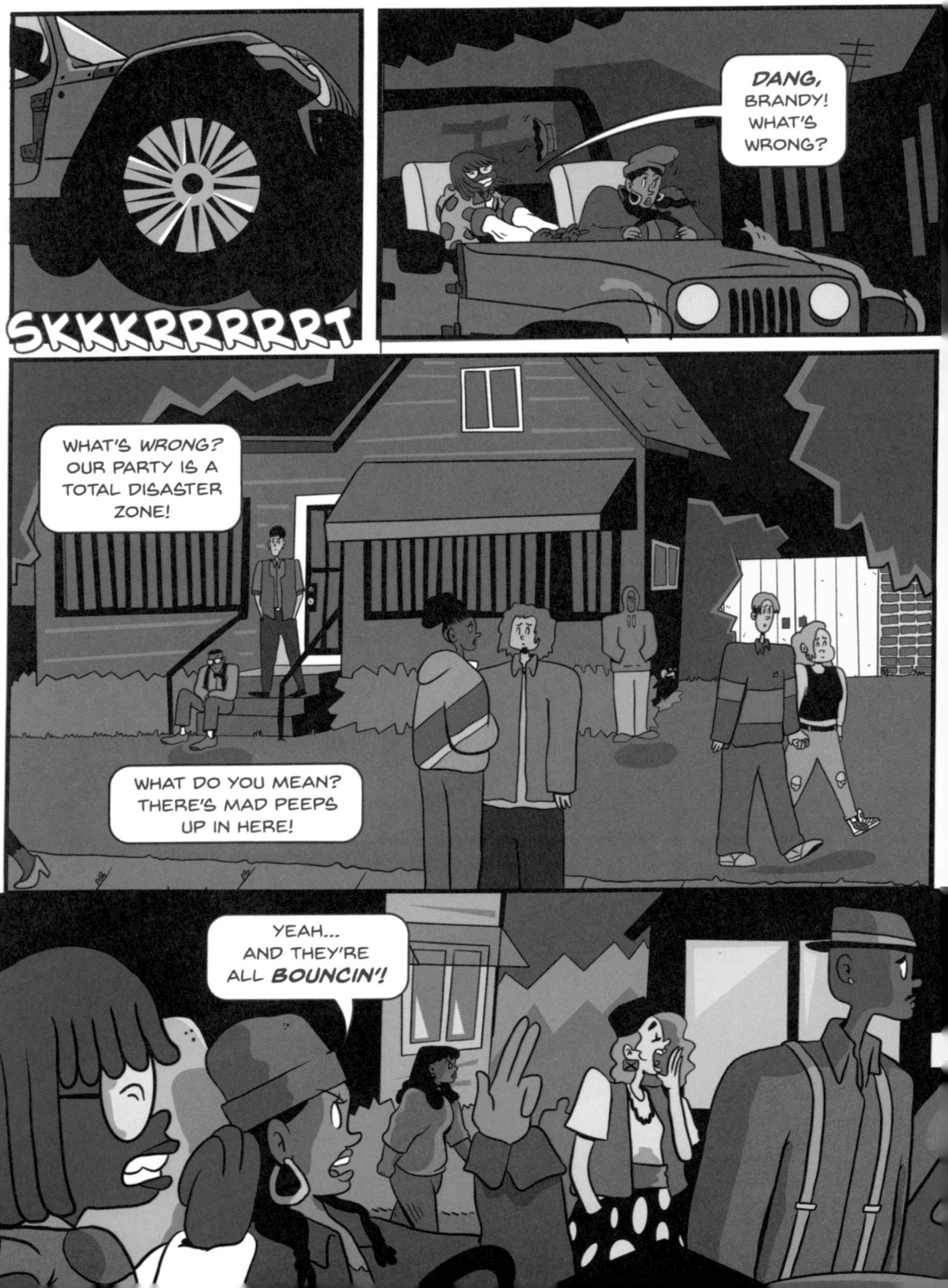
SKKKRRRRRT
DANG, BRANDY! WHAT'S WRONG?
WHAT'S *WRONG*? OUR PARTY IS A TOTAL DISASTER ZONE!
WHAT DO YOU MEAN? THERE'S MAD PEEPS UP IN HERE!
YEAH... AND THEY'RE ALL ***BOUNCIN'***!

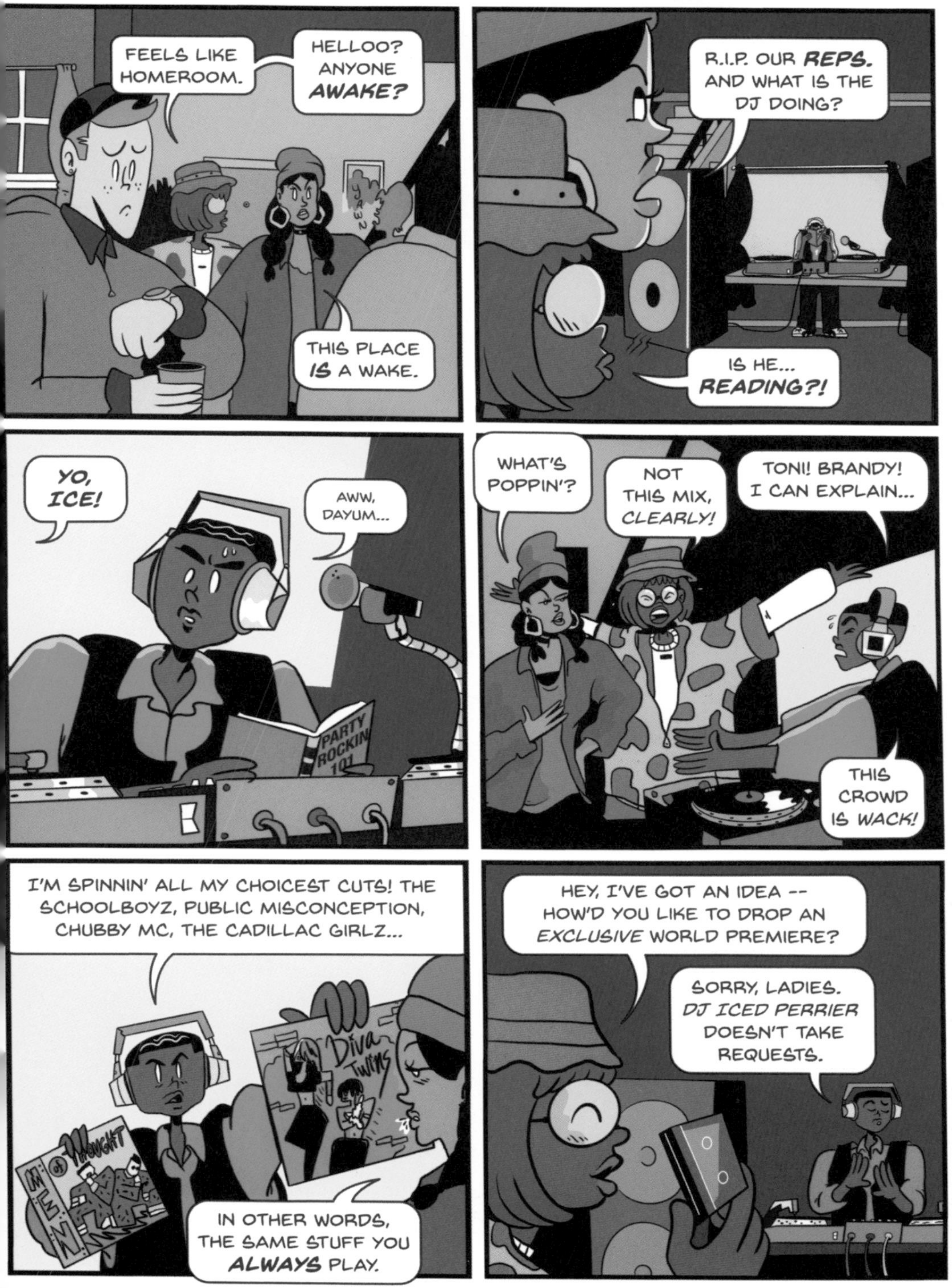
FEELS LIKE HOMEROOM.
HELLOO? ANYONE AWAKE?
THIS PLACE IS A WAKE.
R.I.P. OUR REPS. AND WHAT IS THE DJ DOING?
IS HE... READING?!
YO, ICE!
AWW, DAYUM...
PARTY ROCKIN 101
WHAT'S POPPIN'?
NOT THIS MIX, CLEARLY!
TONI! BRANDY! I CAN EXPLAIN...
THIS CROWD IS WACK!
I'M SPINNIN' ALL MY CHOICEST CUTS! THE SCHOOLBOYZ, PUBLIC MISCONCEPTION, CHUBBY MC, THE CADILLAC GIRLZ...
Diva Twins
IN OTHER WORDS, THE SAME STUFF YOU ALWAYS PLAY.
HEY, I'VE GOT AN IDEA -- HOW'D YOU LIKE TO DROP AN EXCLUSIVE WORLD PREMIERE?
SORRY, LADIES. DJ ICED PERRIER DOESN'T TAKE REQUESTS.

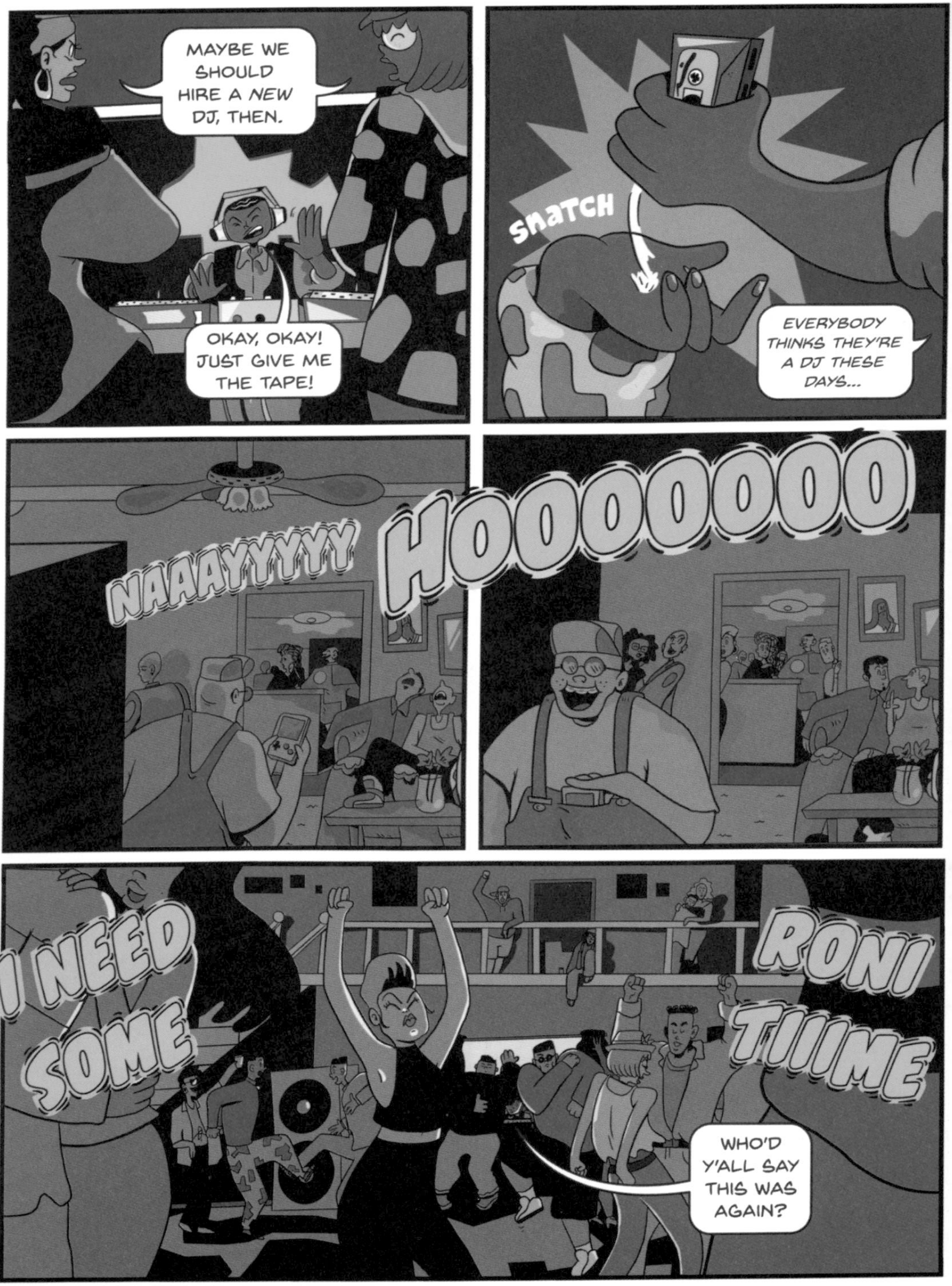
MAYBE WE SHOULD HIRE A *NEW* DJ, THEN.
OKAY, OKAY! JUST GIVE ME THE TAPE!
SNATCH
EVERYBODY THINKS THEY'RE A DJ THESE DAYS...
NAAAYYYYY
HOOOOOOOO
I NEED SOME
RONI TIIIME
WHO'D Y'ALL SAY THIS WAS AGAIN?

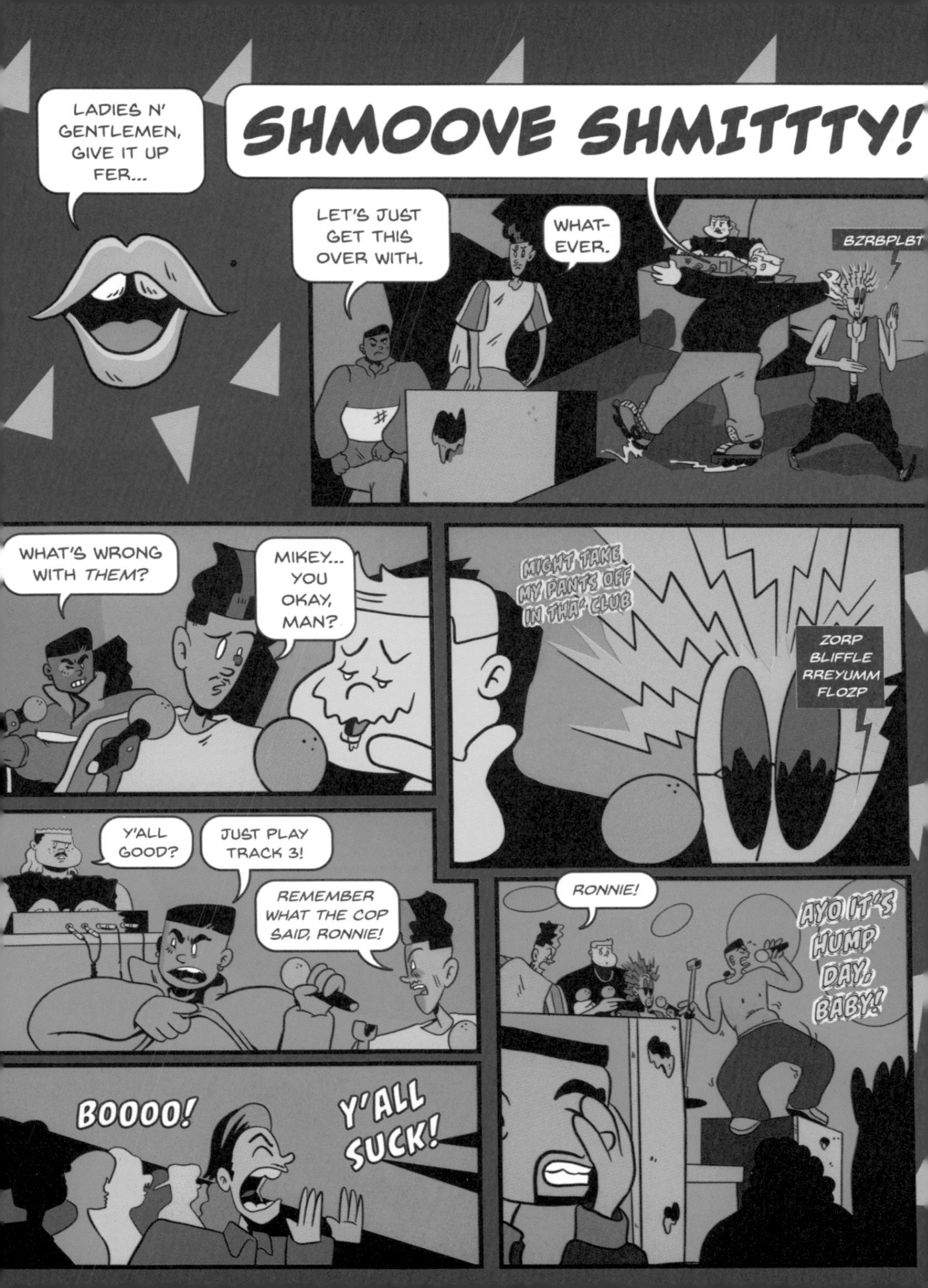
LADIES N' GENTLEMEN, GIVE IT UP FER...
SHMOOVE SHMITTTY!
LET'S JUST GET THIS OVER WITH.
WHAT-EVER.
BZRBPLBT
WHAT'S WRONG WITH THEM?
MIKEY... YOU OKAY, MAN?
MIGHT TAKE MY PANTS OFF IN THA' CLUB
ZORP BLIFFLE RREYUMM FLOZP
Y'ALL GOOD?
JUST PLAY TRACK 3!
REMEMBER WHAT THE COP SAID, RONNIE!
RONNIE!
AYO IT'S HUMP DAY, BABY!
BOOOO!
Y'ALL SUCK!

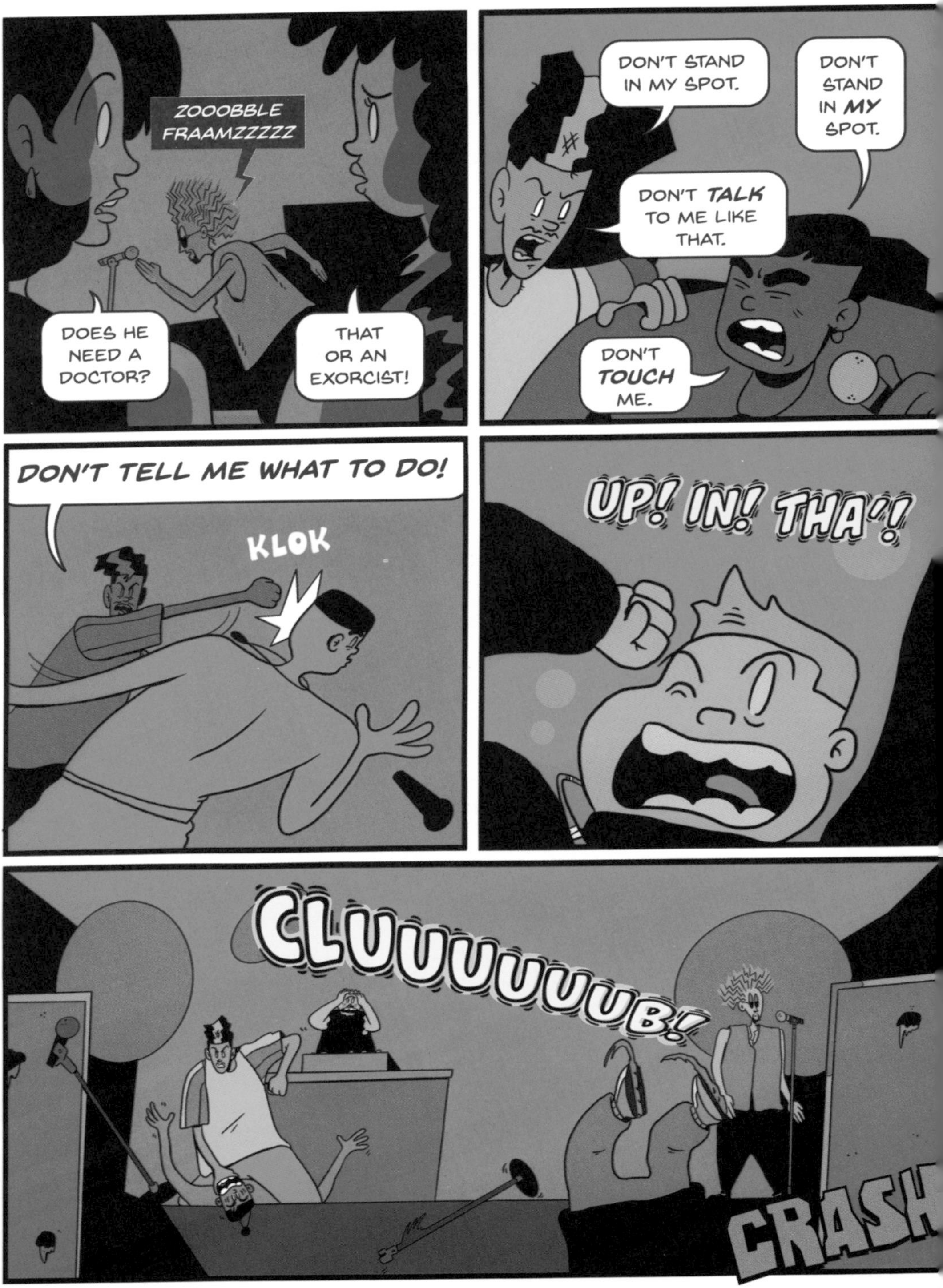
ZOOOBBLE FRAAMZZZZZ
DOES HE NEED A DOCTOR?
THAT OR AN EXORCIST!
DON'T STAND IN MY SPOT.
DON'T STAND IN MY SPOT.
DON'T TALK TO ME LIKE THAT.
DON'T TOUCH ME.
DON'T TELL ME WHAT TO DO!
KLOK
UP! IN! THA'!
CLUUUUUUUB!
CRASH

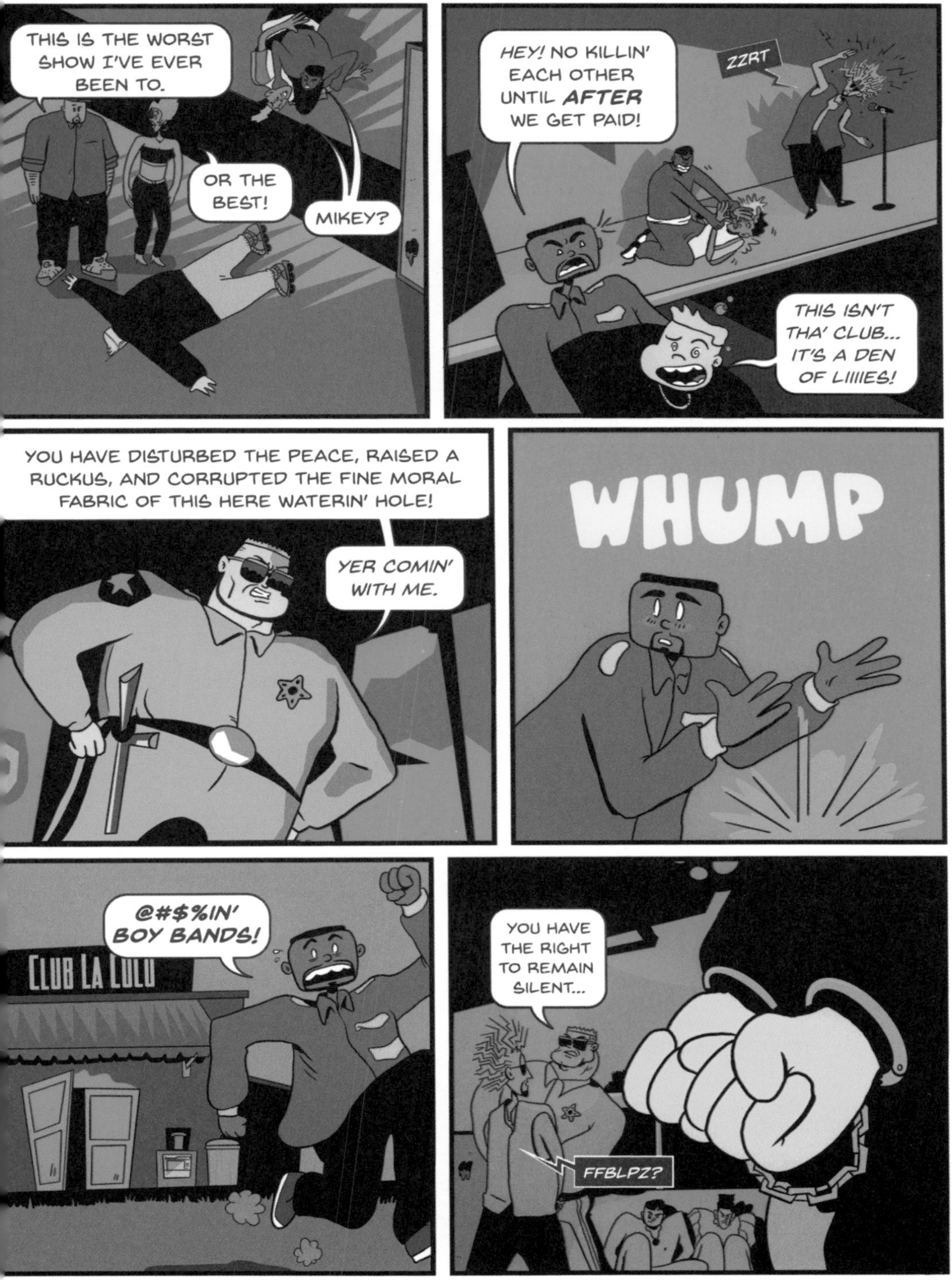
THIS IS THE WORST SHOW I'VE EVER BEEN TO.
OR THE BEST!
MIKEY?
HEY! NO KILLIN' EACH OTHER UNTIL AFTER WE GET PAID!
ZZRT
THIS ISN'T THA' CLUB... IT'S A DEN OF LIIIIES!
YOU HAVE DISTURBED THE PEACE, RAISED A RUCKUS, AND CORRUPTED THE FINE MORAL FABRIC OF THIS HERE WATERIN' HOLE!
YER COMIN' WITH ME.
WHUMP
@#$%IN' BOY BANDS!
CLUB LA LULU
YOU HAVE THE RIGHT TO REMAIN SILENT...
FFBLPZ?

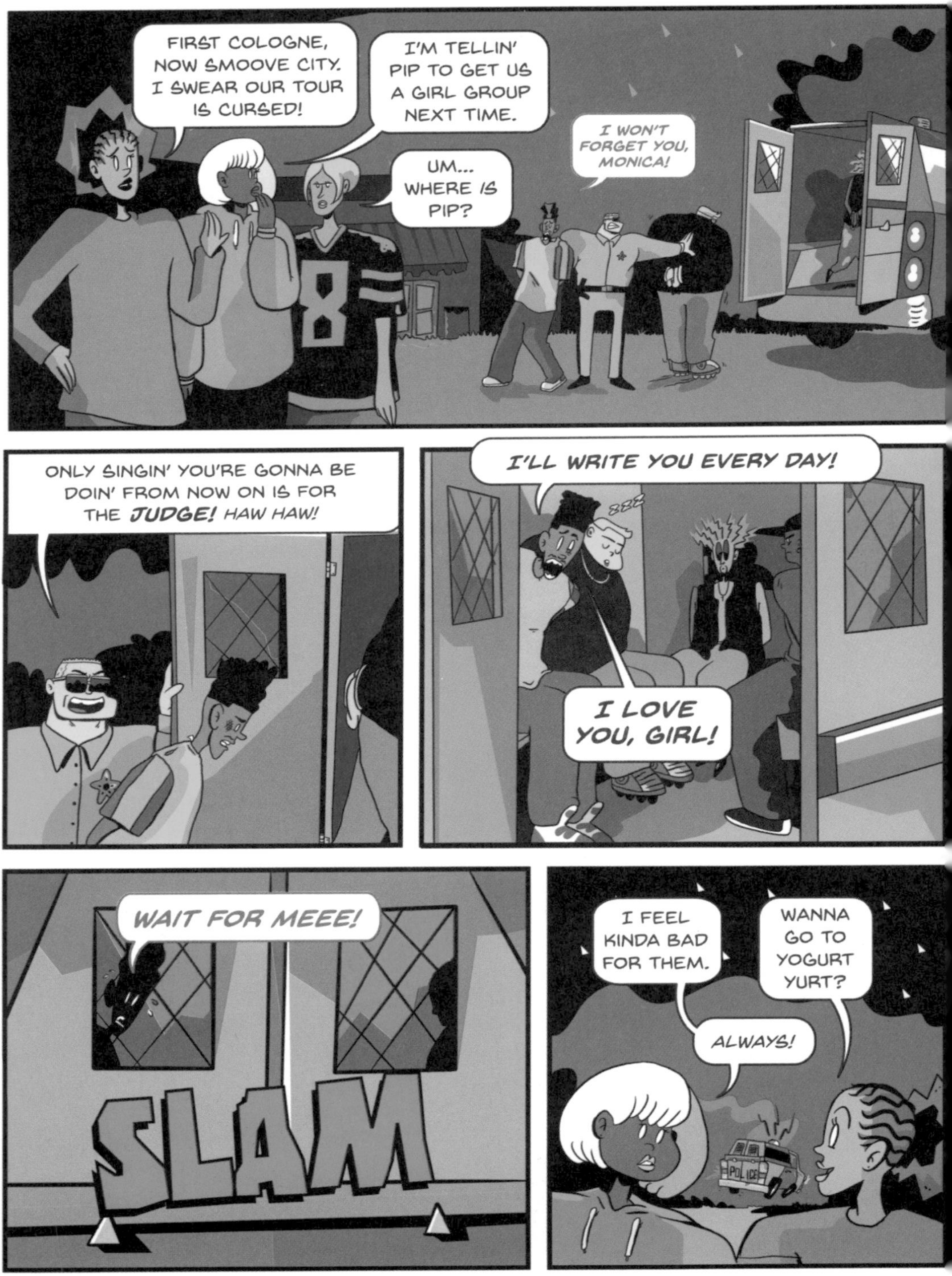
FIRST COLOGNE, NOW SMOOVE CITY. I SWEAR OUR TOUR IS CURSED!
I'M TELLIN' PIP TO GET US A GIRL GROUP NEXT TIME.
UM... WHERE IS PIP?
I WON'T FORGET YOU, MONICA!
ONLY SINGIN' YOU'RE GONNA BE DOIN' FROM NOW ON IS FOR THE JUDGE! HAW HAW!
I'LL WRITE YOU EVERY DAY!
ZZZ
I LOVE YOU, GIRL!
WAIT FOR MEEE!
SLAM
I FEEL KINDA BAD FOR THEM.
WANNA GO TO YOGURT YURT?
ALWAYS!
POLICE

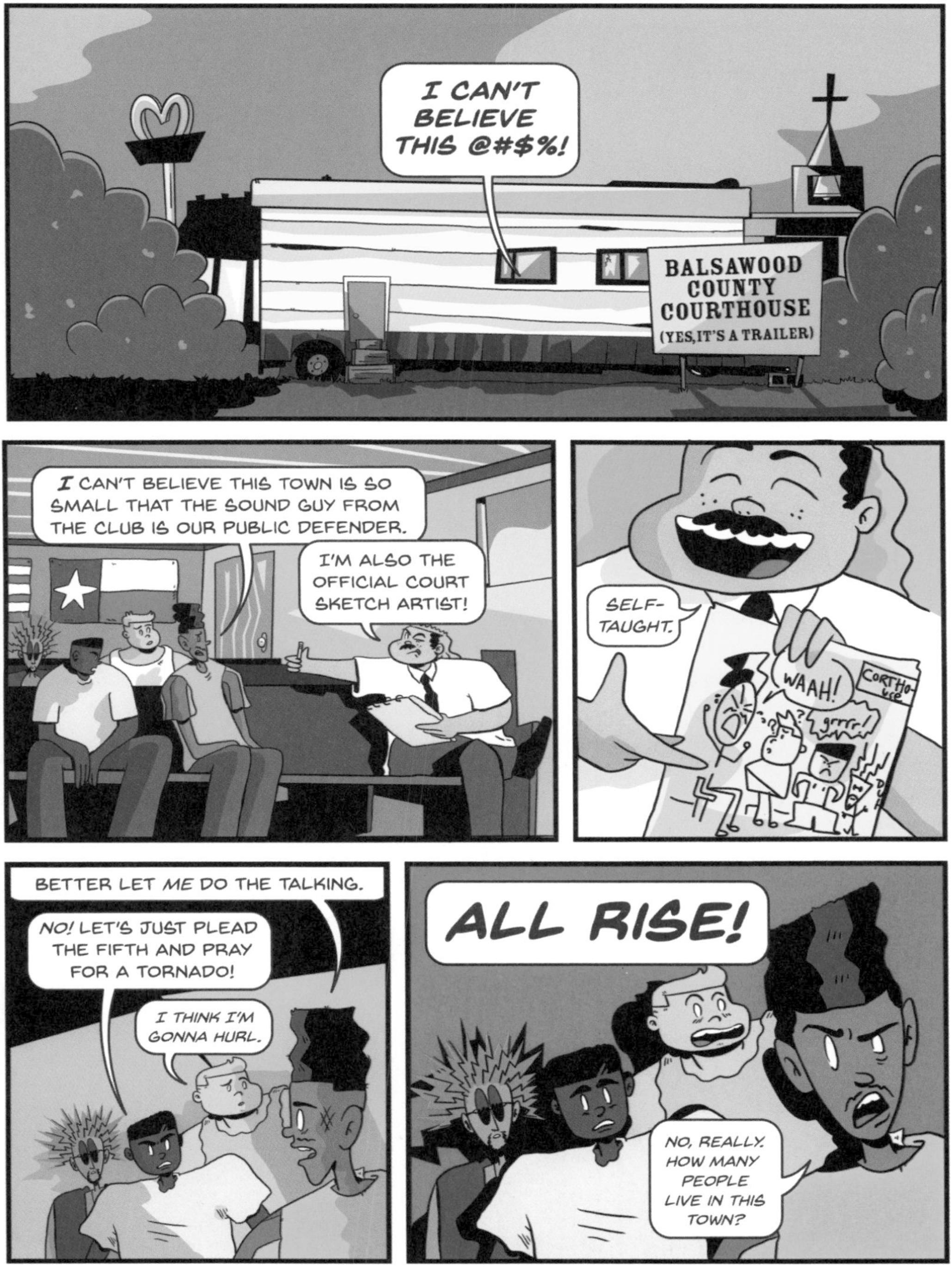
I CAN'T BELIEVE THIS @#$%!
BALSAWOOD COUNTY COURTHOUSE (YES, IT'S A TRAILER)
I CAN'T BELIEVE THIS TOWN IS SO SMALL THAT THE SOUND GUY FROM THE CLUB IS OUR PUBLIC DEFENDER.
I'M ALSO THE OFFICIAL COURT SKETCH ARTIST!
SELF-TAUGHT.
WAAH!
CORTHOuse
grrrr!
BETTER LET ME DO THE TALKING.
NO! LET'S JUST PLEAD THE FIFTH AND PRAY FOR A TORNADO!
I THINK I'M GONNA HURL.
ALL RISE!
NO, REALLY. HOW MANY PEOPLE LIVE IN THIS TOWN?

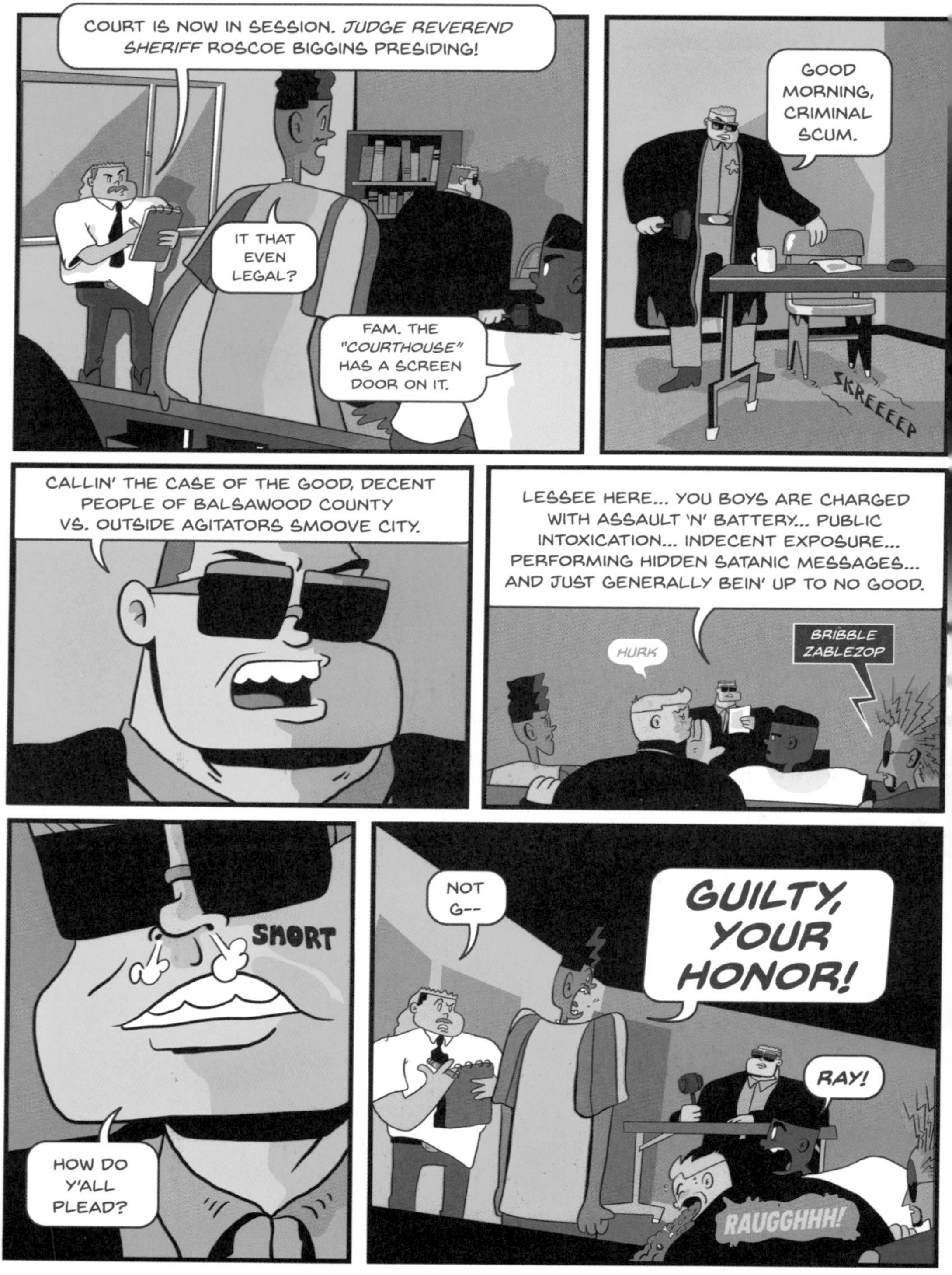
COURT IS NOW IN SESSION. JUDGE REVEREND SHERIFF ROSCOE BIGGINS PRESIDING!
IT THAT EVEN LEGAL?
FAM. THE "COURTHOUSE" HAS A SCREEN DOOR ON IT.
GOOD MORNING, CRIMINAL SCUM.
SKREEEEEP
CALLIN' THE CASE OF THE GOOD, DECENT PEOPLE OF BALSAWOOD COUNTY VS. OUTSIDE AGITATORS SMOOVE CITY.
LESSEE HERE... YOU BOYS ARE CHARGED WITH ASSAULT 'N' BATTERY... PUBLIC INTOXICATION... INDECENT EXPOSURE... PERFORMING HIDDEN SATANIC MESSAGES... AND JUST GENERALLY BEIN' UP TO NO GOOD.
HURK
BRIBBLE ZABLEZOP
SNORT
HOW DO Y'ALL PLEAD?
NOT G--
GUILTY, YOUR HONOR!
RAY!
RAUGGHHH!

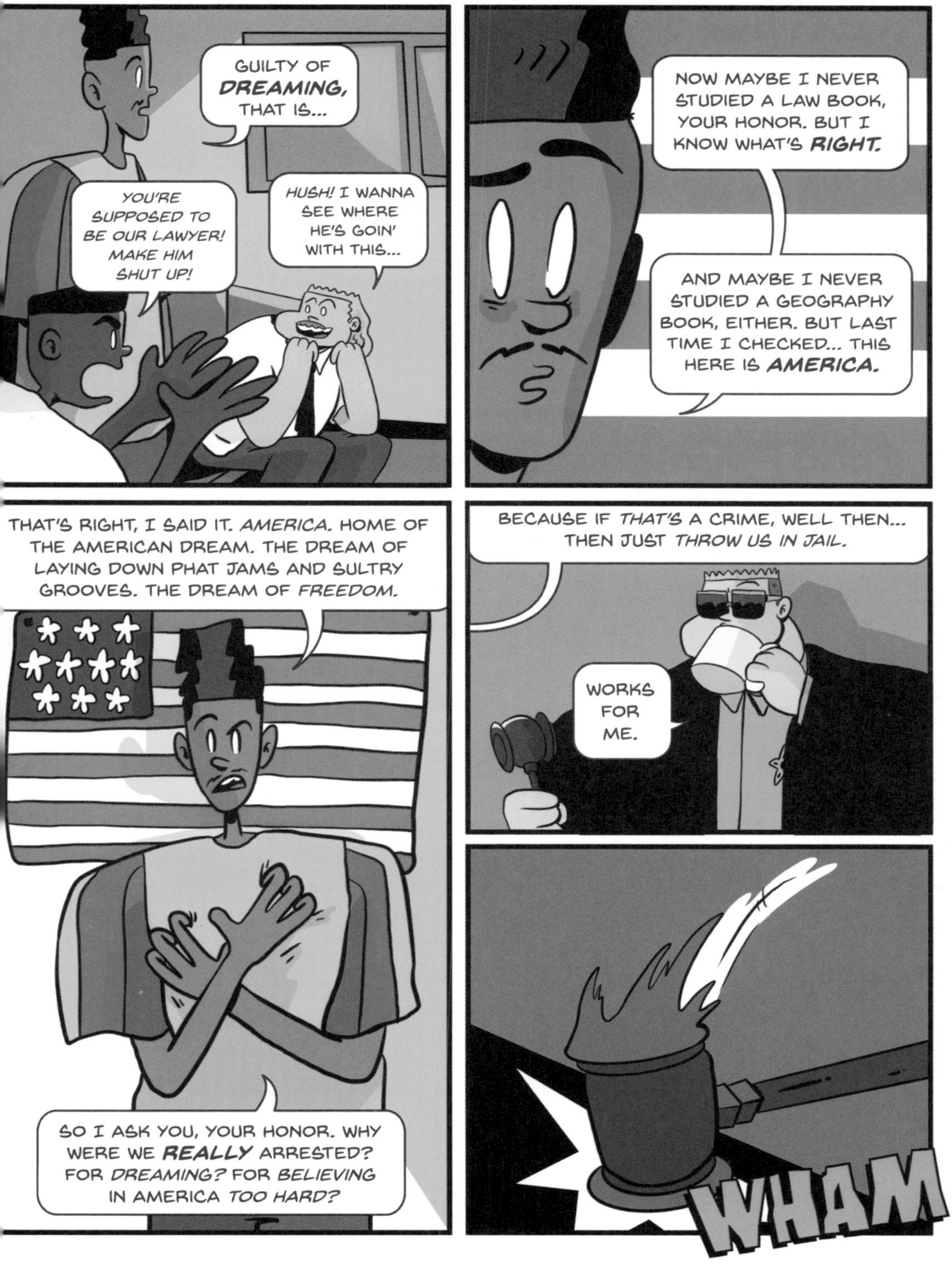
GUILTY OF *DREAMING,* THAT IS...
YOU'RE SUPPOSED TO BE OUR LAWYER! MAKE HIM SHUT UP!
HUSH! I WANNA SEE WHERE HE'S GOIN' WITH THIS...
NOW MAYBE I NEVER STUDIED A LAW BOOK, YOUR HONOR. BUT I KNOW WHAT'S ***RIGHT.***
AND MAYBE I NEVER STUDIED A GEOGRAPHY BOOK, EITHER. BUT LAST TIME I CHECKED... THIS HERE IS ***AMERICA.***
THAT'S RIGHT, I SAID IT. *AMERICA.* HOME OF THE AMERICAN DREAM. THE DREAM OF LAYING DOWN PHAT JAMS AND SULTRY GROOVES. THE DREAM OF *FREEDOM.*
SO I ASK YOU, YOUR HONOR. WHY WERE WE ***REALLY*** ARRESTED? FOR *DREAMING?* FOR *BELIEVING* IN AMERICA *TOO HARD?*
BECAUSE IF *THAT'S* A CRIME, WELL THEN... THEN JUST *THROW US IN JAIL.*
WORKS FOR ME.
WHAM

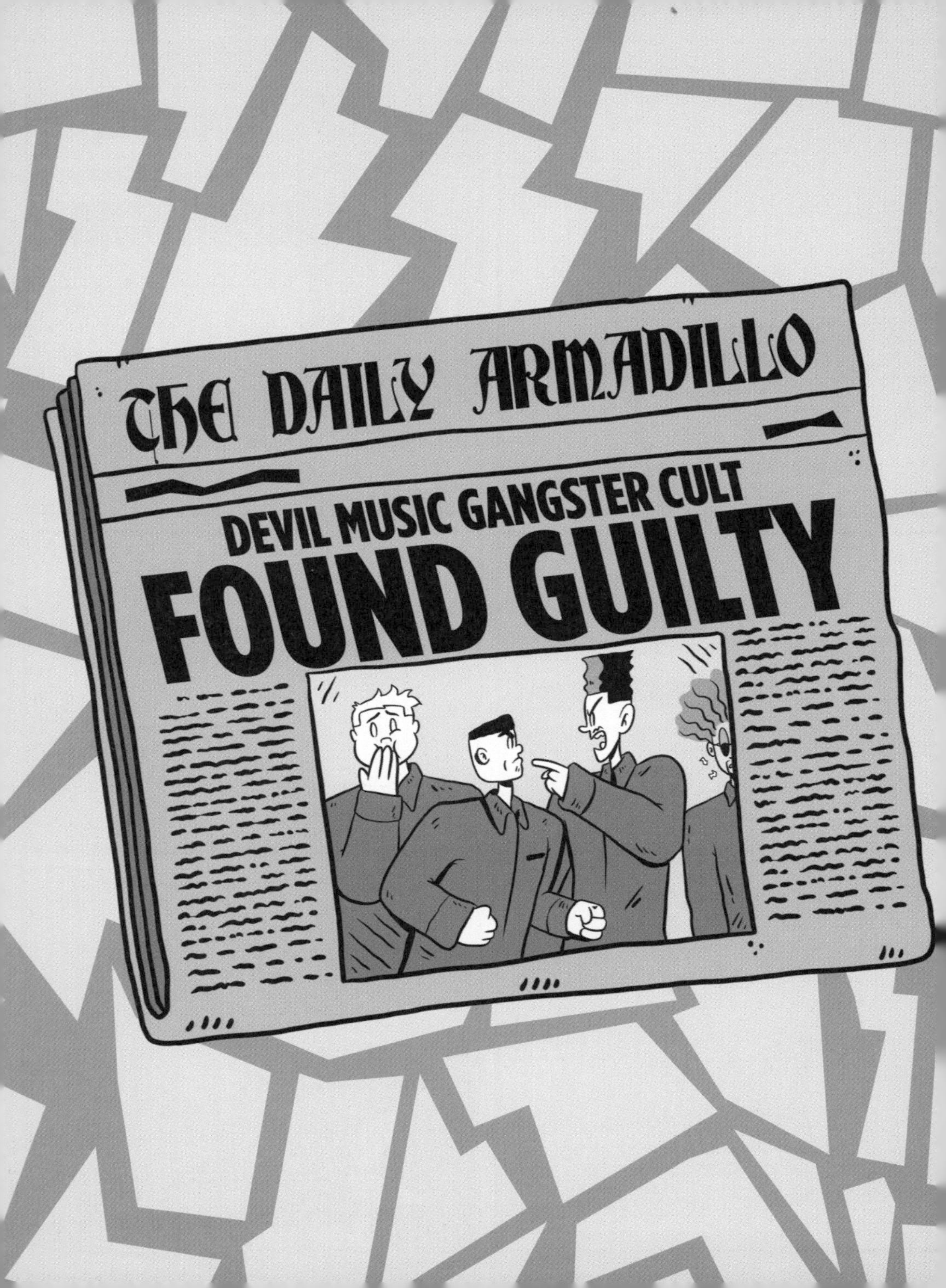
THE DAILY ARMADILLO
DEVIL MUSIC GANGSTER CULT
FOUND GUILTY

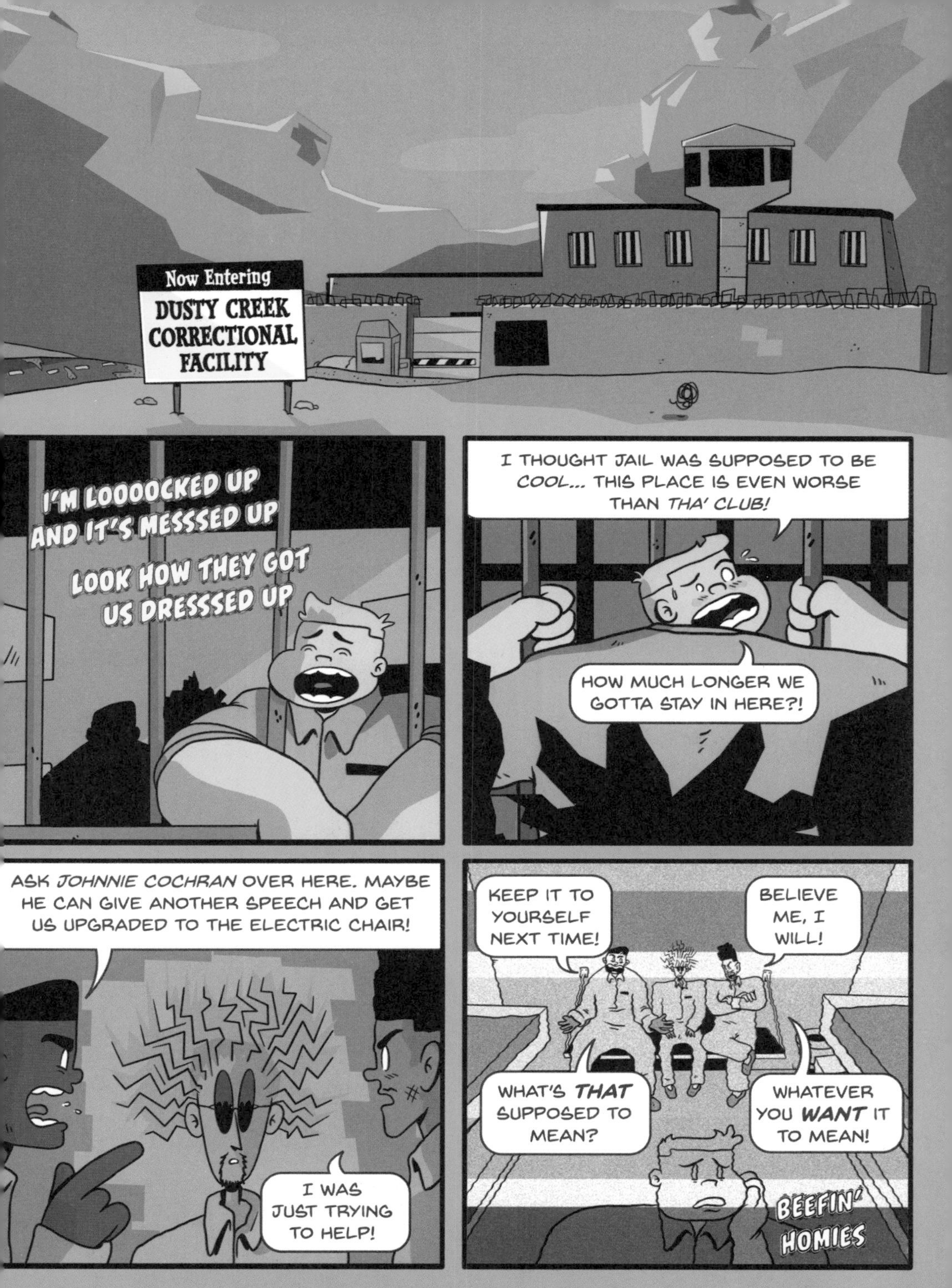

Now Entering
DUSTY CREEK CORRECTIONAL FACILITY
I'M LOOOOCKED UP AND IT'S MESSSED UP
LOOK HOW THEY GOT US DRESSSED UP
I THOUGHT JAIL WAS SUPPOSED TO BE COOL... THIS PLACE IS EVEN WORSE THAN THA' CLUB!
HOW MUCH LONGER WE GOTTA STAY IN HERE?!
ASK JOHNNIE COCHRAN OVER HERE. MAYBE HE CAN GIVE ANOTHER SPEECH AND GET US UPGRADED TO THE ELECTRIC CHAIR!
I WAS JUST TRYING TO HELP!
KEEP IT TO YOURSELF NEXT TIME!
BELIEVE ME, I WILL!
WHAT'S THAT SUPPOSED TO MEAN?
WHATEVER YOU WANT IT TO MEAN!
BEEFIN' HOMIES

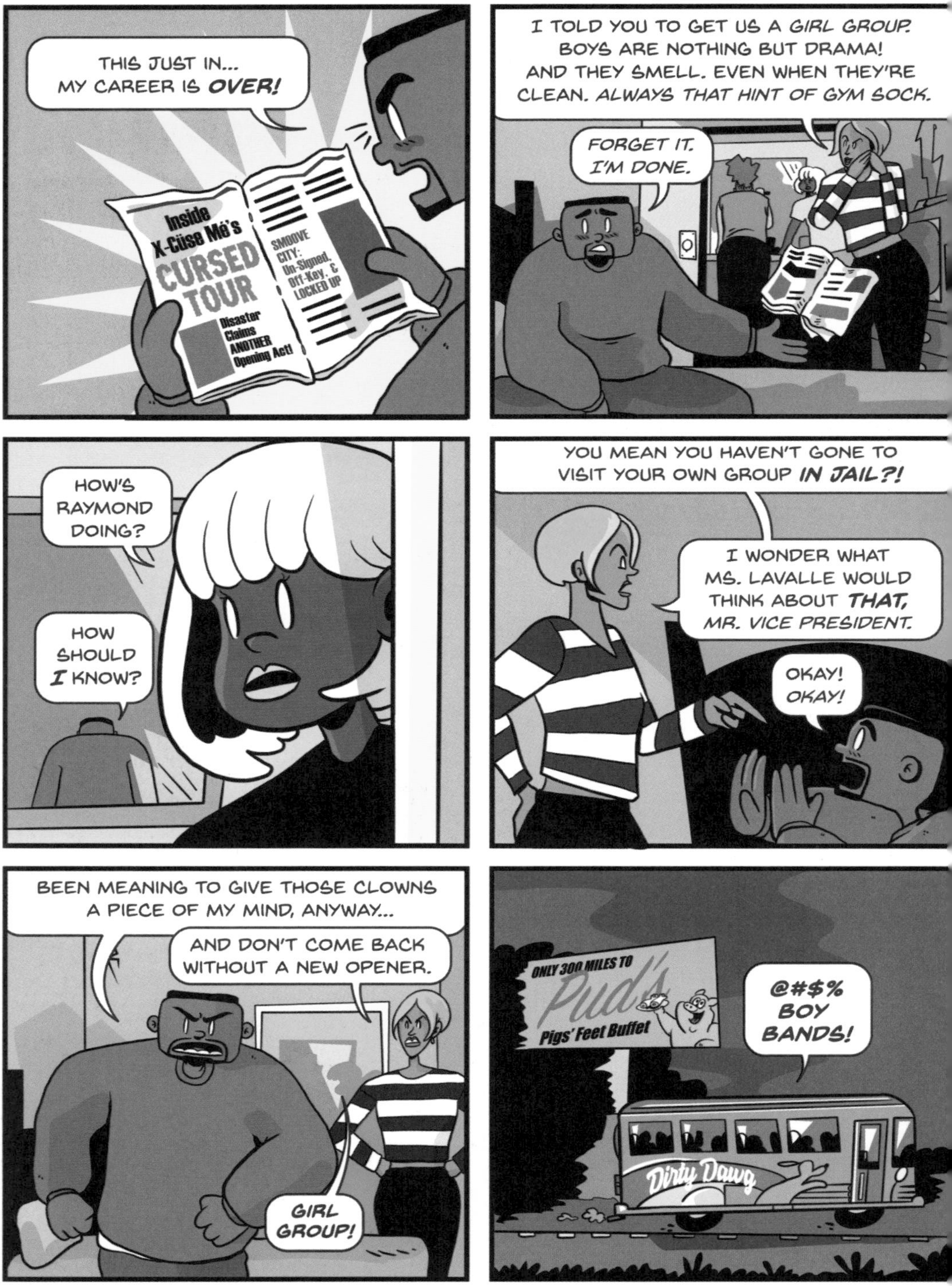
THIS JUST IN...
MY CAREER IS OVER!
Inside X-Cüse Mé's CURSED TOUR
Disaster Claims ANOTHER Opening Act!
SMOOVE CITY: Un-Signed, Off-Key, & LOCKED UP
I TOLD YOU TO GET US A GIRL GROUP. BOYS ARE NOTHING BUT DRAMA! AND THEY SMELL. EVEN WHEN THEY'RE CLEAN. ALWAYS THAT HINT OF GYM SOCK.
FORGET IT. I'M DONE.
HOW'S RAYMOND DOING?
HOW SHOULD I KNOW?
YOU MEAN YOU HAVEN'T GONE TO VISIT YOUR OWN GROUP IN JAIL?!
I WONDER WHAT MS. LAVALLE WOULD THINK ABOUT THAT, MR. VICE PRESIDENT.
OKAY! OKAY!
BEEN MEANING TO GIVE THOSE CLOWNS A PIECE OF MY MIND, ANYWAY...
AND DON'T COME BACK WITHOUT A NEW OPENER.
GIRL GROUP!
ONLY 300 MILES TO Pud's Pigs' Feet Buffet
@#$% BOY BANDS!
Dirty Dawg

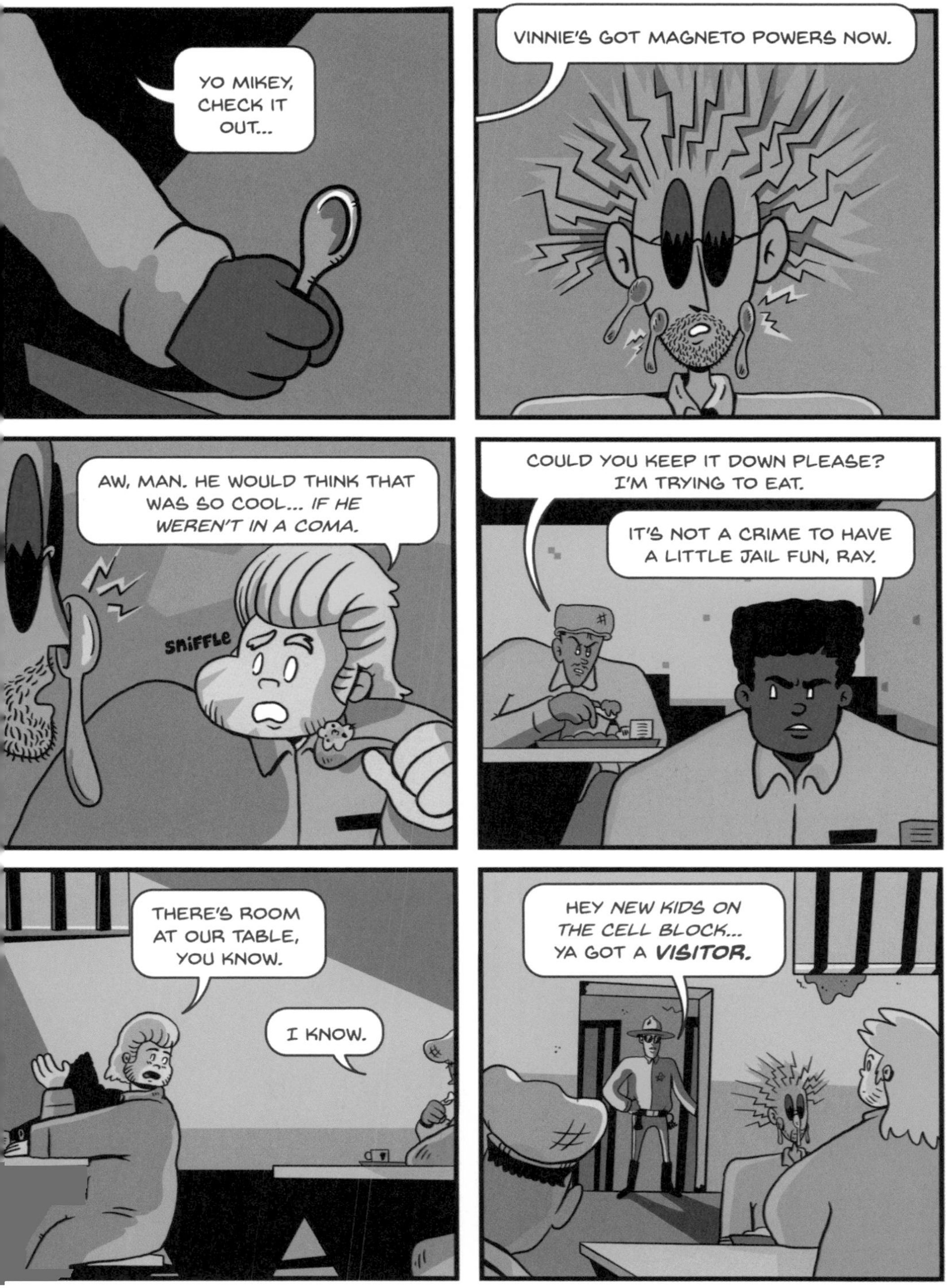
YO MIKEY, CHECK IT OUT...
VINNIE'S GOT MAGNETO POWERS NOW.
AW, MAN. HE WOULD THINK THAT WAS SO COOL... *IF HE WEREN'T IN A COMA.*
SNIFFLE
COULD YOU KEEP IT DOWN PLEASE? I'M TRYING TO EAT.
IT'S NOT A CRIME TO HAVE A LITTLE JAIL FUN, RAY.
THERE'S ROOM AT OUR TABLE, YOU KNOW.
I KNOW.
HEY *NEW KIDS ON THE CELL BLOCK...* YA GOT A ***VISITOR.***

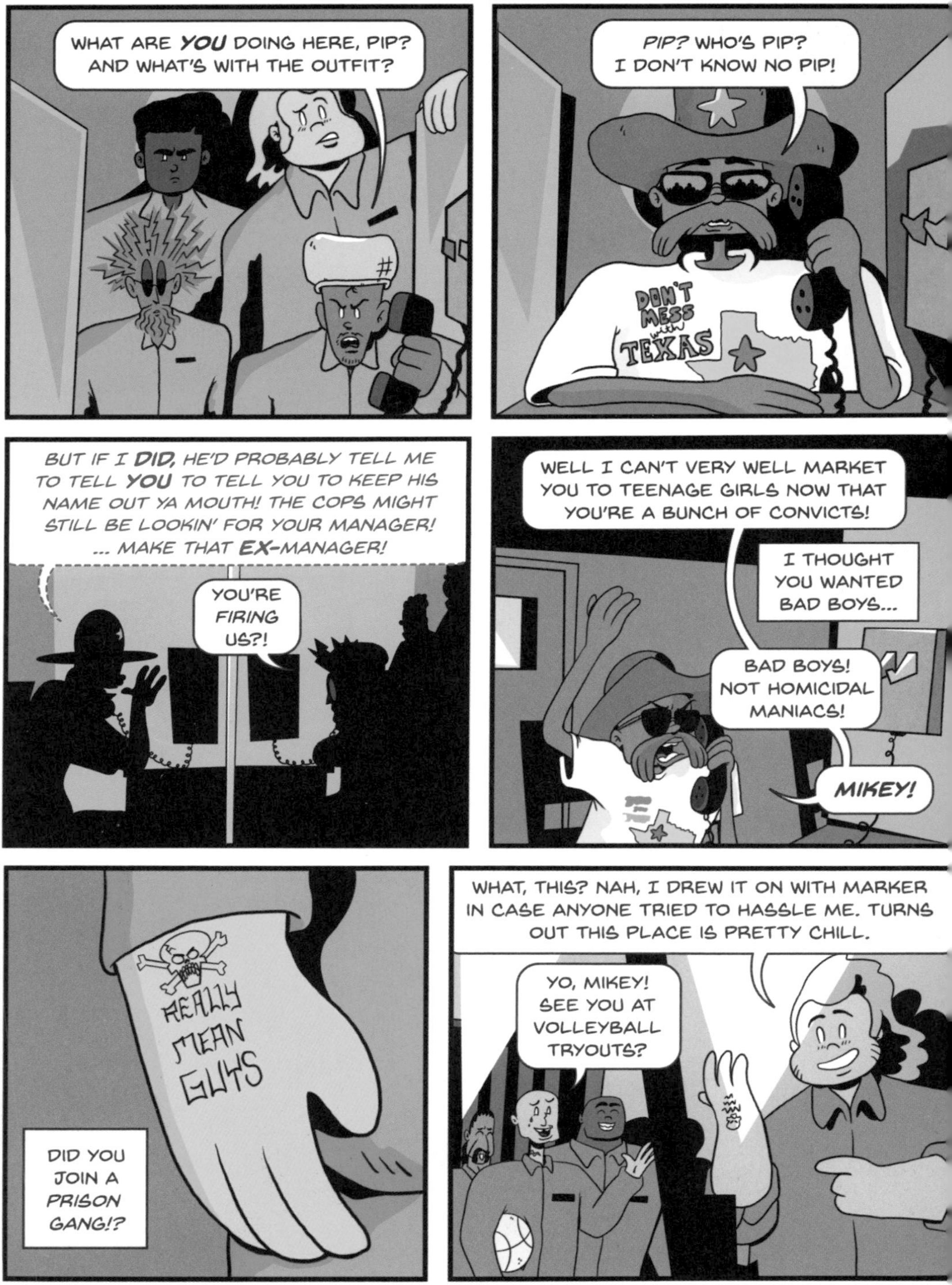
WHAT ARE YOU DOING HERE, PIP? AND WHAT'S WITH THE OUTFIT?
PIP? WHO'S PIP? I DON'T KNOW NO PIP!
DON'T MESS with TEXAS
BUT IF I DID, HE'D PROBABLY TELL ME TO TELL YOU TO TELL YOU TO KEEP HIS NAME OUT YA MOUTH! THE COPS MIGHT STILL BE LOOKIN' FOR YOUR MANAGER! ... MAKE THAT EX-MANAGER!
YOU'RE FIRING US?!
WELL I CAN'T VERY WELL MARKET YOU TO TEENAGE GIRLS NOW THAT YOU'RE A BUNCH OF CONVICTS!
I THOUGHT YOU WANTED BAD BOYS...
BAD BOYS! NOT HOMICIDAL MANIACS!
MIKEY!
REALLY MEAN GUYS
DID YOU JOIN A PRISON GANG!?
WHAT, THIS? NAH, I DREW IT ON WITH MARKER IN CASE ANYONE TRIED TO HASSLE ME. TURNS OUT THIS PLACE IS PRETTY CHILL.
YO, MIKEY! SEE YOU AT VOLLEYBALL TRYOUTS?

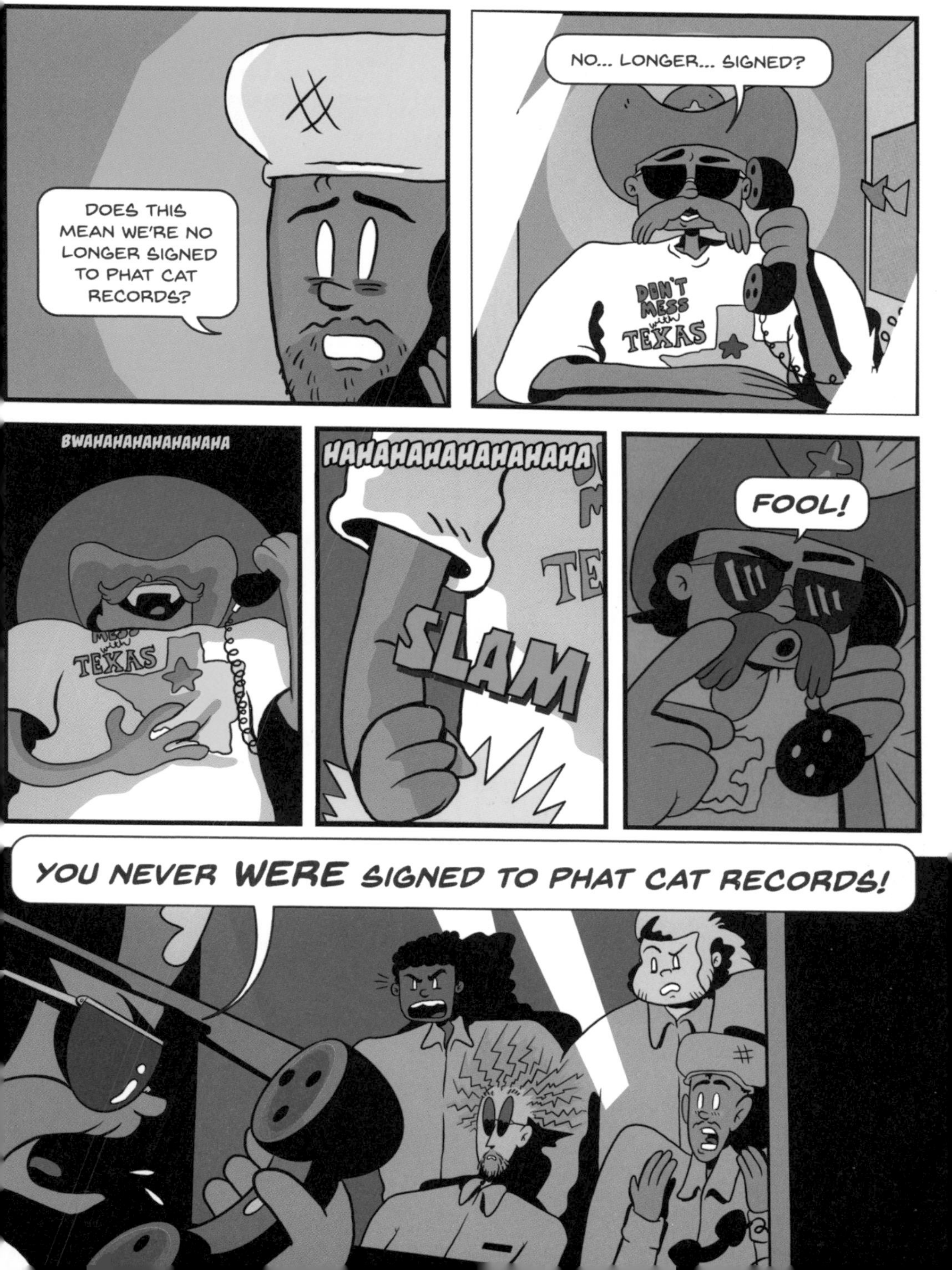
DOES THIS MEAN WE'RE NO LONGER SIGNED TO PHAT CAT RECORDS?
NO... LONGER... SIGNED?
DON'T MESS with TEXAS
BWAHAHAHAHAHAHAHA
HAHAHAHAHAHAHAHA
SLAM
FOOL!
YOU NEVER WERE SIGNED TO PHAT CAT RECORDS!

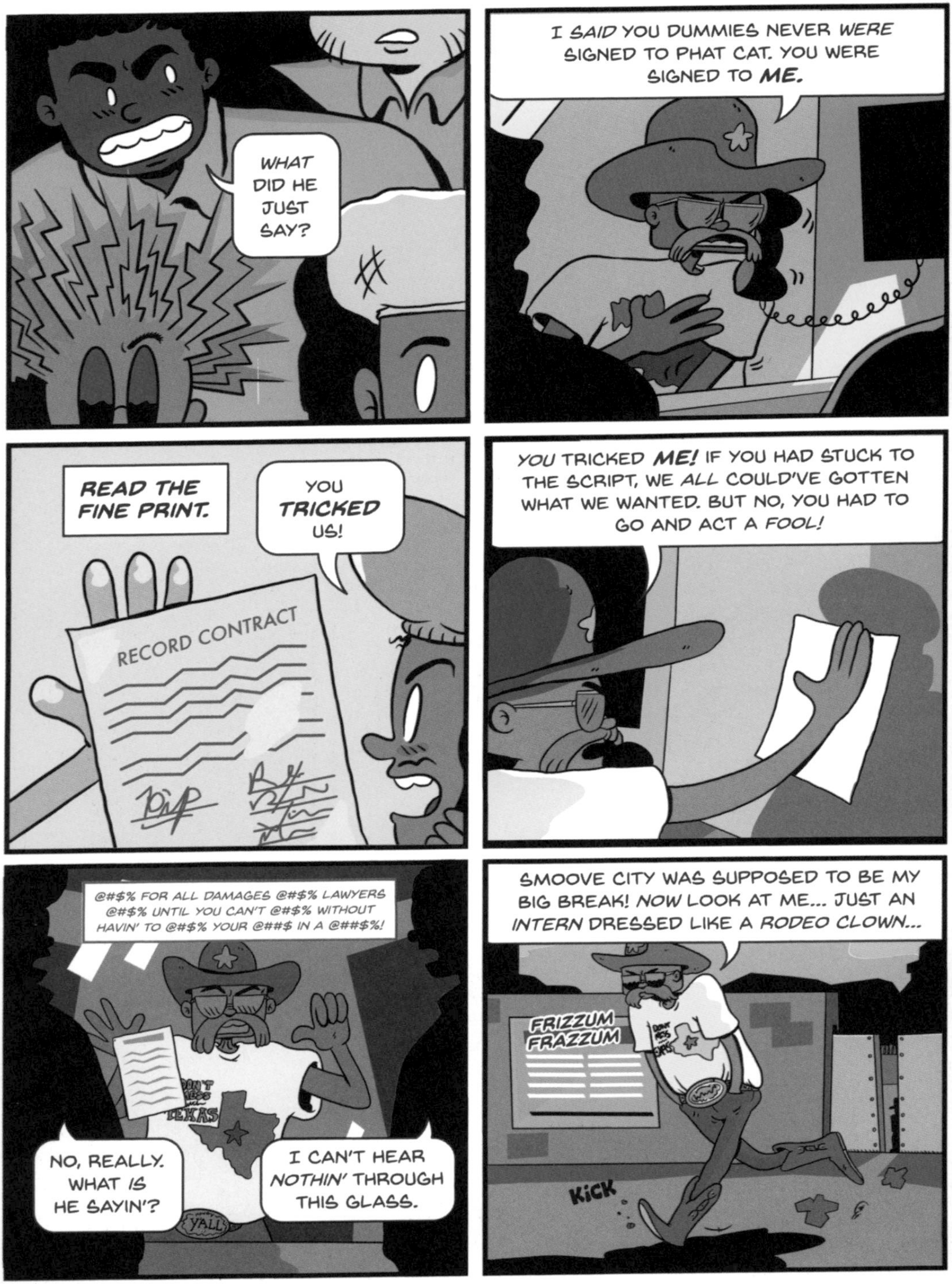

WHAT DID HE JUST SAY?
I SAID YOU DUMMIES NEVER WERE SIGNED TO PHAT CAT. YOU WERE SIGNED TO ME.
READ THE FINE PRINT.
YOU TRICKED US!
RECORD CONTRACT
YOU TRICKED ME! IF YOU HAD STUCK TO THE SCRIPT, WE ALL COULD'VE GOTTEN WHAT WE WANTED. BUT NO, YOU HAD TO GO AND ACT A FOOL!
@#$% FOR ALL DAMAGES @#$% LAWYERS @#$% UNTIL YOU CAN'T @#$% WITHOUT HAVIN' TO @#$% YOUR @##$ IN A @##$%!
TEXAS
NO, REALLY. WHAT IS HE SAYIN'?
I CAN'T HEAR NOTHIN' THROUGH THIS GLASS.
YALL
SMOOVE CITY WAS SUPPOSED TO BE MY BIG BREAK! NOW LOOK AT ME... JUST AN INTERN DRESSED LIKE A RODEO CLOWN...
FRIZZUM FRAZZUM
KICK

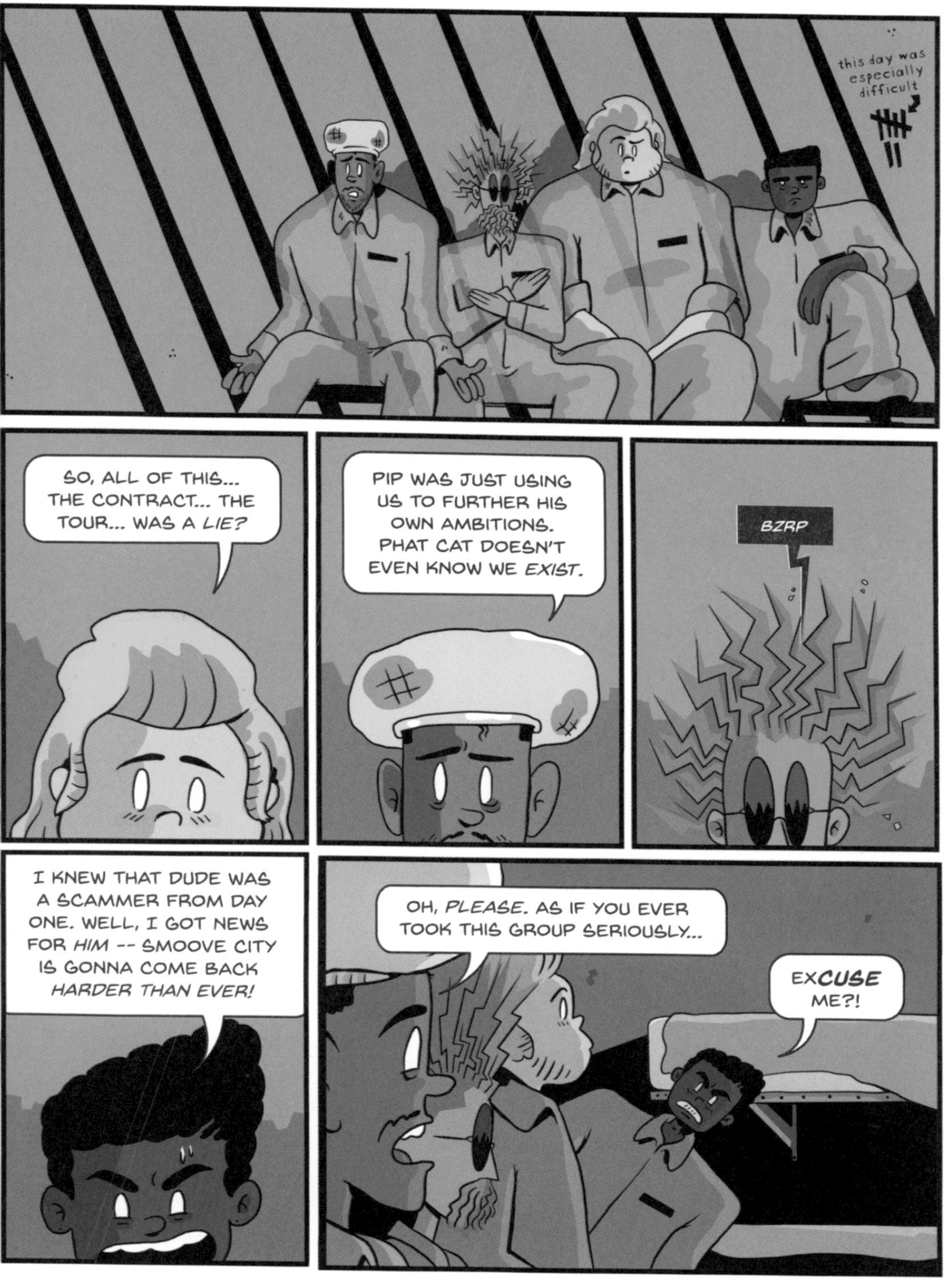
this day was especially difficult
SO, ALL OF THIS... THE CONTRACT... THE TOUR... WAS A *LIE?*
PIP WAS JUST USING US TO FURTHER HIS OWN AMBITIONS. PHAT CAT DOESN'T EVEN KNOW WE *EXIST.*
BZRP
I KNEW THAT DUDE WAS A SCAMMER FROM DAY ONE. WELL, I GOT NEWS FOR *HIM* -- SMOOVE CITY IS GONNA COME BACK *HARDER THAN EVER!*
OH, *PLEASE.* AS IF YOU EVER TOOK THIS GROUP SERIOUSLY...
EX**CUSE** ME?!

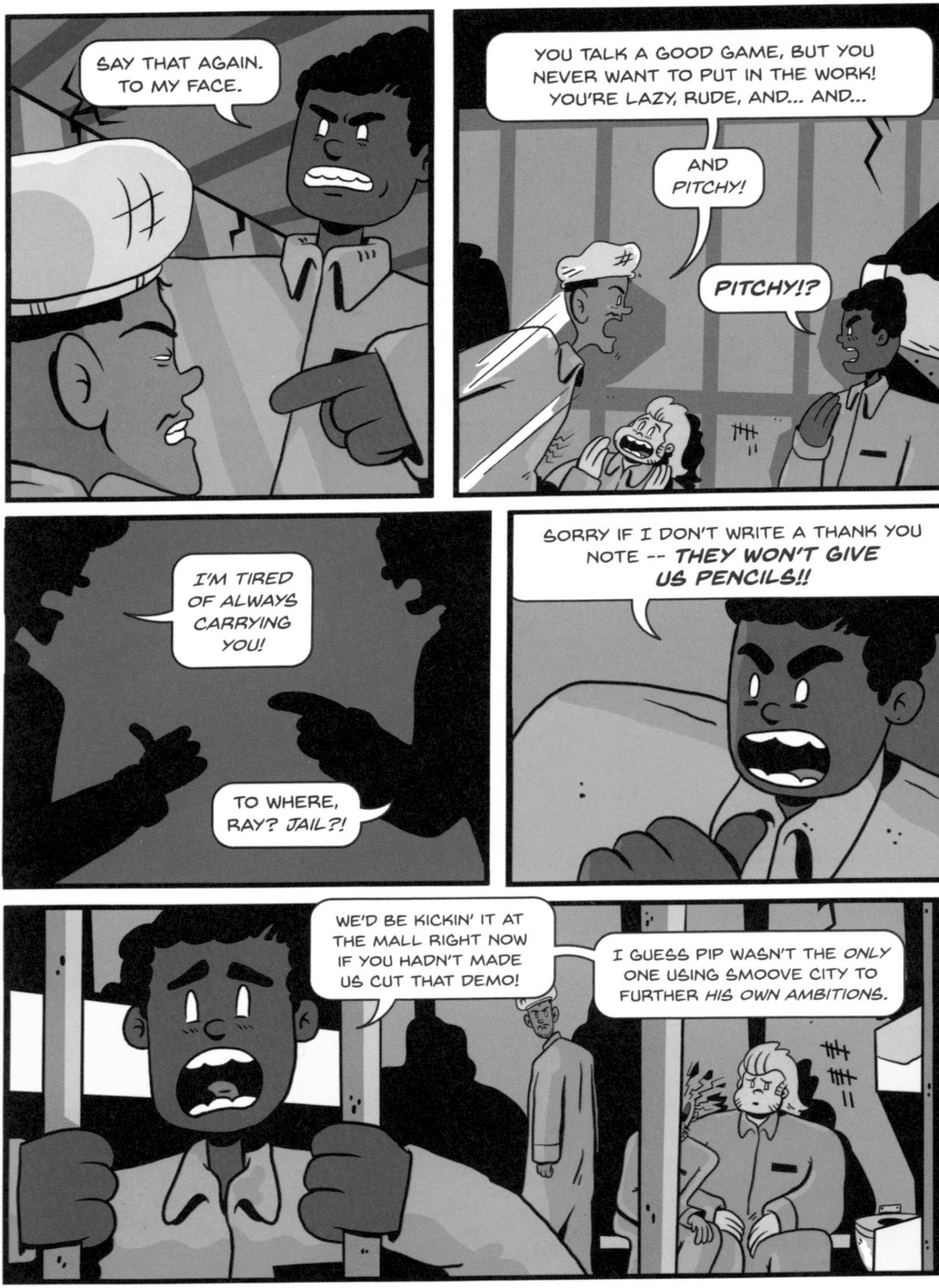
SAY THAT AGAIN. TO MY FACE.
YOU TALK A GOOD GAME, BUT YOU NEVER WANT TO PUT IN THE WORK! YOU'RE LAZY, RUDE, AND... AND...
AND PITCHY!
PITCHY!?
I'M TIRED OF ALWAYS CARRYING YOU!
TO WHERE, RAY? JAIL?!
SORRY IF I DON'T WRITE A THANK YOU NOTE -- THEY WON'T GIVE US PENCILS!!
WE'D BE KICKIN' IT AT THE MALL RIGHT NOW IF YOU HADN'T MADE US CUT THAT DEMO!
I GUESS PIP WASN'T THE ONLY ONE USING SMOOVE CITY TO FURTHER HIS OWN AMBITIONS.

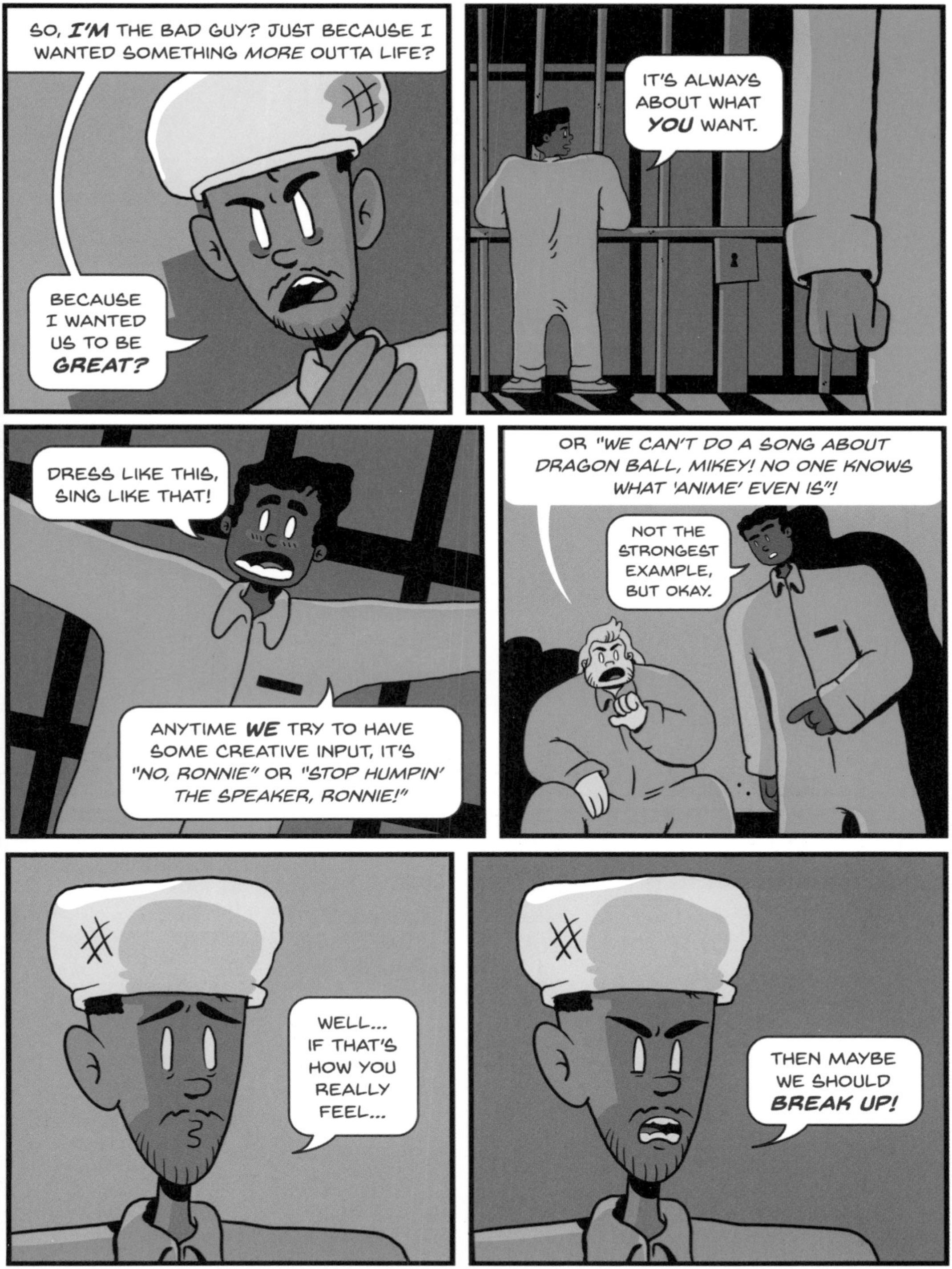
SO, I'M THE BAD GUY? JUST BECAUSE I WANTED SOMETHING MORE OUTTA LIFE?
BECAUSE I WANTED US TO BE GREAT?
IT'S ALWAYS ABOUT WHAT YOU WANT.
DRESS LIKE THIS, SING LIKE THAT!
ANYTIME WE TRY TO HAVE SOME CREATIVE INPUT, IT'S "NO, RONNIE" OR "STOP HUMPIN' THE SPEAKER, RONNIE!"
OR "WE CAN'T DO A SONG ABOUT DRAGON BALL, MIKEY! NO ONE KNOWS WHAT 'ANIME' EVEN IS"!
NOT THE STRONGEST EXAMPLE, BUT OKAY.
WELL... IF THAT'S HOW YOU REALLY FEEL...
THEN MAYBE WE SHOULD BREAK UP!

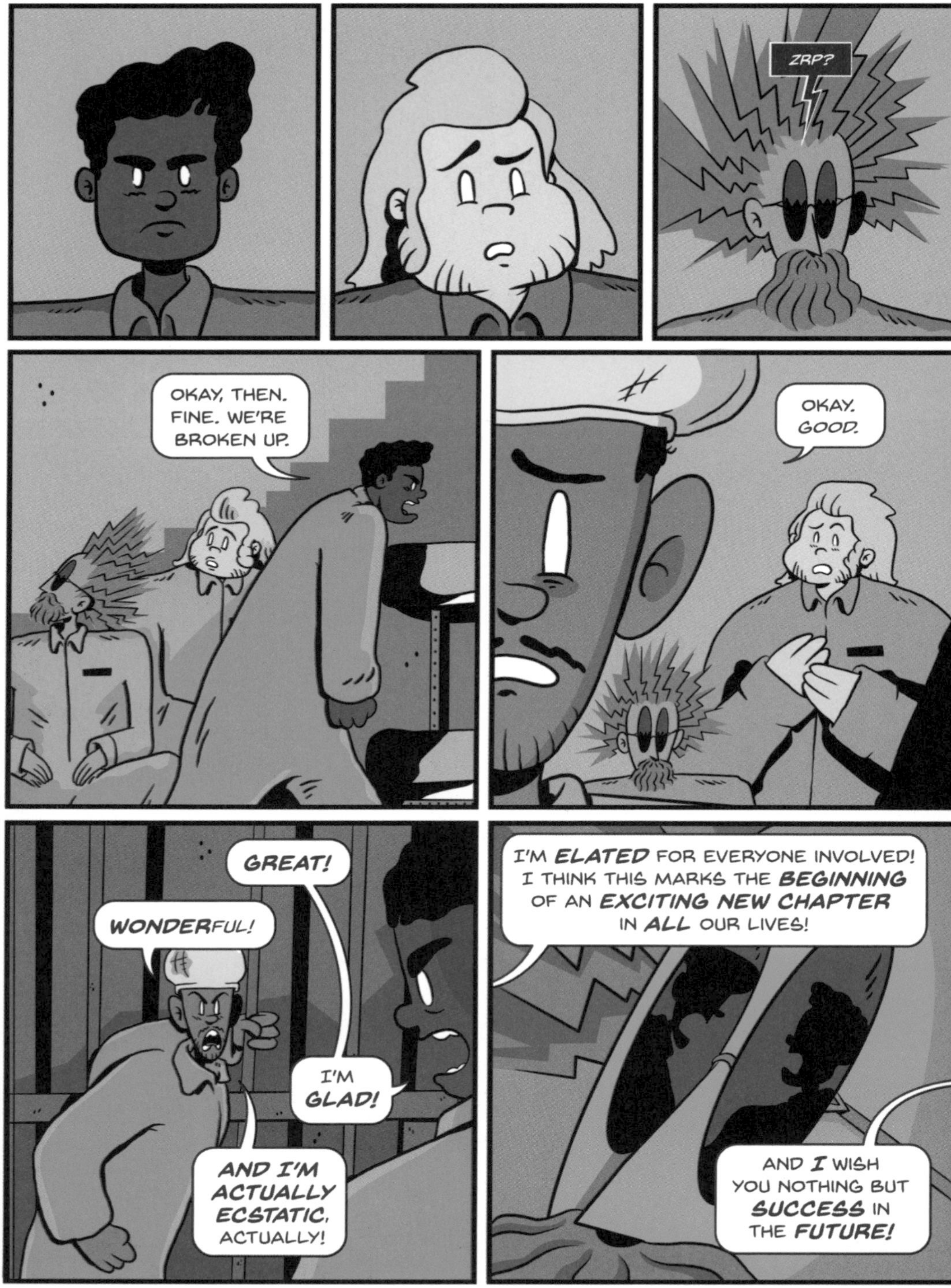
ZRP?
OKAY, THEN. FINE. WE'RE BROKEN UP.
OKAY. GOOD.
GREAT!
WONDERFUL!
I'M GLAD!
AND I'M ACTUALLY ECSTATIC, ACTUALLY!
I'M ELATED FOR EVERYONE INVOLVED! I THINK THIS MARKS THE BEGINNING OF AN EXCITING NEW CHAPTER IN ALL OUR LIVES!
AND I WISH YOU NOTHING BUT SUCCESS IN THE FUTURE!

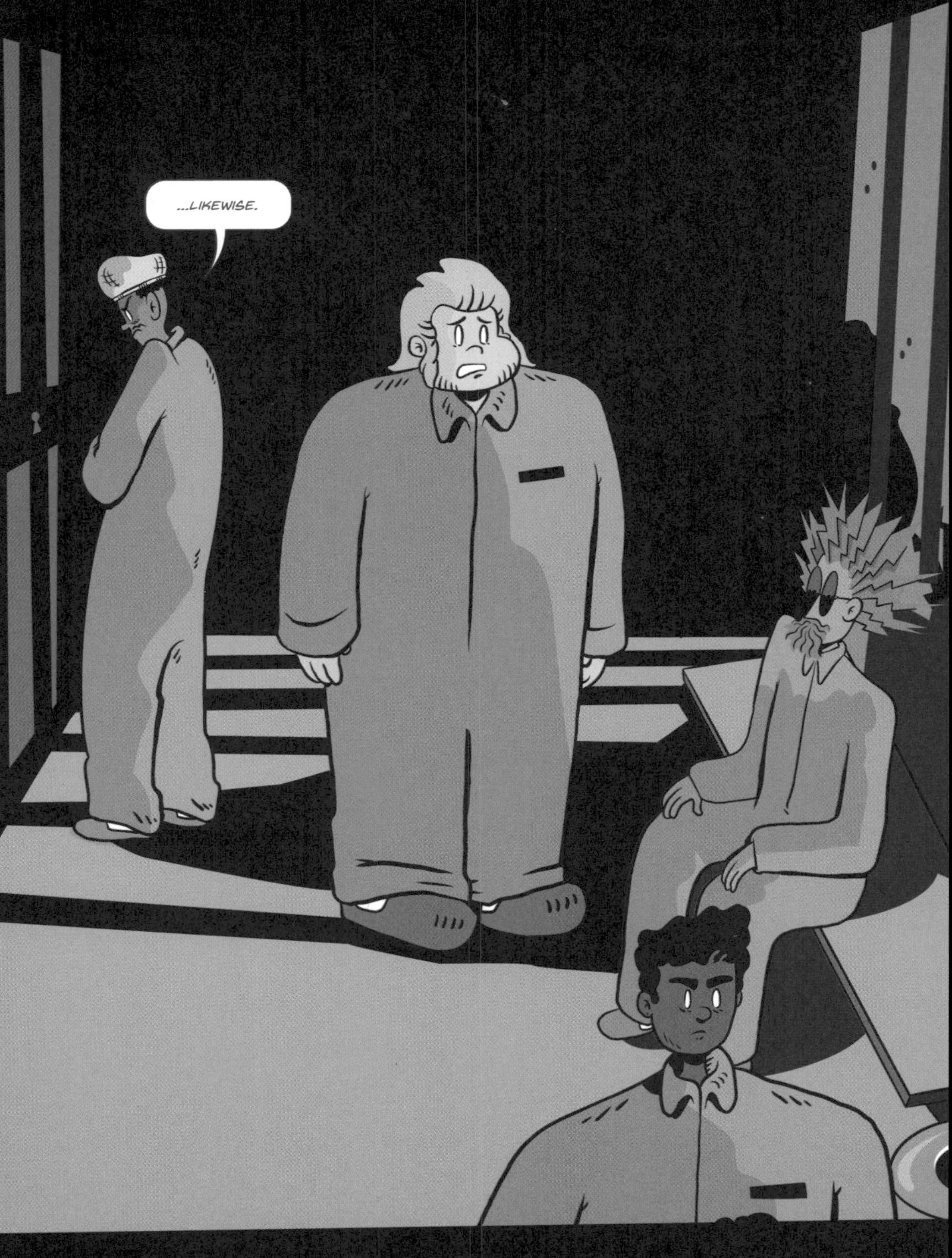
...LIKEWISE.

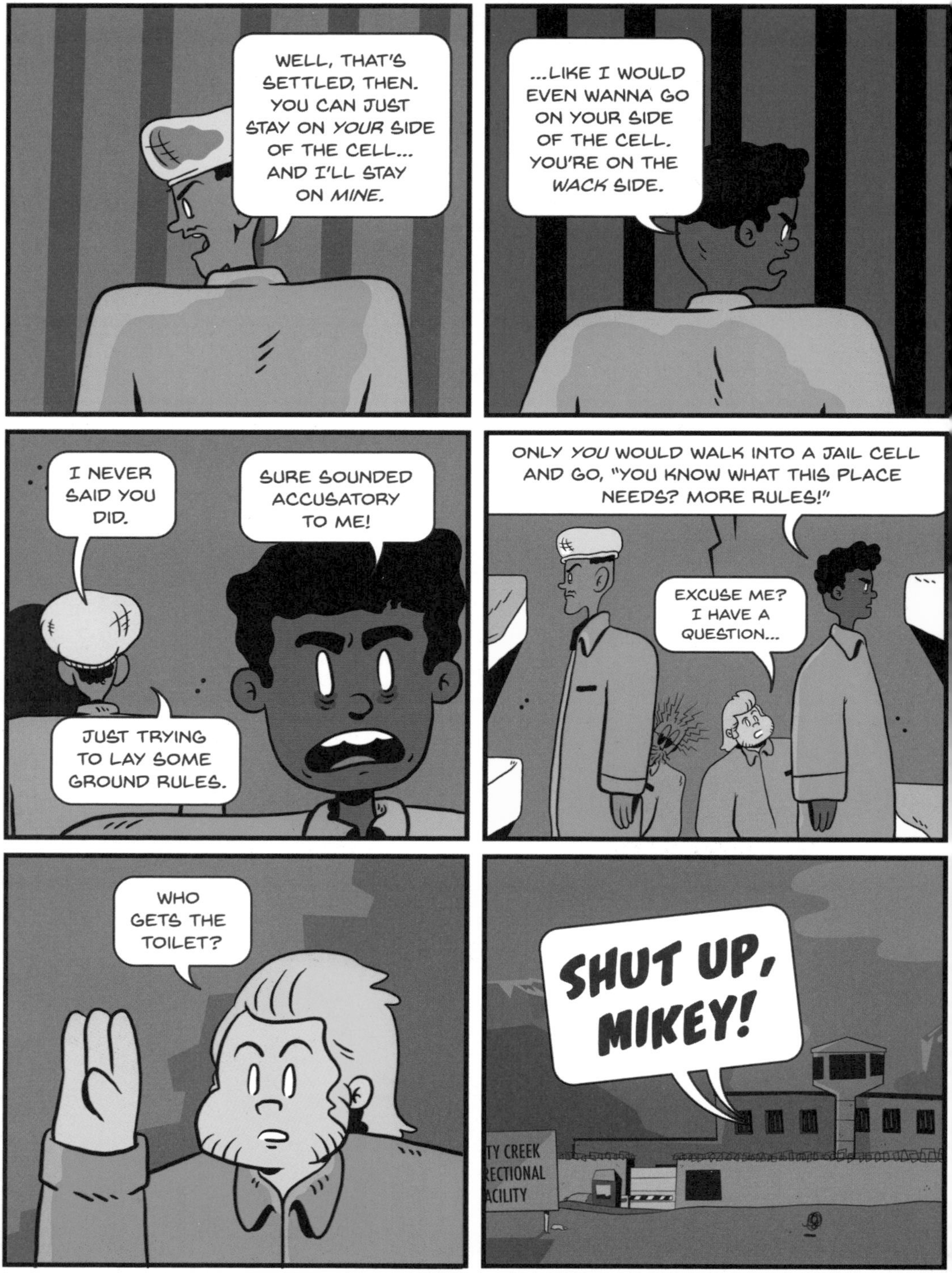
WELL, THAT'S SETTLED, THEN. YOU CAN JUST STAY ON *YOUR* SIDE OF THE CELL... AND I'LL STAY ON *MINE.*
...LIKE I WOULD EVEN WANNA GO ON YOUR SIDE OF THE CELL. YOU'RE ON THE *WACK* SIDE.
I NEVER SAID YOU DID.
SURE SOUNDED ACCUSATORY TO ME!
JUST TRYING TO LAY SOME GROUND RULES.
ONLY *YOU* WOULD WALK INTO A JAIL CELL AND GO, "YOU KNOW WHAT THIS PLACE NEEDS? MORE RULES!"
EXCUSE ME? I HAVE A QUESTION...
WHO GETS THE TOILET?
SHUT UP, MIKEY!
TY CREEK
RECTIONAL
ACILITY

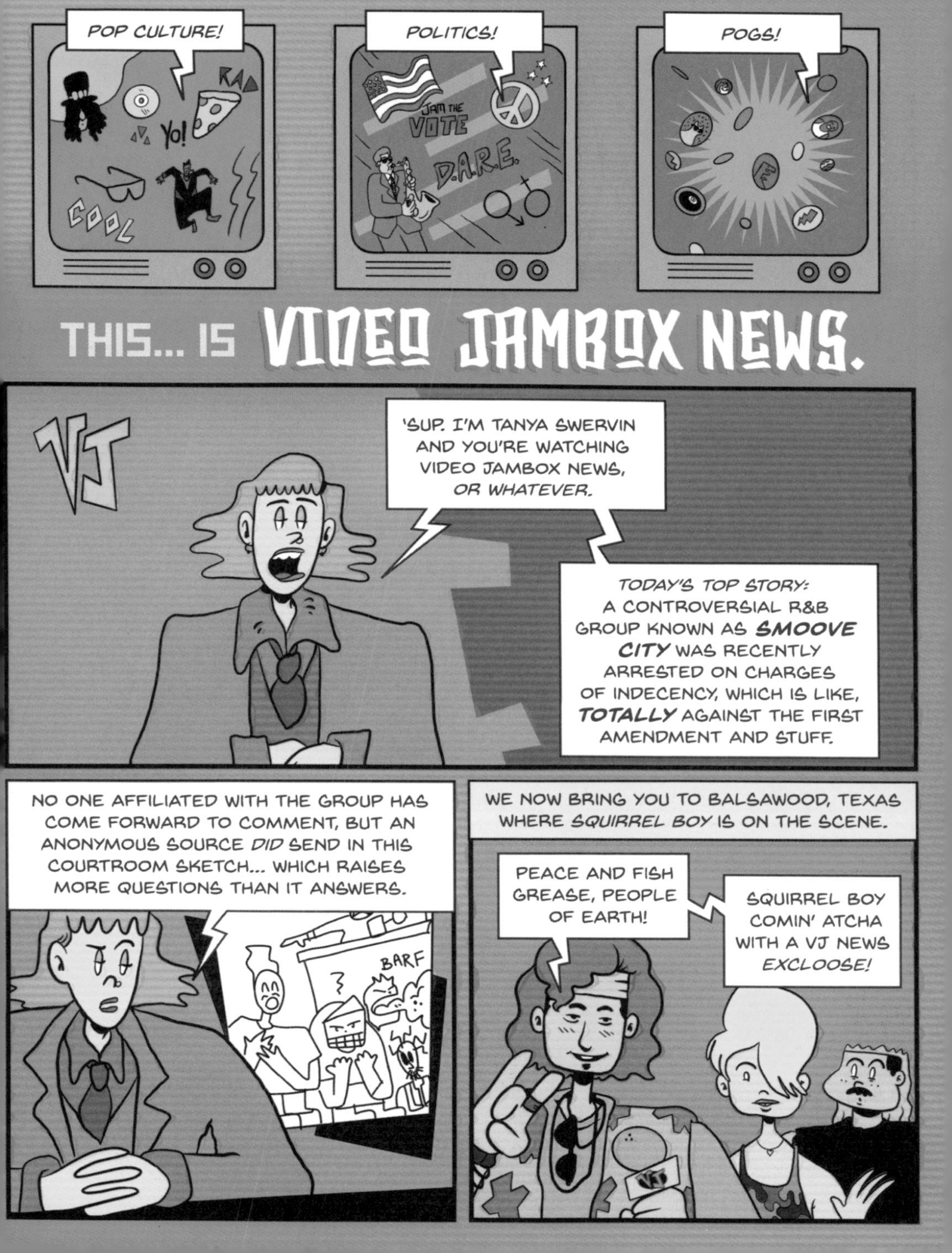
POP CULTURE!
RAD
YO!
COOL
POLITICS!
JAM THE VOTE
D.A.R.E.
POGS!
THIS... IS VIDEO JAMBOX NEWS.
VJ
'SUP. I'M TANYA SWERVIN AND YOU'RE WATCHING VIDEO JAMBOX NEWS, OR WHATEVER.
TODAY'S TOP STORY: A CONTROVERSIAL R&B GROUP KNOWN AS SMOOVE CITY WAS RECENTLY ARRESTED ON CHARGES OF INDECENCY, WHICH IS LIKE, TOTALLY AGAINST THE FIRST AMENDMENT AND STUFF.
NO ONE AFFILIATED WITH THE GROUP HAS COME FORWARD TO COMMENT, BUT AN ANONYMOUS SOURCE DID SEND IN THIS COURTROOM SKETCH... WHICH RAISES MORE QUESTIONS THAN IT ANSWERS.
BARF
WE NOW BRING YOU TO BALSAWOOD, TEXAS WHERE SQUIRREL BOY IS ON THE SCENE.
PEACE AND FISH GREASE, PEOPLE OF EARTH!
SQUIRREL BOY COMIN' ATCHA WITH A VJ NEWS EXCLOOSE!

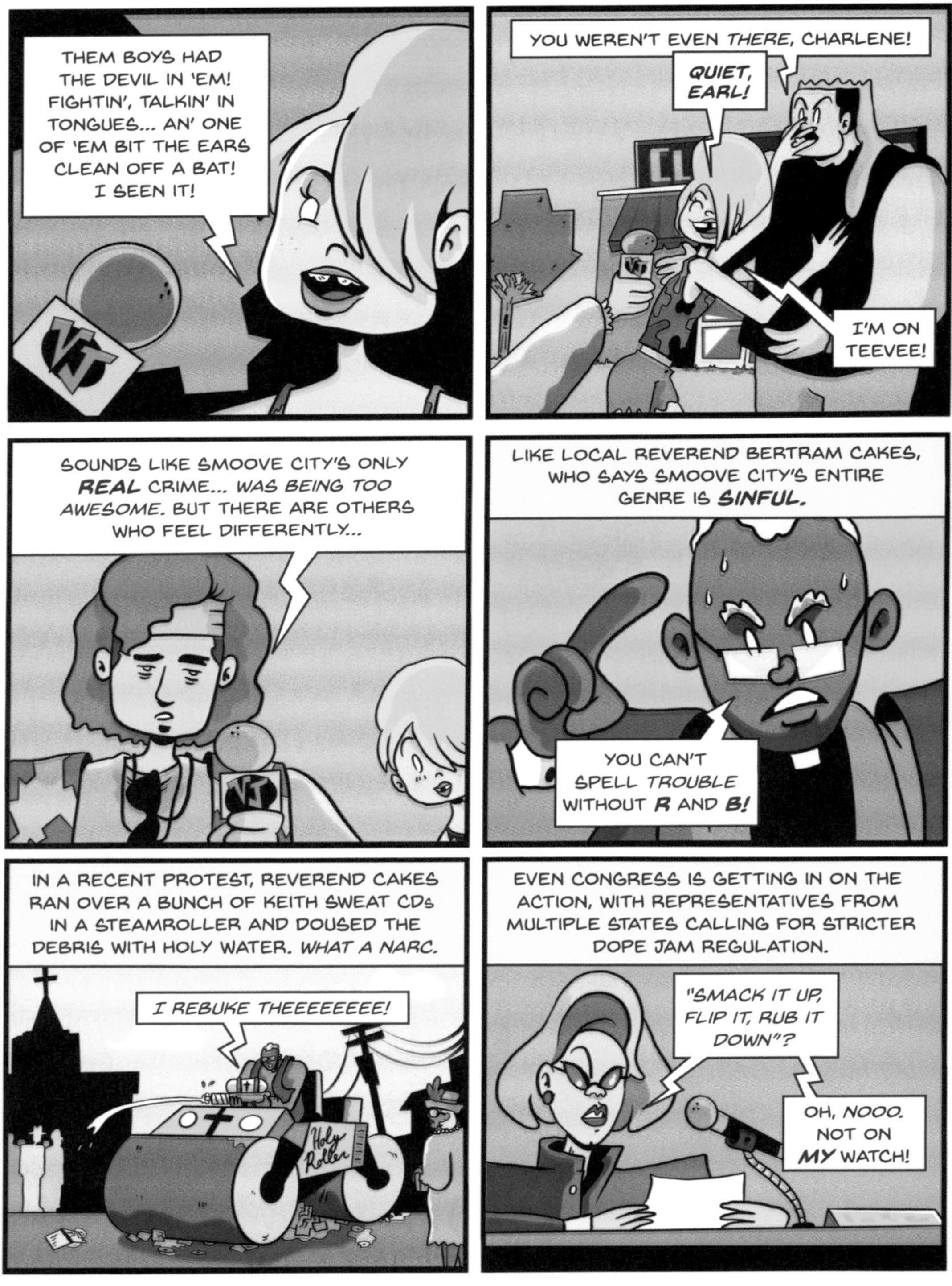
THEM BOYS HAD THE DEVIL IN 'EM! FIGHTIN', TALKIN' IN TONGUES... AN' ONE OF 'EM BIT THE EARS CLEAN OFF A BAT! I SEEN IT!
YOU WEREN'T EVEN *THERE*, CHARLENE!
QUIET, EARL!
I'M ON TEEVEE!
SOUNDS LIKE SMOOVE CITY'S ONLY ***REAL*** CRIME... *WAS BEING TOO AWESOME.* BUT THERE ARE OTHERS WHO FEEL DIFFERENTLY...
LIKE LOCAL REVEREND BERTRAM CAKES, WHO SAYS SMOOVE CITY'S ENTIRE GENRE IS ***SINFUL.***
YOU CAN'T SPELL *TROUBLE* WITHOUT ***R*** AND ***B!***
IN A RECENT PROTEST, REVEREND CAKES RAN OVER A BUNCH OF KEITH SWEAT CDs IN A STEAMROLLER AND DOUSED THE DEBRIS WITH HOLY WATER. *WHAT A NARC.*
I REBUKE THEEEEEEEE!
Holy Roller
EVEN CONGRESS IS GETTING IN ON THE ACTION, WITH REPRESENTATIVES FROM MULTIPLE STATES CALLING FOR STRICTER DOPE JAM REGULATION.
"SMACK IT UP, FLIP IT, RUB IT DOWN"?
OH, *NOOO.* NOT ON ***MY*** WATCH!

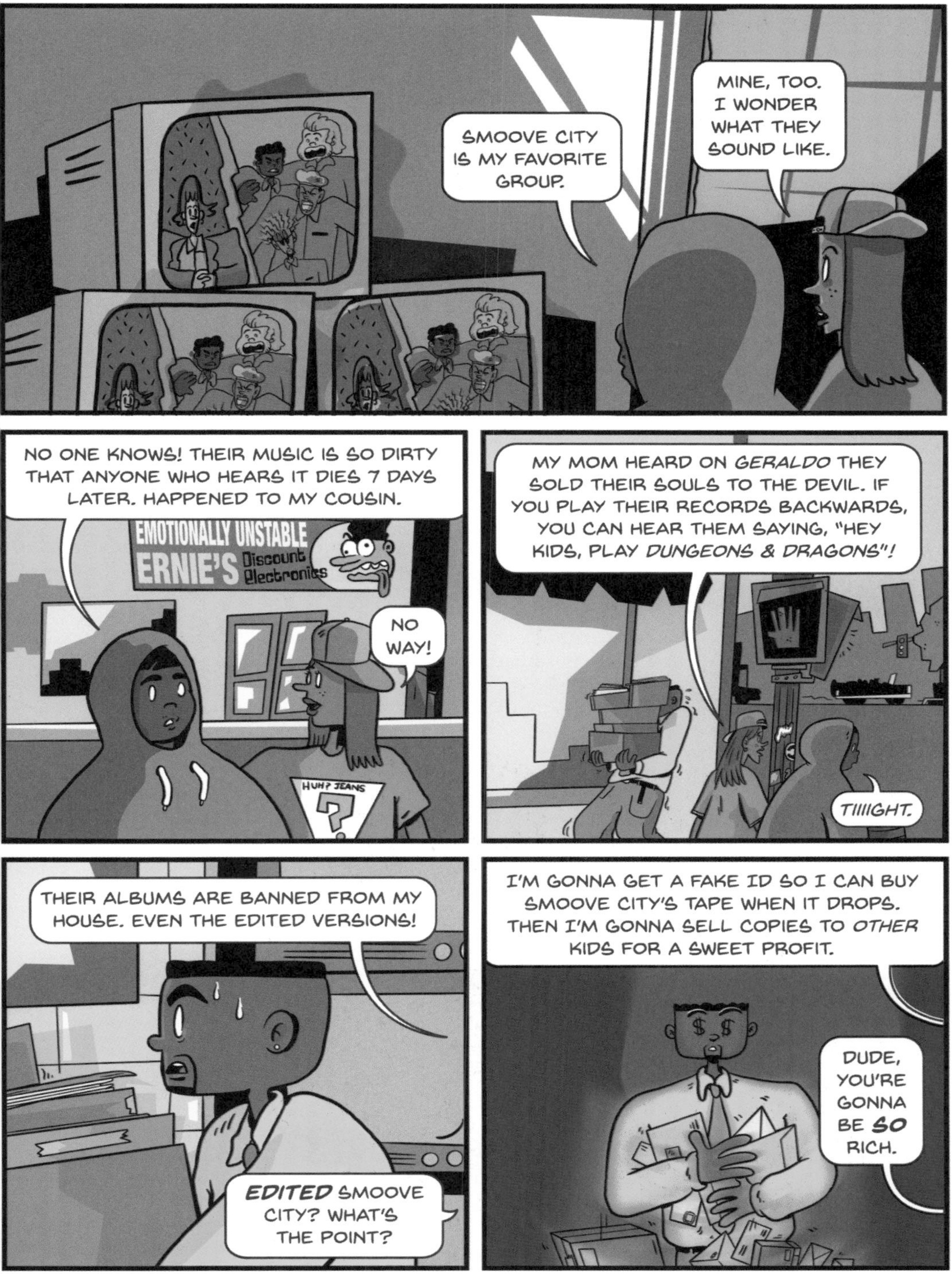
SMOOVE CITY IS MY FAVORITE GROUP.
MINE, TOO. I WONDER WHAT THEY SOUND LIKE.
NO ONE KNOWS! THEIR MUSIC IS SO DIRTY THAT ANYONE WHO HEARS IT DIES 7 DAYS LATER. HAPPENED TO MY COUSIN.
EMOTIONALLY UNSTABLE ERNIE'S Discount Electronics
NO WAY!
HUH? JEANS
MY MOM HEARD ON *GERALDO* THEY SOLD THEIR SOULS TO THE DEVIL. IF YOU PLAY THEIR RECORDS BACKWARDS, YOU CAN HEAR THEM SAYING, "HEY KIDS, PLAY *DUNGEONS & DRAGONS*"!
TIIIIGHT.
THEIR ALBUMS ARE BANNED FROM MY HOUSE. EVEN THE EDITED VERSIONS!
EDITED SMOOVE CITY? WHAT'S THE POINT?
I'M GONNA GET A FAKE ID SO I CAN BUY SMOOVE CITY'S TAPE WHEN IT DROPS. THEN I'M GONNA SELL COPIES TO *OTHER* KIDS FOR A SWEET PROFIT.
DUDE, YOU'RE GONNA BE ***SO*** RICH.

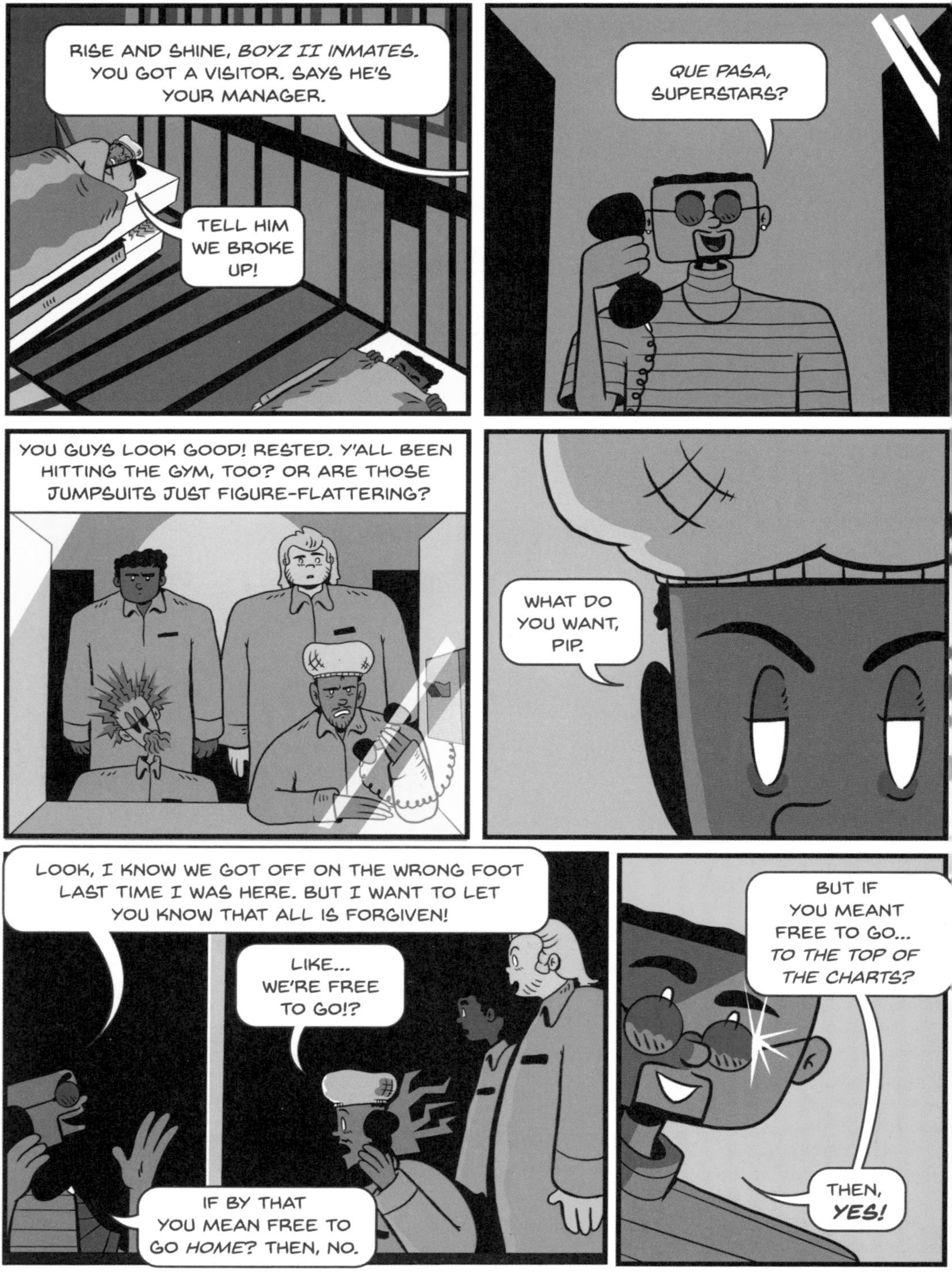
RISE AND SHINE, *BOYZ II INMATES.* YOU GOT A VISITOR. SAYS HE'S YOUR MANAGER.
TELL HIM WE BROKE UP!
QUE PASA, SUPERSTARS?
YOU GUYS LOOK GOOD! RESTED. Y'ALL BEEN HITTING THE GYM, TOO? OR ARE THOSE JUMPSUITS JUST FIGURE-FLATTERING?
WHAT DO YOU WANT, PIP.
LOOK, I KNOW WE GOT OFF ON THE WRONG FOOT LAST TIME I WAS HERE. BUT I WANT TO LET YOU KNOW THAT ALL IS FORGIVEN!
LIKE... WE'RE FREE TO GO!?
IF BY THAT YOU MEAN FREE TO GO *HOME?* THEN, NO.
BUT IF YOU MEANT FREE TO GO... *TO THE TOP OF THE CHARTS?*
THEN, ***YES!***

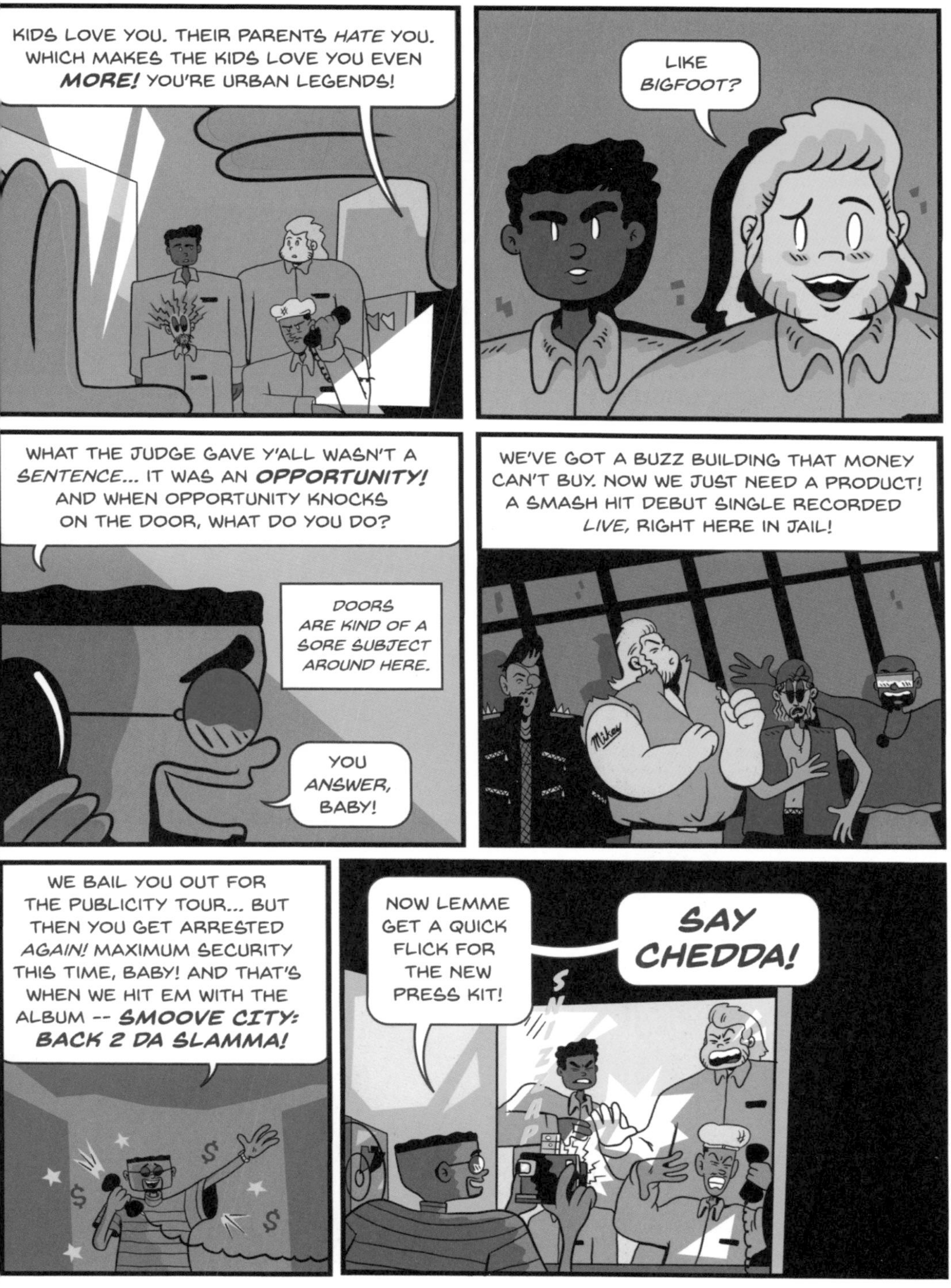

KIDS LOVE YOU. THEIR PARENTS *HATE* YOU. WHICH MAKES THE KIDS LOVE YOU EVEN **MORE!** YOU'RE URBAN LEGENDS!
LIKE *BIGFOOT?*
WHAT THE JUDGE GAVE Y'ALL WASN'T A *SENTENCE*... IT WAS AN **OPPORTUNITY!** AND WHEN OPPORTUNITY KNOCKS ON THE DOOR, WHAT DO YOU DO?
DOORS ARE KIND OF A SORE SUBJECT AROUND HERE.
YOU *ANSWER,* BABY!
WE'VE GOT A BUZZ BUILDING THAT MONEY CAN'T BUY. NOW WE JUST NEED A PRODUCT! A SMASH HIT DEBUT SINGLE RECORDED *LIVE,* RIGHT HERE IN JAIL!
Mikey
WE BAIL YOU OUT FOR THE PUBLICITY TOUR... BUT THEN YOU GET ARRESTED *AGAIN!* MAXIMUM SECURITY THIS TIME, BABY! AND THAT'S WHEN WE HIT EM WITH THE ALBUM -- ***SMOOVE CITY: BACK 2 DA SLAMMA!***
NOW LEMME GET A QUICK FLICK FOR THE NEW PRESS KIT!
SAY CHEDDA!
SNIZZAP

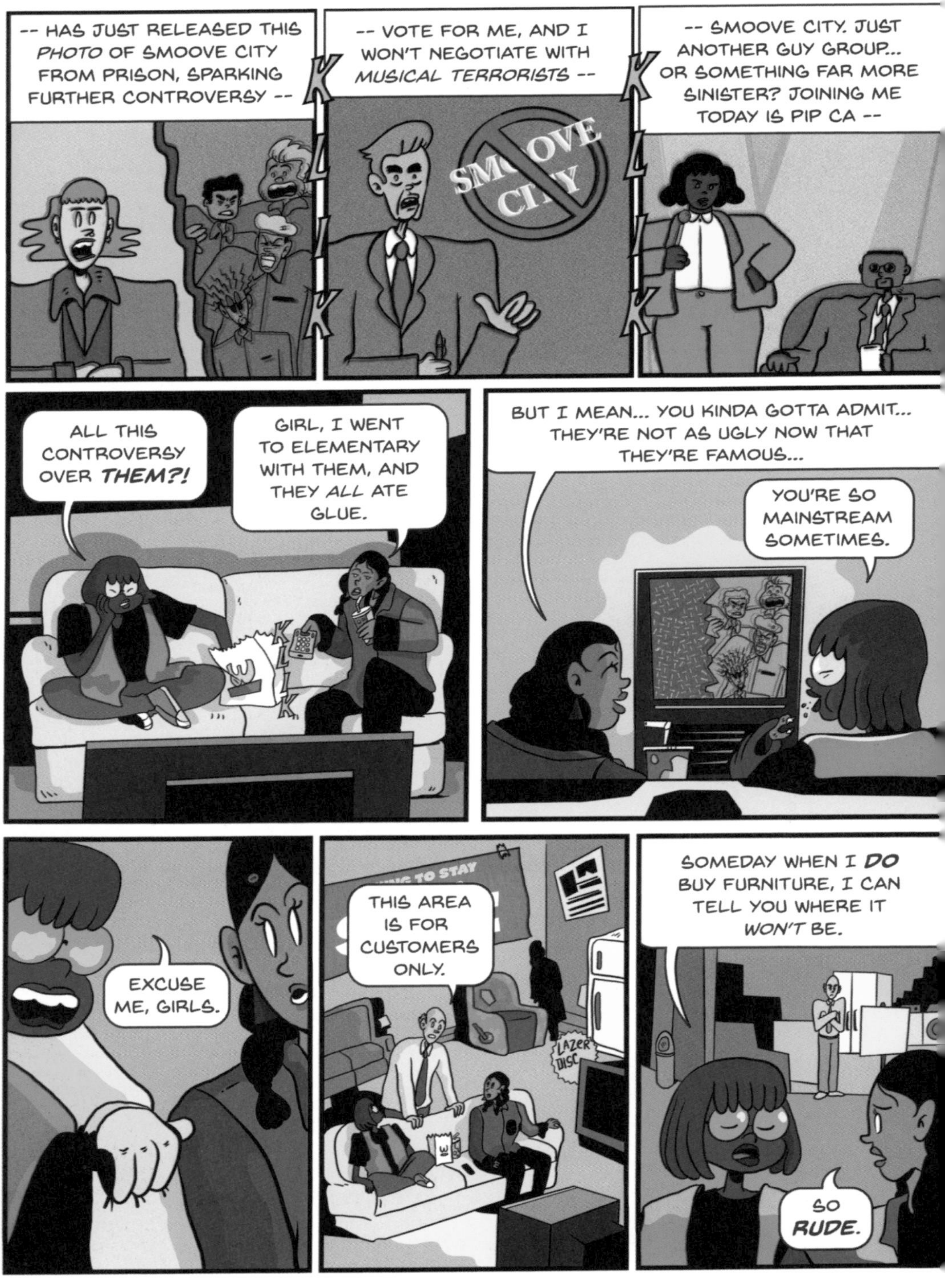
-- HAS JUST RELEASED THIS PHOTO OF SMOOVE CITY FROM PRISON, SPARKING FURTHER CONTROVERSY --
KLIK
-- VOTE FOR ME, AND I WON'T NEGOTIATE WITH MUSICAL TERRORISTS --
SMOOVE CITY
KLIK
-- SMOOVE CITY. JUST ANOTHER GUY GROUP... OR SOMETHING FAR MORE SINISTER? JOINING ME TODAY IS PIP CA --
ALL THIS CONTROVERSY OVER THEM?!
GIRL, I WENT TO ELEMENTARY WITH THEM, AND THEY ALL ATE GLUE.
KLIK
BUT I MEAN... YOU KINDA GOTTA ADMIT... THEY'RE NOT AS UGLY NOW THAT THEY'RE FAMOUS...
YOU'RE SO MAINSTREAM SOMETIMES.
EXCUSE ME, GIRLS.
THIS AREA IS FOR CUSTOMERS ONLY.
LAZER DISC
SOMEDAY WHEN I DO BUY FURNITURE, I CAN TELL YOU WHERE IT WON'T BE.
SO RUDE.

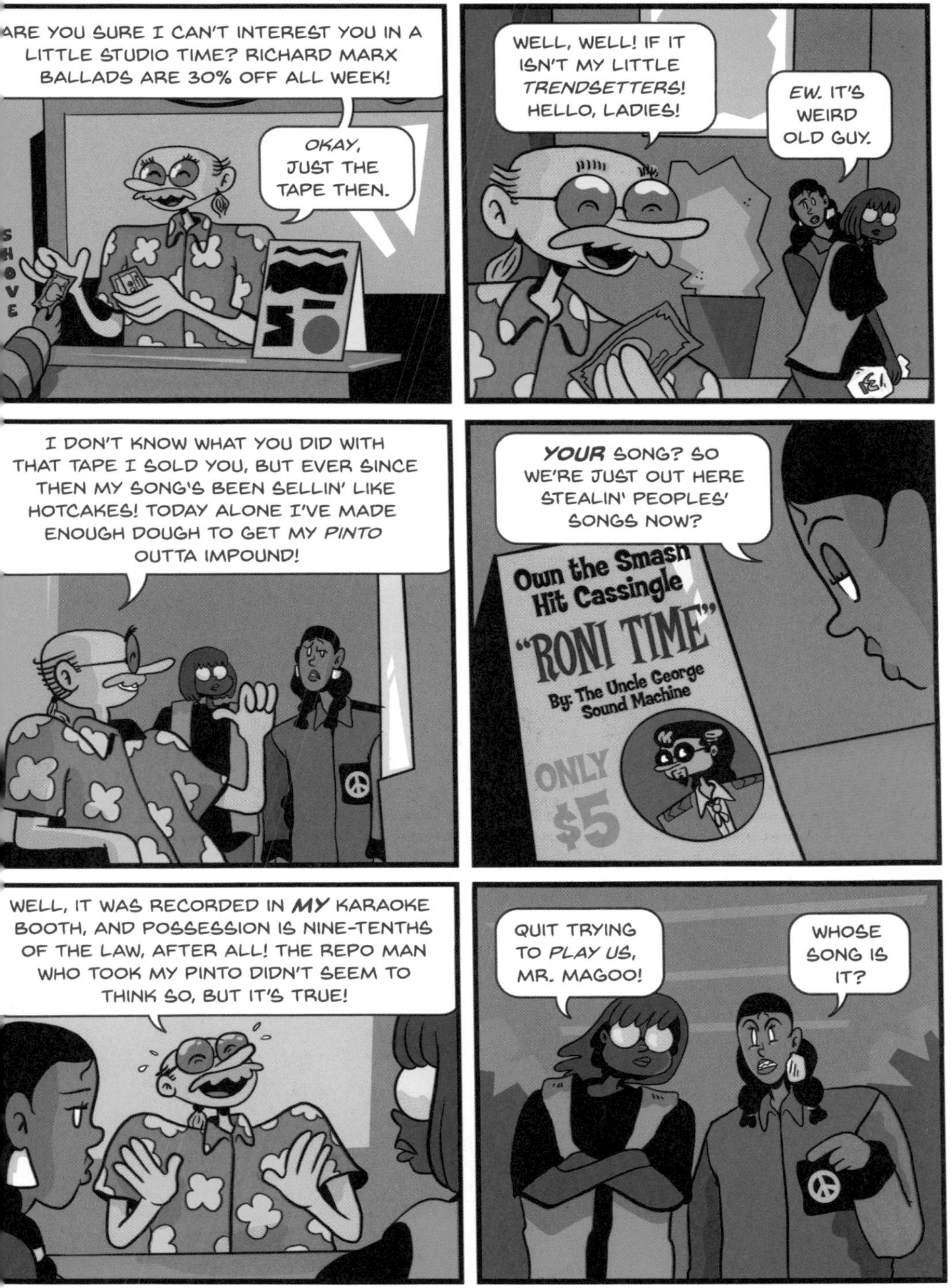
ARE YOU SURE I CAN'T INTEREST YOU IN A LITTLE STUDIO TIME? RICHARD MARX BALLADS ARE 30% OFF ALL WEEK!
OKAY, JUST THE TAPE THEN.
SHOVE
WELL, WELL! IF IT ISN'T MY LITTLE *TRENDSETTERS!* HELLO, LADIES!
EW. IT'S WEIRD OLD GUY.
I DON'T KNOW WHAT YOU DID WITH THAT TAPE I SOLD YOU, BUT EVER SINCE THEN MY SONG'S BEEN SELLIN' LIKE HOTCAKES! TODAY ALONE I'VE MADE ENOUGH DOUGH TO GET MY *PINTO* OUTTA IMPOUND!
YOUR SONG? SO WE'RE JUST OUT HERE STEALIN' PEOPLES' SONGS NOW?
Own the Smash Hit Cassingle
"RONI TIME"
By: The Uncle George Sound Machine
ONLY $5
WELL, IT WAS RECORDED IN ***MY*** KARAOKE BOOTH, AND POSSESSION IS NINE-TENTHS OF THE LAW, AFTER ALL! THE REPO MAN WHO TOOK MY PINTO DIDN'T SEEM TO THINK SO, BUT IT'S TRUE!
QUIT TRYING TO *PLAY US,* MR. MAGOO!
WHOSE SONG IS IT?

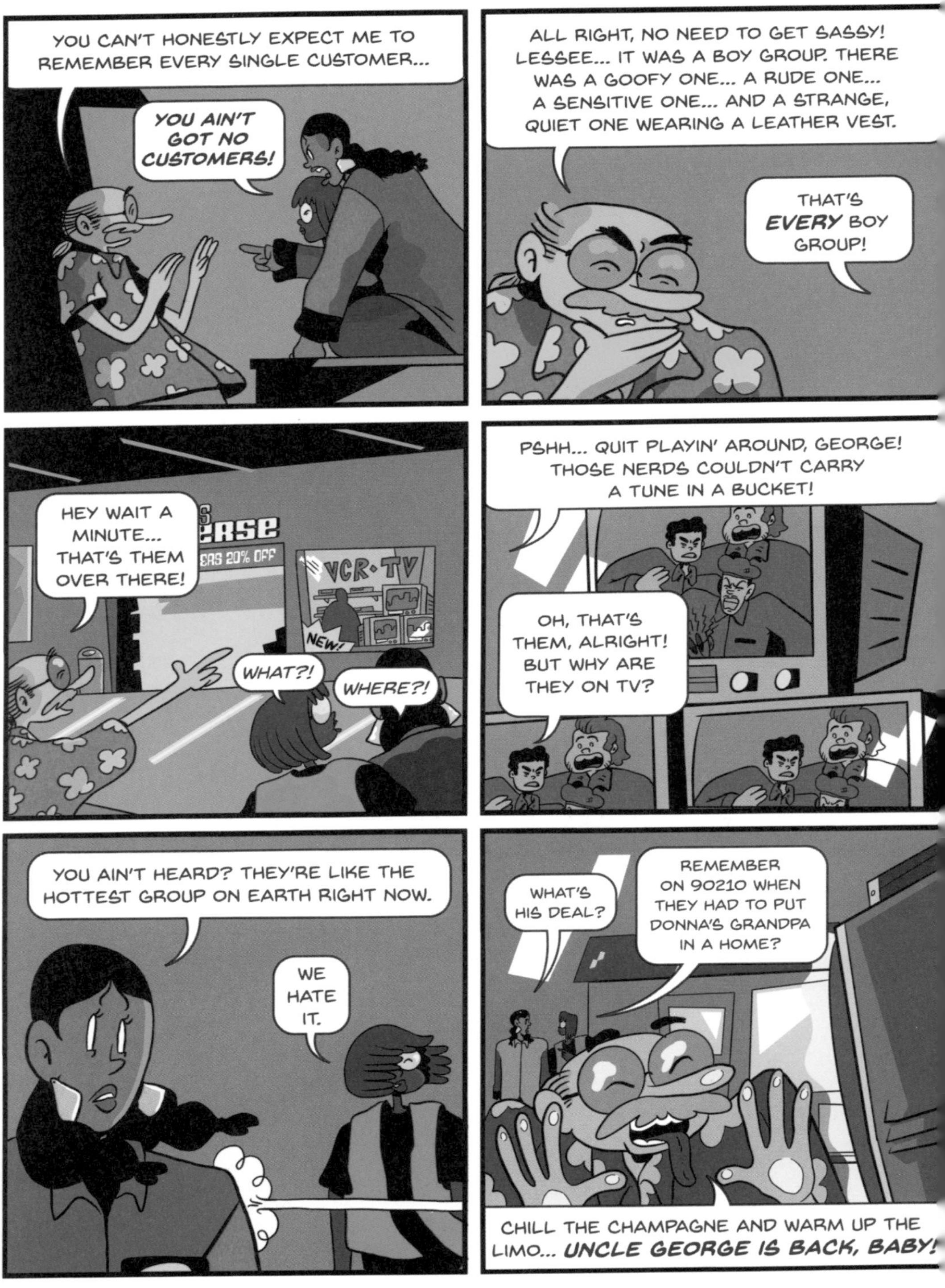
YOU CAN'T HONESTLY EXPECT ME TO REMEMBER EVERY SINGLE CUSTOMER...
YOU AIN'T GOT NO CUSTOMERS!
ALL RIGHT, NO NEED TO GET SASSY! LESSEE... IT WAS A BOY GROUP. THERE WAS A GOOFY ONE... A RUDE ONE... A SENSITIVE ONE... AND A STRANGE, QUIET ONE WEARING A LEATHER VEST.
THAT'S EVERY BOY GROUP!
HEY WAIT A MINUTE... THAT'S THEM OVER THERE!
ERS 20% OFF
VCR·TV
NEW!
WHAT?!
WHERE?!
PSHH... QUIT PLAYIN' AROUND, GEORGE! THOSE NERDS COULDN'T CARRY A TUNE IN A BUCKET!
OH, THAT'S THEM, ALRIGHT! BUT WHY ARE THEY ON TV?
YOU AIN'T HEARD? THEY'RE LIKE THE HOTTEST GROUP ON EARTH RIGHT NOW.
WE HATE IT.
WHAT'S HIS DEAL?
REMEMBER ON 90210 WHEN THEY HAD TO PUT DONNA'S GRANDPA IN A HOME?
CHILL THE CHAMPAGNE AND WARM UP THE LIMO... UNCLE GEORGE IS BACK, BABY!

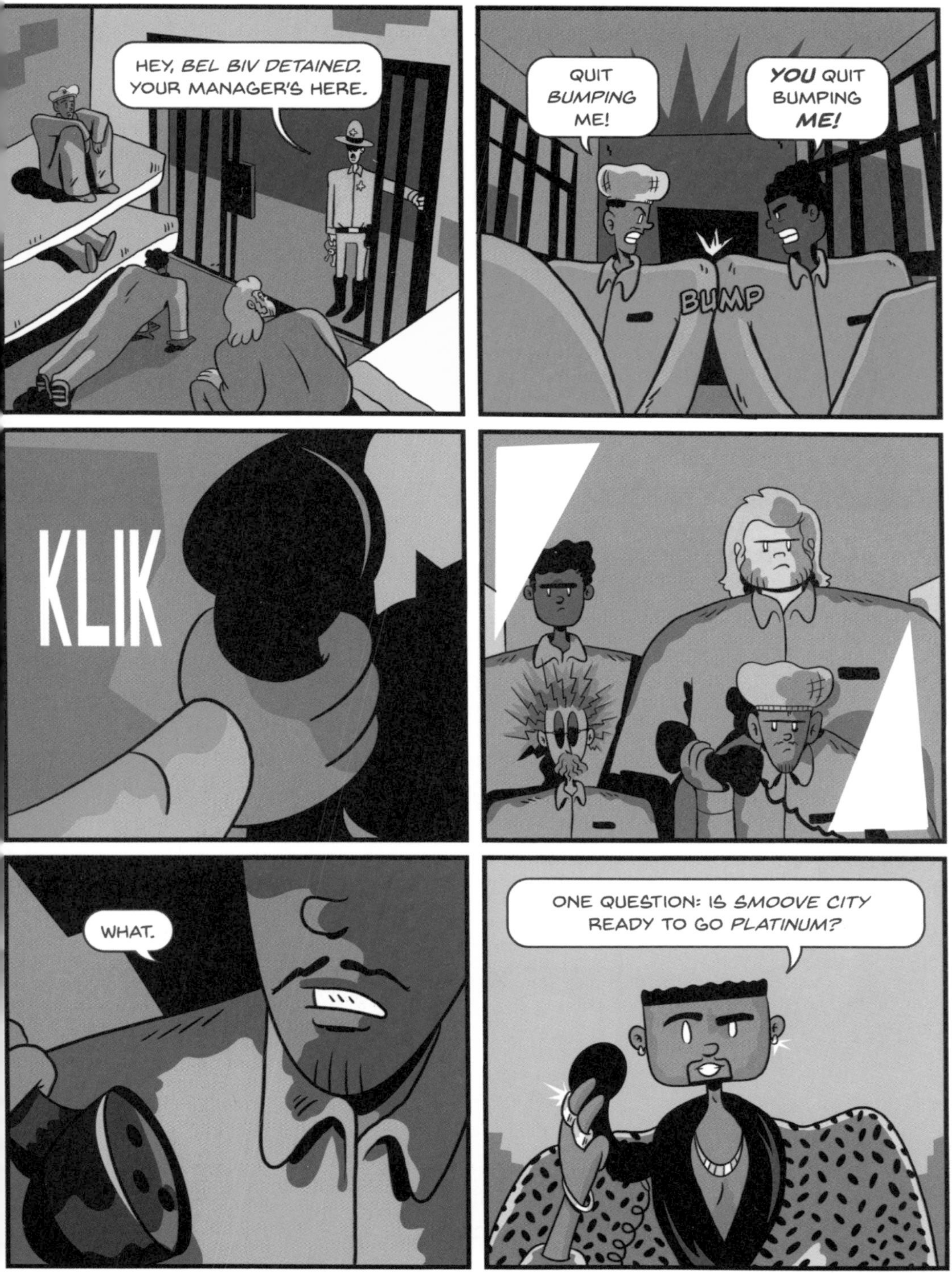
HEY, BEL BIV DETAINED. YOUR MANAGER'S HERE.
QUIT BUMPING ME!
YOU QUIT BUMPING ME!
BUMP
KLIK
WHAT.
ONE QUESTION: IS SMOOVE CITY READY TO GO PLATINUM?

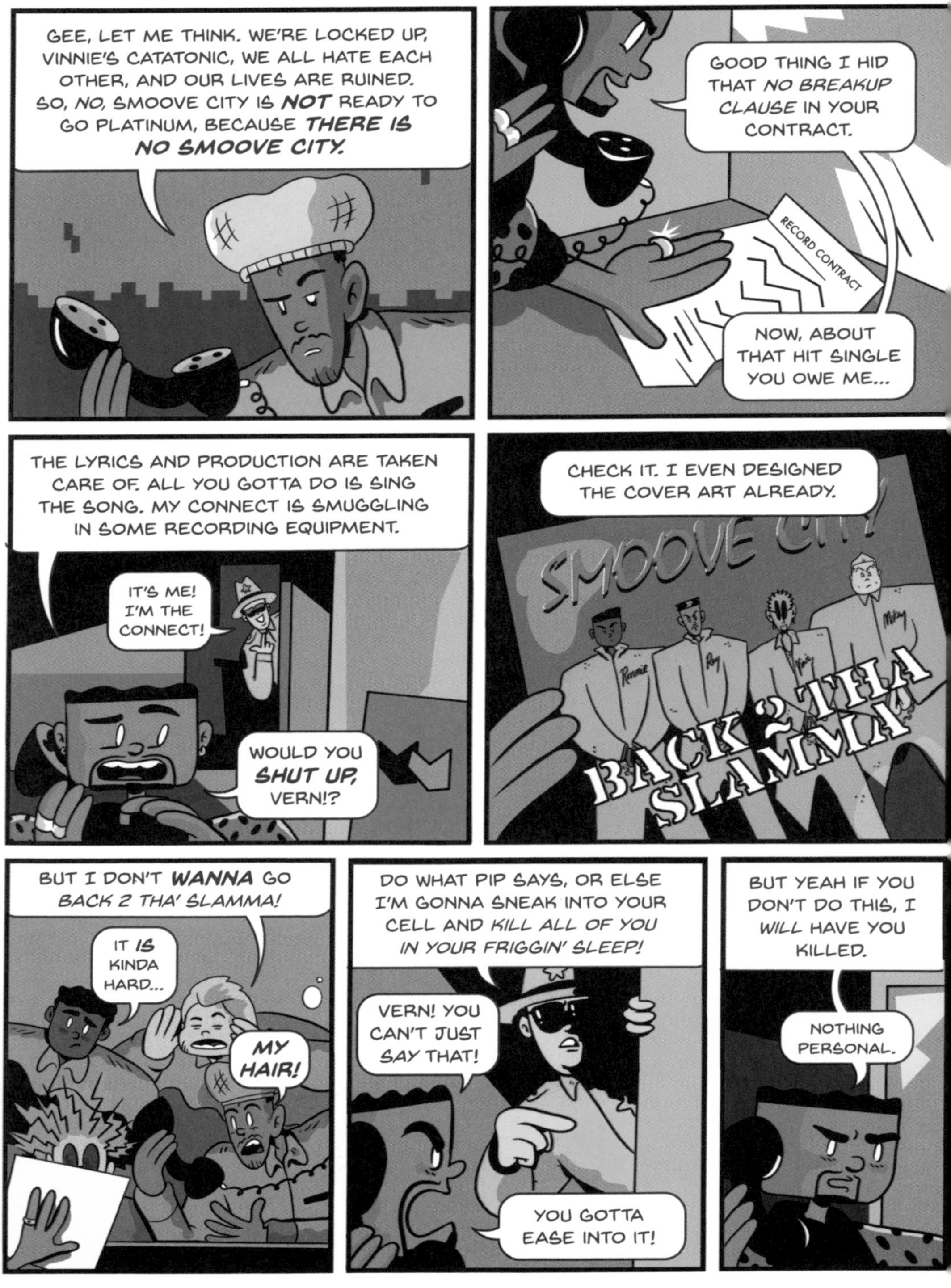
GEE, LET ME THINK. WE'RE LOCKED UP, VINNIE'S CATATONIC, WE ALL HATE EACH OTHER, AND OUR LIVES ARE RUINED. SO, NO, SMOOVE CITY IS NOT READY TO GO PLATINUM, BECAUSE THERE IS NO SMOOVE CITY.
GOOD THING I HID THAT NO BREAKUP CLAUSE IN YOUR CONTRACT.
RECORD CONTRACT
NOW, ABOUT THAT HIT SINGLE YOU OWE ME...
THE LYRICS AND PRODUCTION ARE TAKEN CARE OF. ALL YOU GOTTA DO IS SING THE SONG. MY CONNECT IS SMUGGLING IN SOME RECORDING EQUIPMENT.
IT'S ME! I'M THE CONNECT!
WOULD YOU SHUT UP, VERN!?
CHECK IT. I EVEN DESIGNED THE COVER ART ALREADY.
SMOOVE CITY
BACK 2 THA SLAMMA
BUT I DON'T WANNA GO BACK 2 THA' SLAMMA!
IT IS KINDA HARD...
MY HAIR!
DO WHAT PIP SAYS, OR ELSE I'M GONNA SNEAK INTO YOUR CELL AND KILL ALL OF YOU IN YOUR FRIGGIN' SLEEP!
VERN! YOU CAN'T JUST SAY THAT!
YOU GOTTA EASE INTO IT!
BUT YEAH IF YOU DON'T DO THIS, I WILL HAVE YOU KILLED.
NOTHING PERSONAL.

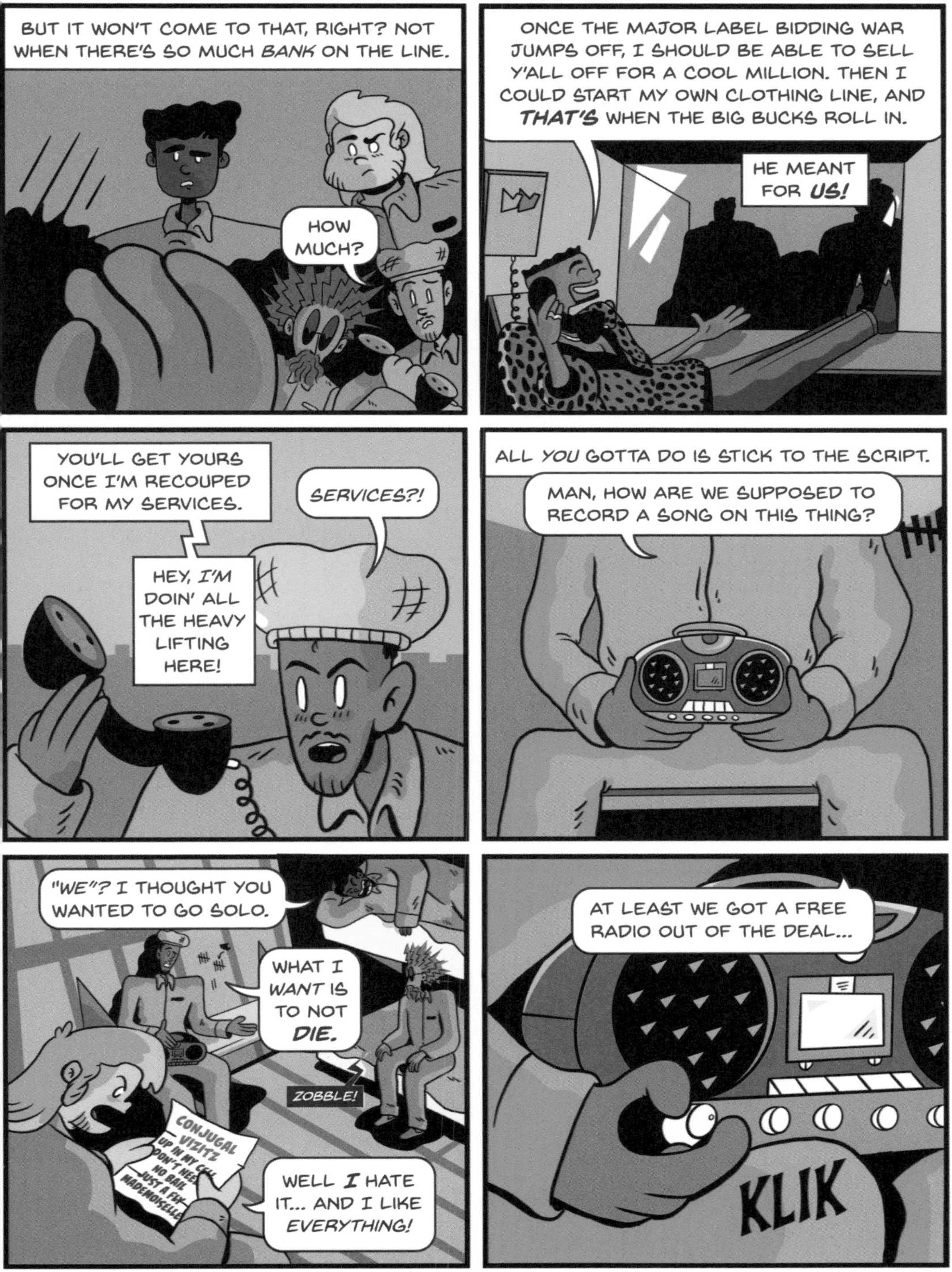

BUT IT WON'T COME TO THAT, RIGHT? NOT WHEN THERE'S SO MUCH *BANK* ON THE LINE.
HOW MUCH?
ONCE THE MAJOR LABEL BIDDING WAR JUMPS OFF, I SHOULD BE ABLE TO SELL Y'ALL OFF FOR A COOL MILLION. THEN I COULD START MY OWN CLOTHING LINE, AND ***THAT'S*** WHEN THE BIG BUCKS ROLL IN.
HE MEANT FOR ***US!***
YOU'LL GET YOURS ONCE I'M RECOUPED FOR MY SERVICES.
SERVICES?!
HEY, *I'M* DOIN' ALL THE HEAVY LIFTING HERE!
ALL *YOU* GOTTA DO IS STICK TO THE SCRIPT.
MAN, HOW ARE WE SUPPOSED TO RECORD A SONG ON THIS THING?
"*WE*"? I THOUGHT YOU WANTED TO GO SOLO.
WHAT I *WANT* IS TO NOT ***DIE.***
ZOBBLE!
CONJUGAL
VIZITZ
NO BAIL
MADEMOISELLE
WELL ***I*** HATE IT... AND I LIKE *EVERYTHING!*
AT LEAST WE GOT A FREE RADIO OUT OF THE DEAL...
KLIK

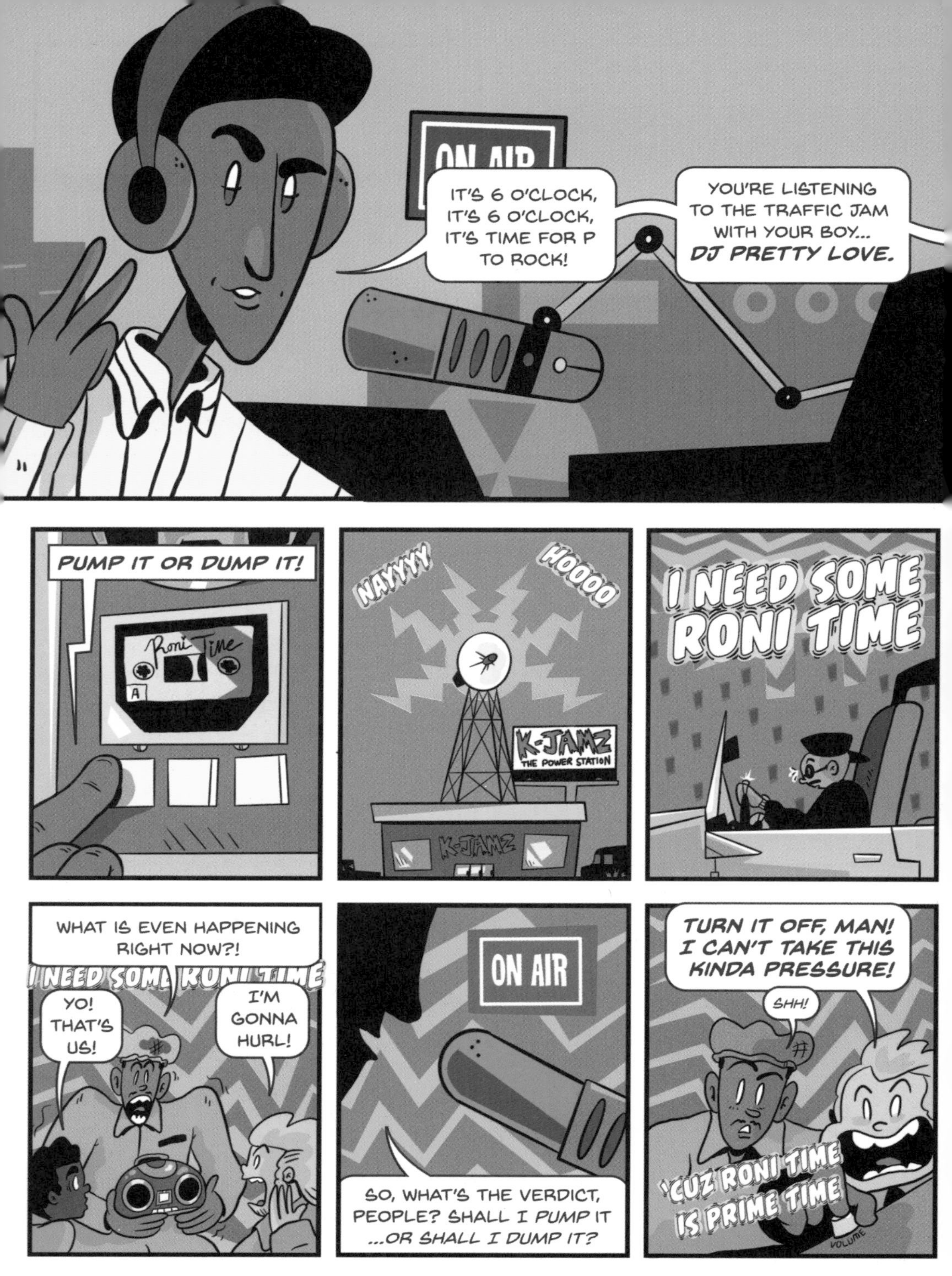
ON AIR
IT'S 6 O'CLOCK, IT'S 6 O'CLOCK, IT'S TIME FOR P TO ROCK!
YOU'RE LISTENING TO THE TRAFFIC JAM WITH YOUR BOY... DJ PRETTY LOVE.
PUMP IT OR DUMP IT!
Roni Time
A
NAYYYY
HOOOO
K-JAMZ THE POWER STATION
K-JAMZ
I NEED SOME RONI TIME
WHAT IS EVEN HAPPENING RIGHT NOW?!
I NEED SOME RONI TIME
YO! THAT'S US!
I'M GONNA HURL!
ON AIR
SO, WHAT'S THE VERDICT, PEOPLE? SHALL I PUMP IT ...OR SHALL I DUMP IT?
TURN IT OFF, MAN! I CAN'T TAKE THIS KINDA PRESSURE!
SHH!
'CUZ RONI TIME IS PRIME TIME
VOLUME

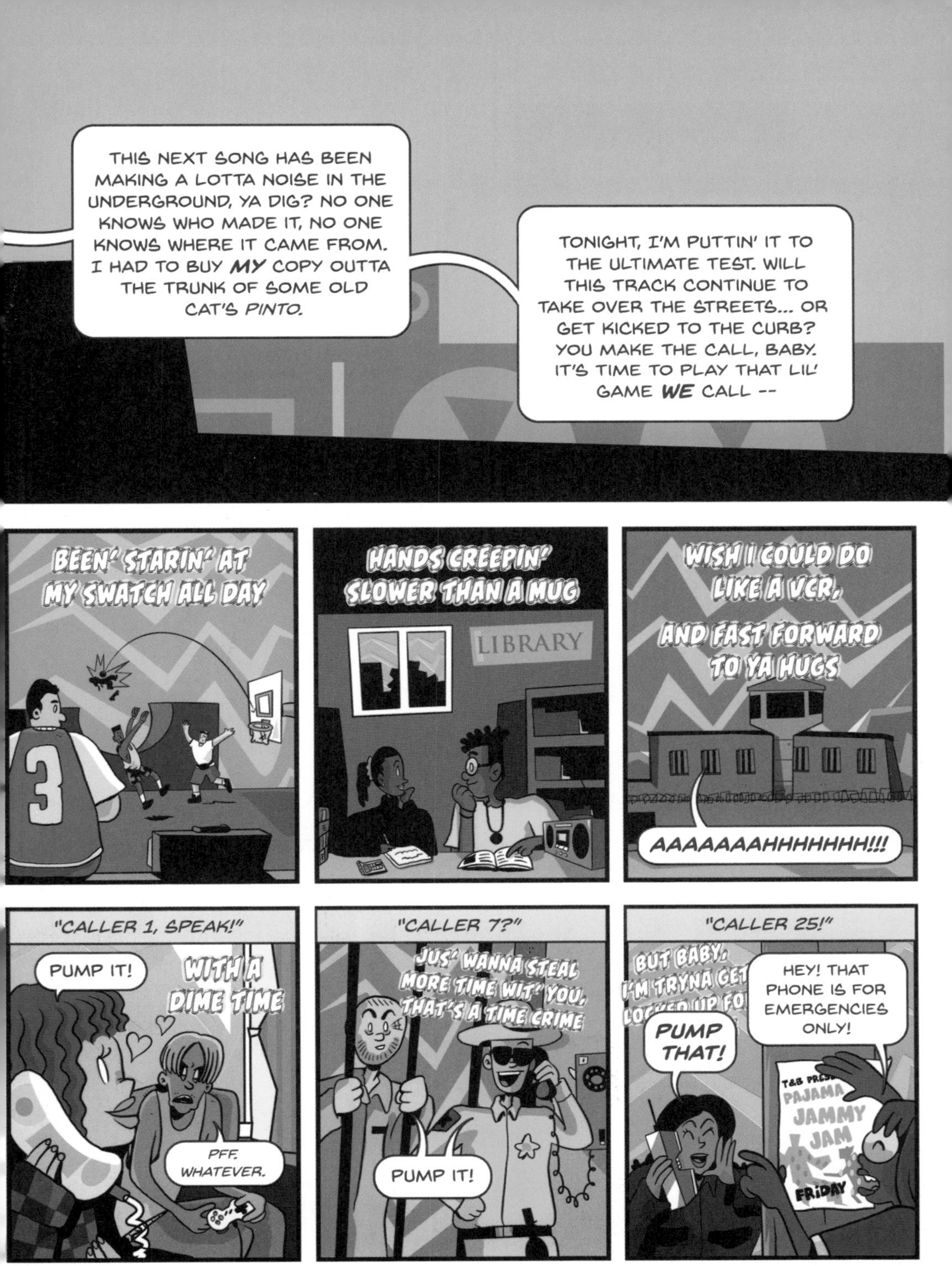

THIS NEXT SONG HAS BEEN MAKING A LOTTA NOISE IN THE UNDERGROUND, YA DIG? NO ONE KNOWS WHO MADE IT, NO ONE KNOWS WHERE IT CAME FROM. I HAD TO BUY MY COPY OUTTA THE TRUNK OF SOME OLD CAT'S PINTO.
TONIGHT, I'M PUTTIN' IT TO THE ULTIMATE TEST. WILL THIS TRACK CONTINUE TO TAKE OVER THE STREETS... OR GET KICKED TO THE CURB? YOU MAKE THE CALL, BABY. IT'S TIME TO PLAY THAT LIL' GAME WE CALL --
BEEN' STARIN' AT MY SWATCH ALL DAY
3
HANDS CREEPIN' SLOWER THAN A MUG
LIBRARY
WISH I COULD DO LIKE A VCR,
AND FAST FORWARD TO YA HUGS
AAAAAAAHHHHHHH!!!
"CALLER 1, SPEAK!"
PUMP IT!
WITH A DIME TIME
PFF. WHATEVER.
"CALLER 7?"
JUS' WANNA STEAL MORE TIME WIT' YOU, THAT'S A TIME CRIME
PUMP IT!
"CALLER 25!"
BUT BABY, I'M TRYNA GET
PUMP THAT!
HEY! THAT PHONE IS FOR EMERGENCIES ONLY!
PAJAMA JAMMY JAM
FRIDAY

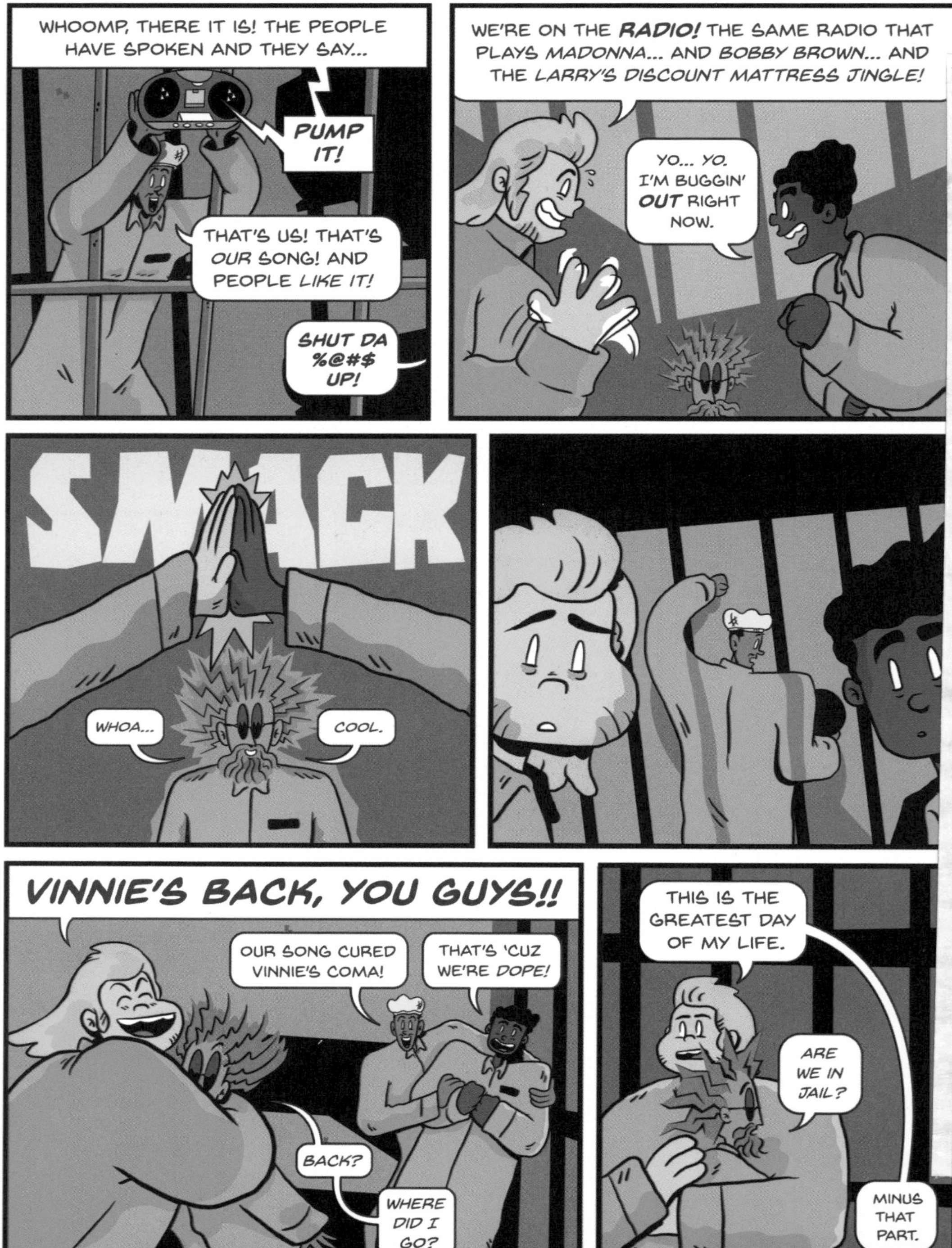
WHOOMP, THERE IT IS! THE PEOPLE HAVE SPOKEN AND THEY SAY...
PUMP IT!
THAT'S US! THAT'S OUR SONG! AND PEOPLE LIKE IT!
SHUT DA %@#$ UP!
WE'RE ON THE RADIO! THE SAME RADIO THAT PLAYS MADONNA... AND BOBBY BROWN... AND THE LARRY'S DISCOUNT MATTRESS JINGLE!
YO... YO. I'M BUGGIN' OUT RIGHT NOW.
SMACK
WHOA...
COOL.
VINNIE'S BACK, YOU GUYS!!
OUR SONG CURED VINNIE'S COMA!
THAT'S 'CUZ WE'RE DOPE!
BACK?
WHERE DID I GO?
THIS IS THE GREATEST DAY OF MY LIFE.
ARE WE IN JAIL?
MINUS THAT PART.

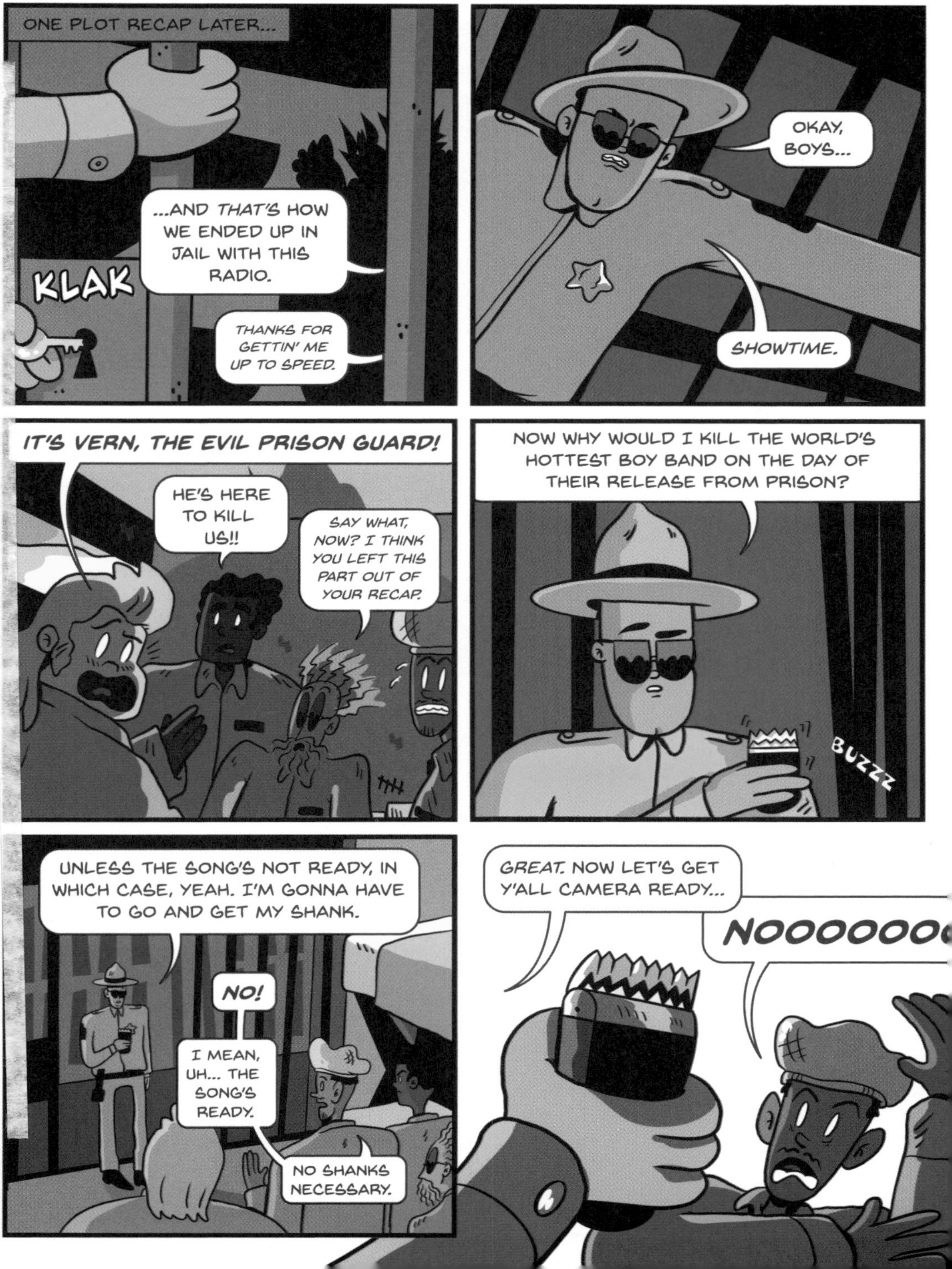
ONE PLOT RECAP LATER...
...AND THAT'S HOW WE ENDED UP IN JAIL WITH THIS RADIO.
KLAK
THANKS FOR GETTIN' ME UP TO SPEED.
OKAY, BOYS...
SHOWTIME.
IT'S VERN, THE EVIL PRISON GUARD!
HE'S HERE TO KILL US!!
SAY WHAT, NOW? I THINK YOU LEFT THIS PART OUT OF YOUR RECAP.
NOW WHY WOULD I KILL THE WORLD'S HOTTEST BOY BAND ON THE DAY OF THEIR RELEASE FROM PRISON?
BUZZZ
UNLESS THE SONG'S NOT READY, IN WHICH CASE, YEAH. I'M GONNA HAVE TO GO AND GET MY SHANK.
NO!
I MEAN, UH... THE SONG'S READY.
NO SHANKS NECESSARY.
GREAT. NOW LET'S GET Y'ALL CAMERA READY...
NOOOOOOO

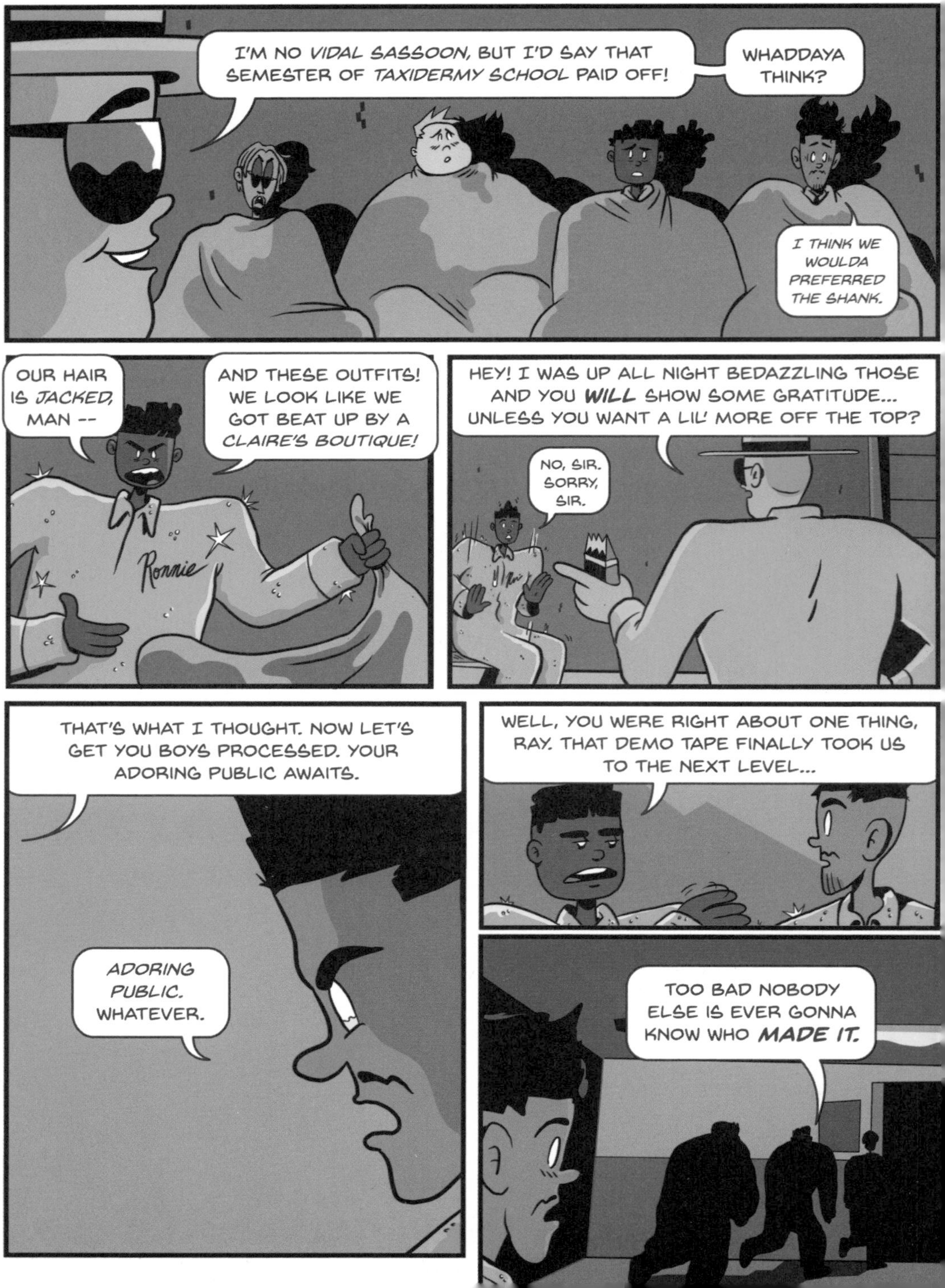
I'M NO *VIDAL SASSOON*, BUT I'D SAY THAT SEMESTER OF *TAXIDERMY SCHOOL* PAID OFF!
WHADDAYA THINK?
I THINK WE WOULDA PREFERRED THE SHANK.
OUR HAIR IS *JACKED*, MAN --
AND THESE OUTFITS! WE LOOK LIKE WE GOT BEAT UP BY A *CLAIRE'S BOUTIQUE!*
Ronnie
HEY! I WAS UP ALL NIGHT BEDAZZLING THOSE AND YOU ***WILL*** SHOW SOME GRATITUDE... UNLESS YOU WANT A LIL' MORE OFF THE TOP?
NO, SIR. SORRY, SIR.
THAT'S WHAT I THOUGHT. NOW LET'S GET YOU BOYS PROCESSED. YOUR ADORING PUBLIC AWAITS.
ADORING PUBLIC. WHATEVER.
WELL, YOU WERE RIGHT ABOUT ONE THING, RAY. THAT DEMO TAPE FINALLY TOOK US TO THE NEXT LEVEL...
TOO BAD NOBODY ELSE IS EVER GONNA KNOW WHO ***MADE IT.***

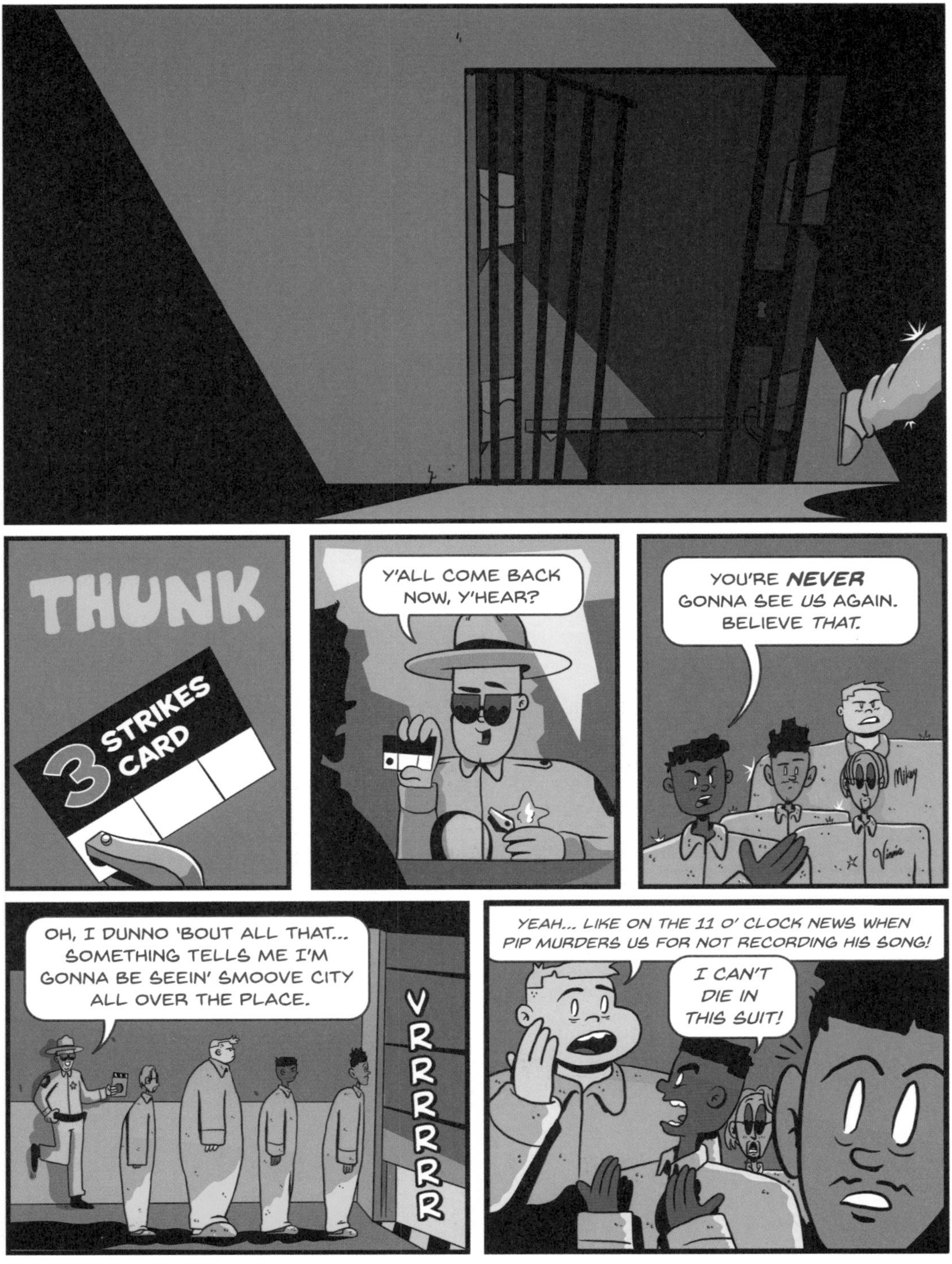
THUNK
3 STRIKES CARD
Y'ALL COME BACK NOW, Y'HEAR?
YOU'RE **NEVER** GONNA SEE US AGAIN. BELIEVE *THAT.*
OH, I DUNNO 'BOUT ALL THAT... SOMETHING TELLS ME I'M GONNA BE SEEIN' SMOOVE CITY ALL OVER THE PLACE.
VRRRRRR
YEAH... LIKE ON THE 11 O' CLOCK NEWS WHEN PIP MURDERS US FOR NOT RECORDING HIS SONG!
I CAN'T DIE IN THIS SUIT!

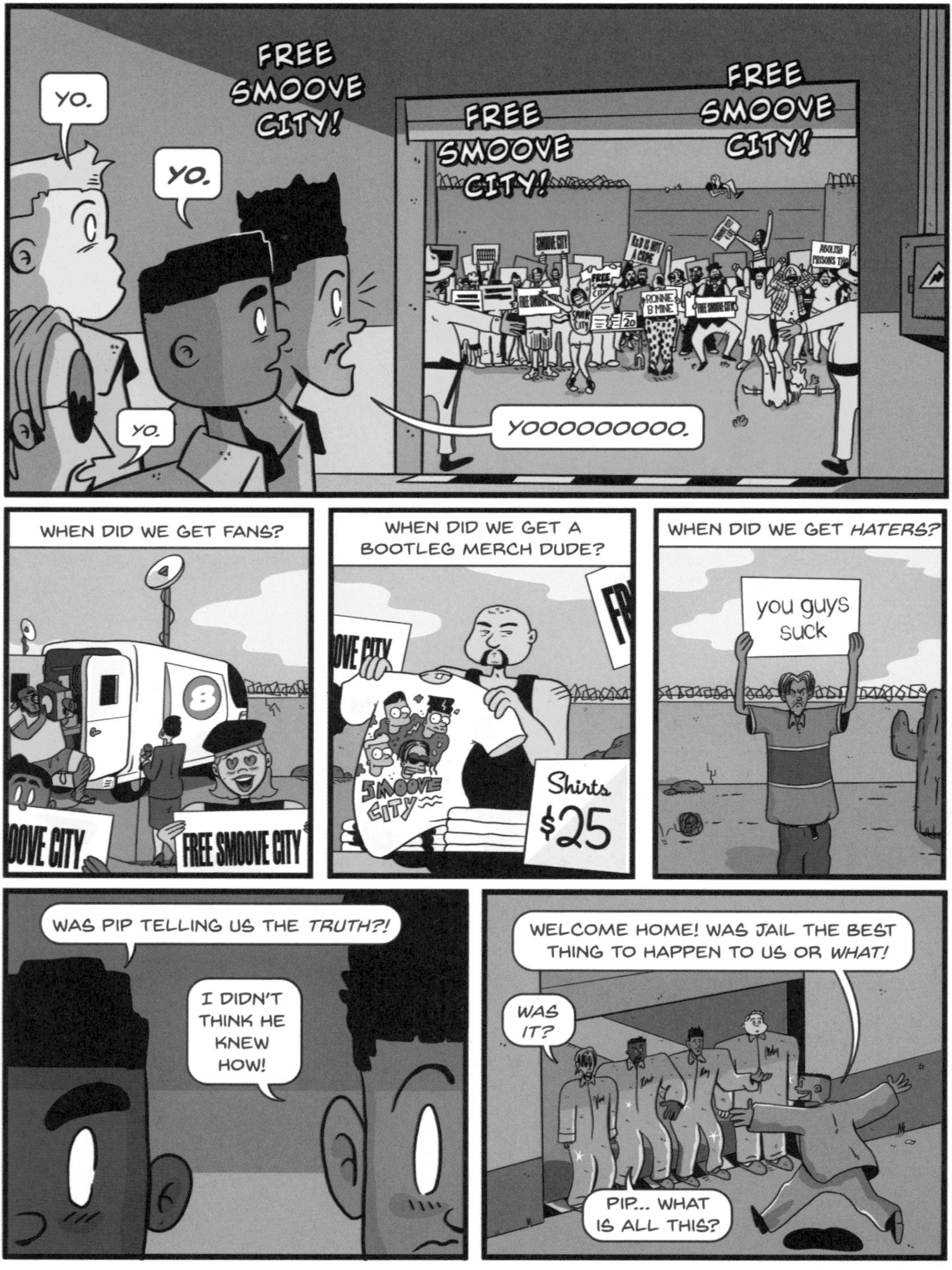
YO.
FREE SMOOVE CITY!
YO.
FREE SMOOVE CITY!
FREE SMOOVE CITY!
YO.
YOOOOOOOOO.
WHEN DID WE GET FANS?
OVE CITY
FREE SMOOVE CITY
WHEN DID WE GET A BOOTLEG MERCH DUDE?
SMOOVE CITY
Shirts $25
WHEN DID WE GET HATERS?
you guys suck
WAS PIP TELLING US THE TRUTH?!
I DIDN'T THINK HE KNEW HOW!
WELCOME HOME! WAS JAIL THE BEST THING TO HAPPEN TO US OR WHAT!
WAS IT?
PIP... WHAT IS ALL THIS?

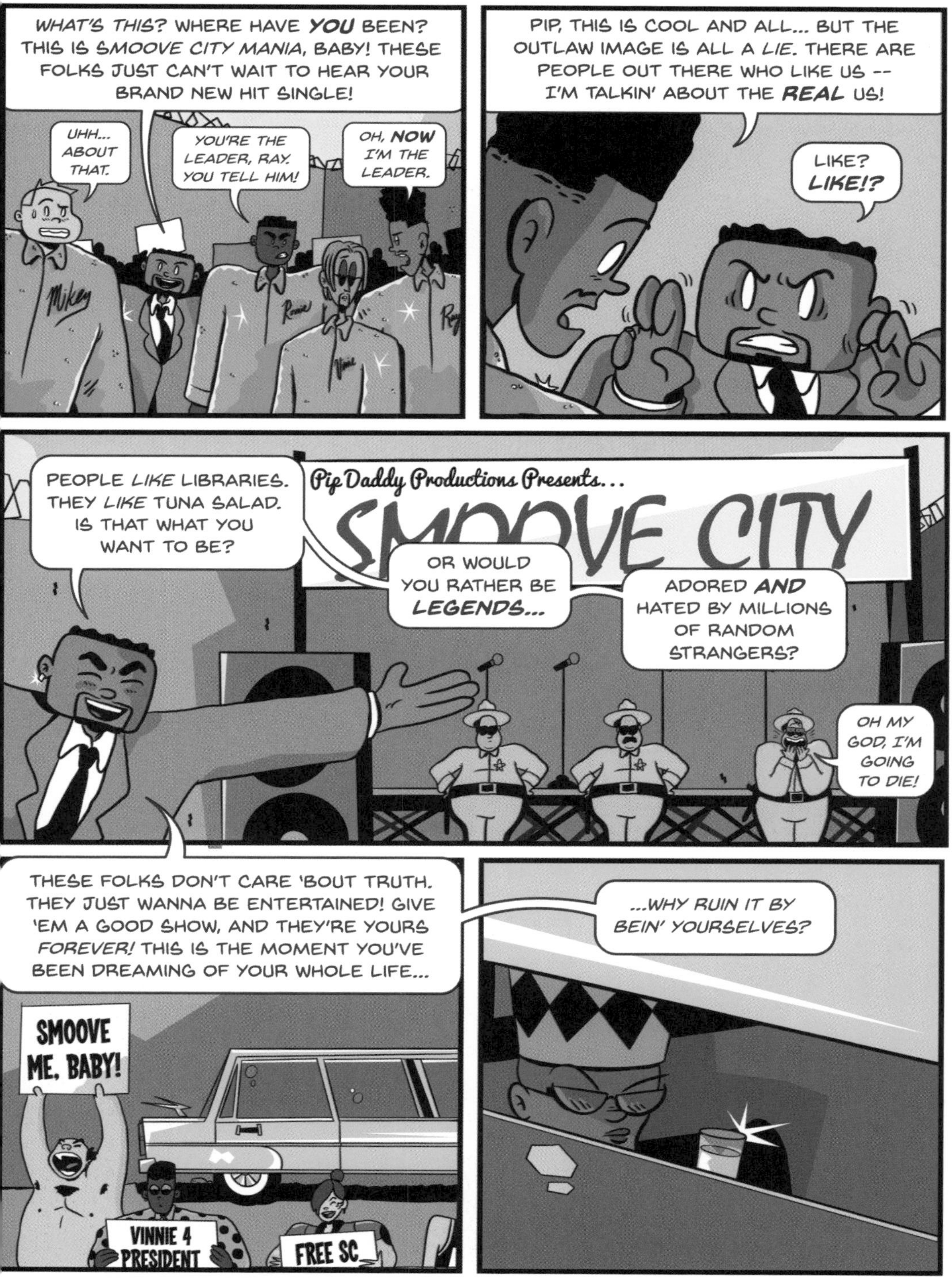
WHAT'S THIS? WHERE HAVE YOU BEEN? THIS IS SMOOVE CITY MANIA, BABY! THESE FOLKS JUST CAN'T WAIT TO HEAR YOUR BRAND NEW HIT SINGLE!
UHH... ABOUT THAT.
YOU'RE THE LEADER, RAY. YOU TELL HIM!
OH, NOW I'M THE LEADER.
Mikey
Ronnie
Vinnie
Ray
PIP, THIS IS COOL AND ALL... BUT THE OUTLAW IMAGE IS ALL A LIE. THERE ARE PEOPLE OUT THERE WHO LIKE US -- I'M TALKIN' ABOUT THE REAL US!
LIKE? LIKE!?
Pip Daddy Productions Presents...
SMOOVE CITY
PEOPLE LIKE LIBRARIES. THEY LIKE TUNA SALAD. IS THAT WHAT YOU WANT TO BE?
OR WOULD YOU RATHER BE LEGENDS...
ADORED AND HATED BY MILLIONS OF RANDOM STRANGERS?
OH MY GOD, I'M GOING TO DIE!
THESE FOLKS DON'T CARE 'BOUT TRUTH. THEY JUST WANNA BE ENTERTAINED! GIVE 'EM A GOOD SHOW, AND THEY'RE YOURS FOREVER! THIS IS THE MOMENT YOU'VE BEEN DREAMING OF YOUR WHOLE LIFE...
...WHY RUIN IT BY BEIN' YOURSELVES?
SMOOVE ME, BABY!
VINNIE 4 PRESIDENT
FREE SC

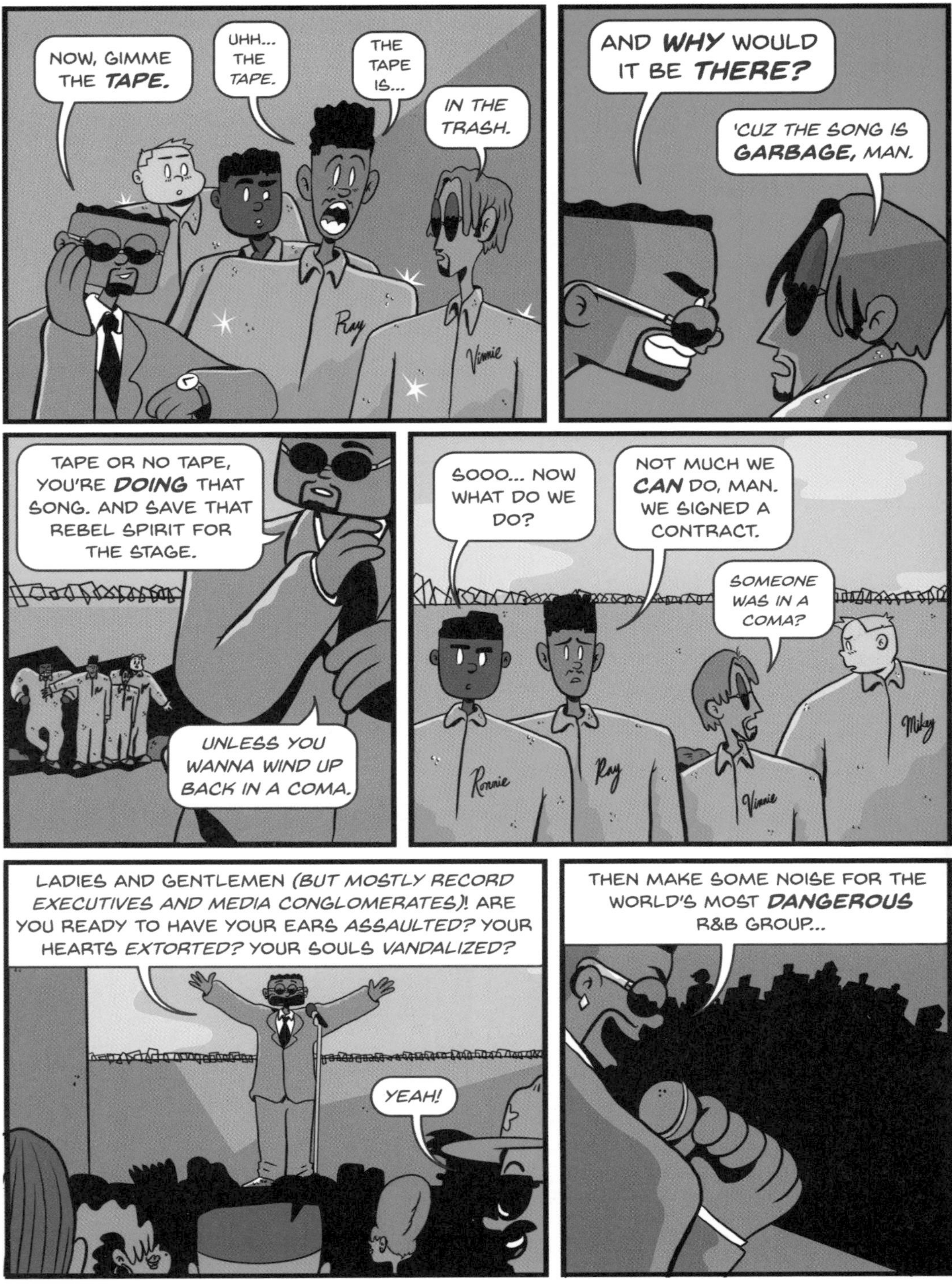
NOW, GIMME THE TAPE.
UHH... THE TAPE.
THE TAPE IS...
IN THE TRASH.
Ray
Vinnie
AND WHY WOULD IT BE THERE?
'CUZ THE SONG IS GARBAGE, MAN.
TAPE OR NO TAPE, YOU'RE DOING THAT SONG. AND SAVE THAT REBEL SPIRIT FOR THE STAGE.
UNLESS YOU WANNA WIND UP BACK IN A COMA.
SOOO... NOW WHAT DO WE DO?
NOT MUCH WE CAN DO, MAN. WE SIGNED A CONTRACT.
SOMEONE WAS IN A COMA?
Ronnie
Ray
Vinnie
Mikey
LADIES AND GENTLEMEN (BUT MOSTLY RECORD EXECUTIVES AND MEDIA CONGLOMERATES)! ARE YOU READY TO HAVE YOUR EARS ASSAULTED? YOUR HEARTS EXTORTED? YOUR SOULS VANDALIZED?
YEAH!
THEN MAKE SOME NOISE FOR THE WORLD'S MOST DANGEROUS R&B GROUP...

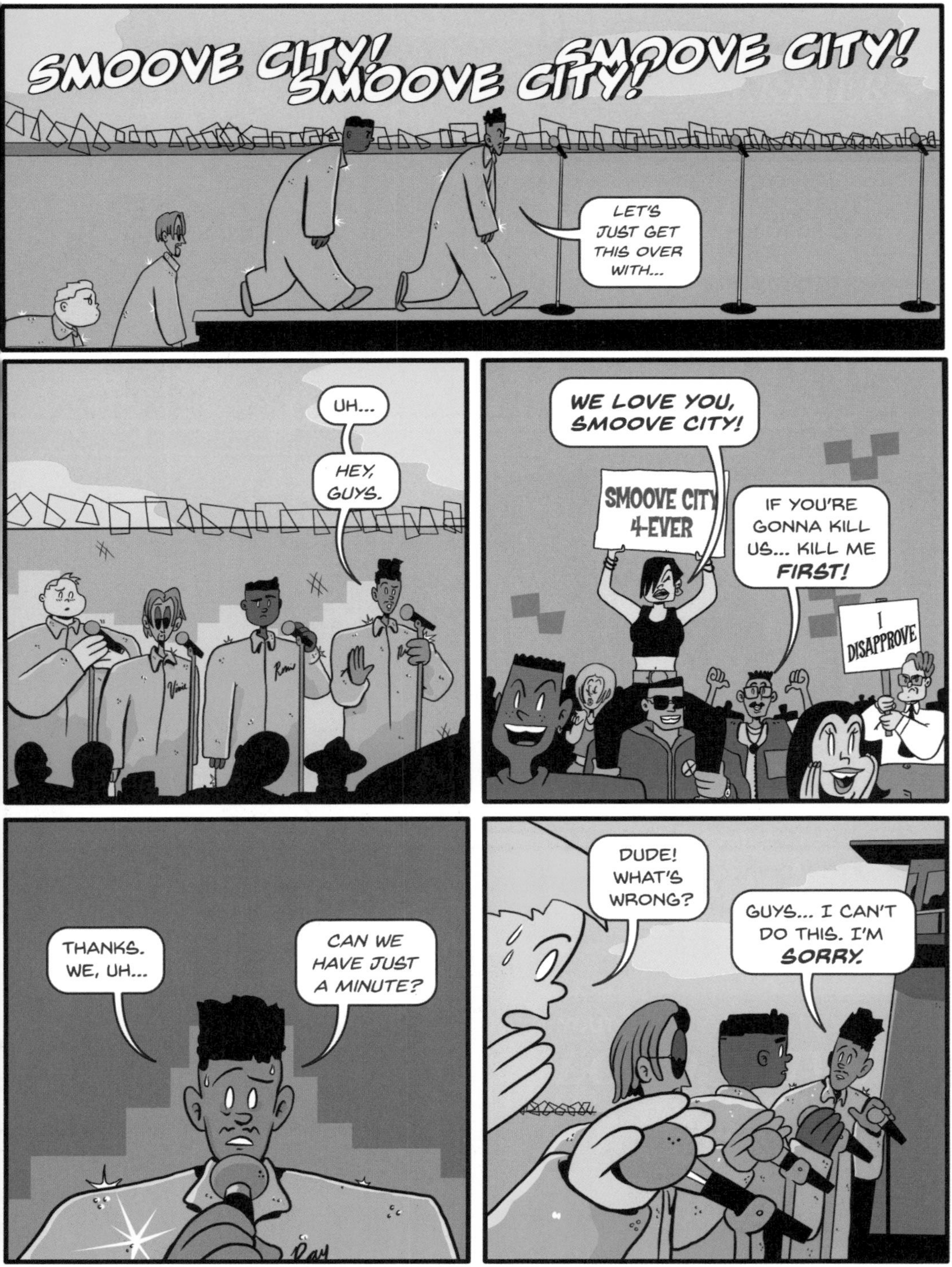
SMOOVE CITY! SMOOVE CITY! SMOOVE CITY!
LET'S JUST GET THIS OVER WITH...
UH...
HEY, GUYS.
WE LOVE YOU, SMOOVE CITY!
SMOOVE CITY 4-EVER
IF YOU'RE GONNA KILL US... KILL ME FIRST!
I DISAPPROVE
THANKS. WE, UH...
CAN WE HAVE JUST A MINUTE?
DUDE! WHAT'S WRONG?
GUYS... I CAN'T DO THIS. I'M SORRY.

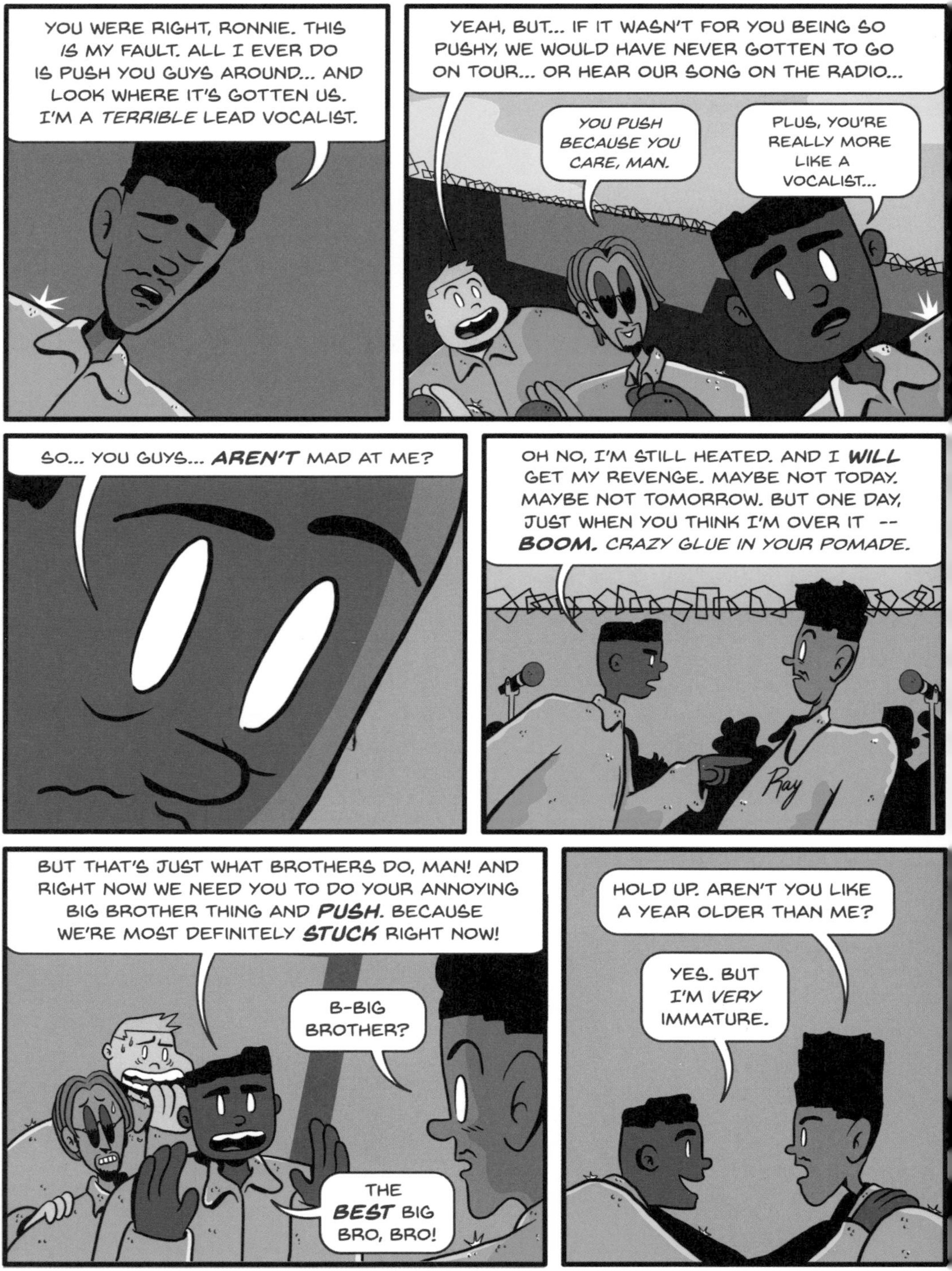
YOU WERE RIGHT, RONNIE. THIS IS MY FAULT. ALL I EVER DO IS PUSH YOU GUYS AROUND... AND LOOK WHERE IT'S GOTTEN US. I'M A TERRIBLE LEAD VOCALIST.
YEAH, BUT... IF IT WASN'T FOR YOU BEING SO PUSHY, WE WOULD HAVE NEVER GOTTEN TO GO ON TOUR... OR HEAR OUR SONG ON THE RADIO...
YOU PUSH BECAUSE YOU CARE, MAN.
PLUS, YOU'RE REALLY MORE LIKE A VOCALIST...
SO... YOU GUYS... AREN'T MAD AT ME?
OH NO, I'M STILL HEATED. AND I WILL GET MY REVENGE. MAYBE NOT TODAY. MAYBE NOT TOMORROW. BUT ONE DAY, JUST WHEN YOU THINK I'M OVER IT -- BOOM. CRAZY GLUE IN YOUR POMADE.
Ray
BUT THAT'S JUST WHAT BROTHERS DO, MAN! AND RIGHT NOW WE NEED YOU TO DO YOUR ANNOYING BIG BROTHER THING AND PUSH. BECAUSE WE'RE MOST DEFINITELY STUCK RIGHT NOW!
B-BIG BROTHER?
THE BEST BIG BRO, BRO!
HOLD UP. AREN'T YOU LIKE A YEAR OLDER THAN ME?
YES. BUT I'M VERY IMMATURE.

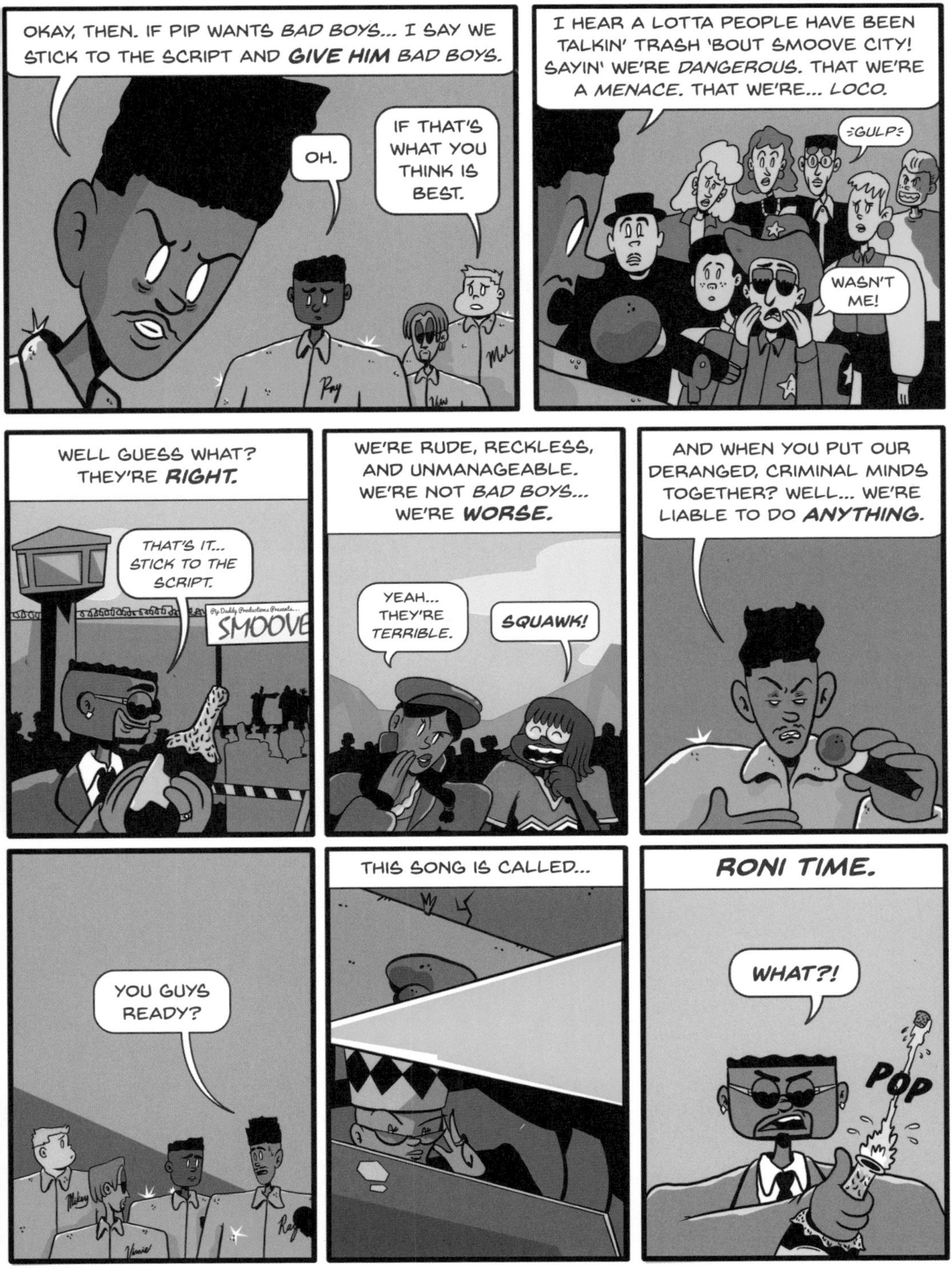

OKAY, THEN. IF PIP WANTS BAD BOYS... I SAY WE STICK TO THE SCRIPT AND GIVE HIM BAD BOYS.
OH.
IF THAT'S WHAT YOU THINK IS BEST.
I HEAR A LOTTA PEOPLE HAVE BEEN TALKIN' TRASH 'BOUT SMOOVE CITY! SAYIN' WE'RE DANGEROUS. THAT WE'RE A MENACE. THAT WE'RE... LOCO.
GULP
WASN'T ME!
WELL GUESS WHAT? THEY'RE RIGHT.
THAT'S IT... STICK TO THE SCRIPT.
Pip Daddy Productions Presents...
SMOOVE
WE'RE RUDE, RECKLESS, AND UNMANAGEABLE. WE'RE NOT BAD BOYS... WE'RE WORSE.
YEAH... THEY'RE TERRIBLE.
SQUAWK!
AND WHEN YOU PUT OUR DERANGED, CRIMINAL MINDS TOGETHER? WELL... WE'RE LIABLE TO DO ANYTHING.
YOU GUYS READY?
THIS SONG IS CALLED...
RONI TIME.
WHAT?!
POP

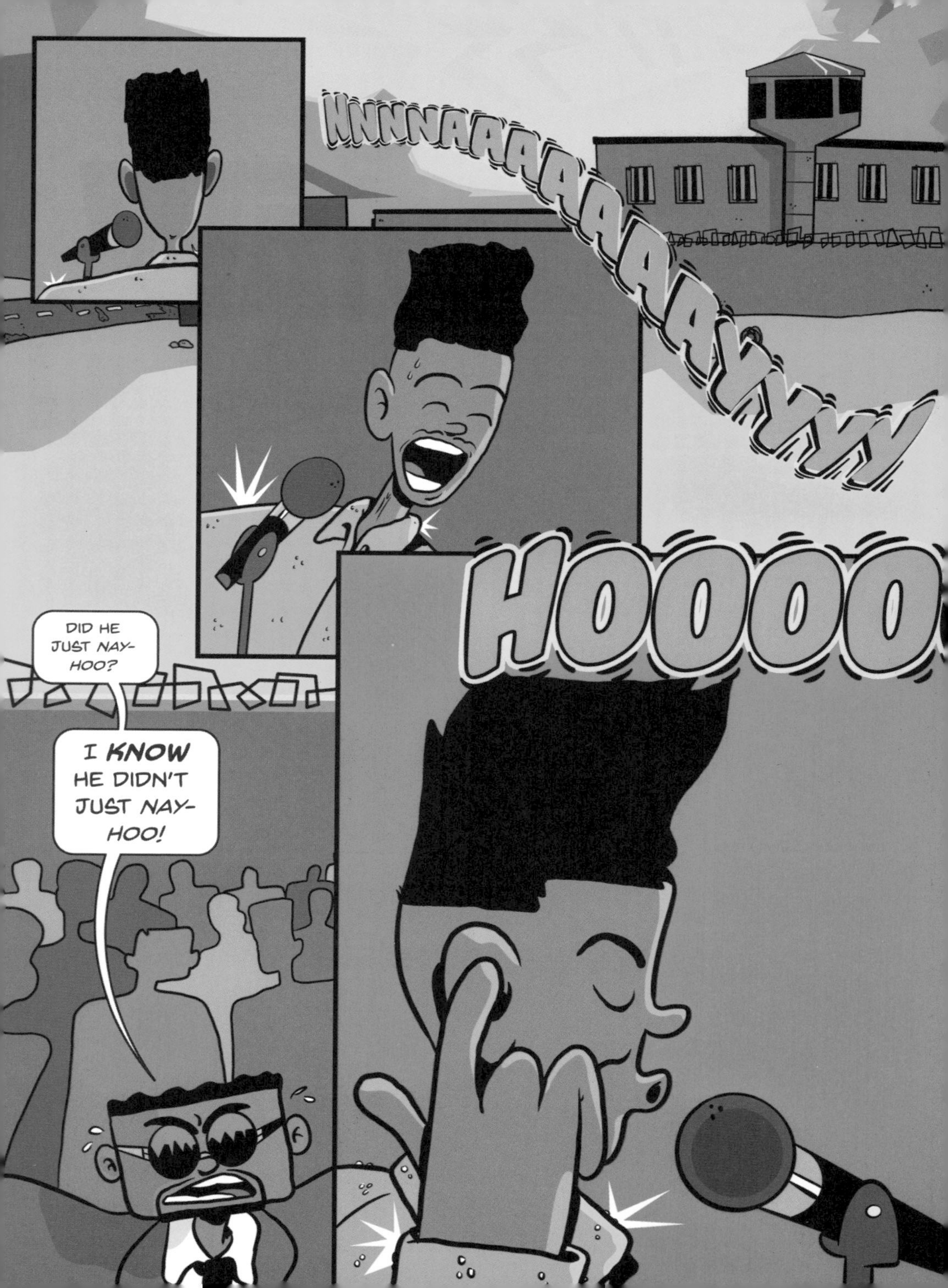
NNNNAAAAAAAAAAYYYY
HOOOOO
DID HE JUST NAY-HOO?
I KNOW HE DIDN'T JUST NAY-HOO!

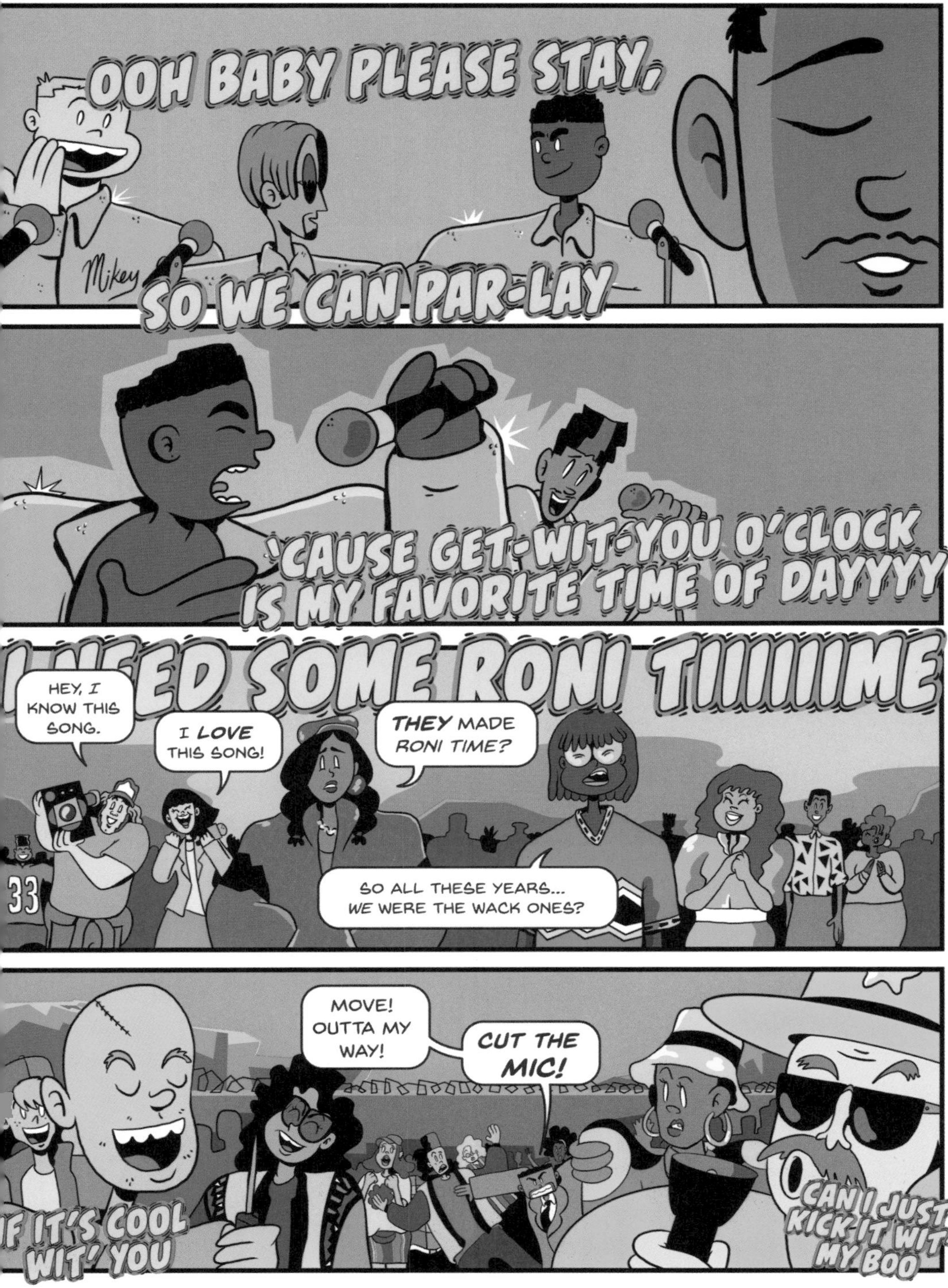
OOH BABY PLEASE STAY,
Mikey
SO WE CAN PAR-LAY
'CAUSE GET-WIT-YOU O'CLOCK IS MY FAVORITE TIME OF DAYYYY
I NEED SOME RONI TIIIIIIME
HEY, I KNOW THIS SONG.
I LOVE THIS SONG!
THEY MADE RONI TIME?
SO ALL THESE YEARS... WE WERE THE WACK ONES?
F IT'S COOL WIT' YOU
MOVE! OUTTA MY WAY!
CUT THE MIC!
CAN I JUST KICK IT WIT' MY BOO

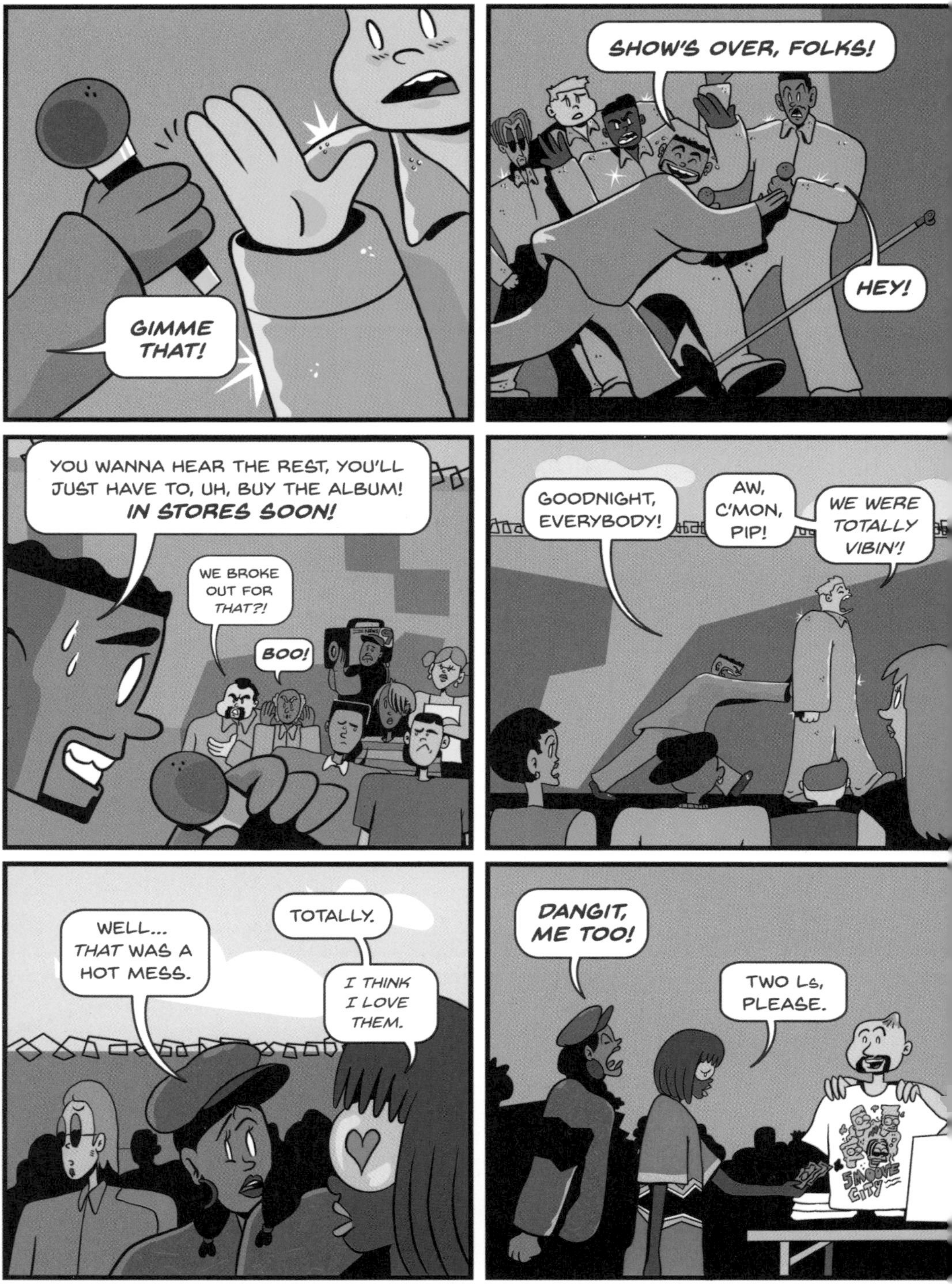
GIMME THAT!
SHOW'S OVER, FOLKS!
HEY!
YOU WANNA HEAR THE REST, YOU'LL JUST HAVE TO, UH, BUY THE ALBUM! IN STORES SOON!
WE BROKE OUT FOR THAT?!
BOO!
GOODNIGHT, EVERYBODY!
AW, C'MON, PIP!
WE WERE TOTALLY VIBIN'!
WELL... THAT WAS A HOT MESS.
TOTALLY.
I THINK I LOVE THEM.
DANGIT, ME TOO!
TWO Ls, PLEASE.
SMOOVE CITY

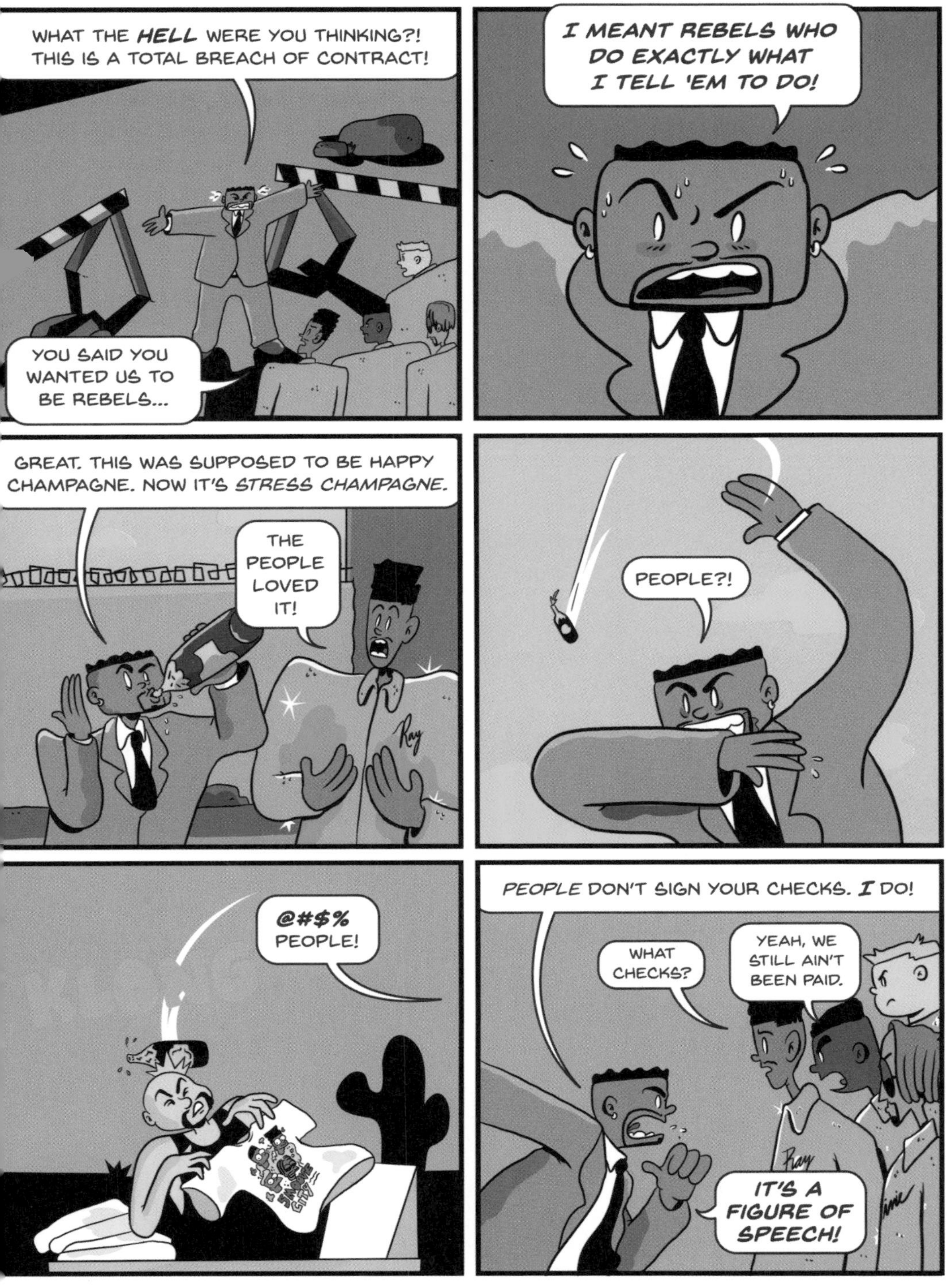
WHAT THE HELL WERE YOU THINKING?! THIS IS A TOTAL BREACH OF CONTRACT!
YOU SAID YOU WANTED US TO BE REBELS...
I MEANT REBELS WHO DO EXACTLY WHAT I TELL 'EM TO DO!
GREAT. THIS WAS SUPPOSED TO BE HAPPY CHAMPAGNE. NOW IT'S STRESS CHAMPAGNE.
THE PEOPLE LOVED IT!
Ray
PEOPLE?!
@#$% PEOPLE!
PEOPLE DON'T SIGN YOUR CHECKS. I DO!
WHAT CHECKS?
YEAH, WE STILL AIN'T BEEN PAID.
IT'S A FIGURE OF SPEECH!

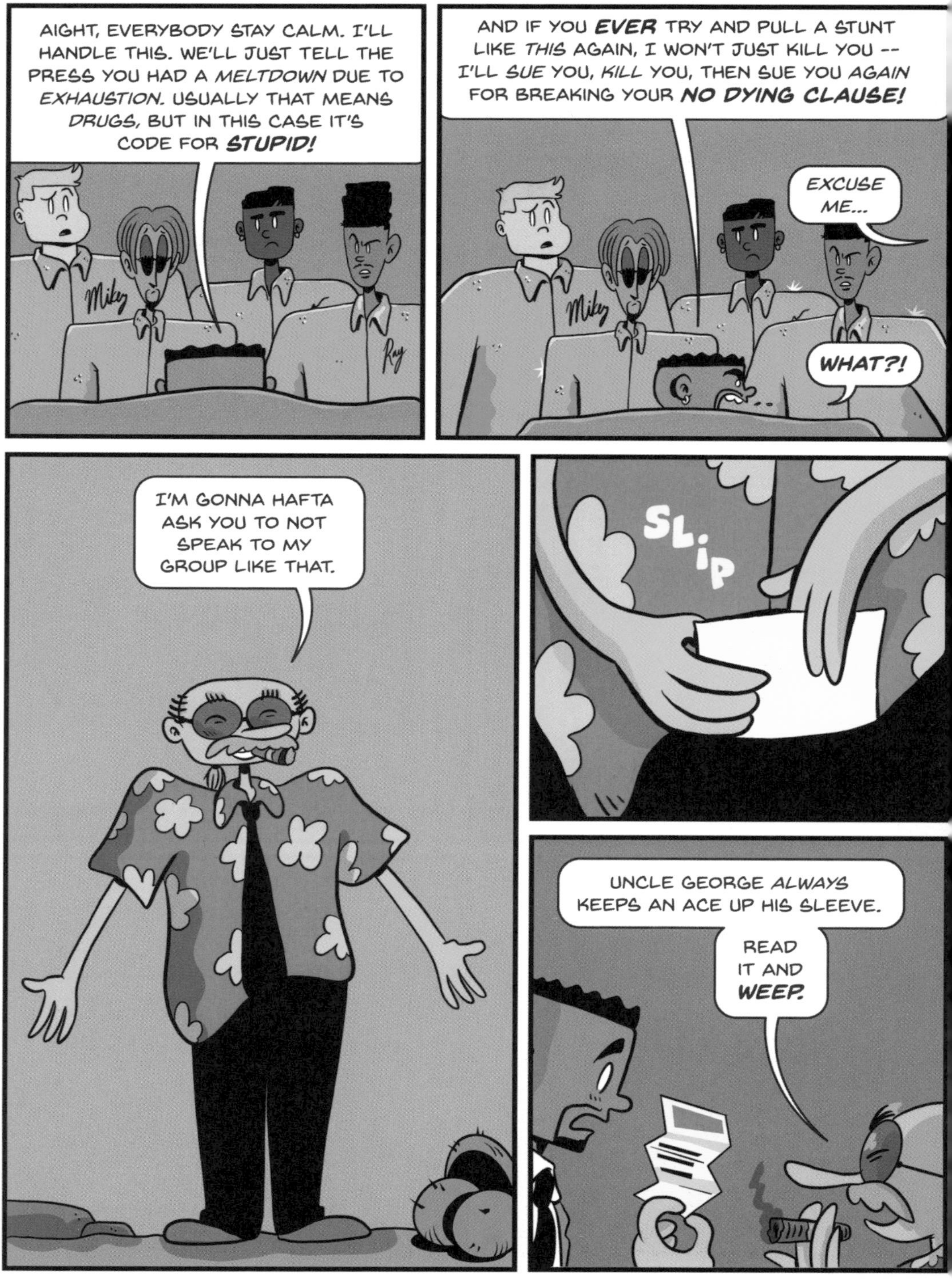
AIGHT, EVERYBODY STAY CALM. I'LL HANDLE THIS. WE'LL JUST TELL THE PRESS YOU HAD A *MELTDOWN* DUE TO *EXHAUSTION*. USUALLY THAT MEANS *DRUGS*, BUT IN THIS CASE IT'S CODE FOR ***STUPID!***
Miky
Ray
AND IF YOU ***EVER*** TRY AND PULL A STUNT LIKE *THIS* AGAIN, I WON'T JUST KILL YOU -- I'LL *SUE* YOU, *KILL* YOU, THEN SUE YOU *AGAIN* FOR BREAKING YOUR ***NO DYING CLAUSE!***
EXCUSE ME...
Miky
WHAT?!
I'M GONNA HAFTA ASK YOU TO NOT SPEAK TO MY GROUP LIKE THAT.
SLIP
UNCLE GEORGE *ALWAYS* KEEPS AN ACE UP HIS SLEEVE.
READ IT AND ***WEEP.***

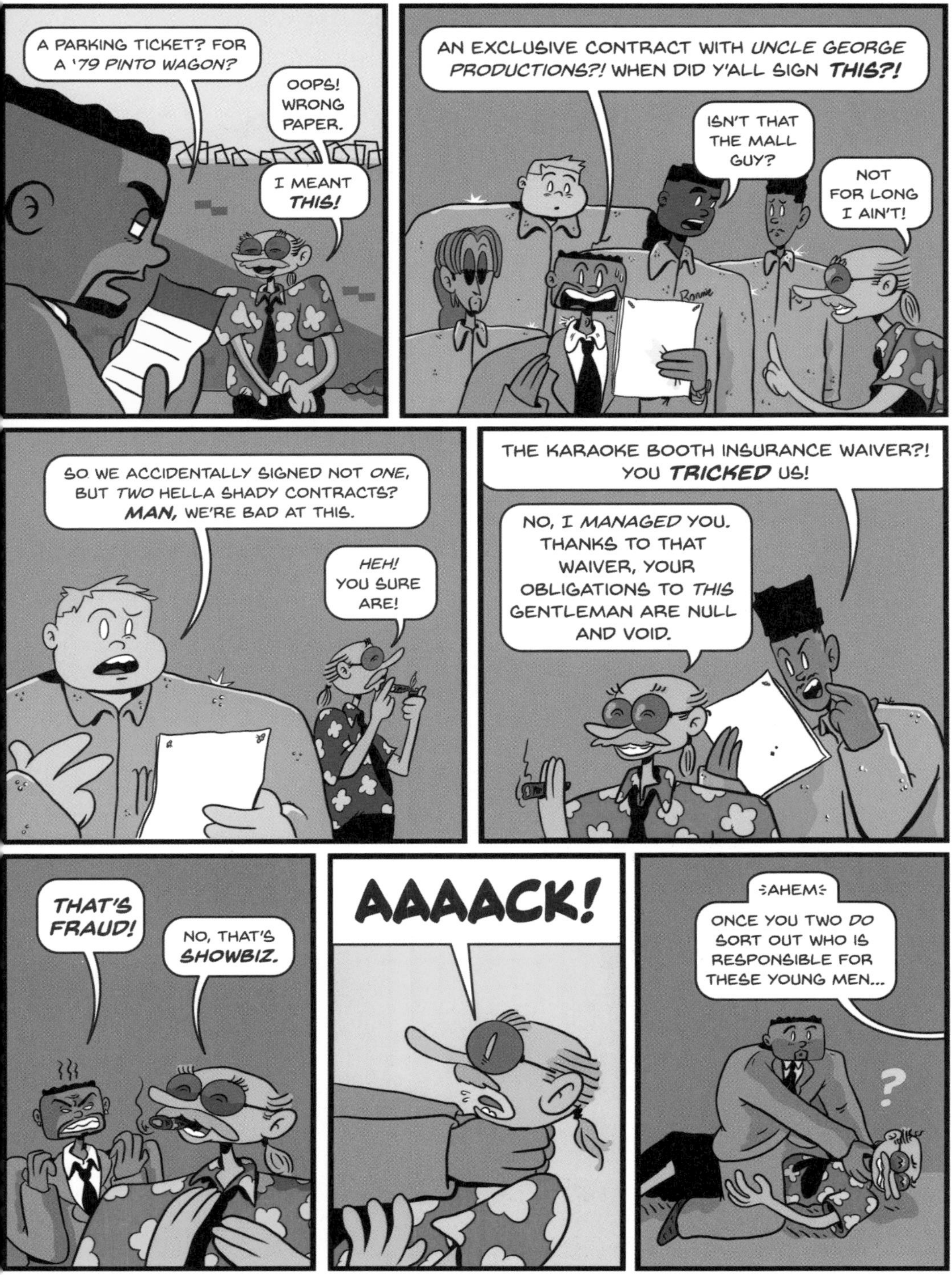
A PARKING TICKET? FOR A '79 PINTO WAGON?
OOPS! WRONG PAPER.
I MEANT THIS!
AN EXCLUSIVE CONTRACT WITH UNCLE GEORGE PRODUCTIONS?! WHEN DID Y'ALL SIGN THIS?!
ISN'T THAT THE MALL GUY?
NOT FOR LONG I AIN'T!
Ronnie
SO WE ACCIDENTALLY SIGNED NOT ONE, BUT TWO HELLA SHADY CONTRACTS? MAN, WE'RE BAD AT THIS.
HEH! YOU SURE ARE!
THE KARAOKE BOOTH INSURANCE WAIVER?! YOU TRICKED US!
NO, I MANAGED YOU. THANKS TO THAT WAIVER, YOUR OBLIGATIONS TO THIS GENTLEMAN ARE NULL AND VOID.
THAT'S FRAUD!
NO, THAT'S SHOWBIZ.
AAAACK!
AHEM
ONCE YOU TWO DO SORT OUT WHO IS RESPONSIBLE FOR THESE YOUNG MEN...
?

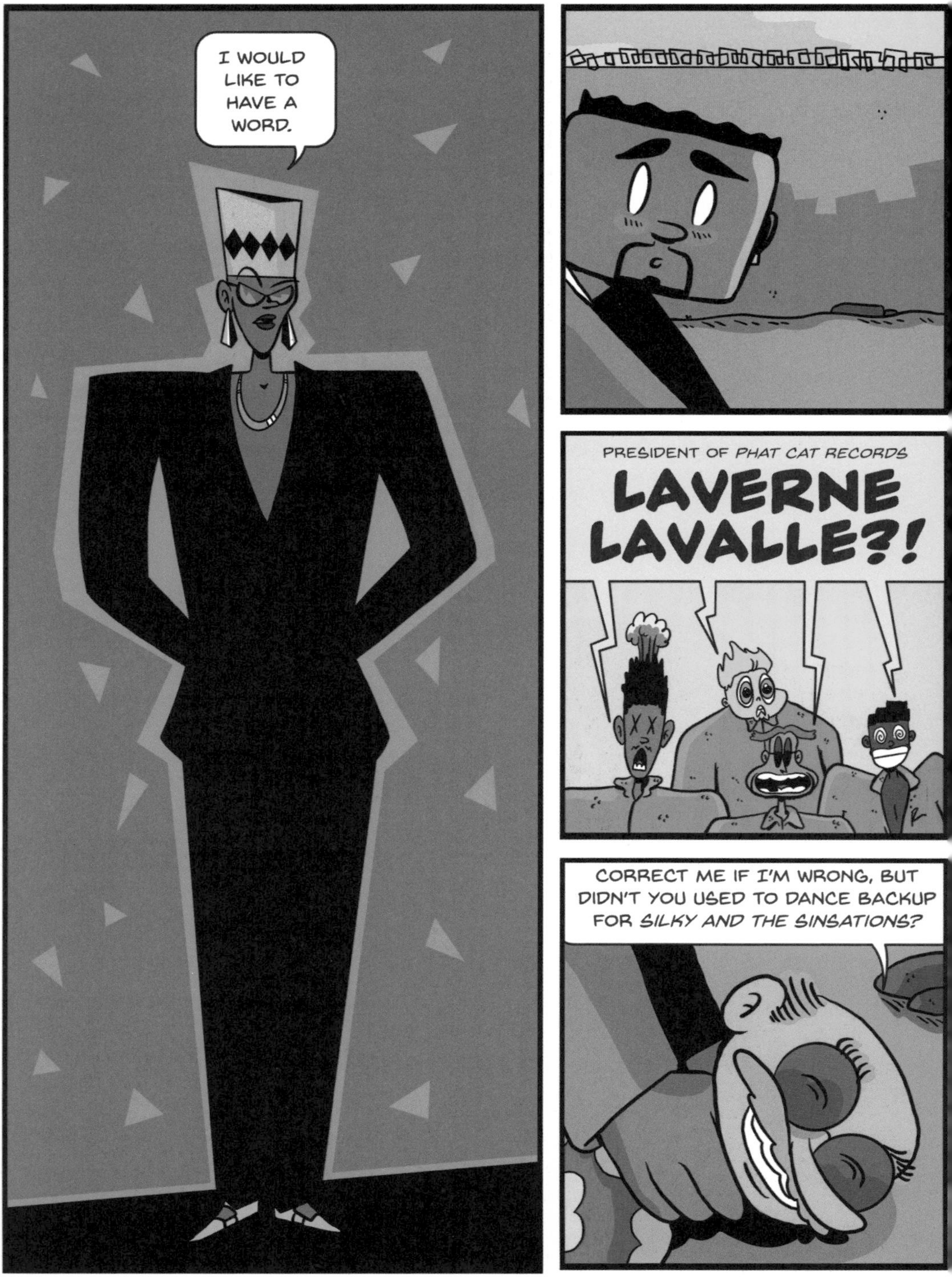
I WOULD LIKE TO HAVE A WORD.
PRESIDENT OF PHAT CAT RECORDS
LAVERNE LAVALLE?!
CORRECT ME IF I'M WRONG, BUT DIDN'T YOU USED TO DANCE BACKUP FOR SILKY AND THE SINSATIONS?

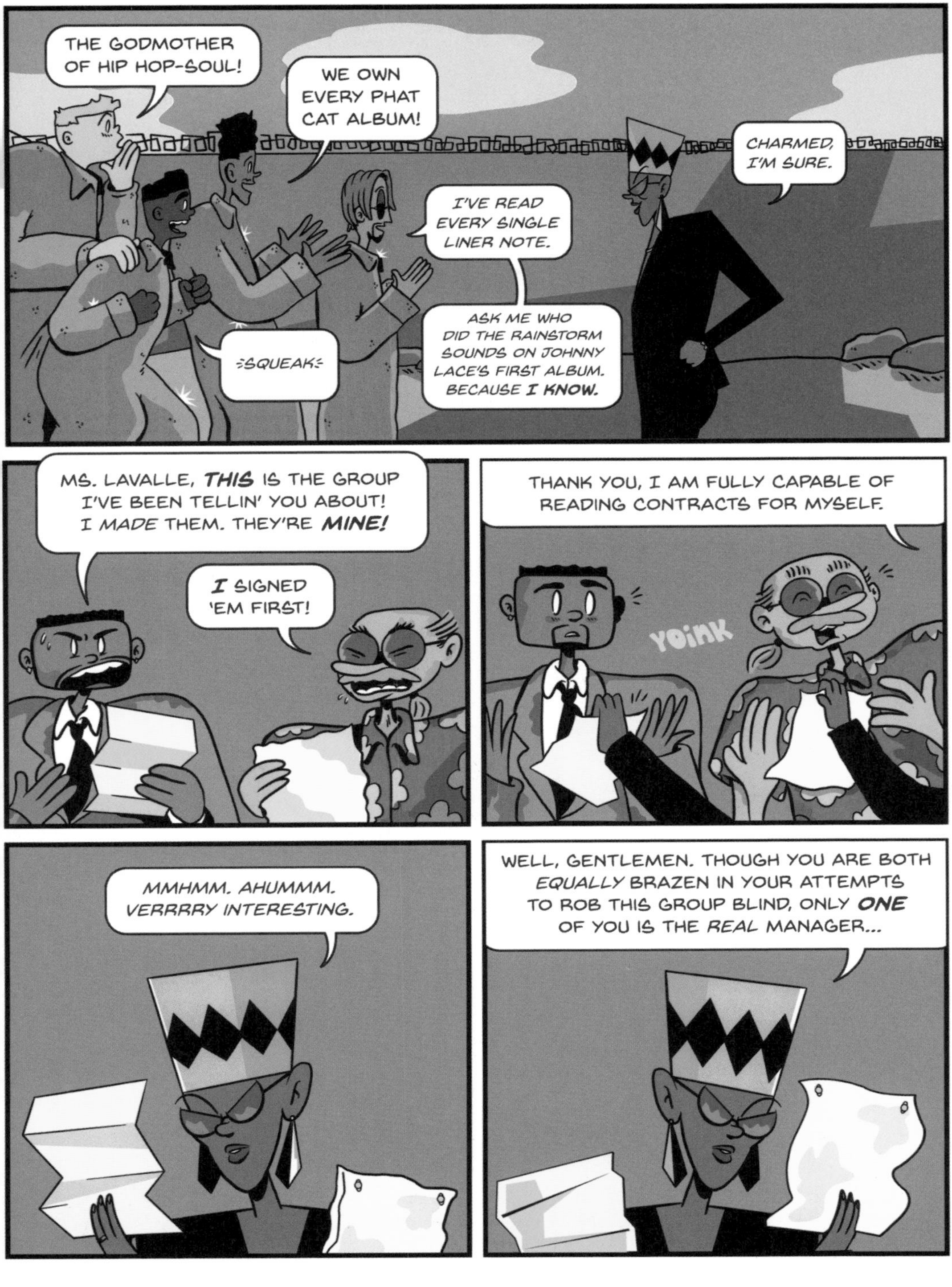
THE GODMOTHER OF HIP HOP-SOUL!
WE OWN EVERY PHAT CAT ALBUM!
CHARMED, I'M SURE.
I'VE READ EVERY SINGLE LINER NOTE.
ASK ME WHO DID THE RAINSTORM SOUNDS ON JOHNNY LACE'S FIRST ALBUM. BECAUSE I KNOW.
SQUEAK
MS. LAVALLE, THIS IS THE GROUP I'VE BEEN TELLIN' YOU ABOUT! I MADE THEM. THEY'RE MINE!
I SIGNED 'EM FIRST!
THANK YOU, I AM FULLY CAPABLE OF READING CONTRACTS FOR MYSELF.
YOINK
MMHMM. AHUMMM. VERRRRY INTERESTING.
WELL, GENTLEMEN. THOUGH YOU ARE BOTH EQUALLY BRAZEN IN YOUR ATTEMPTS TO ROB THIS GROUP BLIND, ONLY ONE OF YOU IS THE REAL MANAGER...

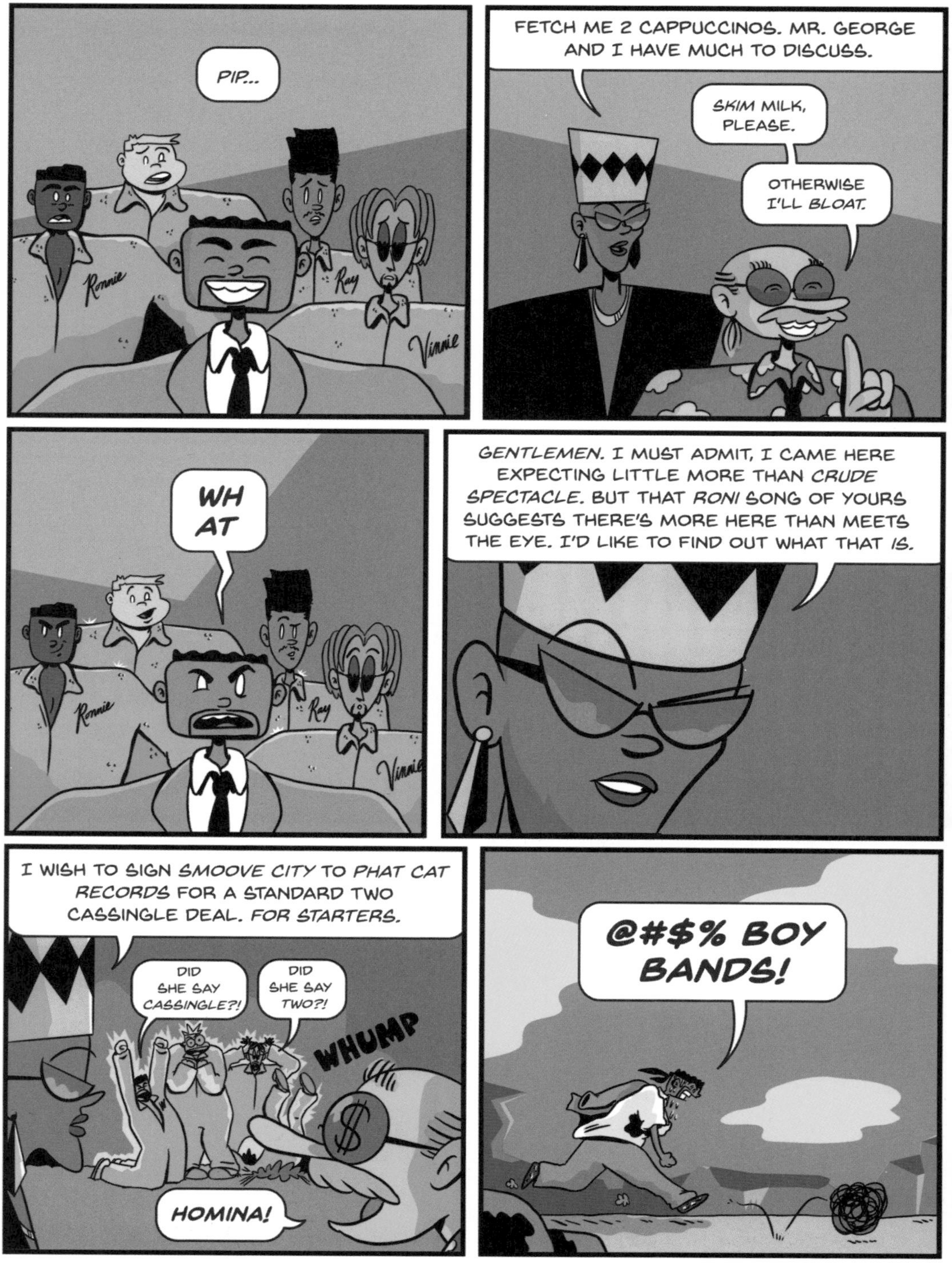
PIP...
Ronnie
Ray
Vinnie
FETCH ME 2 CAPPUCCINOS. MR. GEORGE AND I HAVE MUCH TO DISCUSS.
SKIM MILK, PLEASE.
OTHERWISE I'LL BLOAT.
WH AT
Ronnie
Ray
Vinnie
GENTLEMEN. I MUST ADMIT, I CAME HERE EXPECTING LITTLE MORE THAN CRUDE SPECTACLE. BUT THAT RONI SONG OF YOURS SUGGESTS THERE'S MORE HERE THAN MEETS THE EYE. I'D LIKE TO FIND OUT WHAT THAT IS.
I WISH TO SIGN SMOOVE CITY TO PHAT CAT RECORDS FOR A STANDARD TWO CASSINGLE DEAL. FOR STARTERS.
DID SHE SAY CASSINGLE?!
DID SHE SAY TWO?!
WHUMP
HOMINA!
@#$% BOY BANDS!

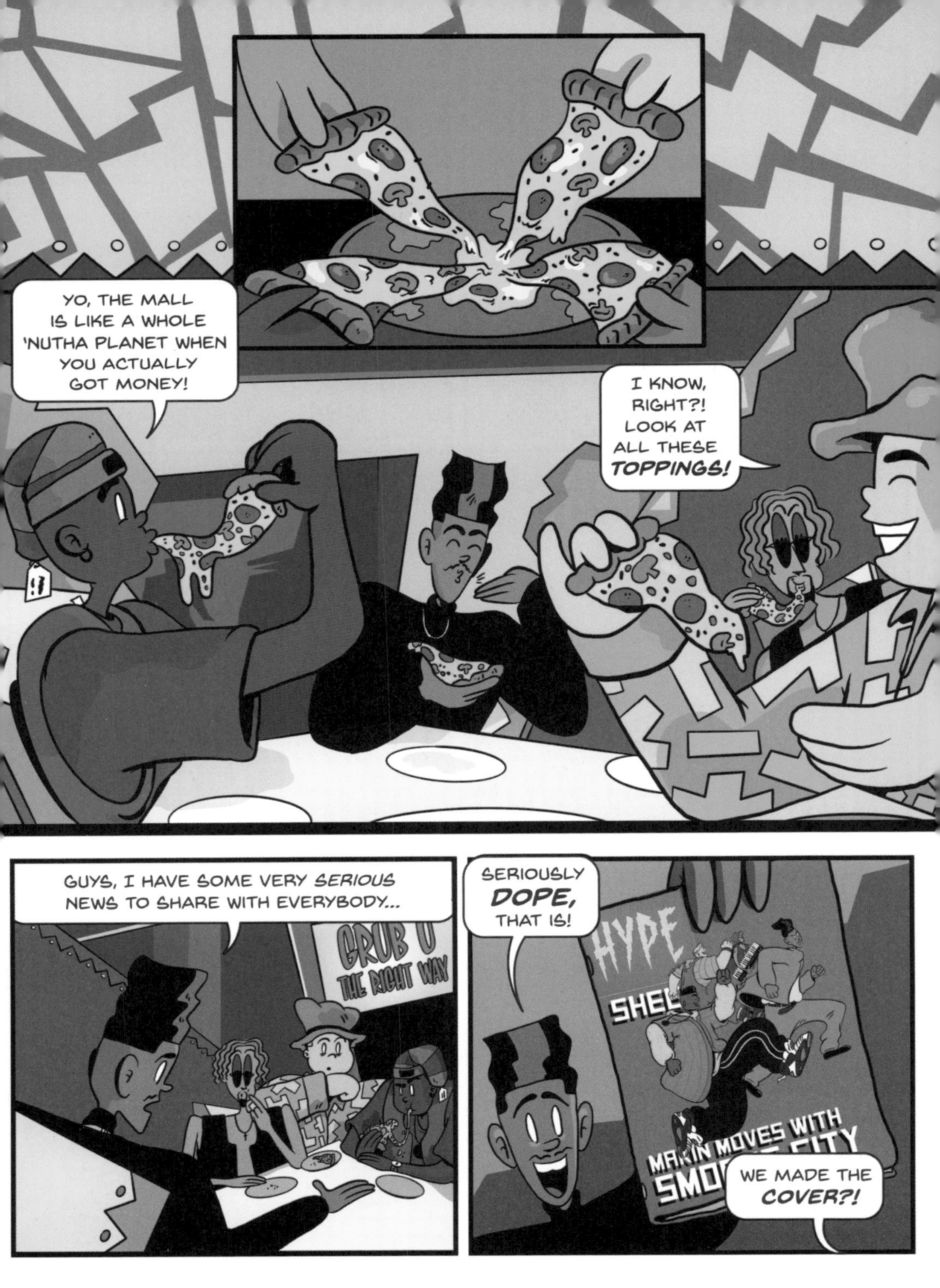

YO, THE MALL IS LIKE A WHOLE 'NUTHA PLANET WHEN YOU ACTUALLY GOT MONEY!
I KNOW, RIGHT?! LOOK AT ALL THESE *TOPPINGS!*
GUYS, I HAVE SOME VERY *SERIOUS* NEWS TO SHARE WITH EVERYBODY...
GRUB U THE RIGHT WAY
SERIOUSLY **DOPE,** THAT IS!
HYPE
WE MADE THE *COVER?!*

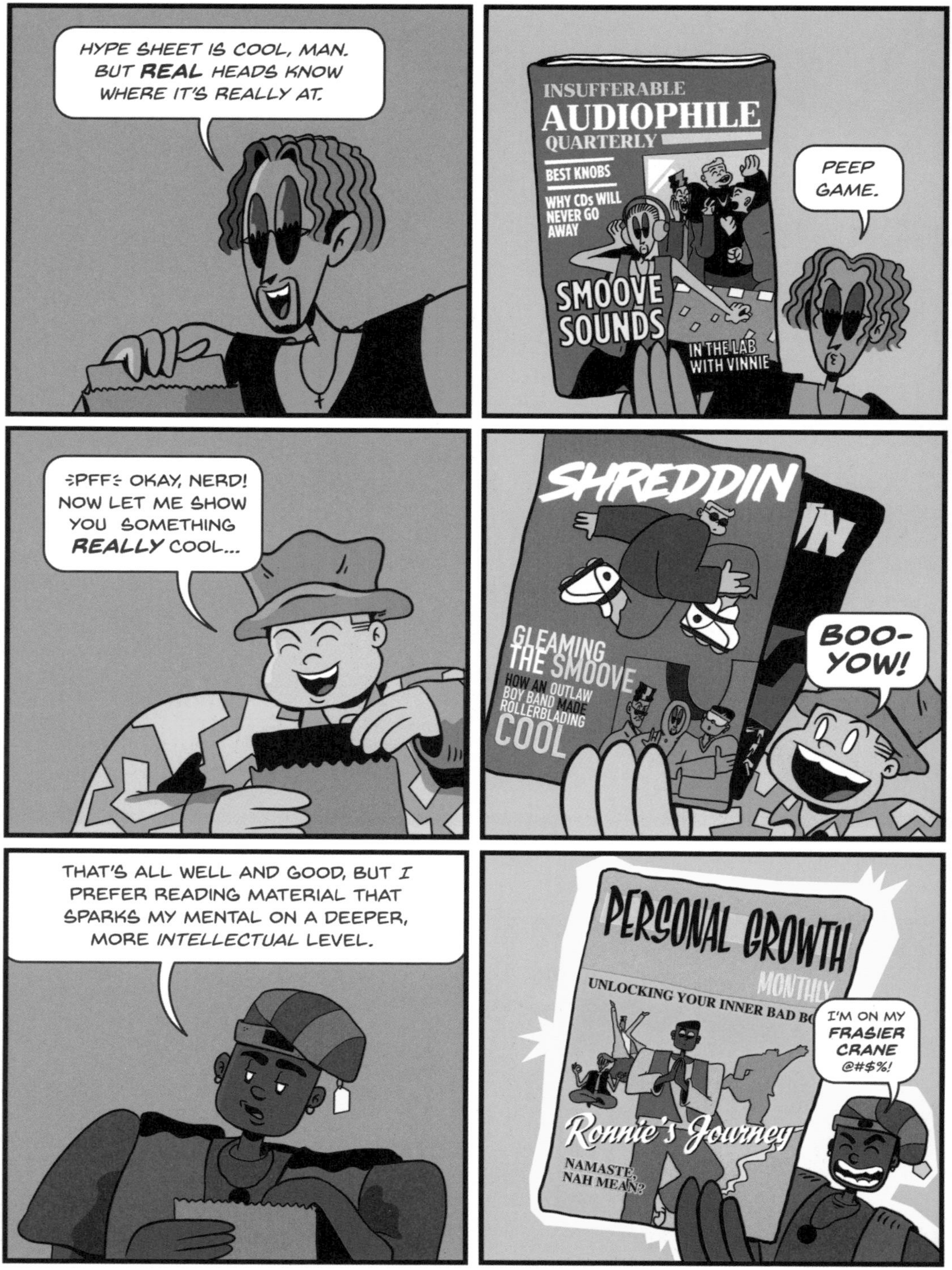
HYPE SHEET IS COOL, MAN. BUT REAL HEADS KNOW WHERE IT'S REALLY AT.
INSUFFERABLE AUDIOPHILE QUARTERLY
BEST KNOBS
WHY CDs WILL NEVER GO AWAY
SMOOVE SOUNDS
IN THE LAB WITH VINNIE
PEEP GAME.
=PFF= OKAY, NERD! NOW LET ME SHOW YOU SOMETHING REALLY COOL...
SHREDDIN
GLEAMING THE SMOOVE
HOW AN OUTLAW BOY BAND MADE ROLLERBLADING COOL
BOO-YOW!
THAT'S ALL WELL AND GOOD, BUT I PREFER READING MATERIAL THAT SPARKS MY MENTAL ON A DEEPER, MORE INTELLECTUAL LEVEL.
PERSONAL GROWTH MONTHLY
UNLOCKING YOUR INNER BAD BO
Ronnie's Journey
NAMASTE, NAH MEAN?
I'M ON MY FRASIER CRANE @#$%!

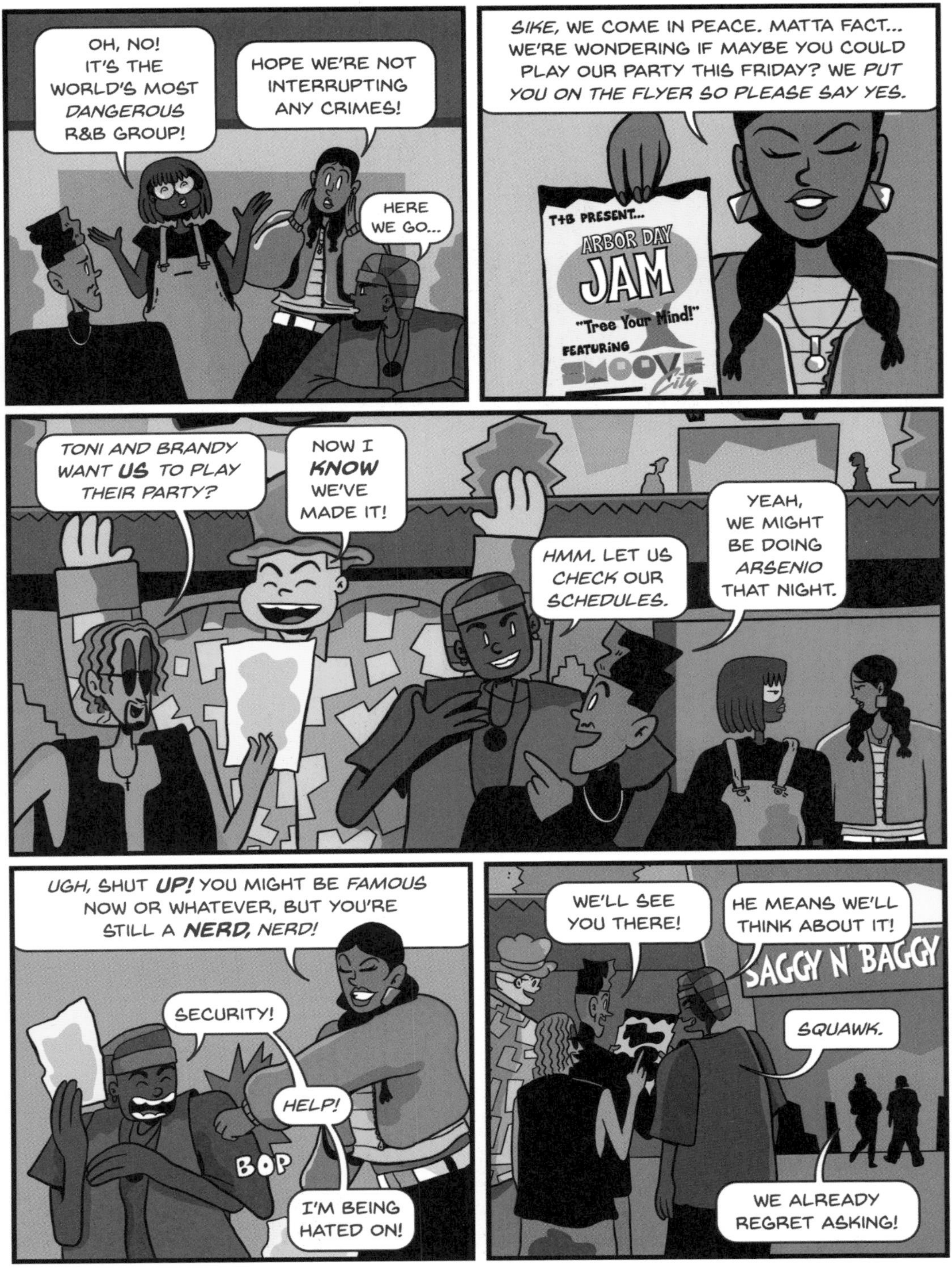
OH, NO! IT'S THE WORLD'S MOST DANGEROUS R&B GROUP!
HOPE WE'RE NOT INTERRUPTING ANY CRIMES!
HERE WE GO...
SIKE, WE COME IN PEACE. MATTA FACT... WE'RE WONDERING IF MAYBE YOU COULD PLAY OUR PARTY THIS FRIDAY? WE PUT YOU ON THE FLYER SO PLEASE SAY YES.
T+B PRESENT...
ARBOR DAY JAM
"Tree Your Mind!"
FEATURING
SMOOVE City
TONI AND BRANDY WANT US TO PLAY THEIR PARTY?
NOW I KNOW WE'VE MADE IT!
HMM. LET US CHECK OUR SCHEDULES.
YEAH, WE MIGHT BE DOING ARSENIO THAT NIGHT.
UGH, SHUT UP! YOU MIGHT BE FAMOUS NOW OR WHATEVER, BUT YOU'RE STILL A NERD, NERD!
SECURITY!
HELP!
BOP
I'M BEING HATED ON!
WE'LL SEE YOU THERE!
HE MEANS WE'LL THINK ABOUT IT!
SAGGY N' BAGGY
SQUAWK.
WE ALREADY REGRET ASKING!

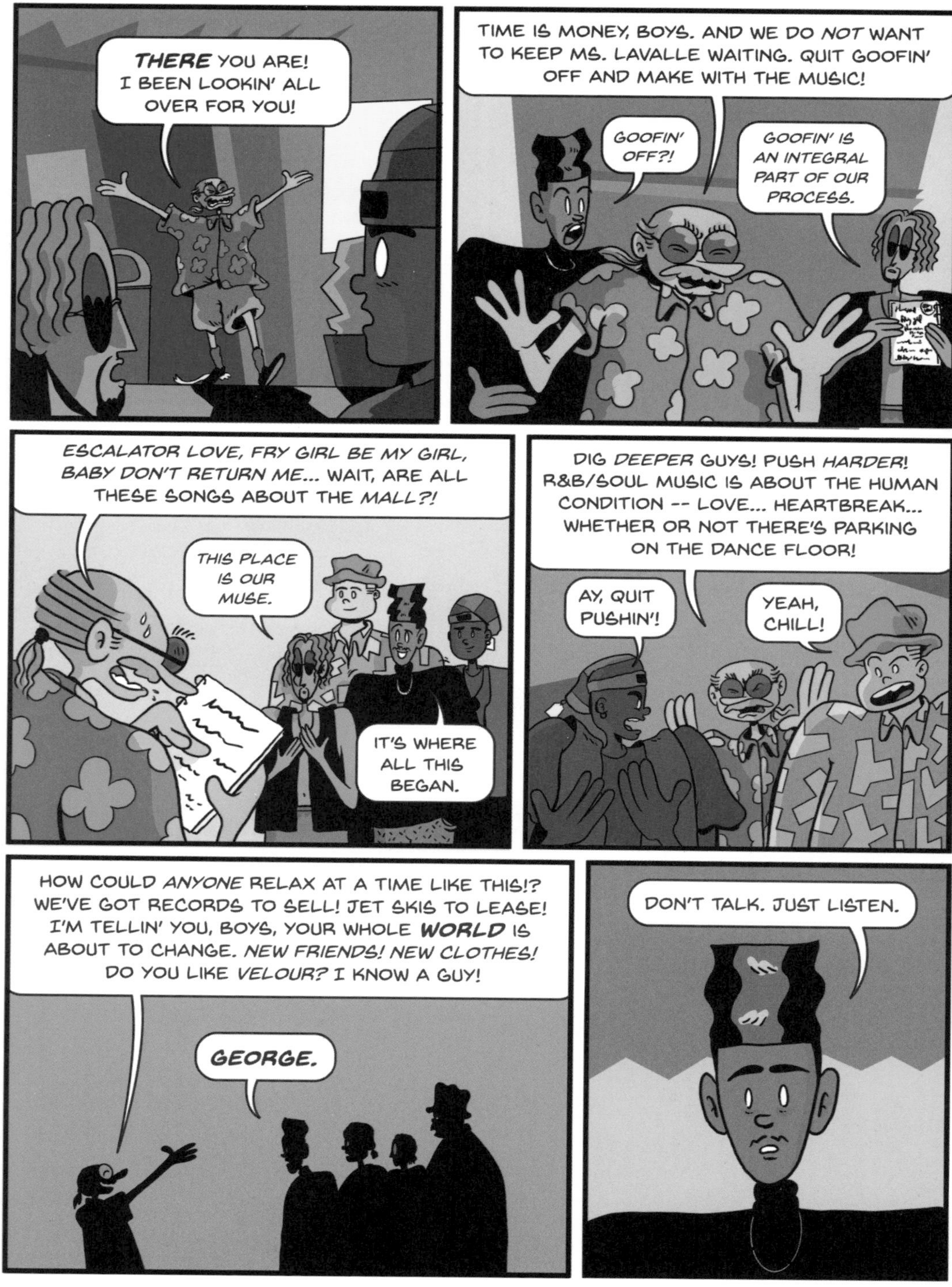
THERE YOU ARE! I BEEN LOOKIN' ALL OVER FOR YOU!
TIME IS MONEY, BOYS. AND WE DO NOT WANT TO KEEP MS. LAVALLE WAITING. QUIT GOOFIN' OFF AND MAKE WITH THE MUSIC!
GOOFIN' OFF?!
GOOFIN' IS AN INTEGRAL PART OF OUR PROCESS.
ESCALATOR LOVE, FRY GIRL BE MY GIRL, BABY DON'T RETURN ME... WAIT, ARE ALL THESE SONGS ABOUT THE MALL?!
THIS PLACE IS OUR MUSE.
IT'S WHERE ALL THIS BEGAN.
DIG DEEPER GUYS! PUSH HARDER! R&B/SOUL MUSIC IS ABOUT THE HUMAN CONDITION -- LOVE... HEARTBREAK... WHETHER OR NOT THERE'S PARKING ON THE DANCE FLOOR!
AY, QUIT PUSHIN'!
YEAH, CHILL!
HOW COULD ANYONE RELAX AT A TIME LIKE THIS!? WE'VE GOT RECORDS TO SELL! JET SKIS TO LEASE! I'M TELLIN' YOU, BOYS, YOUR WHOLE WORLD IS ABOUT TO CHANGE. NEW FRIENDS! NEW CLOTHES! DO YOU LIKE VELOUR? I KNOW A GUY!
GEORGE.
DON'T TALK. JUST LISTEN.

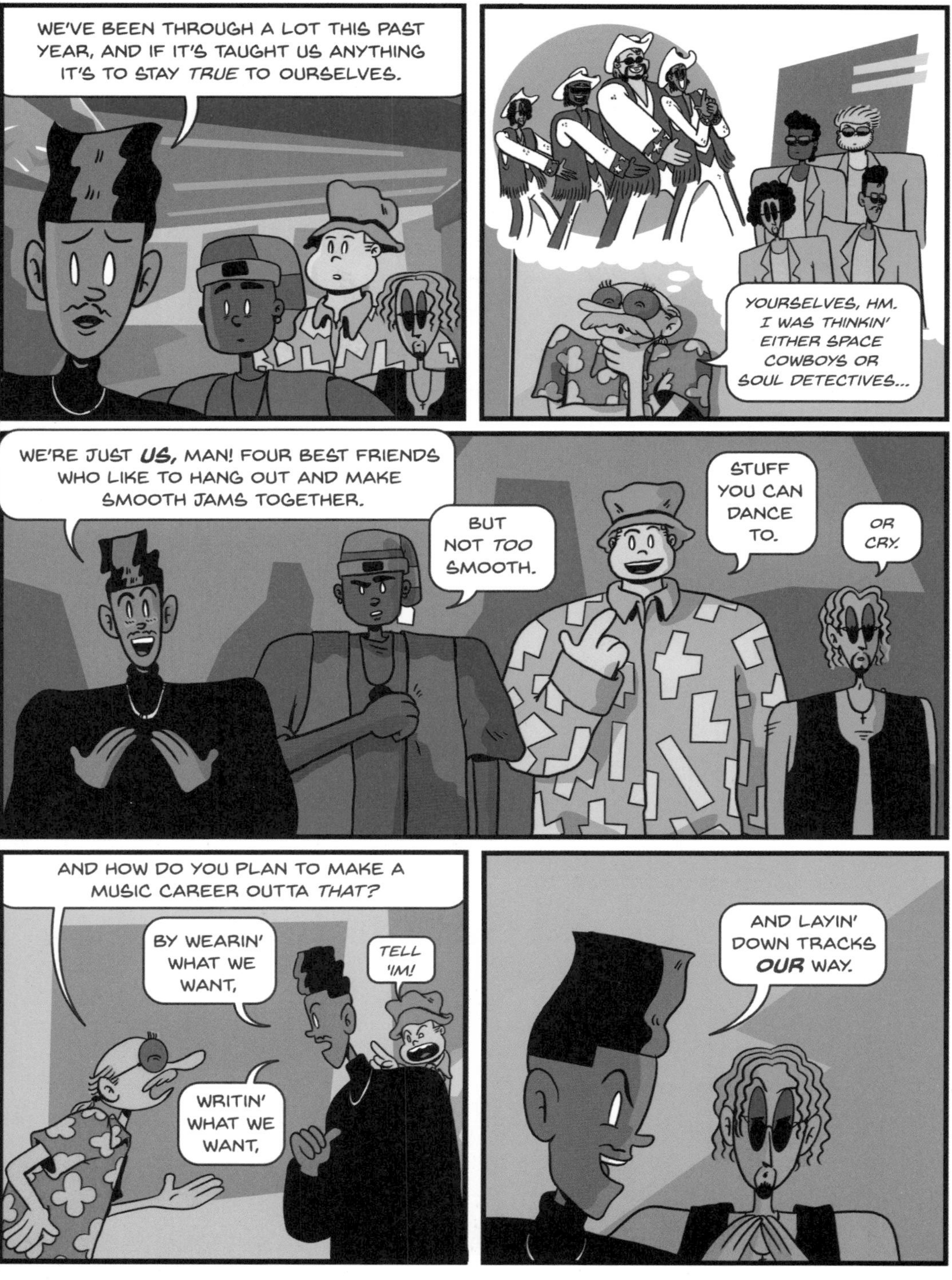
WE'VE BEEN THROUGH A LOT THIS PAST YEAR, AND IF IT'S TAUGHT US ANYTHING IT'S TO STAY *TRUE* TO OURSELVES.
YOURSELVES, HM. I WAS THINKIN' EITHER SPACE COWBOYS OR SOUL DETECTIVES...
WE'RE JUST ***US,*** MAN! FOUR BEST FRIENDS WHO LIKE TO HANG OUT AND MAKE SMOOTH JAMS TOGETHER.
BUT NOT *TOO* SMOOTH.
STUFF YOU CAN DANCE TO.
OR CRY.
AND HOW DO YOU PLAN TO MAKE A MUSIC CAREER OUTTA *THAT?*
BY WEARIN' WHAT WE WANT,
TELL 'IM!
WRITIN' WHAT WE WANT,
AND LAYIN' DOWN TRACKS ***OUR*** WAY.

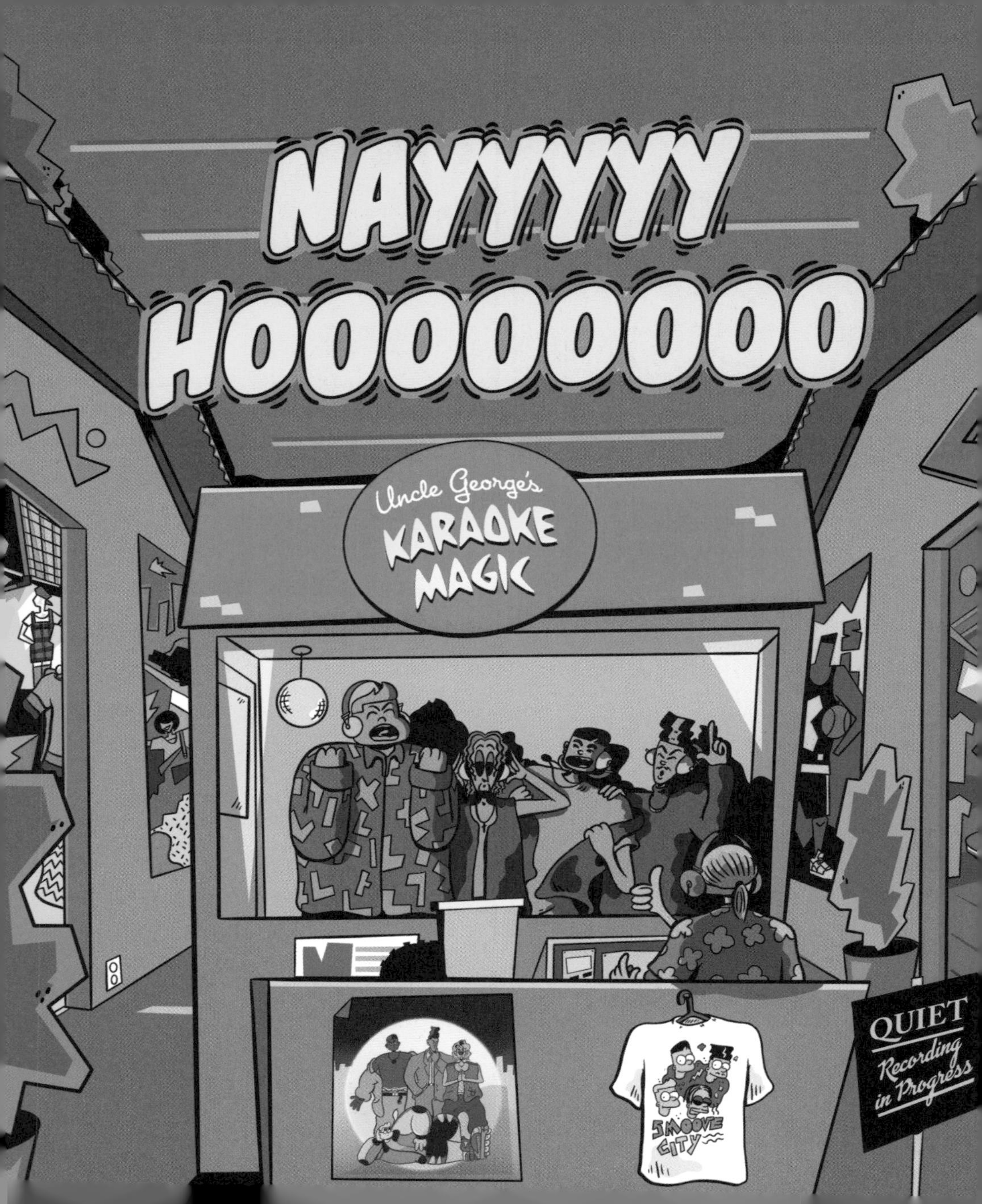
NAYYYYY
HOOOOOOOO
Uncle George's
KARAOKE
MAGIC
SMOOVE
CITY
QUIET
Recording
in Progress

PEACE OUT • ONE LOVE • AUDI 5000

THE END

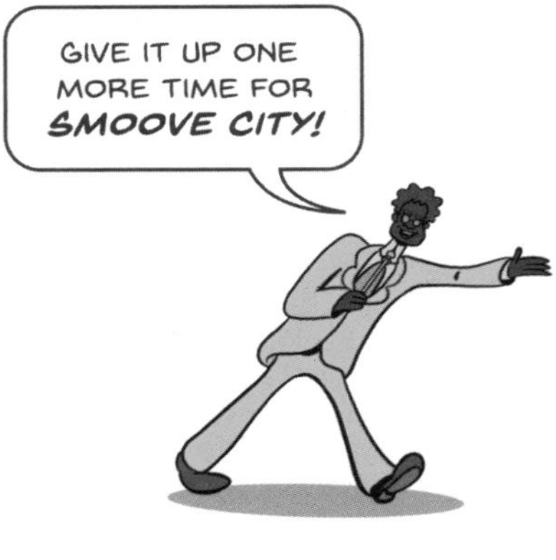
GIVE IT UP ONE MORE TIME FOR *SMOOVE CITY!*

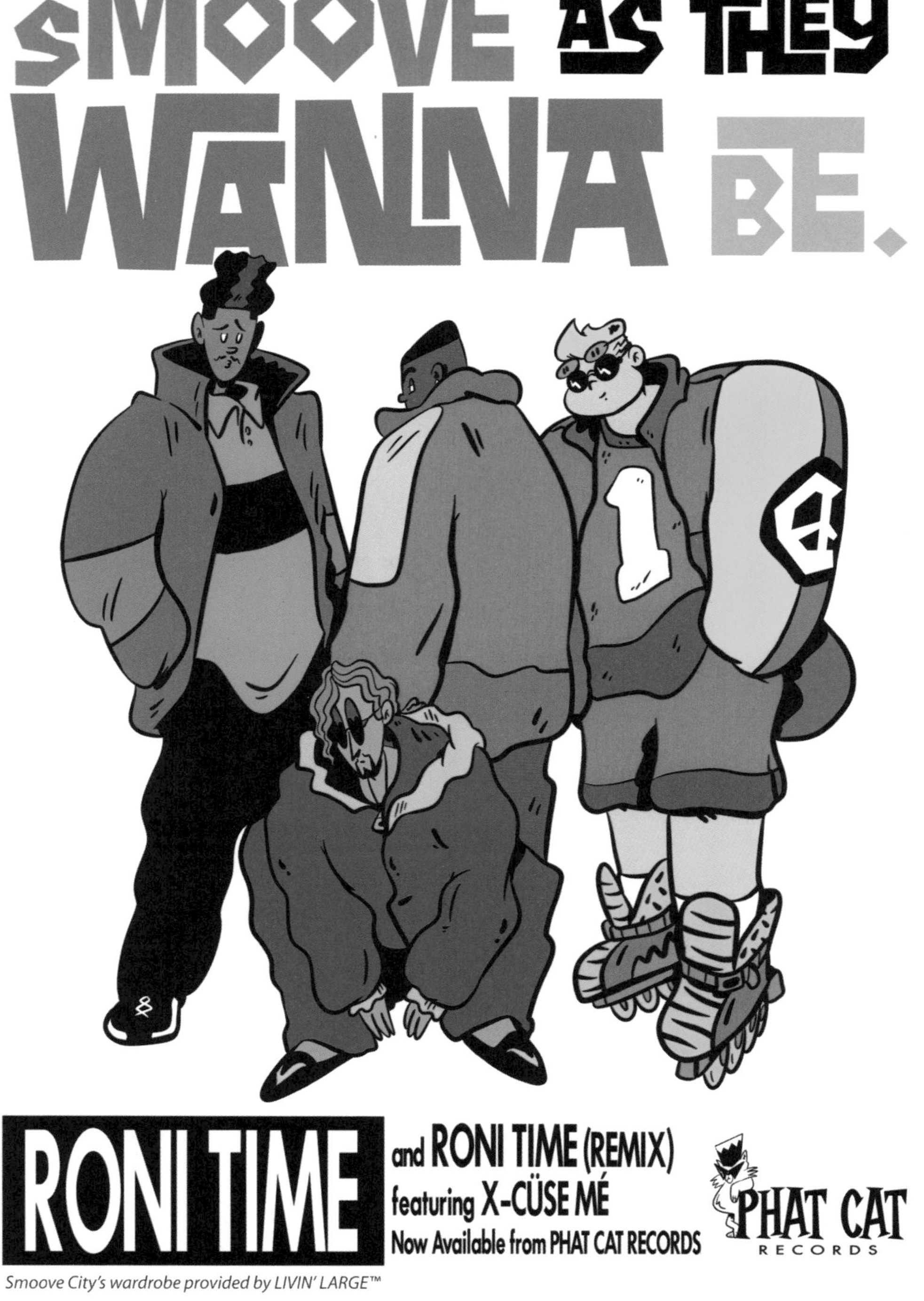
SMOOVE AS THEY WANNA BE.
RONI TIME
and RONI TIME (REMIX)
featuring X-CÜSE MÉ
Now Available from PHAT CAT RECORDS
PHAT CAT
RECORDS
Smoove City's wardrobe provided by LIVIN' LARGE™

FAN CLUB

JOIN NOW

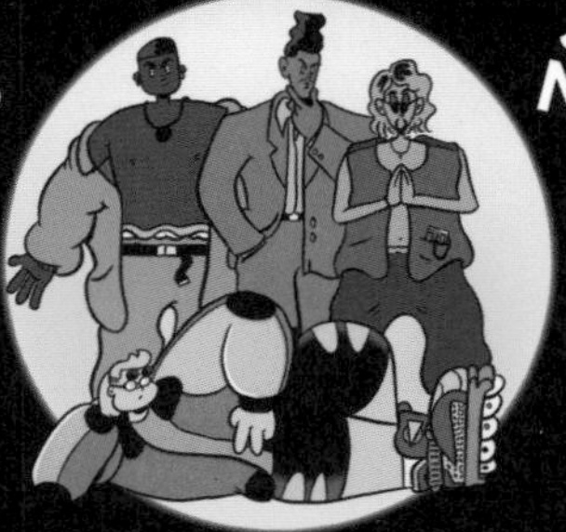

SMOOVE City

Send $10 and a SASE to
Phat Cat Records, c/o Pip the Intern

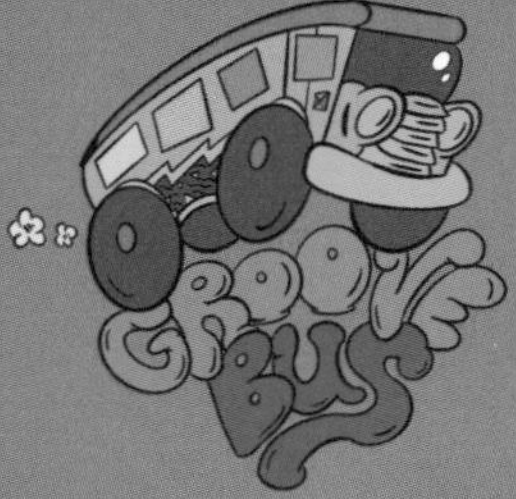
GROOVE BUS

GROOVE BUS

TUESDAYS
at 4:45 A.M.
New Time Slot,
Same Groove

Uncle George's KARAOKE MAGIC

Present this coupon for
50% OFF
of the first 10 seconds of
YOUR NEXT RECORDING SESSION

If you have been injured while busting a move, you may be entitled to financial compensation.

Call Kid N' Plea,
Dance Floor Attorneys

DJ ICED PERRIER

"Party Rocker Extraordinaire"

I get parties pumpin', weddings wylin', & bat mitzvahs bumpin'! NO REQUESTS
(Lawn care services also available.)
Call Now: 555-GO DJ

INTRODUCING...

GIGANTOR

19-Disc CD Changer

"You'll never need to upgrade again!"

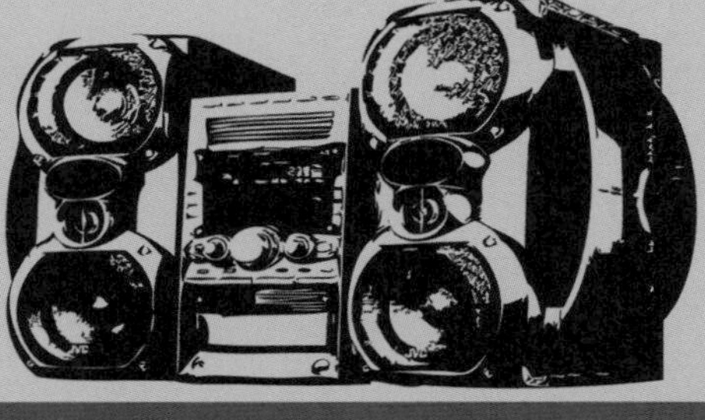

Only at Emotionally Unstable Ernie's

OPENING ACT WANTED

Girl group sensation X-Cüse Mé is looking for a new opening act. *Again.*
Must be clean, punctual,
law abiding, and drama-free.
Boy bands need not apply.

ATTN: YOUTHS! Call Your Local DJ & Request

LORD, 4GIVE ME 4 GROOVIN'

By Reverend Bertram Cakes
from his upcoming album,
"JAMMIN' 4 JESUS"

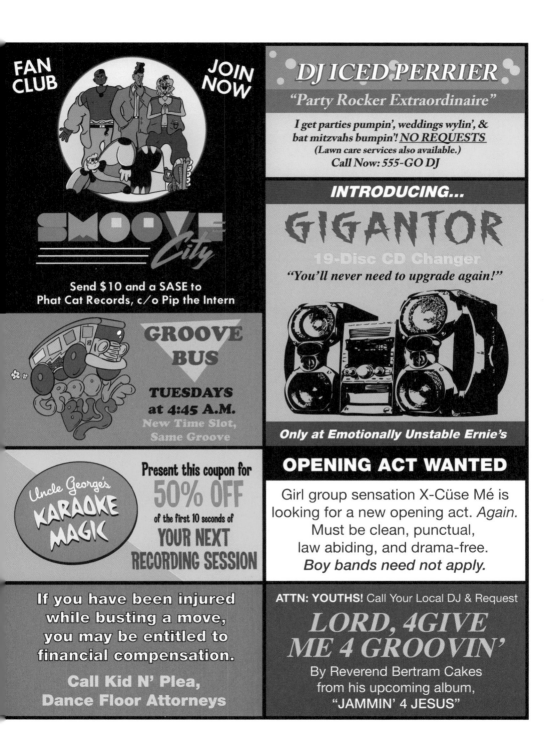

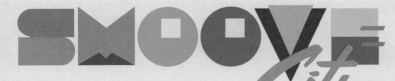

SMOOVE City

THE MIXTAPE

Bump the full playlist on Spotify.
(Or just come over and I'll burn you a CD.)

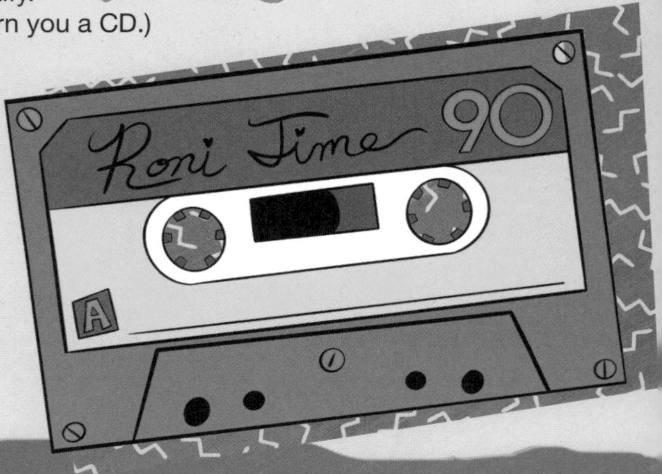
Roni Time
90
A

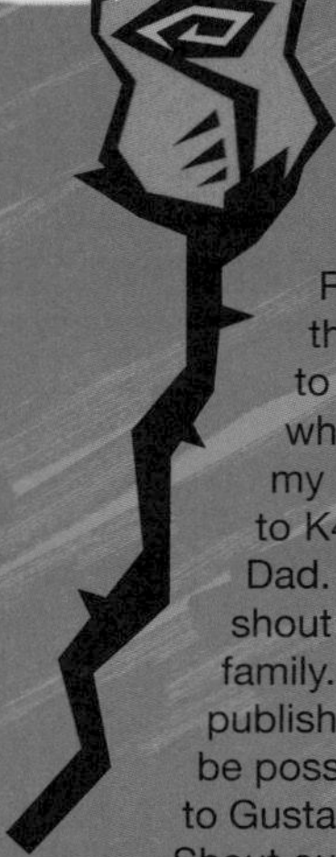

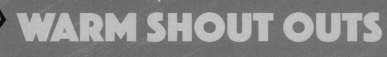

WARM SHOUT OUTS

Remember squinting at the liner notes trying to read all the fine print shout-outs in the "Acknowledgements" section? Good times. This might be my only chance in life to do that, so let's go: First off, shout out to God, the Universe, the Force, the Creator who makes all creation possible. I am blessed to do what I do. Shout out to my homie, my wifey, and my 'roni: Ro! All the good love songs make me think of you. Shout out to K4! You are my life's joy and inspiration. Shout out to my Mom, yo! Shout out to my Dad. Shout out to Sarah. Shout out to my sisters and brothers from another mother, shout out to my nieces and nephews, Mom and Dad Nacino, shout out to my entire family. Aunts, uncles, cousins, manangs, everybody. Shout out to Lion Forge and Oni for publishing this book. Shout out to Amanda Meadows, without whom this book would not be possible, nor funny, coherent, etc. Shout out to the entire Devastator Squad! Shout out to Gustavo and Alma! Shout out to anyone who's ever stopped by the Chamanvision booth! Shout out to Jessica! Shout out to DJ Patrick Reed and the whole Hip Hop & Comics Panel crew. Shout out to Motion Family! Shout out to Diwang, Becca, and Santi. Shout out to Cobra Chi. Shout out to Cashew Co. Shout out to Bobby. Shout out to everyone out there grinding in these comic streets. Shout out to Keith Knight. Shout out to Los Bros Hernandez. Shout out to Jack Kirby. Shout out to Dan DeCarlo, Daniel Clowes, and Danny DeVito. Shout out to Coop and House Industries. Shout out to Archie and Jughead and them. Shout out to Alfred E. Neuman. Shout out to Ryan Flanders. Shout out to John Ficarra and Dave Croatto. Shout out